A Biblical Study of the End Times For These Times
WINSOME WARRIORS

Copyright © 2012 by David M. Guerrin. All rights reserved.

All scripture quotations, unless otherwise indicated, are taken from the Holy Bible, New International Version®, NIV®. Copyright ©1973, 1978, 1984, 2011 by Biblica, Inc.™ Used by permission of Zondervan. All rights reserved worldwide. www.zondervan.com

The "NIV" and "New International Version" are trademarks registered in the United States Patent and Trademark Office by Biblica, Inc.™

Cover design by David M. Guerrin

Contact the author directly through his website, www.winsomewarriors.com.

Guerrin, David,
Winsome Warriors: a biblical study of the end times for these times/ David M. Guerrin

Includes references.
ISBN-13: 978-1470006761
Christian life. Non-fiction

Dedication

To Di. You are and have always been, "my reason for reason."

Table of Contents

Chapter 1
Why This Stuff Matters........................... 1

Chapter 2
Mining for Gold in God's Word....... 16

Chapter 3
Can God Tell Time?............................ 31

Chapter 4
The Prince of Peace?......................... 61

Chapter 5
Jesus' great "Wintervention"................ 90

Chapter 6
The Great Reign Robbery............... 120

Chapter 7
Is Jesus A Fan Of Big Love?............ 144

Chapter 8
Will The Real Antichrist Please Stand Up?................................. 202

Chapter 9
The (not very secret) rapture............ 266

Chapter 10
The Wait Of The World............... 309

CHAPTER 11
A SCROLL DOWN MEMORY LANE; PART 1 349

CHAPTER 12
A SCROLL DOWN MEMORY LANE; PART 2 368

CHAPTER 13
A SCROLL DOWN MEMORY LANE; PART 3 417

CHAPTER 14
HOW THEN SHALL WE LIVE? 464

APPENDIX 1 THE EARLY CHURCH 482

APPENDIX 2 ISRAEL AND THE CHURCH 486

APPENDIX 3 THE CHURCH IS THE TRUE ISRAEL 496

APPENDIX 4 SCRIPTURE INDEX 503

Preface

This is not an academic book. It is intended to be devotional and motivational. Still, footnotes are provided where appropriate. What began as a sermon series, evolved into a Bible study. Upon the prompting of those who participated in that study, I have finally put those ideas into book form. The main thrust of the pages that follow is the Word of God. I urge every reader to have in one hand a copy of this book, and in the other, a copy of The Book. More than ever, we have become a people without a Standard. We are quick to proclaim we believe in a divine Being (whatever that may mean) but we have lost any sense of a divine Text.

Even those of us who proclaim allegiance to both a Divine Being and a Divine Text have become woefully ignorant of the latter, making us dolefully out of touch with the former. But even a casual reading of Scripture introduces us to an undeniable tension. We live *in* the world, but are not *of* the world. Our feet are planted on earth, but our minds and hearts are called to Heaven. That tension is heightened when we consider the Kingdom of God. On the one hand, it is here. The victory has been won, and Christ reigns.

On the other hand, we are not there yet, at least not completely. Today, we at least intuit that tension, but we are lost as to what to do with it. A solution has come in the form of endless predictions and charts and graphs and diagrams, all designed to make peace between our minds and our spirits. The outcome has been that we have made peace between neither, but with the World instead. We run the very real risk of succumbing to the thinking that plagued first-century Judaism and accounted for its destruction. The Kingdom will not come through a church or denomination, a nation, a program of social justice or even world-wide evangelism. It will come at the hands of winsome warriors whose minds and hearts are in the grip of the risen Christ.

The history of God's People reveals a cavalier attitude toward the radical ethic to which we are called, and the mission to the nations that is our covenant responsibility. Instead, an entire industry has grown up around a relatively new set of doctrines concerning the end times. It is known by a number of names, but it is nothing more or less than the prevailing and popular teachings surrounding the "end times." It has spawned best-selling novels, major motion pictures, popular television programs, and countless popular books.

Using that body of teaching as our touchstone, we will examine the Kingdom of God as the Bible unwraps it. God willing, this will be only the first in a series of books dedicated to fleshing out the meaning of The Kingdom of God and the implications of its presence on earth today. The value of this or any work is measured solely on the basis of the degree to which it brings glory to God. To that end, I offer the following.

A brief note to the reader; Due to my own reading preference, I have included the text of many scriptures in the body of the book. Quite simply, I dislike reading a Scripture reference and then having to take the time to look it up. (I know. I have not yet memorized the entire Bible.) I also know that others prefer to simply read the Biblical reference and move on. For that reason, I have highlighted all of the longer texts and indented them slightly. If you are in the latter category, feel free to skip over those sections. For those like myself, enjoy!

Introduction

I saw it again today—another ad promising to finally reveal the truth about Revelation. It was a full page insert advertising a book signing. The author explained that *for over forty years I have been researching the mysteries of Revelation... Through passion, inspiration, and persistence, the hidden meaning of Revelation became for the first time, clear to me. By understanding the symbolism and metaphors in the Bible, I began to analyze and synthesize segments of Daniel and Revelation. I attained enough understanding to discover that Biblical prophecy was in essence, paralleling modern day events. A deep feeling of urgency came to me to deliver a message, especially aimed at New York City...*

Seriously? Seriously. Apparently, for the last two thousand years the church has gotten it wrong and just recently we have found what was missing. Who knew that Revelation was about New York City? And it's not just the end-times or the book of Revelation that get passed off as the next new thing: Emergent, seeker-sensitive, incarnational, dispensational, *sola mea*, double-brewed, fire-breathed, Spirit led power encounters of the barking kind—that will fix it. Conferences abound—*carpe nauseum*. The church machine, despite all the cogs and blogs, is still searching for that one thing that will cause the World to sit down and take us seriously. Culture wars, Bible-camp s'mores, church of the revolving door—and impotence is the still the order of the day for the Church.

Through it all, the post-modern mantra, like the modern one before it, is the same—"new is always better." So the search continues for something that no one else has discovered before. When we find it, we lap it up like parched pups who are far too sophisticated for the tricks of old-dogs.

Despite all the new iterations of the faith, we are still plagued by an old problem. We don't seem to be making much of a difference. **Is it possible that our impotence in the present is related to our misunderstanding of the past and our feeble hope for the future?**

And could it be that we have grossly misunderstood the CURRENT role that Jesus Christ plays in our world? Ricky Bobby, the character played by Will Ferrell in *Talladega Nights: The Legend of Ricky Bobby* is fond of praying to the "little baby Jesus." "Dear Tiny Jesus, in your golden fleece diapers with your tiny, little fat balled up fists..." To all appearances, it would seem that most Christ followers today embrace a similar perspective. We prefer the "meek and mild" version of Jesus—cute and cuddly, espousing a message of peace and love, as if those ideas are something other than radical weapons in the hands of a no-holds barred combatant who will not rest until the works of the Devil are destroyed. As Bobby's wife, Carley (actress Lesley Bibb) objects during his prayer to the "tiny but still omnipotent" Jesus, "Hey, um... you know, sweetie, Jesus did grow up." He has "grown up" indeed! He sits at the right hand of the Father, far above all rule and authority, and He is systematically putting everything under His feet. He is our Warrior King, and He invites you and me to join Him in waging war against everyone and everything that dares to oppose His rule.

The lessons from 9/11 are legion, not the least of which is the impact that people who live for the future can have. Rooted in its understanding of "yesterday," radical Islam represents a worldview that is pregnant with expectations regarding "tomorrow." Misguided and misinformed, most militant Muslims are at least consistent. This life is to be lived for the sake of the next. That's a game-changer.

Almost every contemporary evangelical commentator argues that **when** Christ "comes again," **when** the "last days" are here, and **when** the "end of the age" arrives, Christ's Kingdom will flourish like never before. But what if, in the very sense in which Jesus intended, He HAS returned? What if the "end" has come and gone? What if the "last days" are now the past days? The Kingdom of Heaven is here, and it's high time we started living like people who believe that. My prayer is that, together, we will uncover a great catalyst to loving service in the name of Jesus Christ. My hope is that we will uncover an inspiration to courage and daring. I pray that when we are done, we will be motivated to infiltrate the Kingdom of darkness like subversives who are determined to destroy anything that sets itself up against the Lordship of the one true King, the Lord Jesus. I pray that we will redouble our efforts at becoming winsome warriors, gentle and respectful, audacious and lethal, gladly bearing the fallout of the offense of the cross.

As we journey together through God's Word, we will discover that the message of Jesus Christ was profoundly simple: "Repent, the Kingdom is here." To put it in the vernacular, "Abandon your own Kingdoms—Now! The promised rule of the one true King is here, accessible to all people like never before."

If this is true, then a new era dawned with the first coming of Jesus, and it will not end until He appears again. For those of us living in the "in-between" time, everything has changed. What might happen if we lived as if that were true? What might happen if we believed that, far from getting worse and worse, things are actually getting better and brighter? What if we believed that the "gloom and doom" industry that so many peddle has to do with things that have already come to pass? What if we took Christ's teaching seriously, and began to pray with greater fervency, "Your Kingdom come, Your will be done, ON EARTH as it is in Heaven?

Regardless of the details, one thing is certain—one day, Jesus will crack open the sky and we will hear Him shout, "Enough," only this time, there will be no in-between—The game is up. The King is afoot—for good. "Maranatha!"

Acknowledgments

I am deeply indebted to members of that first Bible study. Without your encouragement (nagging?) this book would never have been written.

I am also overwhelmed by the incredible contributions of Saints who have gone before us. The "great cloud of witnesses" that surround us is filled with courageous and brilliant practitioners of the ways of the Kingdom of God.

I am so grateful to those who gave countless hours of their time to editing, reviewing, making suggestions, and most of all, encouraging me to press on and complete this project. A special thanks to Crissa Boyink. Her tireless efforts went far beyond anything I had asked for. Without her help, I would never have plumbed the depths of the meaning of the popular but widely misunderstood "em-dash."

Finally, I am more thankful than they could know to my family. My parents, my wife of thirty-three years, my six children, five in-laws, and six grand-children continue to inspire me to be a better husband, a better father, and a better man.

CHAPTER 1
Why This Stuff Matters

VICTORY OR DEFEAT

> For what I received I passed on to you as of first importance: that Christ died for our sins according to the Scriptures, that he was buried, that he was raised on the third day according to the Scriptures...
> 1 CORINTHIANS 15:3-4

> I'm a "pan-millennialist;" everything will pan out in the end.
> SEMINARY STUDENT

It's easy to become frustrated when we study Biblical prophecy or the end times. The mind-boggling array of charts and timelines is enough to set our heads spinning. Our goal here is to look carefully at the Biblical texts and see if we can't come to some conclusions ourselves. Of course, all these things *will* pan out in the end. And a study of the end times, while significant, is not a matter of "first importance." But our understanding of the there and then can make a huge difference in how we live in the here and now. Any attempt at developing a vigorous Christian worldview must include an understanding of the end times. Rather than spending our time refuting one position or comparing a number of views, our focus will be God's Word. What did Biblical writers mean by the words they wrote? While reading this book won't answer every question, it will accomplish several things.

Why This Stuff Matters

It Will Force us to Read the Scriptures Carefully

"So you mean that if I don't agree with what's in this book, then I haven't been reading the Bible carefully?" Not exactly. It could mean that many of us have simply taken the word of end-times "experts" without really looking at the passages of Scripture ourselves. Have you listened recently to a TV preacher explain the end times? Every other sentence is peppered with a Biblical reference. Have you ever taken the time to carefully look up each passage, read it in context and then ask yourself, "What did the original author mean?"

We live in such an information-rich age, that it is easy for us to live our spiritual lives vicariously through the teaching or preaching of others. Regardless of whether or not you agree with the contents of this book, if you will carefully work through it, at the very least, you will be "forced" to pore over God's Word.

The focus of this study will be just that—God's Word. We will be reading and studying passages ourselves. We will be using the classic 3-Step "inductive" method of Bible study—Observation, Interpretation, and Application. If nothing else, when you turn the last page, you will be better prepared to *present yourself to God as one approved, a workman who does not need to be ashamed and who correctly handles the Word of Truth.* (2 Timothy 2:15) **What none of us can afford to do is react dismissively to an interpretation that doesn't fit with our preconceived notions.** If you don't agree with an interpretation, articulate an alternative that is firmly rooted in God's Word.

It Will Acquaint us With Our Rich Christian Heritage

We should always be suspicious of new interpretations of Scripture that have little or no historical precedent. That's not to say that we can never discover anything new in Scripture—new **applications** of passages are possible every day! But humility as well as wisdom requires that we look at where we have come from. What have Christ followers believed about the end times since Christ's first coming? As we move deeper into this study, we will discover that **interpretations we have never heard of are really those views with the best historical pedigree, while those views that are currently the most popular are really quite new!** (See Appendix #1 for a sketch of that history.)

It Will Provide Us With Hope And Joy Now!

So much of today's end-time teaching is characterized by dismal predictions and ominous warnings. "Things are bad, and they are only going to get worse." Many end-times *experts* are only too happy to catalog for us how the downward spiral toward a great tribulation is only minutes away, and we had better get ready for the worst. Someday, in the future, Christ will reign; but for now, Satan and his minions call the shots. Our best hope is to hang on and be raptured before everything goes to Babylon in a bread basket!

History shows that a great number of Biblical scholars have held a very different view of "the end." By focusing on Jesus' teaching that "The Kingdom is here," many of them envisioned a much brighter future. If that is true, that the Kingdom is here, then we have no choice but to live like Kingdom citizens now. We are to fight against anything that fails to recognize the one True King and His reign. As Paul urged the Ephesians,

> *I pray that the eyes of your heart may be enlightened in order **that you may know the hope** to which he has called you, the riches of his glorious inheritance in his holy people, and his incomparably great power for us who believe. That power is the same as the mighty strength he exerted when he raised Christ from the dead and seated him at his right hand in the heavenly realms, far above all rule and authority, power and dominion, and every name that is invoked, **not only in the present age** but also in the one to come* (Ephesians 1:18-21).

The church in Thyatira was assured that the reign of Christ was to be shared by ALL believers:

> *To the one who is **victorious** and does my will to the end, **I will give authority over the nations**—that one 'will rule them with an iron scepter and will dash them to pieces like pottery'—**just as I have received authority from my Father*** (Revelation 2:26-27).

Living like the Kingdom is here now also contributes to joy. Every June, papers and television networks remember June 6, 1944. While veterans of the actual D-Day landings are becoming harder to find, the celebration is no less profound. In the weeks following the initial invasion, French cities were razed, farms and churches were burned, and livestock were killed or commandeered. Most of the destruction had come at the hands of the allies as part of their attempts to dislodge German defenders. Bombs from air raids and artillery shells fell like rain in many places. Many American GIs wondered how the French people would respond to the army that had caused so much destruction.

One of hardest hit cities was the town of Vire. On August 29, 1944, the city was officially "liberated." It had been leveled. Not a single building emerged unscathed. Trepidation was understandably the mood of the American troops who rolled into Vire that day in late August. One of the men who was part of that group remembers that they had expected a formal reception by a small delegation of the city fathers. "Instead the entire populace was out on the sidewalk with American flags, screaming madly," he said. "Basically for four hours, the entire town threw us a party. It was truly one of the highlights of my life." [1]

What prompted this kind of delirium in the face of unimaginable loss? The French people knew that this was the beginning of the end for the German occupiers. Again and again, the Scriptures urge us to live with the same kind of expectant joy. From the announcement of Christ's birth (Luke 1:13-17), to the ascension of the Christ, (Luke 24:50-53), joy is the hallmark of God's people.

The toughest part of the conflict is the battle of faith—fighting the tendency to draw conclusions on what the eyes of sight tell us. **DESPITE what we see, Christ reigns NOW, and the Kingdom is coming more fully each day! Like the Kingdom, joy is here now! Like the Kingdom, hope is here now!**

It Will Solve Many Problematic Passages in Scripture

It is no surprise that there are people who don't believe

---

[1] *French showed joy Iraqis don't feel.* August 22, 2004 The Baltimore Sun By Michael Hill, SUN STAFF

that the Bible is God's infallible word. But most people are not aware of how much of a role Biblical prophecy plays in their attacks on Scripture. **There are many passages in Scripture, including direct quotations from Christ himself, which defy explanation if we believe that most prophecy points to events in the distant future.** Liberal scholars in particular observe that the Bible is rife with time-frame references that seem to suggest an imminent "return" of Christ. Jesus made bold claims about His imminent return. Bible critics argue that this is proof-positive that the Bible is not reliable. Still others argue that since Jesus predicted His imminent return, He was not truly the Son of God, or He would have known better.

Other, more conservative scholars will often refer to the "over-realized eschatology" of Biblical authors. Jesus' first century followers were so anxious for the promised return of Christ, that they projected their longing onto their readers, making it *appear* as if Jesus would return in their lifetime. Still other conservative scholars go to great lengths to argue that seemingly clear passages don't mean what they look like they mean. Since Jesus did not "return" in the first century, the passages that suggest He did must mean something else.

Perhaps no Biblical book has presented readers more "time-frame issues" than the book of Revelation. While it fascinates most, it is usually met with fear and frustration when it comes to studying it. "That book is so confusing! How could anyone possibly keep track of all those angels and seals and trumpets and beasts...?" *This* book is designed to take some of the mystery out of those hard to understand passages, and to make sense of the many seemingly out of place time-frame references throughout the New Testament.

On the other hand, we need to be honest and admit that NO TEACHING REGARDING THE END TIMES OR BIBLICAL PROPHECY IS WITHOUT ITS PROBLEMS. If that were not so, we would all believe the same thing, and no books like this one would be necessary. But the interpretations offered in this book will go a long way in clearing up some of the confusion by providing simple, straightforward explanations of passages that may very well mean what they look like they mean.

It Will Enhance Our Understanding Of God's Glory

How has the God of the Bible chosen to reveal Himself, especially in relationship to His people? How is history moving in a clear, God-guided direction? Who is at the heart of God's affections? What is the one thing that God desires above all others? Studying Biblical prophecy for answers to questions like these is a thrilling pursuit. My prayer is that what will emerge from the pages of this book is a fuller picture of God's glory. I want each of us to "taste and see" a picture of the sovereign God of all creation, guiding and moving history to a spectacular conclusion. Our heart rate should quicken as we consider a God who avenges those who are persecuted, a God who pursues justice, and a God who fights for those who are His. God is on the march, and He is working everything together for His greater glory and our greater good. **There are few places that provide us a better vantage point from which to drink in the beauty of God's glory than a study of the end times.**

The only-wise God has chosen to restore and redeem our fallen world—to cause it to conform to the values and prerogatives of heaven itself. Like the God who conceived them, those values and prerogatives are "holy;" they are "other," not of this world. He is most glorified when things *look* the worst, when the enemy *seems* to have the upperhand, and when the only devices left at the disposal of His saints are weapons that *appear* hopelessly outmatched. *Sola Gloria Deo!*

It Will Change the Way we Behave

Closely related to the having "hope and joy now," "this stuff" matters because the interpretational conclusions that we will reach have the potential to change us from survivalists into subversives. We are talking practical implications of the highest order. We are on the winning side—NOW. Rather than living in fear, rarely venturing far from the safety of the church, we are transformed into aggressive warriors. Using weapons that are totally unfamiliar to the world, we destroy everything that sets itself up in opposition to the Lordship of Christ. By engaging in prayer, loving our enemies, doing good to those who persecute us, engaging in worship and promoting racial reconciliation, just to name a few, we push back the Kingdom of Darkness. By examining how the story ends, we begin to live like people who know the compelling "secret" to life. By affirming our citizenship of the only Kingdom that will truly last, everything changes; from our attitudes, to the way we interpret world events, from the way we worship, to the way we spend our money, from the way we love to the way we live. The end times, far from being a study reserved for spiritual heavyweights or seminary professors is a study that will plant our feet firmly on holy ground, while our minds and hearts soar to the heavenly Jerusalem. **Our study of the end times** will transform us into people that are so heavenly minded that we become people of inestimable earthly good.

It Will Provide Us With A Robust Philosophy Of History

Say what? I admit, the words "robust" and "philosophy of history" seem mismatched. Unfortunately, the Church is woefully ill-equipped to articulate a clear, and yes, robust philosophy of history.

True Confessions: I love "first-person shooter" games. For the uninitiated, FPS's are video/computer games in which the player is a one-man wrecking crew, armed with an arsenal that would make Rambo blush (And yes, I love MMA as well, as brutish a sport as there ever was which certainly appeals to my more "base" instincts—If you are not familiar with MMA, Google it). In each level of a FPS game, the player has a "task" that involves moving through enemy territory. Sometimes I get lost. No worries. In the upper left or right of the screen, there is usually a compass. It highlights the player's position and always points true North, the direction you have to move to reach your goal. It's a great resource—whenever lost or confused, look for true North. A good philosophy of history is much the same. It's easy for us to "get lost." What is the true North for all of history? The Kingdom.

John Bright, in his brilliant exposition of the role of the Kingdom in Scripture put it this way in commenting on Mark 1:14-15: *"Mark thus makes it plain that the burden of Jesus' preaching was to announce the Kingdom of God; that was the central thing with which He was concerned. A reading of the teachings of Jesus as they are found in the Gospels only serves to bear this statement out. Everywhere the Kingdom of God is on His lips, and it is always a matter of desperate importance."*[2]

One more confession--I have a bad habit of always heading for work whenever I leave the house. Regardless of where I'm going, I absent-mindedly head for work. When my wife is with me and she recognizes I may be doing this, she will ask "Do you know where you're going?" To which I will often respond, "No. But I'm making great time." Without a robust philosophy of history, we are destined to make great time without really knowing where we're headed. The truth is that we are going somewhere. Some have postulated that we are headed for Armageddon, or a Rapture, or an earthly Kingdom. None of these find much support in Scripture. What we know for certain is that Christ taught us to pray, "Your Kingdom come, Your will be done, on earth, *as it is heaven.*" **Something about heavenly realities are destined for earth. Those realities are best captured in the word, "Kingdom."**

One of the blessings of catechism (yes, I took catechism, and yes, it was a blessing, and yes, I lament its ouster in many churches) was that I learned at an early age that the "big picture" could be summarized in three words: Creation, Fall, Redemption. Those three trains of thought need to be hooked up to the engine of the Kingdom. In the pages ahead we will see how God's Word fits together perfectly to paint a picture of ultimate triumph and victory. We can be certain that our labor is not in vain (1 Corinthians 15:58), and that Christ is taking us for the ride of our lives. He

---

[2] John Bright, *The Kingdom of God* (Nashville, TN: Abingdon Press, 1953), Location 96 of 4274 in Kindle Version of the book, first page of Chapter 1.

is systematically making everything His "footstool," and, everything but death will come under His rule in **this life**. Christ will gather up all the posers and pretenders, everything that denies His authority, every power, every dominion, every nation, all bundled up and offered to the Father. And what do the Scriptures call this collection of dominions and powers that Christ will hand over to the Father? You guessed it:

> *Then the end will come, when he hands over **the Kingdom** to God the Father after he has destroyed all dominion, authority and power. **For he must reign** until he has put all his enemies under his feet. The last enemy to be destroyed is death* (1 Corinthians 15:24-26).

There you have it. This is what Jesus is about, and this is where history is headed. All aboard!

It Will Equip Us To Fight!

IF Christ is reigning now, and IF He has already begun to put *all His enemies under His feet*, and IF a battle rages all around us as Christ continues *to destroy the works of the Devil* (1 John 3:8), then a very real war is being waged, and we are in the thick of it. Christ has offered us a template for how this battle is to be waged, and a template for the role that we play. There is an understandable uneasiness in this day and age whenever "religious" people use the language of war. As we will see, this is a very different battle, against a very different enemy, fought with very different weapons. Despite the unique nature of the conflict, a study of the end times will leave no doubt that we are, in fact, at war. If you doubt it, consider this.

WHY THIS STUFF MATTERS

What is the most quoted or referred to Psalm in the entire New Testament? Psalm 23? Psalm 100? Nope. It is Psalm 110.[3] Why is that significant? Because Psalm 110 is "fightin' words."

> *The LORD says to my lord: "Sit at my right hand until I make your enemies a footstool for your feet." The LORD will extend your mighty scepter from Zion, saying, "Rule in the midst of your enemies!" Your troops will be willing on your day of battle. Arrayed in holy splendor, your young men will come to you like dew from the morning's womb. The LORD has sworn and will not change his mind: "You are a priest forever, in the order of Melchizedek." The Lord is at your right hand; He will crush kings on the day of his wrath. He will judge the nations, heaping up the dead and crushing the rulers of the whole earth. He will drink from a brook along the way, and so he will lift his head high* (Psalm 110).

It comes as a surprise to many believers that the Bible most often describes our lives in terms of warfare. There is good reason. Our life is warfare because our leader is a Warrior. "Virtually every book of the Bible—Old and New Testaments—and almost every page tells us about God's warring activity."[4] As we dive into God's Word over the next few pages, we will find inspiration for daring raids and audacious forays against the Kingdom of darkness. We will learn that the weapons at our disposal are "powerful," and that our Leader has modeled for us the proper way to fight. We

---
[3] Ben Patterson, *Muscular Faith* (Carol Stream, IL: Tyndale House Publishers, 2011), pp. 16-17.

[4] Dr. Dan Allender and Tremper Longman III, *Bold Love* (Colorado Springs, CO: Navpress, 1992), p. 111.

will learn to fight, not as people who *act* as if they have already won, *but as People who in fact have won and are reigning with Christ now*. Best of all, we will continue to look to our great Leader, Our Divine Warrior King, for both the "want to" and the "can do" that are critical in achieving the consummate victory.

Conclusion

If given the opportunity to visit Milan, Italy, I am told that the great Duomo Cathedral is a must-see. Six centuries in the making, it is the fourth (some say the second) largest cathedral in the world. Most impressive is its bank of one-hundred twenty stained glass windows that adorn the front of the church. Replaced in the mid-19th century, the subject for the windows is not what one would expect. There are no Old Testament stories depicted, no images from the life of Christ, no manger, no cross, no empty tomb. Instead, the artist has dedicated this magnificent bank of windows to the book of Revelation. R. Geoffrey Brown in a sermon entitled "Look! A Great White Horse" describes it this way:

"The afternoon sun strains in, turning the window into a sea of glass mingled with fire. You see the vials being outpoured; the trumpets, Michael and his angels in battle against the dragon, the great angel with the rainbow upon his head and one foot upon the earth and the other upon the heaven, declaring in the name of him who lives forever and ever that time shall be no longer. Bound with a chain, Satan is thrown into the bottomless pit at last. The great white throne glows in the sunlight.

"Most impressive of all is the great, white horse. Upon the horse sits a still greater Rider with the armies of

heaven behind him. He comes to set everything straight at last for everyone of us who has hoped in Him, and for everyone who has been subjected to the pain and prejudice of living for Jesus Christ in a world seemingly gone mad."[5]

Just as all the natural light that spills onto that altar is filtered through those windows, so the light of God's glory that shines on us is filtered through the great events of the book of Revelation. As we will see, the vision Christ gave to John inspired his first-century readers to do more than just hang on. They were inspired to overcome! The same light of God's glory shines on us today, this generation of winsome warriors.

Chapter Summary

We are at war—Not a culture war, not a military struggle, but a conflict between Kingdoms. They are NOT equal combatants. Despite the continued growth of the kingdom of darkness, Christ's Kingdom continues to expand and overcome. We are approaching the day when Christ will "fill everything in every way…" (Ephesians 1:23). In the time between His first coming and His final appearing, the Church is the vehicle through which Christ will achieve the ultimate victory. It is critical that we understand that.

Although a study of the end-times is not a matter of first importance, it is essential in developing a dynamic Christian worldview. Among the many reasons why such a

---

[5] R. Geoffrey Brown, *"Look! A Great White Horse!,"* Preaching Today, Tape No. 111

study is important, there are several that stand out. A study like this will:

- Force us to Read the Scriptures Carefully
- Acquaint Us With Our Rich Christian Heritage
- Provide Us With Hope And Joy Now!
- Solve Many Problematic Passages in Scripture
- Enhance Our Understanding Of God's Glory
- Change the Way We Behave
- Provide Us With A Robust Philosophy Of History
- Equip Us To Fight!

The goal of this study is, through the careful exploration of the Scriptures, to connect us with our rich Christian heritage and discover truths that will energize us to continue fighting the good fight. By discovering that Jesus and His disciples meant precisely what it looks like they meant, we will not only be able to make sense of difficult passages, but we will uncover a great source of motivation and inspiration to change the way we live and to embrace our calling as witnesses with renewed passion and joy. Like never before, we will rally around our currently-reigning Leader to lift up His name and advance the Kingdom that He came to establish.

CHAPTER 2

Mining For Gold In God's Word

DRILLING DOWN

The aim of good interpretation is not uniqueness; one is not trying to discover what no one else has ever seen before...the aim of good interpretation is simple; to get at the 'plain meaning of the text.
Gordon Fee and Douglas Stuart; *Reading the Bible For All it's Worth*

Do your best to present yourself to God as one approved, a worker who does not need to be ashamed and who correctly handles the word of truth.
2 Timothy 3:15

For several years, my family lived on the banks of a tributary to the Big Applegate River, which fed the Rogue River of Southern Oregon. "Our" river was cleverly named "The Little Applegate." No more than twenty or thirty feet across in most spots, the Little Applegate made its way through some of the most beautiful country in the world. The "worth" of the beauty of that river was largely lost on me as a late teen. It was a great place to swim and fish. That was about it. All that changed on the day when our family made the "great discovery." There was gold in the Little Applegate. I'm talking real gold. Solid gold. Late teen or not, that certainly got my attention. For years, miners had turned up that river bed to mine gold. The remains of the late 19th century slues boxes could still be seen on the mountainside above our home. Although official mining had stopped decades earlier, rumor had it that there was still gold to be found there. That, coupled with the meteoric rise in gold prices at that time, inspired my family to try their hand at prospecting. Prospect we did.

And we did find gold. At first, armed with only a shovel, a pail, and a gold pan, we worked the banks of that river. Early minor successes caused us to take our work more seriously. We studied gold-mining—Gold tends to fall on the "down-current" side of large rocks on the river bottom. We bought more sophisticated equipment—we purchased a portable, gas powered dredge (a big vacuum cleaner-like machine set atop an inflated inner tube) with a built in riffle board (a one-foot wide, 3 foot long ribbed slide, angled down at 45 degrees to the water, which sand and rocks spilled over on their way from the top of the board back into the river.) That's where the gold would be—stuck on the carpet that lined the bottom of the riffle board. Of course, you couldn't just pick it up. The rice-sized pieces of pure gold would be nestled in among the heavier rocks and the jet-black sand that was inevitably there (we later learned that the "sand" was actually iron ore, ground down over time into a fine powder the consistency of powdered sugar and its exact opposite in color). After spending an hour sucking up sand and rocks and the occasional crayfish, we would empty the material left on the riffle board into buckets. Then we would pan.

Obviously, gold is heavy. It's that dynamic that makes panning for gold a consistently effective way to find it. After you've filled a gold-pan (a pan that looks like a Chinese wok with a shallower bottom) with material from the bucket, you start to pan. You dip the pan into the water at the river's edge and rotate the water around the pan in a rhythmic, circular motion. Lighter stones wash out first, then heavier ones, and so on. You refill the pan with water and repeat the process. What you are left with is the iron "sand" dotted with small flakes or kernels of pure gold. Against the backdrop of the ink-black sand, the gold stands out dramatically, like the burst of flash bulbs in a dark room.

Believe it or not, we actually got pretty good at panning gold. We supplemented our income with tidy sums of money from our monthly trips to the assayer's office in Medford. It was never a lot, but it was enough to make it worth the effort. While most of the gold we found was turned over for a profit, we kept some of the gold we found. Most of what we kept we had made into jewelry. Local artisans were only too happy to make suggestions for how to incorporate our gold into their designs.

So what does all this have to do with our study of the end-times? Just this: The pieces of gold jewelry that we had made would have fetched the same price as any other gold. Whatever the going rate per ounce was, that was what you could expect to be paid. But the gold that we used to make that jewelry was worth much more to *us*. It was not because they represented fine pieces of art. **It was because they were made from gold that we had personally mined. The value of** the gold increased dramatically to us because we had worked so hard to find it in the first place.

The same is true for the Word of God. The truths we find in God's word are worth the same "per-ounce" regardless of where they come from. If you read them in a book, hear them in a sermon, or listen to them on a CD, their "value" is roughly the same—but the truth that you mine yourself? There is a special value attached to that. Those truths are more precious and will be far more meaningful to us than any truth we have handed to us. This is why we need to do a little "study" and perhaps purchase some other "equipment" before we jump into the world of the end-times. By taking these introductory steps, we set ourselves up for greater success. In the end, there is no truth more precious than the truth we mine ourselves.

A Brief Lesson In Biblical Interpretation

Although it's a big word, "hermeneutics" is something that we all do, even if we've never heard the word before. Hermeneutics is simply a set of rules or principles for interpreting the Bible. The word itself means "to interpret." I know we are all anxious to dive into Biblical prophecy, but if we are to avoid some of the mistakes that others have made, we need to be as prepared as possible when it comes to knowing where to look and how to find the kernels of truth we seek—and that means that we need to bring the right tools with us before we "dig in."

Background

God is nothing if He is not THE God of history. God is always busy, always active. He is moving ALL of humanity in a clear direction, with one overriding purpose; to bring glory to His name and to spread His fame throughout the galaxy. (Exodus 9:13-16; 2 Samuel 7:23; Ezekiel 36:20-23) God has determined, from the beginning, to spread His fame throughout the earth (Habakkuk 3:2) in the context of what the Scriptures call, "The Kingdom." We will look in much greater detail later at what this Kingdom includes: when and where it is, and how we should live as citizens of that Kingdom.

The thing to remember at this point is that this Kingdom is not imaginary, and it is not experienced on some spiritual plane to which only the truly enlightened are privy. This Kingdom is displacing all the other Kingdoms of the world, both political and personal. There are not two histories—world history and Kingdom history. They are inextricably linked. Like a great divine steam roller, the Kingdom of God is moving through history, crushing everyone and everything that opposes it. Our spiritual fathers and mothers understood this. It would be unthinkable to imagine a radical distinction between what God is doing and what the "world" is doing—they are one and the same.

What Do You Think It Means?

gen·re (noun): *one of the categories, based on form, style, or subject matter, into which works of all kinds can be divided...* The Bible is composed of many different types or genres of literature. Within each type, other types appear. The Bible is composed of narrative history, poetry, letters, parables, and more. Each demands that we approach it with the right interpretive "grid."

We may be tempted to read each genre in the same way, but we sacrifice understanding the meaning of many passages by doing so. Biblical prophecy or apocalyptic literature is one genre. As such, it has its own rules for interpretation. More on that later.

Taking the Bible "Literally"

There was a time in the history of the Church when Biblical interpretation was given over to an "allegorical" or "mystical" method. Despite the ominous undertones of the word "mystical," many of the early Church fathers employed this method. They were devout Christ followers who held to the inerrancy and authority of God's word. Popularized in the Eastern Church, men like Clement of Alexandria, (155-216 AD) Origen, and even the great St. Augustine (354-430 AD) approached the Bible in this way. Rather than work from the clear or straightforward meaning of a text, they would look for "deeper" meaning, especially as it applied to the Old Testament. Jesus employed a popular allegorical method of teaching using parables. Many of the stories that Jesus told were not intended to have us focus, for example, on farmers and seeds and fields, but on the fact that those images represented disciples, the message of the Kingdom, and the world. The danger inherent in such an approach to Scripture is obvious. With little effort, it is possible to come up with meanings that are a far cry from what the author originally intended.

In response to the abuses of the allegorical method of interpretation, the Reformers, e.g. Martin Luther (1483-1546) and John Calvin (1509-1564), recommended taking the Bible "literally." This did NOT mean that these giants of the faith rejected the idea that many things in the Bible are intended symbolically or figuratively. They understood that the Bible is filled with figures of speech and symbols. But unless there is good reason to believe that the Biblical author intended us to interpret what they wrote symbolically or figuratively, then we should understand their words in their normal and customary sense.

Unfortunately, in our day, the word "literal" has become an evangelical hot-potato. It is **the** litmus test for "true, conservative Biblical scholarship." Any interpreter, the argument goes, who suggests that a passage may not mean exactly what it appears to mean, must obviously be a "liberal." By that criterion, every one of the greatest Biblical expositors in the history of the Church would be branded a heretic. Even those who hold to today's understanding of a "literal" hermeneutic do not stick to it in every situation. A "star" is clearly a celestial body, emanating light that is visible only at night. But a trip to Hollywood would undoubtedly expose us to a plethora of stars that have little relation to "stars" (although the Hollywood versions are also most visible at night). In the same way, a literal interpretation of Jesus' words, "I am the gate" would leave the reader confused and frustrated.

As we study God's word, we need to take each passage literally, in the classic sense that the Reformers used that word. This is why it is critical that we employ good common sense in our reading of prophetic or apocalyptic literature. A stiff, wooden literalism will most certainly move us further away from the author's meaning. Prophetic writing, especially the book of Revelation is rife with vivid and dramatic symbols. Some symbols have a uniform meaning, while at other times the same symbol is used to describe something different. In many cases, these symbols are explained to us in the text itself. Other times, we are left to determine the meaning of a symbol from the immediate context, or other uses of the same symbol in another passage or other prophecy. Regardless of the method we use to determine the meaning of symbols, we must never lose sight of the fact that they are just that—symbols. They stand for or signify something else. Whether the writer is using numbers, descriptions of stars or stones, bones or bowls, we must always ask ourselves, "what did the author mean by using that symbol in that way?"

There is no need to guess at the danger of reading prophecy with a wooden literalism. History records the gross failure of just such a group of individuals—the Scribes and Pharisees. As they pored over Biblical prophecy, a picture of the coming Messiah began to take shape that made it virtually impossible for them to recognize Him when He actually came. Their expectations regarding the coming Kingdom were terribly disappointing precisely because of their literal interpretations. When they read the promises of God to David in 2 Samuel, they anticipated a King in the warrior tradition of David, one who would reign from Jerusalem and restore the political fortunes of Israel. It was literal interpretations like that that blinded them to the coming of their own Messiah. We dare not make the same mistake, or we, too, will turn a blind eye to the very real and present King.

Interpreting A Passage

"The Bible is such a difficult book to understand. There are so many interpretations for every passage." We have all heard ourselves or someone else say something like that. At first glance, that seems right. But when a

Biblical writer, under the inspiration of the Holy Spirit, wrote something down, did they mean for their words to be understood in a certain way? Did they mean many things by what they wrote, leaving it up to the individual reader to decide what their words meant? This is not a "harmless" question. It raises an issue that is at the heart of everything that is both right and wrong in our world today. Let me put it another way; when it comes to reading something, anything, do we *discover* meaning or do we *create* meaning? There is a popular and powerful school of thought, even in the Church today that would lean heavily to the latter—we create meaning. Some would argue that it is impossible to know what the original author meant; therefore it is futile to try. This kind of thinking throws the doors open wide to a kind of relativism that takes one of our most important weapons out of our hands, rendering us harmless and ineffective. This kind of relativism can subtly creep into our own lives.

How often have you been part of a Bible study where the facilitator asked the group, "So what do you think this passage means?" We understand the *intent* of the question, but it is a terribly poor choice of words! IT IS IRRELEVANT WHAT I THINK A PASSAGE MEANS! And it is irrelevant what YOU think a passage means. The first and most important question we need to ask is, "what did the PERSON WHO WROTE IT mean?" When Biblical writers wrote, they meant only ONE thing. Our goal in interpreting a passage is to answer the question, "What did the writer of these words mean for his original readers to understand?"

"But I have often read the same passage and been able to apply it to my life in different ways—or I know other people who read the same passage I did, and they get something entirely different out of it." Absolutely true! But we are not using our words carefully. What we really mean to say is, "Once I understand the *meaning* of a passage, there are many possible *applications* of that meaning—for me and for you." *For every passage of Scripture, there is only one meaning, many applications.*

Of course, it's not that simple. Sometimes, the MEANING of a passage is hard to determine. This is why we need to work hard at determining the original meaning. If we get the meaning wrong, there's a very good chance that we will make poor applications as well. Even if we get the meaning right, we must be careful not to apply a passage in a way that completely loses sight of the meaning. For example, we might read Romans 8:28 and rightly understand Paul to be saying that no matter what the circumstances of our life are, God will work all those things together for our good. A bad application would be that we can adopt any lifestyle we choose, because no matter how much we drink, eat, sleep around, etc., God will work all those things together for our good.

While this idea of there being only one meaning to every passage may seem patently obvious to you or me, it's important to remember that there are many people, even among those who profess to be evangelical Christians, who would not agree. They would argue that it is IMPOSSIBLE to know what someone meant who wrote something hundreds or even thousands of years ago. As we proceed, you will discover that this book flatly rejects that idea. We CAN know what Biblical writers meant when they wrote. The degree to which we carefully unpack the meaning of a passage is the degree to which we can apply it to our lives in healthy and profitable ways.

The Text In The Context

Another key to good interpretation is understanding the context of a passage. Context is everything when it comes to Biblical interpretation. Imagine that someone walks up to you and exclaims, "I am mad about my flat." Obviously, this person means something by those words, and they mean only one thing. But if the "context" of those words is London, England, it will mean something quite different than if the context is Chicago, Illinois. The former would be making a declaration about their new apartment--they just love it! The latter would be talking on a cell phone on the shoulder of the Dan Ryan Expressway, lamenting the fact that one of the tires on their car is now without air. When we read the Bible, context is determined by reading around a passage, moving from the larger (the entire book) to the smaller (a word or phrase). Background information is another important element to determining context: who is writing, to whom are they writing, when are they writing, and what are the larger themes in a particular chapter, book, or section of the Bible?

Are We Clear?

A final principle for good Biblical interpretation may be the most important of all. We've already acknowledged that some passages are hard to understand. **This is why it is critical for us to let clearer passages help us interpret the less clear passages.** For example, read Luke 14:26-27 and then tell me how we are to feel about our relatives.

> *"If anyone comes to me and does not hate father and mother, wife and children, brothers and sisters—yes, even their own life—such a person cannot be my disciple. And whoever does not carry their cross and follow me cannot be my disciple"* (Luke 14:26-27).

Did you get the right meaning? A person who read only this passage might come to some very inappropriate conclusions about how Christians should feel about their immediate family. So, what could we do to get a fuller understanding of Jesus' words here? Use your study Bible's to "cross reference" this passage and then, based on those other passages, give another interpretation of Jesus' words. In this case, we would cross-reference Matthew 10, where we read,

> *"Anyone who loves their father or mother more than me is not worthy of me; anyone who loves their son or daughter more than me is not worthy of me. Whoever does not take up their cross and follow me is not worthy of me. Whoever finds their life will lose it, and whoever loses their life for my sake will find it"* (Matthew 10:37-39).

Jesus is not urging us to "hate" our family—He is reminding us to make sure that our priorities are straight. We must never let any earthly relationship take precedence over our commitment to Jesus Christ.

Inductive Bible Study

Now let's pull it all together. For every passage we look at, we need to do three things: Observe, Interpret, and Apply. Here is a simple chart to help us study God's Word most effectively.

MINING FOR GOLD IN GOD'S WORD

Focus:	OBSERVATION The Text	INTERPRETATION The Meaning	APPLICATION My Life
Key Question	*What does it say?*	*What does it mean?*	*What should I do?*
Additional Questions	*Who is writing?* *To Whom are they writing?* *When was it written?* *Are words/ideas repeated?*	*What genre of literature is this?* *What does the immediate context tell me?* *Are there other Scriptures that address the same issues?*	*How might this passage change the way I think, act, feel?* *Is the Holy Spirit speaking to me in a specific way through this passage?*
Study Helps	Other Translations	Cross-References, Commentaries, Bible Dictionaries	Bible Studies, Sermons, Study Guides, Seminars

Chapter Summary

God's Word is unlike any other book ever written. God's Word is just like any other book ever written. Huh? Was that a

28

typo? No. They are both true. On the one hand, the words on the pages of Scripture are literally "alive." They breathe. They have the power to change hearts and renew minds. Unlike any other sacred text, the Bible brings together the unique personalities and objectives of forty different authors and the divine movement of the Spirit of God Himself. Without obliterating each authors' uniqueness, God's Spirit compelled those same authors to record precisely what He intended to convey.

On the other hand, the Bible is literature. It is composed of various genres, and each author had an objective in mind when he wrote. They meant something by their words, and they fully expected their readers to understand what they meant.

It is incumbent upon us to respect both of those truths. We are handling spiritual nitro glycerin! But we must also rely on good principles of interpretation just as we rely on the Spirit of God to reveal the truth of His Word to us. That means that we must keep in mind several "keys" to "rightly dividing the Word of Truth." We must assume that the Bible is to be taken "literally," not in a stiff, wooden sense, but in the way that the Reformers understood the word "literal." Each passage is a type of literature, and the same rules that we would apply to reading that type of literature anywhere else must be applied to Scripture. Prophetic literature cannot be read like an epistle, nor can poetry be understood in the same way as narrative history. Given those interpretational parameters, we should always assume that a passage means what it looks like it means, unless there is good reason to assume otherwise.

Our goal in reading the Bible literally is first of all to understand the meaning of the passage. Before we rush toward applying a passage, we must first answer the question, "what did the writer mean for his initial readers to understand?" Getting at the meaning of a passage includes looking carefully at the words themselves and then reading around those words to discover both the immediate and the broader context. As we encounter difficult passages, our first recourse is to look to other scriptures that deal with similar themes and ideas in order to let clearer passages help us understand less clear passages. Once we are confident that we have understood the author's meaning, we are then free to ask, "what are the implications of this passage for me, my family, and my world?" By employing this method, often referred to as "inductive" study, we will find that the fruit of our labor is nothing short of nuggets of pure, spiritual gold.

Finally, we must remember that the first step in any attempt at understanding God's Word is to consult with the ultimate author, God Himself. Who knows the heart of God like the Spirit of God (1 Corinthians 2:10-12)? That same Spirit will guide us through our study. Every time we look to God's Word, we should preface our study with the words of David in Psalm 119:18—"Open my eyes, that I might see wonderful things in your law." Prepare yourself, for "wonderful things."

CHAPTER 3

CAN GOD TELL TIME?

DRILLING DOWN

Most Muslims acknowledge Jesus as a prophet, but seek to discredit His Deity and destroy the credibility of Christianity by pointing out alleged errors and inconsistencies contained in the Bible concerning His non-return. They recognize the logical implications of the Bible's time statements as having a direct bearing on the Messianic and divine claims of Christ. But Jesus and the apostles must have lied about His imminent return and other eschatological matters, they argue. Or, if Jesus sincerely prophesied His time-restricted return and it has not been fulfilled, then He is a false prophet. The net result is to crumble the inspiration and inerrancy of the Bible and open the door for the acceptance of the Koran and Islam.
JOHN NOE IN *7 DEMANDING EVIDENCES*

"I am concerned with Christ as He appears in the Gospel narrative as it stands, and there one does find some things that do not seem to be very wise. For one thing, He certainly thought that His second coming would occur in clouds of glory before the death of all the people who were living at the time. There are a great many texts that prove it...where it is quite clear that He believed that His coming would happen during the lifetime of many then living. That was the belief of His earlier followers, and it was the basis of a good deal of His moral teaching."

BERTRAND RUSSELL -- WELL-KNOWN ATHEIST, IN HIS BOOK, *WHY I AM NOT A CHRISTIAN*.

"The vision of the evenings and mornings that has been given you is true, but seal up the vision, for it concerns the distant future..." I heard, but I did not understand. So I asked, "My lord, what will the outcome of all this be?" He replied, "Go your way, Daniel, because the words are rolled up and sealed until the time of the end.
DANIEL 8:26; 12:8-9

Then he told me, "Do not seal up the words of the prophecy of this scroll, because the time is near.
REVELATION 22:10

Truly I tell you, this generation will certainly not pass away until all these things have happened.
MATTHEW 24:34

From that time on Jesus began to preach, "Repent, for the Kingdom of heaven has come near."
MATTHEW 4:17

Time. It flies and heals; it runs out and signals the season to pay the piper. We keep it and kill it, save it and waste it. As much a part of our lives as time is, it may seem strange to start our discussion of the end times here. **But it precisely on the question of "time" that so much of our understanding of the end times turns.** For centuries, the time-frame references in Scripture have caused a great many skeptics to doubt the reliability of the Bible. Even believers have struggled to make sense of what seem to be contradictory references. CS Lewis captured that spirit in commenting on Matthew 24:34. *Truly I tell you, this generation will certainly not pass away until all these things have happened.* "Say what you like," we shall be told, "the apocalyptic beliefs of the first Christians have been proved to be false. It is clear from the New Testament that they all expected the Second Coming in their own lifetime. And, worse still, they had a reason, and one which you will find very embarrassing. Their Master had told them so. He shared, and indeed created, their delusion. He said in so many words, 'this generation shall not pass till all these things are done.' And he was wrong. He clearly knew no more about the end of the world than anyone else. It is certainly the most embarrassing verse in the Bible."[6] References regarding the imminent return of Christ abound. Both Jesus and His best students continually insisted that Jesus would return within the lifetime of His first century followers. Understandable questions follow.

Was Lewis right? Did Jesus know what he was talking about? Did the disciples misunderstand their Teacher? Was Paul simply an overzealous Christ-follower who imposed his personal views on the rest of the early church? Did John Zebedee, the writer of Revelation, editorialize his account of the vision he saw, including time frame references that reflected his own longings rather than what the Angel actually told him? Believe it or not, MANY Biblical teachers/scholars have concluded just that, that Jesus and His disciples were wrong. Are there legitimate reasons for them to think these things, or are they just "liberals" who don't warrant any serious attention?

Why Is When Important?

The questions that swirl around time-frame references in the Bible are about more than just silencing critics. Getting times or dates wrong can have disastrous practical implications as well. I know that we have all been late for something; a meeting, a wedding, a ride. Worse yet, we've all experienced that sinking feeling when we realized we completely missed an appointment.

---

[6] CS Lewis, *The World's Last Night and Other Essays*, (Orlando, Florida: Harcourt, Brace and Co., Inc., 1960), p. 97

CAN GOD TELL TIME?

Imagine the most important meeting of your life. You've worked out of the same office for years, but things are about to change—dramatically. You've entered the date on your Smart Phone or Outlook Calendar. It is several months off. The significance of this meeting couldn't be overstated. Decisions made there will impact your future—your family, your finances, your living arrangements, everything. In addition, you have received a substantial amount of data that you need to filter through in anticipation of that meeting. The data included many references to the correct date and time for the meeting, but, like the meeting itself, you put your preparation off—out of sight...out of mind. It would be months before you would even have to consider getting ready. But you had been misinformed. Or perhaps you just misread the memo alerting you to the time of the meeting. Whatever the reason, what you thought was to take place several months from now, actually took place last week. To make matters worse, no one told you the outcome of the meeting. You continued to live your life; unprepared and unaffected by the changes that were agreed upon at the meeting you missed.

It would be hard to imagine things unfolding that way if this meeting were that important. Your only solace is that of the hundred or so people in the office, most of them missed the meeting as well, because they too got the time wrong. Small consolation, right?

Now, imagine the same problem as it relates to Biblical prophecy. **Depending on whether or not we get the time-frame references right, we could actually become people living "out of time" with our surroundings.** Like spiritual dinosaurs, we have the potential to miss a lot—new values, changed relationships, leadership changes, etc. When it comes to the Kingdom of Heaven, getting the "when" right is critical. What follows is a close look at these many time-frame references.

THE KINGDOM IS "AT HAND"

In the local assembly that I co-pastor, we have a little antiphonal game we play. I say, "Sum up the entire teaching of Jesus Christ in one phrase" to which the congregation responds, "Repent! The Kingdom of Heaven has come near!" Corny? Perhaps. Right on? You betcha! With profound simplicity, we can sum up everything Jesus taught and when this earth-shattering transition occurred. "It's the Kingdom, stupid!"

The word that Jesus used for the "when" of the Kingdom is "near;" the word, *eggus* (εγγυs). When the word is used to describe spatial relationships, it means "close to" or "in proximity to" as in *while they were listening to this, he went on to tell them a parable, because he was **near** Jerusalem* (Luke 19:11). When it is used to describe temporal relationships, it means "soon" or "about to happen" as in *when they sprout leaves, you can see for yourselves and know that summer is **near**. Even so, when you see these things happening, you know that the Kingdom of God is **near**.* (Luke 21:30-31)

The word is actually a compound, composed of the words "εν" meaning "in" or "at" and the word γυιον meaning "appendage" or "hand." In the New Testament, the word first appears in the ministry of John the Baptist.

> *In those days John the Baptist came, preaching in the wilderness of Judea and saying, "Repent, for the Kingdom of heaven has come **near**." This is he who was spoken of through the prophet Isaiah: "A voice of one calling in the wilderness, 'Prepare the way for*

> *the Lord, make straight paths for him'"* (Matthew 3:1-3).

Matthew tips his hand as to his understanding of that word as it relates to time. Concerning the betrayal of Jesus he wrote

> *Then he returned to the disciples and said to them, "Are you still sleeping and resting? Look, the hour has come, and the Son of Man is delivered into the hands of sinners. Rise! Let us go! Here comes my betrayer!"* (Matthew 26:45-46).

There is no reason to believe that Matthew understood the word one way in chapter three and another in chapter 26.

Following the ministry of John the Baptist, Christ also preached that the coming of His Kingdom was near. *From that time on Jesus began to preach, "Repent, for the Kingdom of heaven has come **near**"* (Matthew 4:17). When He commissioned the twelve to spread the Gospel, His instructions were succinct: *As you go, proclaim this message: 'The Kingdom of heaven has come **near**'* (Matthew 10:7). Christ used a variant of the same word in Matthew 24. In responding to the disciples question regarding the destruction of the Temple and the "end of the age" Jesus said

> *"Now learn this lesson from the fig tree: As soon as its twigs get tender and its leaves come out, you know that summer is **near**. Even so, when you see all these things, you know that it is **near**, right at the door"* (Matthew 24:32-33).

Other uses of the εγγυσ word group bear out the idea of imminence.

Luke used this word: *Now the Festival of Unleavened Bread, called the Passover, was **approaching*** (Luke 22:1). In every case where a form of the word εγγυσ is used to describe temporal relationships, it means in a very short period of time on the clock. The same usage can be observed in the epistles.

In attempting to motivate the Philippian believers to good works, Paul wrote, *Rejoice in the Lord always. I will say it again: Rejoice! Let your gentleness be evident to all. The Lord is **near*** (Philippians 4:4-5). While arguing for the superiority of the "new covenant" in Christ, the writer of Hebrews explained that the old covenant was "obsolete" and must be done away with. When would this transition occur? *By calling this covenant "new," He has made the first one obsolete; and what is obsolete and outdated will **soon** disappear* (Hebrews 8:13).

In 1 Peter 4, Peter begins a discussion of how his first-century readers should behave. What does he use to motivate them to live Godly lives? *The end of all things is **near**. Therefore be alert and of sober mind so that you may pray.* Because the end of all things was "near," he encouraged his readers to be clear-minded and self-controlled, given to prayer and love. How could Peter say that the "end of all things" was **near** when we know that it has been nearly 2000 years since Peter wrote those words?

One explanation of Peter's words is that he "overreached" in his hope of an imminent return of his savior. Perhaps he is speaking in a general sense, arguing that we must live ***as if*** Jesus would return soon, or perhaps he simply made a mistake (the non-orthodox answer). Is it possible that he was correct, that the "end of all things" was imminent--that his first century readers should live upright lives because their world would soon come to an end?

In Hebrews we read:

> *And let us consider how we may spur one another on toward love and good deeds, not giving up meeting together, as some are in the habit of doing, but encouraging one another—and all the more as you see the Day **approaching** (nearing) (Hebrews 10:24-25).*

The writer of Hebrews clearly saw a "Day" that was fast approaching. The use of the definite article suggests that the writer had the Day of Judgment or at least some day of judgment in mind.

The half-brother of Jesus, James, is even more explicit than the writer of Hebrews. As James brought his letter to a close, he tried to prepare his readers for the difficult days ahead. He assured them that their suffering would not be indefinite. What should be their motivation for persevering?

> *Be patient, then, brothers and sisters, until the Lord's coming. See how the farmer waits for the land to yield its valuable crop, patiently waiting for the autumn and spring rains. You too, be patient and stand firm, because the Lord's coming is **near** (James 5:7-8).*

By now, we should recognize that word "near." James gets in line with the other New Testament authors in declaring that Jesus was coming back, in his lifetime and/or the lifetime of his readers. He could not have meant the second appearing of Christ. What a cruel encouragement it would have been to tell his readers to take heart, because

Jesus' appearing was near, when in reality, it was still thousands of years off. What could he have meant?

Perhaps the most astounding use of the word "near" or "at hand" appears in Revelation. John provided a perfect parenthesis to the vision he recorded. Although we will look in much greater detail later on, for now, consider the unmistakably clear time-frame references that John gave regarding the "when" of the vision he saw. He began the book by saying, *Blessed is the one who reads aloud the words of this prophecy, and blessed are those who hear it and take to heart what is written in it, because the time is **near*** (Revelation 1:3). So as to leave no doubt, John recorded the final message that the angel delivered to him: *Then he told me, "Do not seal up the words of the prophecy of this scroll, because the time is **near*** (Revelation 22:10).

At this point, the use of the word "near" may have raised more questions than it has answered. At the very least, we have to concede that Christ and his best students taught things that had an air of imminence about them. SOMETHING was going to happen **soon** ($\epsilon\gamma\gamma\upsilon\sigma$). The old covenant expression of the Kingdom was destined to pass away, and the new wine of the Kingdom was being poured in. The transition from the old to the new would not be millennia in the making. A dramatic and radical "day" was "at hand," just as surely as the Kingdom was.

Sealing The Deal

The last passage we looked at (Revelation 22:10) introduced us to the idea of "sealing." John was told, "Do not seal up the words of the prophecy of this scroll, because the time is near." This was not the first time that an angel had communicated such an idea to a prophet. The people of

Israel were taken into exile in 586 B.C. by the Babylonian empire. Daniel was among those taken captive. We know from the book that bears his name that he found favor in the court of Babylon because of his Spirit-inspired ability to interpret dreams and visions. Some of the most stirring visions in all of Scripture are found in Daniel. The question that seems to plague Daniel throughout the entire book is "When?" When were many of the things he saw going to happen? It is a question that he literally lost sleep over (Daniel 8 &10).

Some of the visions he saw were fulfilled in his own lifetime. Daniel 4 and 5 give chilling accounts of God's wrath unleashed upon the kings of Babylon. But other visions, those related to coming Kingdoms and the future disposition of God's people, came with different but very clear time-frame references.

King Nebuchadnezzar had a dream in which he saw a great statue destroyed by a rock that came crashing down the mountainside (We will look at this and other key prophecies in Daniel later). The rock became its own mountain after the other Kingdoms were pulverized. Daniel told his readers that these things would happen "in days to come" (2:27-28). What days? "In the time of those kings," the kings he had just described in his interpretation of the dream. In other words, this prophecy would **not** primarily concern those living at that time. It had to do with Kingdoms yet to be established, especially the fourth Kingdom.

In chapters 7 and 8, and again in chapters 10-12 Daniel is introduced to dreams and visions of his own. Time-frame references abound there as well. They concern things having to do with "the time of the end." (8:17). Daniel is told specifically to "seal up the vision, for it concerns the distant future" (8:26). The angel who gave the interpretation of the visions announced that he had come to "explain to you what will happen to your people in the future, for the vision concerns a time yet to come" (10:14). Because of the disturbing implications of the angel's words, Daniel pressed for a more specific answer. "How long will it be before these astonishing things are fulfilled?" (12:6). The angel reiterated, "Go your way, Daniel, because the words are closed up and sealed until the time of the end."

There is no question among scholars that the fulfillment of what Daniel saw in those chapters was still some time off. The repeated instruction that Daniel was given was to "seal up" his visions and dreams. That is a clear Biblical command describing something that is still in the distant future.

Now, compare those instructions (to "seal up" the prophecy) with the same words that appear in the Revelation of John. As we have seen, the book of Revelation is bracketed with two very clear time-frame references.[7] They are strategically placed to leave the reader with "interpretational bookends."

The very same language that was used in Daniel is used in Revelation. While Daniel was specifically told to "seal up" his prophecy, John was told "Do not seal up the words of the prophecy of this book, because the time is near" (Revelation 22:10). If Daniel's prophecy concerned things in

---

[7] Some have argued that these time-frame references pertain to the first 4 chapters only—the prophecies concerning the seven churches. The argument goes that these prophecies will be fulfilled within a few years. The fact that John **finishes** his account with the same time-frame reference in chapter 22, AND includes other similar time-frame references AFTER chapters 1-4, make this unlikely.

the distant future, what should we conclude regarding John's prophecy? In both cases, the conduits of these visions, Daniel and John, were introduced to the idea of "sealing." One is told to seal up, the other is told NOT to seal up. The implications are clear. Daniel was shown things for a later time, while John was shown things for his own time. If this is not the case, then the specific command regarding "sealing" is meaningless. Of course, it is not meaningless. It means exactly what it looks like it means. Daniel's vision concerned things hundreds of years in the future, while John's had to do with things that would begin happening within just a few years of recording the vision.

You may be wondering at this point, "Why have I never heard this before? I don't even remember reading those things! I know that the book of Revelation is all about things that will happen sometime in the distant future, so what on earth is John talking about?" That is precisely the problem. You HAVE read those things before, but because you were already preconditioned to believe that Revelation is only about the distant future, you missed them!

It is undeniable that John intended his first century readers to take heart at the content of the vision he recorded. The careful placement of time-frame references at the beginning and end of the prophecy (and peppered throughout; 2:16; 3:11; 10:5-7; 11:14 ;) were intentional. The fact that the angel gave John precisely the OPPOSITE instructions he gave Daniel only confirms that the vision John saw concerned things that John and his first-century readers expected to happen within their own lifetimes. And there are many other New Testament references that support this idea of imminence surrounding the end-times.

Do Things Happen Quickly, or Quickly?

En tachai (εν ταχει) is the expression that we translate as "soon" or "quickly." It literally means "in" or "with" "swiftness" or "speed." In Romans 16:17-20, the Apostle Paul encouraged the Roman Christians to persevere in doing good. He assured them that their commitment to what was right would bear fruit—it would result in Satan's defeat.

> *I urge you, brothers and sisters, to watch out for those who cause divisions and put obstacles in your way that are contrary to the teaching you have learned. Keep away from them. For such people are not serving our Lord Christ, but their own appetites. By smooth talk and flattery they deceive the minds of naive people. Everyone has heard about your obedience, so I rejoice because of you; but I want you to be wise about what is good, and innocent about what is evil. The God of peace will **soon** crush Satan under your feet* (Romans 16:17-20 emphasis added).

At first blush, this passage may not seem to have much to do with the end-times. Look closer. The defeat of Satan is a common end-times theme. Paul explained to the Romans that it was **their** feet that God would use to fulfill the promise of Genesis 3:15—"*And I will put enmity between you and the woman, and between your offspring and hers; He will crush your head, and you will strike his heel.*" The final death blow for Satan would be struck, and it would happen "soon."

In addition to the word "at hand," Revelation contains bookended uses of the word *εν ταχει* or "soon." *The revelation from Jesus Christ, which God gave him to show his servants what must **soon** take place. He made it known by sending his angel to his servant John...* (Revelation 1:1). Then, at the close of Revelation:

> *The angel said to me, "These words are trustworthy and true. The Lord, the God who inspires the prophets, sent his angel to show his servants the things that must **soon** take place* (Revelation 22:6).

From start to finish, the Revelation that John was given concerned things that would happen soon, within the lifetime of most of John's readers.

It Can't Mean What It Looks Like It Means

Before we continue, the point needs to be reiterated that **what is keeping you from understanding Biblical prophecy is the ideas that you brought to the "prophecy-table" before we began**. The "*a priori*" assumptions we have will always dramatically color our understanding of God's Word. For example, many liberal Biblical scholars have approached the Bible with their minds already made up: "Miracles are not possible." With that as their starting point, they read the Gospels and systematically explain away all the miracles contained therein. They argue that the "miracles" were nothing more than zealous disciples putting their own spin on who Jesus was. Or they argue that many miracles have perfectly logical explanations. The point? **When you begin reading a passage with a mind that is already made up, your interpretation is a foregone conclusion.**

Is it possible that many readers of the Bible's time-frame references fall prey to the same kind of thinking? They are not always "liberals," but they tend to begin their reading with their minds already made up. "I know that the things in Revelation or talk of the "last days" or the "end" have to do with events in the far distant future, so when I read words that don't fit my preconceptions, I must explain them in some other way."

Kicking The Prophetic Can Down The Road

So, what explanation do good, conservative readers of Scripture give to explain away the obvious meaning of the word εν ταχει, "soon?" They argue that these verses do not tell us *when* these thing will happen, but *how* they will happen, i.e. quickly or suddenly. In other words, this word suggests that **when** the things written about **DO** happen, they will happen quickly, or suddenly. We cannot say *when* these things will unfold, only that when they do, it's "lickity-split" time. Interpreters argue that this word MUST mean quickly, without any specific reference to the passage of time. Is that what the Biblical record shows?

In Matthew 5:25, a form of the same word used in Revelation appears.

> "Settle matters **quickly (soon)** with your adversary who is taking you to court. Do it while you are still together on the way, or your adversary may hand you over to the judge, and the judge may hand you over to the officer, and you may be thrown into prison" (Matthew 5:25).

Jesus warns us not to bring gifts to the altar with unresolved relational issues. Instead, we are told to "settle matters quickly with (y)our adversary." Are we to understand that Jesus is saying, "whenever you get around to it, be reconciled to your brother—but when you do get around to it, make sure that you do it fast?" Obviously, Jesus is saying, don't let a long time pass before you get this done. In fact, you should leave your gift at the altar and deal with it "quickly." Both the "when" and the "how" are assumed in the word we translate "quickly."

The same thing can be said for the admonition of the angel at the tomb of the risen Christ. In Matthew 28:7 we read about the women who found Jesus' empty tomb, only to encounter angels. The women were told, *Then go **quickly** and tell His disciples: 'He has risen from the dead and is going ahead of you into Galilee. There you will see Him.' Now I have told you.* Obviously, they were being urged to move at a rapid pace. But they are **not** being told that it did not matter **when** they decided to move quickly. Implicit in the command was the idea that they should go tell the disciples **now**!

In Acts 25:4, the provincial magistrate Festus indicated that he would be joining Paul in the city of Caesarea "soon." *Festus answered, "Paul is being held at Caesarea, and I myself am going there **soon**."* We might just as easily translate the word "shortly" or even "quickly." In any case, we would know what Festus meant. He was not telling us of his intent to run or ride a horse at a dead gallop to Caesarea. The clear meaning of his words is that in a short period of time, he would go up to Caesarea.

In virtually every instance where the term "shortly" or "soon" is used in the New Testament, it carries a time-frame reference with it. It addresses the question of "when" and not simply the question of "how." This is born out in virtually every Greek Lexicon, which lists the meaning of *tachos* or *en tachai* as "swiftness, quickly, at once, without delay, soon, shortly or very quickly and without delay."[8] It would appear that Biblical writers meant for their first-century readers to take heart in knowing that dramatic, Kingdom-focused things were going to happen soon, in the

---

[8] William F. Arndt and F. Wilbur Gingrich, *A Greek-English Lexicon of the New Testament and Other Early Christian Literature* (Chicago: University of Chicago Press, 1957), p. 814.

very near future. Three final examples of imminence should suffice.

In Romans 13:11-12, Paul wrote:

> *And do this, understanding the present time: The hour has already come for you to wake up from your slumber, because our salvation is nearer now than when we first believed. The night is nearly over;* **the day is almost here.** *So let us put aside the deeds of darkness and put on the armor of light.*

He urged his readers to be agents of love in this world. He motivated them by appealing to the days in which they lived. Paul contrasted "the present time" with "the day." That day was almost there and they should live with a sense of urgency and expectancy. What "day?" It was the day of their (our) salvation, a day when the promised Kingdom would come in a full and fresh way.

To the church at Corinth, Paul referred to that same day in a different way.

> *What I mean, brothers and sisters, is that* **the time is short.** *From now on those who have wives should live as if they do not; those who mourn, as if they did not; those who are happy, as if they were not; those who buy something, as if it were not theirs to keep; those who use the things of the world, as if not engrossed in them. For* **this world in its present form is passing away** (1 Corinthians 7:29-31).

Something was about to occur ("the time is short") that would dramatically change the way the Corinthians lived because the "world in its present form is passing away." Paul gave us a clue as to what he meant by using the same expression (is passing away) later in 2 Corinthians. He wrote:

> *Therefore, since we have such a hope, we are very bold. We are not like Moses, who would put a veil over his face to prevent the Israelites from seeing the end of **what was passing away**. But their minds were made dull, for to this day the same veil remains when the old covenant is read. It has not been removed, because only in Christ is it taken away. Even to this day when Moses is read, a veil covers their hearts. But whenever anyone turns to the Lord, the veil is taken away* (2 Corinthians 3:12-16).

The "world" that was passing away was the world of the Old Covenant. Like Peter, Paul anticipated a decisive moment in the near future that would serve as a break from the old and the introduction of the new. That break would be so profound that it could legitimately be called the "passing away of the world."

Pentecost: Connecting The Dots

As a child, I was fascinated with "activity pages" that had me connect the dots. A seemingly random collection of points on the page soon became a chicken, or a swing set, or a super hero. The issue of Pentecost and "tongues" is not dissimilar. Much more happened on that day than "just" the outpouring of the Holy Spirit. As we connect a number of seemingly unrelated passages, a clearer picture of what was happening will emerge. Listen again to how Peter explained the baffling events of that day. In response to the charge that the believers were drunk, Peter said,

> *"Fellow Jews and all of you who live in Jerusalem, let me explain this to you; listen carefully to what I say. These people are not drunk, as you suppose. It's only nine in the morning! No, this is what was spoken by the prophet Joel: "'**In the last days**, God says, I*

> *will pour out my Spirit on all people. Your sons and daughters will prophesy, your young men will see visions, your old men will dream dreams. Even on my servants, both men and women, I will pour out my Spirit in those days, and they will prophesy. I will show wonders in the heavens above and signs on the earth below, blood and fire and billows of smoke. The sun will be turned to darkness and the moon to blood* **before the coming of the great and glorious day of the Lord.** *And everyone who calls on the name of the Lord will be saved'* (Acts 2:14-21).

As Peter quoted Joel, he made a startling connection: "in the last days…" From Peter's perspective, the last days of which Joel spoke had arrived. According to Joel, and now Peter, more should be expected than just the pouring out of the Spirit. "I will show wonders in the heavens above and signs on the earth below…" etc. Did Peter actually believe that he was living in the "last days" and that a time was fast approaching when these amazing signs would fill the skies and the earth? Apparently so. In fact, Peter was looking to these events as "signs" of something else. They would portend "the coming of the great and glorious day of the Lord." There is no indication that Peter understood Joel to be talking about a gap of thousands of years between the day when the Spirit was poured out and the coming of the signs that would forecast the coming of the "day of the Lord." But our picture is not yet complete. There are more dots.

The Apostle Paul had a great deal to say about "tongues." In 1 Corinthians 14, he pointed to the gift of tongues as a sign that God was judging Israel. The presence of tongues was the fulfillment of the prophecy that God had given to Isaiah. Paul made this connection explicit by quoting from Isaiah in 1 Corinthians 14:21.

> *Brothers and sisters, stop thinking like children. In regard to evil be infants, but in your thinking be adults. In the Law it is written: "With other tongues and through the lips of foreigners I will speak to this people, but even then they will not listen to me, says the Lord." Tongues, then, are a sign, not for believers but for unbelievers* (1 Corinthians 14:20-22).

The specific reference is Isaiah 28:11 and the context of that passage is the judgment of Israel. This helps explain the otherwise cryptic comment that "tongues, then, are a sign, not for believers but for unbelievers." The mostly Jewish congregation to which Paul was writing would have immediately understood his words to mean, "This is what Isaiah foretold, and the presence of tongues serves as a sign to unbelieving Jews who have rebelled against God and His Christ—judgment is coming."

Even a quick reading of Isaiah 28 bears this out. "Ephraim," another name for Israel (cf. Isaiah 7), is going to feel the judgment of God for her apostasy. As a final proof that God was ready to judge Israel, a day would come when "with foreign lips and strange tongues God will speak to His people." *While you or I might never have connected Pentecost and speaking in tongues with God's judgment, Paul did.* That day had come, and Paul, along with Peter, saw it as not only a day of great blessing, but also a day that signaled the end for Israel. For the Apostles, Pentecost was the prelude to Holocaust.

In the film *Ghostbusters*, the three main characters played by Bill Murray (Venkman), Harold Remis (Spengler), and Dan Aykroyd (Stantz), have been called before the mayor of New York City. They are trying to convince him that something "big" will be happening soon.

Dr. Peter Venkman: This city is headed for a disaster of Biblical proportions.
Mayor: What do you mean, "Biblical"?
Dr Ray Stantz: What he means is Old Testament, Mr. Mayor, real wrath of God type stuff.
Dr. Peter Venkman: Exactly.
Dr Ray Stantz: Fire and brimstone coming down from the skies! Rivers and seas boiling!
Dr. Egon Spengler: Forty years of darkness! Earthquakes, volcanoes...
Winston Zeddemore: The dead rising from the grave!
Dr. Peter Venkman: Human sacrifice, dogs and cats living together... mass hysteria!

The world of the first-century was headed for a "disaster" of yes, Biblical proportions. Pentecost forecasted it. That disaster was in some way tied to the Kingdom and it was variously identified with "The Day," "the world in its present form," "the end," and the details of the book of Revelation. Before we try and explain the meaning of all this, we need to look at one more set of Scriptures.

The Most Embarrassing Verse In The Bible

As we have seen, the Gospels are filled with tantalizing clues as to the nature of the future. An overwhelming number of passages pointed to a day that was imminent and that would serve as a clear sign that the Kingdom was entering a new phase. The most well known set of clues is found in a discussion Jesus had with His disciples which has come to be known as "the Olivet Discourse." We have 3 different accounts of this discussion: one in Matthew 24:1-35; Mark 13:1-37; and Luke 21:5-36.

Jesus has just finished a lengthy tongue lashing of the Pharisees. They had failed miserably in their responsibility to prepare the people of Israel for the coming of their Messiah.

He concluded His scathing rebuke of the Pharisees with a mournful prediction regarding the future of the Holy City of Jerusalem. As he left the Temple mount, he gave his disciples a more detailed explanation of the fate of Jerusalem and the Temple. Referring to the Temple Mount and the surrounding buildings, he remarked that "not one stone here will be left on another; every one will be thrown down." It would be impossible for us to imagine the shock of such a statement. The Temple was God's home address. It was where God lived. Every aspect of the Jewish faith was centered in these buildings. It was the equivalent of Jesus saying that God would be abandoning His chosen people.

Understandably, the disciples wanted an answer to the question: when? "When will this happen, and what will be the sign of your coming and of the end of the age?" In Matthew's account, the disciples appear to ask three questions. In Mark and Luke's account of the same event, the disciples' queries are condensed into two questions. In all three Gospels, they want to know: when will the Temple be destroyed, and how can they know that the time was drawing near when Jesus would come again, signaling the end of the present era? Notice the obvious connection that the disciples made between the destruction of the Temple and the end of an era. If one happened, the other would naturally follow.

So Jesus answered their questions, in reverse order. He began by telling them what to look for as the signs of His coming and of the end of the age. Many of us are familiar with the signs he pointed to. We will return to the details of these signs later. At the very least, Jesus told of a time that would be horrific. All of these signs would then culminate in the coming of Jesus, "on the clouds," in the role of a great Judge.

It was only after He pointed to these signs that Jesus answered their first question; "When?" In Matthew 24:34, Mark 13:30 and Luke 21:32, Jesus explained that "this generation will certainly not pass away until all these things have happened." Depending on which translation of the Bible you are reading, you will note that most of them have some indication that there might be an alternative reading to the word "*generation.*" It is most often suggested that the alternative meaning of the word "*generation*" is "*race.*" The logic behind offering such a translation runs something like this: "Jesus cannot be wrong. We know (based on our presuppositions) that He is talking in this chapter about an event in the far distant future. None of those "signs" have come to pass yet. If He meant what it looks like He meant, then He is wrong. Since that cannot be, He must have meant something else." The 'something else" is that He meant "race," not "generation" here.

Of course, this solves any time-frame questions surrounding these passages. If the word for "generation" does in fact mean "race," then these things can happen at any time, so long as the Jewish race continues to exist. We can easily project the "signs" of the Olivet Discourse far into the future. Why then, does the preferred translation of "generation" appear, while the alternate "race" is only offered as a footnote?

Both renderings are within the semantic range of the word *genea (γενεα),* which can be translated either *generation* or *race/people.* But the latter usage is so rare and archaic, that it is hard to imagine a modern parallel. It would be like my use of the word "gay." Although it can mean lighthearted and happy, there are very few instances in which the word would be used in that way today. Such is the case for *genea*. Unless the immediate context **demands** the more archaic understanding, it *always* refers to a group of contemporaries whose life spans thirty to forty years. But this still begs the question—why do so many contemporary scholars agree that *genea* means generation in virtually every other place it appears in the Bible, but NOT in the Olivet Discourse?

It is because these readers are so committed to their preconceived notions about WHEN the events Jesus described would occur, that they cannot imagine that the text means what it looks like it means. This is precisely why CS Lewis described them as the "most embarrassing verse(s) in the Bible." So, if Jesus *really* said that "this race" would not pass away, then Jesus is off the hook, and we can all sleep well tonight. But if Jesus did, in fact, say that "this generation" would not pass away before these "signs" occurred, and "generation" means here what it means everywhere else then we have a problem. Before we look at an alternative explanation, we need to be certain that "generation" in the Olivet Discourse has its usual meaning.

In Matthew 23:36, Jesus used the word γενεα or "generation." In His diatribe against the Pharisees, He informed them of their eternal destination. He predicted that He would send more prophets, just as He had in the past, to warn them of impending doom. They would not listen. In fact, they would continue to do what they had always done—reject the message and kill the messengers. Jesus then warned them that God's patience with this rejection had come to an end. Since the time of Abel, the righteous had suffered at the hands of the unrighteous. Now, God would judge His People for their perpetual rejection. That judgment would befall "this generation." Did Jesus mean that God's judgment would come upon the Jewish race, spread out over millennia? Or did He mean that the very generation he was speaking to would suffer this fate? Before we attempt an answer, let's apply one of the cardinal rules for interpreting Scripture—examine the broader context.

The word *genea (γενεα)*, appears no less than 43 times in the New Testament. Matthew used it 8 times, in 11:16; 12:41,42,45; 16:4; 17:7; 23:36, 24:34. We have already looked at the last two. The three uses in chapter twelve come as part of the response that Jesus gave to the Pharisees request for a sign. Jesus told them that the time for signs was up. "This generation" will not receive a sign. The people asking for a sign had plenty of opportunities to observe one, if they had just looked at Jesus' life and ministry. Their request had to do with themselves and their contemporaries, not themselves as representatives of an entire race. Jesus' reference to "this generation" clearly referred to the Pharisees and their contemporaries.

The appearance of the word in Matthew 11 is part of Jesus' explanation of the role of John the Baptist in the coming of the Kingdom. The poor reception that John received by many was indicative of how Jesus would be received. Again, Jesus' comments are directed at "this generation," the contemporaries of John and Jesus. It is not the Jewish race that had misread the coming of John and Jesus, it was the very group to which they came that missed the hour of their visitation. Again and again, it is this use of the word *genea* that Matthew employs. **Without exception, every use of the word in Matthew refers to a group of contemporaries living during a span of time measuring approximately 30-40 years.**

Hebrews 3:7-10 provides another clue as to the use of *genea (γενεα)*. The writer of Hebrews states:

> *So, as the Holy Spirit says: "Today, if you hear his voice, do not harden your hearts as you did in the rebellion, during the time of testing in the wilderness, where your ancestors tested and tried me, though for* **forty years** *they saw what I did. That is why I was angry with that* **generation**; *I said, 'Their hearts are always going astray, and they have not known my ways.' So I declared on oath in my anger, 'They shall never enter my rest.'*

He referred to them as "that" generation. This seems completely appropriate, since the generation of which he spoke lived hundreds of years earlier. He used the demonstrative pronoun "that" to single out the generation that wandered in the wilderness for forty years. Jesus did the same thing. He always included the demonstrative pronoun "this" when using the word *genea (γενεα)*. Clearly Jesus was distinguishing His own contemporaries from other generations, future and past. In both cases, in Hebrews and in the Gospels, when the demonstrative pronoun is used with *genea*, the meaning of "generation" is a group of contemporaries that share a span of time of thirty to forty years.

At this point it would be wise to employ another cardinal rule of interpreting Scripture—Let other more clear passages help us interpret the less clear passages. In Matthew 10:23 and 16:28, Jesus announced that He would come again. As a word of encouragement, He told His disciples that before they completed their evangelistic work, THEY WOULD SEE THE COMING OF THE SON OF MAN. He assured them that some of His disciples WOULD NOT TASTE DEATH before they witnessed the coming of Jesus (See also Luke 9:27).

At Jesus' trial, when He stood before the Jewish authorities, He was pressed for an answer—"are you the Christ, the Son of God?" Jesus' answer? *"You (those standing before Him) will see the Son of Man sitting at the right hand of the Mighty One and coming on the clouds of heaven"* (Matthew 26:64 parenthesis added). Even John reiterated in The Revelation that when Jesus came in judgment (on the clouds) even "those who pierced Him" would see it, a clear reference to those who participated in His crucifixion (Rev. 1:7). Both to His disciples and to His enemies, Jesus predicted that many of them would live to see His return!

It would seem that Jesus' other comments regarding His return would support the idea that the "generation" to which He was speaking was the very generation that would live to see the events described in Matthew 24, Mark 13, and Luke 21. JESUS TAUGHT, AND HIS DISCIPLES UNDERSTOOD, THAT MANY OF THEM AND THEIR CONTEMPORARIES WOULD LIVE TO SEE THE END OF THE AGE AND THE RETURN OF JESUS. The disciples believed, as a direct result of the teachings of their Leader that they were going to witness a time of great transition between one age and another, between one expression of the Kingdom, and another.

The Gist Of The Grist

But what was it? How is it that Peter, James, John, the Apostle Paul, the writer of Hebrews and Christ Himself all seem to point to a "second coming" of Christ that would be witnessed by the generation living at that time? The answer is that they saw AN end, A coming, that would occur within the lifetime of Jesus' contemporaries, signaling a time of great judgment that would befall the people to whom Jesus came the first time. How then, do people who read the Bible account for this? ALL BIBLICAL SCHOLARS ARE AWARE OF THESE PASSAGES, AND ALL OF THEIR RESPONSES FALL INTO 3 BROAD CATEGORIES:

1. **Jesus was wrong.** Many scholars have argued that Jesus' first century followers, and even Jesus Himself, said things that betrayed their own personal longings, and not necessarily the facts. For some, this confirms that the Bible is not inspired and Jesus was not the Son of God.

2. **Jesus and His best students must have meant something other than what the clear meaning of the text indicates.** These scholars have a clear theology of the "end times," which demands a futuristic interpretation of Biblical prophecy, making it impossible for Jesus and His disciples to have meant what it looks like they meant. Perhaps the most improbable suggestion is that "this generation" refers to the generation that would be living when the "signs" actually appeared. THAT generation, still thousands of years in the future, would not pass away until all the signs were accomplished. In other words, in answer to the disciples' question "when," Jesus never gave an answer. He simply said, "Whenever these signs start unfolding, whatever "generation" happens to be living at that time, that generation will experience them all." Against the backdrop of all the other clear time-frame references this seems a most unlikely interpretation.

3. **Jesus and His disciples meant exactly what it looks like they meant.** WHILE OUR GREATEST HOPE REMAINS THE FINAL, TRIUMPHANT "APPEARING" OF

CHRIST, there was another "coming" of Jesus that signaled the end of one era, and the beginning of another. The coming of Christ to which Jesus and His disciples often referred, was a coming in judgment that ended one expression of the Kingdom of Heaven, and introduced another. Like never before, The Kingdom had come. WHAT WAS THIS "SECOND COMING" OF JESUS TO WHICH ALL THESE CLEAR TIME-FRAME REFERENCES POINT? What are we to make of all the signs to which Jesus pointed as the "beginning of the end?" When did Jesus return "on the clouds?" Is there any series of events that come close to matching the signs that Jesus spoke of, the "end" that Paul and Peter wrote about, and the catastrophic circumstances that John suggested would happen "soon?" In fact, there is, and that will be the focus of chapter 5. First, we need to look at an often overlooked feature of Christ's earthly ministry.

Chapter Summary

Time-frame references abound in Scripture. In the New Testament, most of those references pointed to an imminent event that would occur in the lifetime of Jesus' first-century followers. In preaching that the Kingdom was "at hand," Jesus left no doubt that His incarnation signaled a turning point in the history of mankind. A new way of understanding and accessing the Kingdom had come. Nothing would ever be the same.

Again and again, both Jesus and His disciples pointed to an event that can only be described as Jesus' "second coming." It is incorrect to understand that coming as His final appearing, an event that is still in the future. Jesus and His best students made it abundantly clear that an event was fast approaching that would forever change the world. Closely linked to the Kingdom, this event was foremost in the minds of Jesus' disciples. They wanted to know when this event would occur, and what the signs would be that pointed to its arrival. They were not asking Jesus about His final appearing and the consummation of the Kingdom. They asked, Jesus answered, and they proceeded to tell their fellow first-century disciples that this event would mark the end of the old covenant relationship of God to His people, and mark the beginning of a new relationship. That event would be cataclysmic—it would be attended with signs that can only be described as apocalyptic.

The Olivet Discourse, the prophecies of Daniel, the repeated warnings of Jesus and the Apostles, Pentecost, and the vision recorded in Revelation all point to this event, NOT the second and final appearing of Christ. There is simply no other way to understand the plethora of time-frame references in the New Testament without straining the texts to the point of breaking. Either Jesus and His disciples meant what they said, or they were wrong.

CHAPTER 4

THE PRINCE OF PEACE?

HERE COME DA' JUDGE

"Ooh!" said Susan, "I'd thought he was a man. Is he--quite safe? I shall feel rather nervous about meeting a lion." "That you will, dearie, and no mistake," said Mrs. Beaver, "if there's anyone who can appear before Aslan without their knees knocking, they're either braver than most or else silly." "Then he isn't safe?"said Lucy."Safe?" said Mr. Beaver. "Don't you hear what Mrs. Beaver tells you? Who said anything about safe? 'Course he isn't safe. But he's good. He's the King, I tell you."
CS LEWIS: THE LION, THE WITCH, AND THE WARDROBE

Very truly I tell you, whoever hears my word and believes him who sent me has eternal life and will not be judged but has crossed over from death to life. Very truly I tell you, a time is coming and has now come when the dead will hear the voice of the Son of God and those who hear will live. For as the Father has life in himself, so he has granted the Son also to have life in himself. And he has given him authority to judge because he is the Son of Man.
JOHN 5:24-27

I baptize you with water for repentance. But after me comes one who is more powerful than I, whose sandals I am not worthy to carry. He will baptize you with the Holy Spirit and fire. [12] His winnowing fork is in his hand, and he will clear his threshing floor, gathering his wheat into the barn and burning up the chaff with unquenchable fire
Matthew 3:11-13

The 1970's was the decade of the black comedian: Richard Pryor, Bill Cosby, and Redd Foxx, just to name a few. My personal favorite was Flip Wilson. Wilson earned a Golden Globe and two Emmy's for his variety show, The Flip Wilson Show. He immortalized characters like the "Right Reverend Leroy," pastor of the "Church of What's Happenin' Now." One of his standards was the character Geraldine Jones. Her now famous tag line was, "Here come da judge." Geraldine might just as easily have been paraphrasing what the Bible said about the coming Messiah. To many of the people living in first-century Palestine, Jesus' message was unmistakable: "Here come da judge."

Did Jesus Really Come As Judge?

Yes, and no. Jesus' primary focus in His first coming was to deliver a message of redemption and hope. The old way of accessing the Kingdom of God was ending, and a new era was beginning. The old way, or the "old covenant" was centered in one nation (Israel), one land (Canaan), and a series of kings (beginning with David) to rule over that nation and that land. The hope of Israel was that all the promises under the Old Covenant would be fulfilled in the coming Messiah *in a literal and earthbound way*. The writer of Hebrews went to great lengths to explain that nothing could be more misguided. The coming of Christ confirmed a New Covenant. *By calling this covenant "new," he has made the first one obsolete; and what is obsolete and outdated will soon disappear...* (Hebrews 8:13). The vestiges of the Old Covenant still remained, but a Day was coming when the old, law-centered access to the Kingdom would be destroyed, a time often referred to as "the Day;" *but encouraging one another—and all the more as you see the Day approaching...*(Hebrews 10:25). The time between Christ's first coming and His second "coming" (NOT His final appearing) was that period of transition, culminating in the destruction of the old Temple and the city of Jerusalem.

> *But when Christ came as high priest of the good things that are now already here, he went through the greater and more perfect tabernacle that is not made with human hands, that is to say, is not a part of this creation. He did not enter by means of the blood of goats and calves; but he entered the Most Holy Place once for all by his own blood, thus obtaining eternal redemption. The blood of goats and bulls and the ashes of a heifer sprinkled on those who are ceremonially unclean sanctify them so that they are outwardly clean. How much more, then, will the blood of Christ, who through the eternal Spirit offered himself unblemished to God, cleanse our consciences from acts that lead to death, so that we may serve the living God! For this reason Christ is the mediator of a new covenant, that those who are called may receive the promised eternal inheritance—now that he has died as a ransom to set them free from the sins committed under the first covenant* (Hebrews 9:11-15).

Indeed, the new covenant vitality could not be contained within the old covenant strictures of a racial people, a geographical land, and a typological Temple, for you cannot "put new wine into old wineskins, or else the

THE PRINCE OF PEACE?

wineskins break (and) the wine is spilled" (Matthew 9:17a).[9]

The Judaism of Jesus' day had evolved into a grotesque caricature of what God has always promised. It *did* teach that the coming of the Messiah would be marked by both redemption and judgment: Redemption of His people, Israel, and judgment for those who failed to worship the God of Israel. That hope passed through the political and social realities of each generation. By the time of Jesus, those who believed He was/could be the Messiah were already licking their theological chops at the prospect of the judgment of their current oppressors, the Roman empire. WHILE THEY WERE RIGHT TO EXPECT JUDGMENT, THEY COULD NOT IMAGINE THAT THE FIRST NATION MARKED FOR JUDGMENT WAS ISRAEL ITSELF!

It should come as no surprise that Jesus made his intentions very clear at the beginning of His public ministry. In Luke 4:14-30, Jesus let the cat out of the bag. He visited his hometown of Nazareth. He had been put on the list of "readers" at the synagogue, and the day had arrived for Him to take His turn. He was given the passage from Isaiah 61. Here is the record of what happened.

> *He went to Nazareth, where he had been brought up, and on the Sabbath day he went into the synagogue, as was his custom. He stood up to read, and the scroll of the prophet Isaiah was handed to him. Unrolling it,*

---

[9] Ken Gentry, *As Lightning Comes From the East*, <u>Tabletalk</u>, December 2001, p. 12.

> *he found the place where it is written: "The Spirit of the Lord is on me, because he has anointed me to proclaim good news to the poor. He has sent me to proclaim freedom for the prisoners and recovery of sight for the blind, to set the oppressed free, to proclaim the year of the Lord's favor." Then he rolled up the scroll, gave it back to the attendant and sat down. The eyes of everyone in the synagogue were fastened on him. He began by saying to them, "Today this Scripture is fulfilled in your hearing"* (Luke 4:14-30).

The initial reaction of folks in the pews was positive. But as Moisha elbowed Levi, he muttered, "Isn't there more to verse 2?" Indeed there is. The text from Isaiah actually reads:

> *The Spirit of the Sovereign LORD is on me, because the LORD has anointed me to proclaim good news to the poor. He has sent me to bind up the brokenhearted, to proclaim freedom for the captives and release from darkness for the prisoners, to proclaim the year of the LORD's favor **and the day of vengeance of our God, to comfort all who mourn...*** (Isaiah 61:1-2 emphasis added).

As they pondered Jesus' puzzling omission of some choice words about judgment, He launched into a not-so-thinly-veiled swipe at His own people. Not only was the hoped for judgment of Rome (all Gentiles!) apparently **not** part of *this* Messiah's agenda, He went so far as to hint that their hoped for Messianic Kingdom was going to *include* Gentiles. In fact, there was a good chance that a lot of Israelites were going to be painted out of the picture. By recounting the stories of the widow of Zarephath and

Naaman, (Luke 4:24-27) Jesus had the gall to suggest that Sidonians and Syrians might enter the Kingdom before Judeans and Galileans. The Nazarene's response was instantaneous. "This is obviously not our Man!" In their fury they tried to kill Jesus. "But He walked right through the crowd and went on His way." (Luke 4:28-30)

What Jesus was saying with both His silence and His speech was that He had come to offer redemption to ALL the peoples of the earth, and that the judgment they sought after was coming, but it would not befall the Gentiles, but the Jews. Embedded in the thinking of *all* Jews, not merely the religious leaders was the notion that they were the Chosen People, and nothing could change that. "Now it is not to be supposed that Israel really needed to be reminded of her election. On the contrary, it was a fixed idea with her; she believed it all too well. Her whole tradition asserted with unanimous voice that God had chosen her out of all the families of the nations to be His people, and she cherished that belief with all her heart..."[10] For Israel, the necessary conclusion was inescapable: "The Israelite state is the people of God." Of course, they were wrong. The tree of false religion that had sprung up in the soil of the Promised Land had to come down. Just as He had in the synagogue in Nazareth, Jesus gave many clues as to where the ax would fall.

The Domestication of Jesus

Again and again, Jesus referred to the judgment of His own people, the very people who had failed so

---

[10] John Bright, *The Kingdom of God*, Location 660 of 4274, Kindle Ebook.

miserably in completing the task they had been assigned. (Genesis 12:3) Beyond that, God's people had rarely lived lives that approximated what God's people were supposed to look like. The moral and ethical demands upon God's people were closely tied to being a light to the nations. On every front they had failed. Jesus came in part to announce that God's judgment had come. Unfortunately, contemporary Christianity has effectively "neutered" the Messiah. He has been transformed from a fierce, singularly focused Warrior into a doe-eyed religious do-gooder. Three popular stories will illustrate.

Having Fish For Dinner?

Do you remember sitting in Sunday-school, singing the popular, "I Will Make You Fishers of Men?" I'll bet you can still remember the hand motions. Go ahead. Put the book down and give it a good cast. Remember? It is a delightful little song. But it completely misses the point, just as it did for Jesus' first century followers (Matt. 4:18-22; Mark 1:14-20; Luke 5:2-11; John 1:35-42). Have you ever wondered why Jesus chose this metaphor? Most commentators argue that Jesus was only using a familiar word picture. After all, the disciples He spoke to on this occasion were in fact, fishermen. But there is a deeper meaning.

In the first place, what happens to a fish when it is caught? Do we dialogue with the fish? Have a meaningful discussion? Do we invite the fish into the boat? No. We have the fish over for dinner—OUR DINNER! The fish is killed and then eaten. It's a chilling metaphor. What Jesus is saying is, "I am going to cast the net. We will catch many fish, some to life, and some to death. This will be my method for determining who is for my Kingdom, and who is not. I want you men to join me in this great fishing expedition." Why should we conclude that this is the meaning behind Jesus' words?

Jesus' ministry flowed from the Old Testament. He directly quoted no less than 24 Old Testament books in dozens of separate accounts. He alluded to even more. This is why the "fishing" metaphor is so interesting. When the God of the Old Testament appeared as a fisherman, what did He intend?

> *"But now I will send for many fishermen," declares the LORD, "and they will catch them. After that I will send for many hunters, and they will hunt them down on every mountain and hill and from the crevices of the rocks. My eyes are on all their ways; they are not hidden from me, nor is their sin concealed from my eyes. I will repay them double for their wickedness and their sin, because they have defiled my land with the lifeless forms of their vile images and have filled my inheritance with their detestable idols" (Jeremiah 16:16-18).*

> *Speak to him and say: 'This is what the Sovereign LORD says: "'I am against you, Pharaoh king of Egypt, you great monster lying among your streams. You say, "The Nile belongs to me; I made it for myself." But I will put hooks in your jaws and make the fish of your streams stick to your scales. I will pull you out from among your streams, with all the fish sticking to your scales. I will leave you in the desert, you and all the fish of your streams. You will fall on*

> *the open field and not be gathered or picked up. I will give you as food to the beasts of the earth and the birds of the sky. Then all who live in Egypt will know that I am the LORD* (Ezekiel 29:4-6).

> *The word of the LORD came to me: "Son of man, set your face against Gog, of the land of Magog, the chief prince of[a] Meshek and Tubal; prophesy against him and say: 'This is what the Sovereign LORD says: I am against you, Gog, chief prince of[b] Meshek and Tubal. I will turn you around, put hooks in your jaws and bring you out with your whole army—your horses, your horsemen fully armed, and a great horde with large and small shields, all of them brandishing their swords* (Ezekiel 38:1-4).

> *Hear this word, you cows of Bashan on Mount Samaria, you women who oppress the poor and crush the needy and say to your husbands, "Bring us some drinks!" The Sovereign LORD has sworn by his holiness: "The time will surely come when you will be taken away with hooks, the last of you with fishhooks. You will each go straight out through breaches in the wall, and you will be cast out toward Harmon" declares the LORD* (Amos 4:1-3).

In each case, the individual with a net or a pole comes as a Judge! Jesus is most certainly drawing upon this imagery. The fact that Jesus is going fishing is not good news, at least not for all the fish. This fishing expedition is going to cast a wide net. It will draw in many fish, most of whom will die at the vengeful hand of God because of their disobedience and rejection of the one True King. So as to leave no doubt, Jesus Himself elaborated on the fish metaphor in one of His parables. He said,

> *Once again, the Kingdom of heaven is like a net that was let down into the lake and caught all kinds of fish. When it was full, the fishermen pulled it up on the shore. Then they sat down and collected the good fish in baskets, but threw the bad away. This is how it will be at the end of the age. The angels will come and separate the wicked from the righteous and throw them into the blazing furnace, where there will be weeping and gnashing of teeth. "Have you understood all these things?" Jesus asked. "Yes," they replied* (Matthew 13:47-51).

Unless we are prepared to tell our children the truth about the "fishing" metaphor, perhaps we should stick to teaching them "The B-I-B-L-E."

JESUS HAD A LITTLE LAMB

Another expression of His role as Judge is found in Jesus' reference to the Jewish people as "sheep without a shepherd." (Matthew 9:36; Mark 6:34). Immediately, this conjures up images of a gentle shepherd, tenderly holding a little lamb. Is this ALL that Jesus intended when he said this? Again, the Old Testament is replete with references to a "shepherdless" people. In Ezekiel 34, the entire chapter is dedicated to God's judgment of the "shepherds" of Israel (the religious leaders). In a scathing rebuke, we read that a day would come when those shepherds would be called to account for their behavior. Even the sheep would be called to account.

The Great Shepherd who would come to Israel (Numbers 27:15-17) would separate the sheep into two groups—those who would be saved, and those who would be judged. Jesus' reference to the people as sheep without a shepherd, and, by implication, identifying Himself as the Great Shepherd, is about compassion AND judgment. Those who should have been shepherding God's people to prepare them for His coming had failed. As a result, many of the sheep were clueless. This simply will not do. The Great Shepherd had arrived, and He is not happy! He would judge the shepherds for their woeful lack of faithful leadership. Their fate was sealed. In addition, the sheep fold needed to be purged first, sheep and shepherds alike, and then reopened to many more sheep from many different nations.

> *"I am the good shepherd; I know my sheep and my sheep know me—just as the Father knows me and I know the Father—and I lay down my life for the sheep. I have other sheep that are not of this sheep pen. I must bring them also. They too will listen to my voice, and there shall be one flock and one shepherd. (John 10:14-16).*

The prophet Jeremiah prophesied similarly concerning the shepherds and the sheep.

> *"Woe to the shepherds who are destroying and scattering the sheep of my pasture!" declares the LORD. Therefore this is what the LORD, the God of Israel, says to the shepherds who tend my people: "Because you have scattered my flock and driven them away and have not bestowed care on them, I will bestow punishment on you for the evil you have done," declares the LORD. "I myself will gather the remnant of my flock out of all the countries where I have driven them and will bring them back to their pasture, where they will be fruitful and increase in*

> *number. I will place shepherds over them who will tend them, and they will no longer be afraid or terrified, nor will any be missing," declares the LORD.*
>
> *"The days are coming," declares the LORD, "when I will raise up for David a righteous Branch, a King who will reign wisely and do what is just and right in the land. In his days Judah will be saved and Israel will live in safety. This is the name by which he will be called: The LORD Our Righteous Savior.*
>
> *"So then, the days are coming," declares the LORD, "when people will no longer say, 'As surely as the LORD lives, who brought the Israelites up out of Egypt,' but they will say, 'As surely as the LORD lives, who brought the descendants of Israel up out of the land of the north and out of all the countries where he had banished them.'' Then they will live in their own land* (Jeremiah 23:1-8).

The "shepherds" will be judged and the flock will be culled. The promised "days" of which Jeremiah spoke had arrived. The "wise King" had come, and both punishment and redemption were to follow. Of course both Isaiah and Jeremiah never lost sight of a "remnant." As we will see, this idea figures prominently in Revelation. But the remnant was just that, a small group from the original people who would be saved. What of the rest? The prophet Zechariah provided the most emphatic statement of judgment upon the sheep of Israel.

The "shepherds" of Israel had failed in their calling to care for their sheep. The word of the Lord came to Zechariah, and he was told of a day when the Lord would declare, "the flock detested me, and I grew weary of them and said, "I will not be your shepherd..." The full force of God's displeasure is felt as He "revokes" the covenant with His people (Zechariah 11:10, 14). The sheep had become a "flock marked for slaughter." As God's people rejected their Messianic Shepherd-King judgment would necessarily follow. The providential care of God that had protected Israel would be lifted, and the "nations" (Rome) would be permitted to overrun them. With unmistakable prophetic symbolism, the betrayal and crucifixion of the True Shepherd at the hands of the sheep is foretold:

> *I told them, "If you think it best, give me my pay; but if not, keep it." So they paid me thirty pieces of silver. And the LORD said to me, "Throw it to the potter"— the handsome price at which they valued me! So I took the thirty pieces of silver and threw them to the potter at the house of the LORD* (Jeremiah 11:12-13).

Because they failed to recognize the powerful redemptive work of the Messiah, sheep and shepherd alike would feel the wrath of God.

It would appear that when Jesus spoke of His people as "sheep without a shepherd," He was fulfilling the words of the prophets who spoke of just such a day, when the True Shepherd would come. That Day would bring redemption for a few, the remnant, and judgment for most. Jesus, the "Good Shepherd?" It might be wise to head for cover. Judgment is coming. The most definitive illustration of His role as judge is illustrated in His relationship to the Temple.

Jesus Never "Cleansed" the Temple!

The Temple was the epicenter of the Kingdom quake that Jesus came to announce. The most unambiguous expression of Jesus' rejection of the Temple and all it stood for can be found in Mark 11:12-19 and parallel passages (Matthew 21:12-22; Luke 19:45-47; John 2:13-16). Most church-goin' folk are inclined to read this passage as Jesus' attack on the money changer's greed and His attempt to restore good Temple practice. Such an interpretation couldn't miss the point by a wider margin. **Jesus is not concerned at all with restoring good Temple practice. He is trying to shut the Temple down! For good!**

The story in Mark 11 begins with an apparent digression. Jesus curses a fig tree for not having figs at a time when it was not supposed to have figs! But Jesus goes out of His way (literally—cf. verse 13) to make a point. In the Old Testament, the fig tree, often an allusion to Israel, is also associated with judgment (Isa. 34:4; Jer. 29:17; Hosea 2:12; Hosea 9:10; Joel 1:7; Micah 7:1) Drawing on this Old Testament imagery, Jesus pronounced judgment on something that *looked* good, but had no fruit—all sizzle, and no steak, lots of bark but no bite. It is not the lack of fruit that brought the curse; it is the ***appearance*** of fruitfulness. Israel had not born the fruit of its destiny—to lead all nations to the God of Israel. Israel had not lived as law-keepers, but law-breakers. For centuries they had systematically drawn people OUT of the circle of God's love. Thumbing their nose at what God had originally called them to (Genesis 12:1-3), **His people had now institutionalized the segregation of worshippers by race.** The very architecture of the Temple made a clear statement—"No Gentiles Beyond This Point—You Can Only Go Shofar."

The ugliness of this conceit was in marked contrast to the beauty of the Temple. It was, without dispute, a most magnificent structure. It was the talk of the Near East. It promised worshippers an opportunity to meet God. More specifically, it promised worshippers *from every nation* the opportunity to meet God. But one had only to take a few steps on to the Temple mount to discover that this was a "Jews-only" club. The closer one came to actually meeting the One True God, the more the crowd was thinned out by race. Are we honestly to assume that such a system needed saving—a more pure or refined...what? The argument is often given that Jesus is reacting to this very problem (that Gentiles were marginalized or excluded from worshipping the God of Israel), because the money changers had converted the Court of the Gentiles into a market place. Rather than a place for prayer, the Temple had become a cash cow. But a careful reading of the text shows that this cannot be the case, especially in the context of the cursed fig tree. It is against the backdrop of a fruitless people and fruitless religion that Jesus acts.

Exactly who was it that Jesus drove out of the Temple? Can you, without looking at Matthew 21 or Mark 11 give a definitive answer? I would bet you dollars to doughnuts that you would have answered "he drove the money-changers out." And you would be wrong. It was BOTH "those who were BUYING AND SELLING" there. In the very next verse (Mark 11:17), we are told that Jesus would not allow ANYONE TO CARRY MERCHANDISE through the Temple courts! Read it for yourself.

> *The next day as they were leaving Bethany, Jesus was hungry. Seeing in the distance a fig tree in leaf, he went to find out if it had any fruit. When he reached it, he found nothing but leaves, because it was not the season for figs. Then he said to the tree, "May no one ever eat fruit from you again." And his disciples heard him say it. On reaching Jerusalem, Jesus entered the Temple courts and **began driving out those who were buying and selling there.** He overturned the tables of the money changers and the benches of those selling doves, **and would not allow anyone to carry merchandise through the Temple courts**. And as he taught them, he said, "Is it not written: 'My house will be called a house of prayer for all nations'? But you have made it 'a den of robbers.'" The chief priests and the teachers of the law heard this and began looking for a way to kill him, for they feared him, because the whole crowd was amazed at his teaching. When evening came, Jesus and his disciples went out of the city. In the morning, as they went along, they saw the fig tree withered from the roots. Peter remembered and said to Jesus, "Rabbi, look! The fig tree you cursed has withered!" "Have faith in God," Jesus answered. "Truly I tell you, if anyone says to **this mountain**, 'Go, throw yourself into the sea,' and does not doubt in their heart but believes that what they say will happen, it will be done for them. Therefore I tell you, whatever you ask for in prayer, believe that you have received it, and it will be yours. And when you stand praying, if you hold anything against anyone, forgive them, so that your Father in heaven may forgive you your sins"* (Mark 11:12-26).

Before we unpack this, we need to understand exactly what is happening here.

People were coming from all over the known world for Passover. It was required that they offer sacrifices as part of their observance. Without such sacrifices, there could be no atonement for sin. Rather than drag a cow, or a crate of birds, or a goat for miles, most people bought their sacrifice in one of the four prescribed areas in Jerusalem for making such a purchase. As a convenience to weary travelers, another "animal station" was set up in the Court of the Gentiles to accommodate worshippers.

In addition, each worshipper, along with offerings, had to pay the "Temple tax," a surcharge that was levied to help pay for the Temple's upkeep, utilities, care for the priests, room and board, etc. No Greek or Roman coins could be accepted for this purpose, as they had images of other "deities" on them. Only the shekel and half-shekel Temple coins were acceptable. One of the primary functions of the "money-*changers*" was to exchange unsuitable coins for "Temple coins." Apparently, the "exchange-rate" was usually in favor of the money changers themselves.

So what was Jesus doing by shutting down the money changers and those offering animals for sale? To put it another way, what could NOT happen if this business were not conducted, and if people who had already purchased their sacrifices outside the Temple were not permitted to enter? Obviously, there would be no sacrifices! If people were not able to exchange their coins and pay the Temple tax, the Temple would literally go out of business. **Both commercially and cultically, Jesus is trying to shut the Temple down.** Obviously, Jesus did not prohibit people from entering the Temple permanently. He didn't spend the next several years manning His post prohibiting "anyone" from "carrying merchandise through the Temple courts" (Mark 11:16). At least for that day (He and the disciples leave at night—11:19), He did.

What often pulls commentators and readers off track is Jesus' reference to the passages from Isaiah 56 and Jeremiah 7, respectively (Mark 11:17). The quotation from Isaiah 56:7, when taken in its original context, speaks of the inclusive love of God that is destined to reach people of *all nations*. It is not the money-changers that have kept this from happening; **it is the institutionalized religious bigotry that has become part of the very architecture of the Temple!** The Temple had become a symbol of division, not unity. Besides, the Court of the Gentiles could easily hold 65,000 congregants.[11] Even if the money changers had taken up a great deal of room and were shouting out their rates, there would still have been plenty of room for thousands of Gentiles to pray. Again, the problem was not that space reserved for Gentiles was being used for currency exchange. The problem was the Temple itself and everything it stood for!

The second quotation, from Jeremiah 7:11 has to do with how easy it is for religion to become nothing more

---

[11] This is a conservative number. The Court was 35 acres in size. Roughly 5,000 people can stand on an acre. Do the math.

than a cover, a place for religious posers. Rather than putting their faith in God, they had put their faith in high-sounding religious phrases and lofty spiritual sentiments. God's people had completely divorced faith from life, believing that they could live however they pleased as long as they took refuge in the Temple and its religion. The Temple had become the center of Israel's effort to coerce God into supporting the Kingdom of Israel not the Kingdom of God.

Jesus made His sentiments about the Temple perfectly clear in the next verses (Mark 11:20-23). Again, we have misread this passage about throwing mountains into the sea as if it was a reference to how we should deal with daunting tasks. Jesus used very specific language in this passage. Notice that He used the definite article when describing the mountain. It is "this" mountain that Jesus referred, not "a" mountain, or "any" mountain. As we read those words, the first question that should come to mind is, "what mountain was Jesus referring to?" Given the immediate context, there can be little doubt that he was referring to "this mountain," mount Zion. Given what had just transpired, fig tree and all, it is clear that Faith in God supplants faith in the Temple and all its religious trappings. Rather than put your faith in a beautiful Temple that signifies only vain religion and false hope, put your faith in God. It is no accident that the Temple mount is thrown into "the sea." The sea was a place of death and separation from God—a place where false teachers were thrown and where demon-possessed pigs lived. The sea represented such an anti-God place that in Heaven, there is no sea! (Revelation 21:1). Jesus had no desire to reform or "cleanse" the Temple. He aimed to replace it!

Why was such a "radical" solution needed? "In short, the whole notion of covenant and election had been made a mechanical thing, the deeply moral note inherent in it blurred and obscured. It had been forgotten that the covenant was a bilateral obligation, requiring of its people the worship Of Yahweh alone and the strictest obedience to his righteous law in all human relationships. Or if the obligation was remembered at all, it was imagined that lavish sacrifice and loyal support of the shrines discharged it. The bond between God and people was thus made into a static, pagan thing based on blood and cult—a total perversion of the covenant idea. And religion was accorded an altogether pagan function: to coerce the favor of God by the sedulous manipulation of the ritual so that protection and material benefit might be secured for individual and nation."[12] The Temple had become the crowning achievement of pagan religion. Such a thing cannot be reformed, it must be destroyed.

Jesus not only replaced that Temple, He became the "true Temple." (Revelation 21:22) The blood of animals could only effect "outward" cleansing. That was precisely the problem with the fig tree. It had only the appearance of fruitfulness—outer beauty, but inner corruption. All of the sacrifices that took place in the Temple had become an effort to curry God's favor. They were not merely copies of the powerful, transformational

---

[12] John Bright, *The Kingdom of God*, 668 of 4274.

reality that was coming. They were its antithesis. The blood of Christ, shed only once, did away with all the old "copies," and made us clean from the *inside* out. This is what Jesus declared on that day in the Temple. The beginning of judgment had arrived. It would be only a few short years before that judgment was made complete. In the place of all these animals, the true Lamb of God had arrived. His "once for all" sacrifice would forever supplant the Temple and all it stood for. There is no better Biblical summary of what Jesus was doing on that day than the one provided in Hebrews 9 and 10:

> *In fact, the law requires that nearly everything be cleansed with blood, and without the shedding of blood there is no forgiveness. It was necessary, then, for the copies of the heavenly things to be purified with these sacrifices, but the heavenly things themselves with better sacrifices than these. For Christ did not enter a sanctuary made with human hands that was only a copy of the true one; he entered heaven itself, now to appear for us in God's presence. Nor did he enter heaven to offer himself again and again, the way the high priest enters the Most Holy Place every year with blood that is not his own. Otherwise Christ would have had to suffer many times since the creation of the world.* **But he has appeared once for all at the culmination of the ages to do away with sin by the sacrifice of himself.** *Just as people are destined to die once, and after that to face judgment, so Christ was sacrificed once to take away the sins of many; and he will appear a second time, not to bear sin, but to bring salvation to those who are waiting for him* (Hebrews 9:22-28).

> *The law is only a shadow of the good things that are coming—not the realities themselves. For this reason it can never, by the same sacrifices repeated endlessly year after year, make perfect those who draw near to worship. Otherwise, would they not have stopped being offered? For the worshipers would have been cleansed once for all, and would no longer have felt guilty for their sins. But those sacrifices are an annual reminder of sins. It is impossible for the blood of bulls and goats to take away sins. Therefore, when Christ came into the world, he said:* **"Sacrifice and offering you did not desire, but a body you prepared for me; with burnt offerings and sin offerings you were not pleased.** *Then I said, 'Here I am—it is written about me in the scroll— I have come to do your will, my God'* (Hebrews 10:1-7).

Jesus' activity that day in the Temple had nothing to do with making the Temple better—His message was not one of purification but judgment.

Kill Them In Front Of Me

Perhaps the clearest statement of Jesus' coming in the role of Judge is found in Luke 19. I can honestly say that I have NEVER heard a sermon that dealt specifically with the words of verse 27—*"But those enemies of mine who did not want me to be king over them—bring them here and kill them in front of me."* This is the dénouement of the parable of the Ten Minas. As we have said, the singular focus of Jesus' teaching ministry was the Kingdom. But what of the fate of those who rejected this Kingdom and its King? What of those who were unwilling to receive a Kingdom that had come, and a King who did not match the popular expectations of that time? Death. Jesus declared the fate of all who opposed the Kingdom as He revealed it. Jesus' words have an ominous ring. The fulfillment of those words was less than a generation away.

Are We Clear?

Still doubting that Jesus came to bring a message of judgment for His own people? The above passages may leave a little too much "wiggle room" for those disinclined to believe that Jesus actually brought a message of imminent doom for Israel. But there are plenty of places where Jesus was explicit.

As the forerunner to Christ, John the Baptist articulated the primary thrust of Jesus' ministry. As John's popularity grew, even the leaders of first-century Judaism came to investigate. They couldn't possibly have imagined the response they got.

> *But when he saw many of the Pharisees and Sadducees coming to where he was baptizing, he said to them: "You brood of vipers! Who warned you to flee from **the coming wrath**? Produce fruit in keeping with repentance. And do not think you can say to yourselves, 'We have Abraham as our father.' I tell you that out of these stones God can raise up children for Abraham. The ax is **already** at the root of the trees, and every tree that does not produce good fruit will be cut down and thrown into the fire. "I baptize you with water for repentance. But after me comes one who is more powerful than I, whose sandals I am not worthy to carry. He will baptize you with the Holy Spirit and fire. **His winnowing fork is in his hand, and he will clear his threshing floor, gathering his***

> *wheat into the barn and burning up the chaff with unquenchable fire"* (Matthew 3:7-12).

"Wrath" is coming, and soon. For anyone who has ever split wood or thinned a forest, you know that before you take the first swing, you rest the ax on the anticipated point of impact. What comes next is no surprise. "Whack!" This is precisely the image John uses, and the "tree" is the ethnocentric and morally bankrupt teaching of Judaism that the Pharisees and Sadducees had helped to popularize. Notice as well *where* the ax is laid; it is not on one of the branches, or even the trunk. It is the root, the core, the heart of the religion that Jesus is after. What building symbolized that religion? The Temple. Christ was destined to bring a ministry of "fire" that would prove terminal for the Jewish religion of the day.

Winning Friends?

Not long into His public ministry, Jesus achieved rock-star status. The bulbs of the paparazzi flashed wherever He went. On more than one occasion Jesus stopped to address the large crowds that followed Him. In almost every case, he said things that were *designed to shock His followers*. Case in point:

> *"I have come to bring fire on the earth, and how I wish it were already kindled! But I have a baptism to undergo, and what constraint I am under until it is completed! Do you think I came to bring peace on earth? No, I tell you, but division. From now on there will be five in one family divided against each other, three against two and two against three. They will be divided, father against son and son against father, mother against daughter and daughter against*

> *mother, mother-in-law against daughter-in-law and daughter-in-law against mother-in-law." He said to the crowd: "When you see a cloud rising in the west, immediately you say, 'It's going to rain,' and it does. And when the south wind blows, you say, 'It's going to be hot,' and it is. Hypocrites! You know how to interpret the appearance of the earth and the sky. How is it that you don't know how to interpret this present time?* (Luke 12:49-56).

No single saying or expression completely captures the "why?" of Jesus' first coming. He came "to seek and to save the lost," to "give His life as a ransom for many," and "to destroy the works of the Devil." This passage includes another defining moment in Jesus' ministry: "*I have come to bring fire on the earth...*" So what's the hold up? "I wish it were already kindled! But I have a baptism to undergo...," a clear reference to His crucifixion. In stark contrast to His identity as the "Prince of Peace," this Messiah declared that He had come to bring a sword. He would create division. Among whom? Family members. Which family? *He answered, "I was sent only to the lost sheep of Israel."* It was the house of Israel that would be divided. It was the house of Israel that would feel the fire and the sting of the sword.

Jesus then proceeded to warn His hearers that He was not talking about the distant future. He lamented the fact that they could tell when it was going to rain, but they could not see the obvious signs of impending judgment. They knew when the hot *sirocco* wind from the desert would blow through their cities, but they could not imagine the heat of the fire of His wrath as it fell upon *The*

City. Their troubles were not concerned with some far-off event or prophecy—It was with "the present time."

It would seem that the "Jesus meek and mild" that has been popularized today is a far cry from the real Jesus. The latter came to serve and to save all those who were willing to lay down their own Kingdoms and embrace His--But woe to those who opposed Him. Woe to those who rejected Him. They would be" killed in front of Him."

Conclusion

As winsome warriors, our marching orders come from our Commander-In-Chief. Our inspiration as well as our motivation is rooted in Him. He has modeled for us the way that we should interact with everything and everyone that opposes Him and His Kingdom. WARNING: At *no* time has Christ *ever* endorsed bloodshed or hatred as weapons in our arsenal. Despite the violence surrounding the ultimate destruction of Jerusalem, we should never confuse the just wrath of God with our own calling.

> *Love must be sincere. Hate what is evil; cling to what is good. Be devoted to one another in love. Honor one another above yourselves. Never be lacking in zeal, but keep your spiritual fervor, serving the Lord. Be joyful in hope, patient in affliction, faithful in prayer. Share with the Lord's people who are in need. Practice hospitality. Bless those who persecute you; bless and do not curse. Rejoice with those who rejoice; mourn with those who mourn. Live in harmony with one another. Do not be proud, but be willing to associate with people of low position. Do not be conceited. Do not repay anyone evil for evil. Be careful to do what is right in the eyes of everyone.*

> *If it is possible, as far as it depends on you, live at peace with everyone. Do not take revenge, my dear friends, but leave room for God's wrath, for it is written: "It is mine to avenge; I will repay," says the Lord. On the contrary: "If your enemy is hungry, feed him; if he is thirsty, give him something to drink. In doing this, you will heap burning coals on his head." Do not be overcome by evil, but overcome evil with good* (Romans 12:9-21).

We are to be *winsome* warriors. Our "hatred" for what is evil motivates us to "overcome evil with good." The paradox that Jesus' earthly ministry presents us with should not deter us.

Christ exhibited zero tolerance for false religion, hypocrisy, and an arrogant dismissal of His gracious initiatives. He stridently spoke against them all. The alternative that He offered was rooted in humble submission to the will of the Father. He modeled an attack that was characterized by bold denouncements of anything that opposed The Kingdom. Coupled with stinging rebukes Christ laid down His life for the very people who opposed Him. As He modeled the ethic of the Kingdom, He brought down opposing Kingdoms with love, self-sacrifice and an openness to "sinners" that was unrivaled. He was, quite simply the quintessential Winsome Warrior. We have no alternative but to embrace His mission and to model His methods.

Chapter Summary

It is impossible to distill into one statement the reasons why Jesus came to earth. Among the many, the announcing of impending judgment was clearly one of them. In addition to His repeated appeal to the lost, the suffering, and the sick, Christ also came to earth to sound a warning. His ministry focused almost exclusively on the Jewish people, the "lost sheep of Israel" (Matthew 10:6). It was for His own people that Christ reserved his most scathing rebukes, and it was to them that He issued His most stern warnings.

Drawing heavily upon Old Testament images and metaphors, Christ made it clear that perilous times awaited His people. Their failure to properly understand their own Scriptures had led them and their leaders to institutionalize a kind of racist, man-centered religion that was beyond reformation. At times, Christ spoke obliquely, using Old Testament images of fish, sheep, and fig trees to sound His warning. At other times, He was explicit—He came to bring a sword and to kill those who opposed His Kingdom.

The clearest expression of His scorn for false religion and Judaist exclusivism was expressed in His relationship to the Temple. Its outward beauty belied an inner corruption that was unredeemable. His first-century countrymen understood only too well that Jesus opposed both their religion and the cultic practices that surrounded it. It is no wonder that within only a few years of public ministry, the very people He had come to minister to were calling for His blood. Anyone who repented and believed that Jesus was the Christ, was received with compassion and grace. For those who tenaciously clung to their own understanding of the Messiah and the Kingdom, Jesus could not have been clearer—judgment was coming, and soon. As the coming chapters will show, that judgment came within a generation, or forty years, of Jesus' ascension. With the Great Jewish Revolt and subsequent destruction of Jerusalem in 70 A.D. Jesus' and His disciples' warnings came to pass.

CHAPTER 5

Jesus' Great "Wintervention"

THE END OF THE AGE

Pray that your flight will not take place in winter or on the Sabbath. For then there will be great distress, unequaled from the beginning of the world until now—and never to be equaled again.
MATTHEW 24:20-21

"When Jewish and Christian scholars begin to take this war seriously, when they begin to really study what happened during the terrible years of the siege of Jerusalem, the destruction of the Temple.. when they focus upon the persecution of the Christians in Palestine by the Jews; upon the civil war in Rome in the 60s...as well as the persecutions of the Jews in the Diasporia during this period -- in sum, when all of this dark era is brought into the light of examination -- Bible studies will change."
ANNE RICE, *CHRIST THE LORD, OUT OF EGYPT*

The destruction of Jerusalem was more terrible than anything that the world has ever witnessed, either before or since. Even Titus seemed to see in his cruel work the hand of an avenging God.
CHARLES SPURGEON

Now learn this lesson from the fig tree: As soon as its twigs get tender and its leaves come out, you know that summer is near. Even so, when you see all these things, you know that it is near, right at the door. Truly I tell you, this generation will certainly not pass away until all these things have happened.
MATTHEW 24:32-34

The A & E network has a hit on their hands; it's called *Intervention*. The show follows a person in the throes of active addiction. Each episode culminates in an "intervention," where the addict's family members deliver an ultimatum—get treatment and try to stop, or risk losing contact, income, or other privileges from the loved ones who instigated the intervention. It is painful to watch. No less painful was the "wintervention" (Matthew 24:20-21) initiated by Jesus in what has come to be known as The Olivet Discourse. The people of Jesus' generation had been given an ultimatum—"Repent! The Kingdom is near." Failure to do so would result in the loss of contact with God and the loss of all the privileges that came from being part of God's chosen people. Having rejected their calling as a light to the nations, the "sons of Abraham by blood" were about to experience the end of God's longsuffering. For those who struggle with addictions, you know what your literature says: "We are people in the grip of a continuing and progressive illness whose ends are always the same: jails, institutions, and death."[13] Jesus came to deliver the "sick," but they rejected Him and His ultimatum. The outcome was inevitable: Jails, institutions, and death.

Beginning Of The End

It is impossible for Gentiles living in the West to appreciate the significance of what occurred "that day" and in the years that followed. The impressive Second Temple, and the city of Jerusalem, were both completely destroyed in 70 A.D. by soon to be Roman emperor Titus. While many

---

[13] Narcotics Anonymous, Fifth Edition (Chatsworth, CA: Narcotics Anonymous World Services, Inc., 1988) p. 3

ancient dates are debated, this one is indisputable. On July 30, 70 A.D., the Jewish world and God's relationship to His People changed forever. This was the event that is referred to as the "end of the age," the "coming of the Son of Man on the clouds," and the fulfillment of most of the prophetic words of Jesus and His disciples. Even the first half of the book of Revelation speaks of this horrific era-ending event.

"How could this be?" you might ask. "The passages we have looked at and the first part of the book of Revelation sound nothing like this event!" "The events that Jesus described in Matthew 24 include references to things that clearly have not happened already!" To fully appreciate how this is what Jesus and the disciples spoke of, we need to take a step back and look at the significance of the Temple and the city of Jerusalem to the Jewish people.

God's Post Office Box

While Herod the Great (73 B.C.-4 B.C.) was hated by the Jewish people, they loved one thing about him—the man could build things. And build he did. The landscape of Israel is dotted with the remains of this prolific builder. Perhaps his most impressive building project was the Temple in Jerusalem. Sometimes referred to as "The Second Temple" or "Herod's Temple," the building was awe-inspiring. Gorgeous colonnades, spacious courtyards, marble paths, huge walls, impressive arches, gold overlays and precious stones combined to make this Temple breathtaking. But it was far more than just the architecture that made the Temple significant to the Jewish people.

A brief review of the history of God's dealings with mankind shows an amazing desire on God's part to live with His people. He has always enjoyed their company. From Adam and Eve, with whom he actually walked, to His followers today, God has made it a point to live *with* His people. After Adam and Eve were expelled from the Garden of Eden, God continued His pursuit of mankind. After calling Abraham to be the father of His chosen people, God ordered the construction of a special "dwelling place" for Himself—the Tabernacle. Christians often misunderstand the purpose of the Tabernacle. We tend to think of it as a forerunner to our churches—that it was a place for God's people to go and worship Him, a place to gather and praise God. But this was clearly not the primary purpose of the Tabernacle. God repeatedly gives us the explicit purpose of the Tabernacle:

> *Then have them* (the people of Israel) *make a sanctuary for me, and I will dwell among them"* (Exodus 25:8). *"I will put my dwelling place among you...I will walk among you"* (Leviticus 26:11-12), *"the place the Lord your God will choose as a dwelling place for His name* (Deuteronomy 12:11).

If the God of all creation repeatedly said things like that, what conclusions would you come to regarding the tabernacle? Add to this the fact that the Ark of the Covenant was placed there, and that the Holy of Holies was reserved for the High Priest only, and then only once a year, and you can begin to see the beliefs that grew up around the Tabernacle. It was, quite literally, where God chose to "live."

When Solomon built the first Temple, the same language surrounded its construction. In fact, God goes one step further. He tells Solomon, "*As for the Temple you are building...I will live among the Israelites **and will not abandon My people Israel***" (1 Kings 6:11-13). It is more than merely a curiosity that God chose "to live" in the Temple. His presence there, and, by association, the Temple, represented God's commitment not to abandon His people. It was around this conviction that the practices of the Temple grew up; the sacrifices, the services, the routine of the priests, the prayers of the people, etc. ALL of those practices were conducted under the watchful eye of the God of Abraham, who continued to dwell among His people in the Temple. As long as the Temple was there, God was there.

So, what would the obvious implication be if the Temple were gone? What would it mean if the sacrifices stopped, the services ended, and the priests no longer served as mediators for God's people? **That would be tantamount to God abandoning His people! If the Temple is gone, God is gone!** It is impossible for us to imagine the significance of that building to the Jewish people. The closest parallel would be The World Trade Center. Do you remember where you were on September 11, 2001? Do you remember the effect those attacks had on the American psyche? Now magnify that a hundredfold, and you begin to approach the significance of the Temple to the people of Israel.

The Context Of Matthew 24

Jesus had just finished delivering His most scathing

rebuke of the religious leaders of His day. Matthew 23 begins with the now famous expression, "practice what you preach." The teachers of the law and the Pharisees didn't. In a series of "woes," Jesus brought His disdain for them out of the closet. What would the consequences be of their promotion of false religion?

> *And so upon you will come all the righteous blood that has been shed on earth, from the blood of righteous Abel to the blood of Zechariah son of Berekiah, whom you murdered between the Temple and the altar. Truly I tell you, all this will come on this generation* (Matthew 23:35-36).

Then in a moment of great sorrow, Jesus lamented the fact that the entire city of Jerusalem would be pulled into the circle of judgment that awaited the religious leaders.

> *Jerusalem, Jerusalem, you who kill the prophets and stone those sent to you, how often I have longed to gather your children together, as a hen gathers her chicks under her wings, and you were not willing. Look, your house is left to you desolate. For I tell you, you will not see me again until you say, 'Blessed is he who comes in the name of the Lord'* (Matthew 23:37-39).

Jesus then left the Temple, (Matthew 24:1) where He had just delivered His prophetic rebuke. The disciples were uneasy. "Man, that was awkward." It's not every day you get to sit in on that kind of tongue lashing of the most respected social and religious leaders of the day! The disciples then made a point of drawing Jesus' attention to

JESUS' GREAT "WINTERVENTION"

the entire Temple complex—"Beautiful isn't it?" An alarm should be going off in each of our heads as we read that—"what?" Are the disciples simply trying to change the subject? No! They are following up precisely where Jesus left off. Jesus had just said to the religious leaders, "Your house will be left to you desolate." What house? The Temple![14] Notice that Jesus did not refer to it any longer as "God's house," but as "your house." God had left the building. This is precisely what the prophet Jeremiah had told them would happen.

> *I will forsake my house, abandon my inheritance; I will give the one I love into the hands of her enemies. My inheritance has become to me like a lion in the forest. She roars at me; therefore I hate her* (Jeremiah 12:7-8).

This is precisely what Jesus' disciples understood. Jesus responded to their correct assumption that He was talking about the Temple, and their worst fears were realized. *Truly I tell you, not one stone here will be left on another; every one will be thrown down"* (Matthew 24:2).

With those words, the disciples' curiosity was piqued. They had taken the short trip from the Temple to the Mount of Olives. They were alone, away from the crowds. One of them finally plucked up enough courage to ask what they had all been thinking: *"Tell us,"* they said, *"when will this happen, and what will be the sign of your coming and of the end of the*

---

[14] Virtually every Biblical scholar acknowledges this. Jesus' reference to a "house" is a direct reference to the "house of God," or the Temple. Cf. Barnes Notes, Clarke's Commentary, Wesley's Notes, James Fausset-Brown, Keener, David Brown, John Calvin, C.H. Spurgeon, etc.

age?" (24:3b). I urge every reader at this point to stop and think logically. Set your preconceptions aside for a moment. Given both the immediate and broader context, what exactly are the disciples asking? We are preconditioned to make a huge epochal jump whenever we see the words "coming" and "end." An "end-coming" can only be talking about the Second Appearing of Christ. Stop! As we examine the disciples' questions in their immediate context, we see that they were actually asking two questions: "when" will the Temple complex be "thrown down" and "what" will be the signs that precede this cataclysmic event?

As we have seen, ALL New Testament writers understood that the destruction of the Temple would be occasioned by *A* coming of the Lord, which would necessarily indicate the end of the age. It was to *this* event that all those imminent time-frame references were pointing. God's judgment of Jerusalem and the Temple would happen "soon" — it was "at hand" —it was the fast approaching "day" to which they spoke. As we have seen, the absence of the Temple was tantamount to the abandonment of God. As we have seen, even Old Testament prophets spoke of just such a day. Are we really to believe that the disciples are in effect asking "When will the Temple be destroyed and, by the way, what will be the signs of your coming thousands of years later after we are all dead and gone?"

It strains credulity to suspect that this was what was going through the disciples' minds. They knew that something "big" was coming. Their own personal "devotions" had given every indication that they were on the cusp of new realities and new expressions of the Kingdom. They had been sitting at the feet of Christ for years, listening and learning, picking up hints that everything was about to change. They had just been warned that THE decisive transitional moment was coming. When?!

Before we dive into the particulars, we need to be reminded of the interpretational key to Jesus' answer. Matthew 24:34 is that key. *"I tell you the truth, this generation will certainly not pass away until all these things have happened."* What could Jesus possibly mean? Are we to believe that "all these things" occurred in the decades leading up to 70 AD, when the Temple was completely destroyed?

One final bit of groundwork. As we read, we will be employing the "literal" hermeneutic described in chapter 2. **We should understand words in their usual and customary way, unless there is good BIBLICAL reason to do otherwise.** That said, how did Jesus answer the disciples' questions?

False Christ's

Jesus began by answering the second part of their question: "What will be the signs?" He warned them of false Messiahs (Matthew 24:4-5). Many, they were told, would come, declaring that they were the returning Messiah. The history of Israel following the Ascension of Jesus is replete with references to such "messiahs." These pseudo-Christs included Menahem, the son or perhaps grandson of Judas the Galilean, Shim'on bar Giora, and Lukuas, just to name a few.[15] Josephus pointed to "false prophets" as the very occasion of the destruction of the Temple and the city. *A false prophet was the occasion of*

---

[15] Harris Lenowitz, *The Jewish Messiahs, From Galilee to Crown Heights* (New York, NY Oxford University Press: 1998), p. 27

these people's destruction, who had made a public proclamation in the city that very day, that God commanded them to get upon the Temple, and that there they should receive miraculous signs of their deliverance. Now there was then a great number of false prophets suborned by the tyrants to impose on the people, who denounced this to them, that they should wait for deliverance from God; and this was in order to keep them from deserting, and that they might be buoyed up above fear and care by such hopes. Now a man that is in adversity does easily comply with such promises; for when such a seducer makes him believe that he shall be delivered from those miseries which oppress him, then it is that the patient is full of hopes of such his deliverance.[16]

Wars and Rumors of Wars

You will hear of wars and rumors of wars, but see to it that you are not alarmed. Such things must happen, but the end is still to come. Nation will rise against nation, and Kingdom against Kingdom (Matthew 24:6-7a).

There is nothing especially time specific about this sign. Just as with today, we can find examples of these things in any number of places. What IS significant is that at the time Jesus spoke these words, Jerusalem WAS at peace. In an unparalleled way, Jesus' first century followers had known peace like few generations before them. The *Pax Romana* was the order of the day. To speak of wars and political unrest would have been hard to believe for His first century audience. But within a decade of Jesus' ascension, four Roman emperors met violent ends, all within an 18-month period. This triggered a season of bloody and violent wars, local conflicts, attempted coups, and general unrest in the

---

[16] Josephus, *War of the Jews*, Trans. William Whiston (Thomas Nelson: 1998) Book 6, Chapter 5, sections 2, 3. Pp. 889-890

years just preceding the destruction of Jerusalem in 70 A.D.[17] As Jesus predicted, this was precisely what happened just prior to His coming in 70 A.D.

FAMINES AND EARTHQUAKES

There will be famines and earthquakes in various places. All these are the beginning of birth pains. (Matthew 24:7b-8) Acts 11:27-28 reads as follows:

> *During this time some prophets came down from Jerusalem to Antioch. One of them, named Agabus, stood up and through the Spirit predicted that a severe famine would spread over the entire Roman world. (This happened during the reign of Claudius.)*

Claudius reigned from 41-54 AD. The Roman historian Tacitus recounted: *This year (51 AD) witnessed many prodigies. Ill-omened birds settled on the Capitol (Rome). Houses were flattened by repeated earthquakes...Further portents were seen in a shortage of corn, resulting in famine.*[18] In the years after Christ's ascension but before 70 AD there were dozens of reported earthquakes, many of which occurred in places not known for seismic activity, including Campania, Chios, Colossae, Create, Hierapolis, Judea, Laodicea, Miletus, Rome, Smyrna, and Samos.

HANDED OVER TO BE PERSECUTED

> *Then you will be handed over to be persecuted and put to death, and you will be hated by all nations because of me. At that time many will turn away from the faith and*

---

[17] Tacitus, *Histories*, Translated by Alfred John Church and William Jackson Brodribb (Internet Classic Archive) 1:2.; Josephus, *War of the Jews*, 2.18.2, pp.751-752

[18] Tacitus, *Annals*, Translated by Alfred John Church and William Jackson Brodribb (Internet Classic Archive) p. 271.

> *will betray and hate each other, and many false prophets will appear and deceive many people. Because of the increase of wickedness, the love of most will grow cold, but the one who stands firm to the end will be saved* (Matthew 24:9-13).

Jesus then warned His disciples of the impending persecution that they would face. With the exception of Judas Iscariot and John Zebedee, all the disciples died a martyr's death, and John died in exile on the island of Patmos. Stephen was stoned to death by the mob in Jerusalem (Acts 7:54-60). James, the brother of Jesus was killed by Herod Agrippa (Acts 12). Paul was brought before numerous authorities, including the proconsul of Achaia (Acts 18:12), Roman governor Felix (Acts 24) and King Agrippa (Acts 25). The persecution of which Jesus spoke would come from two sources—The Jewish religious establishment, and the Roman Empire. The judgment of both these enemies of the Kingdom is given in chilling detail in the book of Revelation, a topic we will return to later. For now, it is enough to observe that Jesus pulled no punches with His followers. Their persecution would be imminent and ultimate and a sign of the coming judgment (Matthew 24:9-13).

The Whole World Hears The Gospel

Matthew 24 Verse 14 is problematic in the context of the clear time frame reference that Jesus gave in verse 34. Are we to believe that the Gospel was preached across the entire globe by 70 AD? Before we reconcile these words with Jesus' time frame reference, we need to address a potential objection. Thus far, we have argued for the clear and simple meaning of the Scriptures. If a text tells us that something will happen soon, we should understand that to mean that it will happen soon. If we are informed that the people who heard Jesus' words would not die until His prophetic utterances were fulfilled, then we should take that to mean exactly what it looks like it means. Is it not contradictory then, to argue that this verse does *not* mean what it clearly seems to mean? Again, the INTERPRETIVE KEY to this passage is the time frame reference that Jesus gives. As we have shown, that assumption is built on the corroborative teaching of Jesus' best students, as well as numerous other clear statements that Jesus Himself made. **The natural assumption must be that there is a simple explanation of verse 14 that honors the time frame reference in verse 34.** In fact, there is.

The Gospel of the Kingdom WAS preached to the whole world prior to the destruction of the Temple in 70 A.D. We have this on no less an authority than the apostle Paul himself. In Colossians 1, Paul stated emphatically that the Gospel was *"bearing fruit all over the world,"* and that this same Gospel has been *"preached to every creature under heaven"* (6, 23). He told the Church in Rome that their faith, rooted in the Gospel of the Kingdom was being *"reported all over the world."* (Romans 1:8) In responding to the objection that perhaps some Jews could be excused for not responding to the Gospel because they had never heard it, Paul noted that the voice of the Gospel had gone out *"into all the earth"* and the word of life *"to the ends of the world."* (Romans 10:18) In explaining to Timothy the "mystery" of godliness, Paul urged him to consider that *"He (Jesus) appeared in a body, was vindicated by the Spirit, was seen by angels, was preached among the nations, was believed on in the world..."* (1 Timothy 3:16). Even by the day of Pentecost, the Gospel of the

Kingdom had reached the entire world. We are told by Luke that God-fearing Jews *"from every nation under heaven"* were present (Acts 2:5).

It is not surprising that in Mark's account of the Olivet discourse (Mark 13:9-11), Jesus' pronouncement that the whole world would hear the Gospel is sandwiched between references to the persecution of His followers. Just as in Matthew 24, Jesus warned His followers in Mark 13 that they would be persecuted for spreading the Gospel.

> *"You must be on your guard. You will be handed over to the local councils and flogged in the synagogues. On account of me you will stand before governors and kings as witnesses to them. And the Gospel must first be preached to all nations. Whenever you are arrested and brought to trial, do not worry beforehand about what to say. Just say whatever is given you at the time, for it is not you speaking, but the Holy Spirit"* (Mark 13:9-11).

Why would Jesus warn His first-century followers that they would be persecuted, then in the next verse, reference something that (supposedly) would be accomplished thousands of years in the future, and then in the next verse, return to a discussion of how to handle persecution? By that logic, Jesus said, "You will be persecuted for preaching the Gospel of the Kingdom, and FYI, people whom you have never heard of, thousands of years from now, will spread that Gospel across the globe, and...where was I? That's right, when you are suffering persecution for spreading the Gospel, don't worry about what you will say—The Holy Spirit has you covered." It makes no logical sense. THEY would be the ones who would be persecuted, THEY would be responsible for preaching the Gospel to the world, and THEY could be assured that God would give them the words they needed in their defense. If we take His words in verse 10 to mean an event that would happen thousands of years later, then Jesus emerges as a very poor teacher.

When Jesus declared that the Gospel would be "preached in the whole world," He meant that in precisely the same way that Luke and Paul meant it. By "whole world," they each meant the **known** world or the world at that time. Whatever nations were known to first-century Jews, or were considered part of the Roman Empire, were considered to be the entire world. Even the great Dr. Luke understood this when he described events surrounding Jesus' birth: *In those days Caesar Augustus issued a decree that a census should be taken of the entire Roman world* (Luke 2:1). Luke never actually mentioned "the entire Roman world." He used exactly the same word that Jesus used in Matthew 24—"the inhabited earth," ($οικουμένη$), which the editors of the NIV properly translate "entire Roman world." They mean the same thing.

A fair question would be "doesn't this interpretation rob us of a great incentive to preach the Gospel to all the nations?" No. To argue from *this* Scripture that Jesus will not appear a second time before the nations hear the Gospel, and, correspondingly, that we should strive for this in order to hasten His appearing is incorrect. But there are plenty of *other* Scriptures that DO provide us ample incentive to bring the Gospel of the Kingdom to the nations. A few chapters later in Matthew, Christ commissioned His first-century disciples (and us, by application) to do just this.

> *Then Jesus came to them and said, "All authority in heaven and on earth has been given to me. Therefore go and make disciples of all nations, baptizing them in the name of the Father and of the Son and of the Holy Spirit, and teaching them to obey everything I have commanded you* (Matthew 28:18-20).

Our desire to preach the Gospel of the Kingdom to the nations finds ample inspiration in other places.

Drawing directly upon the teaching of Isaiah 49:6, Paul defended his ministry this way:

> *On the next Sabbath almost the whole city gathered to hear the word of the Lord. When the Jews saw the crowds, they were filled with jealousy. They began to contradict what Paul was saying and heaped abuse on him. Then Paul and Barnabas answered them boldly: "We had to speak the word of God to you first. Since you reject it and do not consider yourselves worthy of eternal life, we now turn to the Gentiles. For this is what the Lord has commanded us: "'I have made you a light for the Gentiles, that you may bring salvation to the ends of the earth.'" When the Gentiles heard this, they were glad and honored the word of the Lord; and all who were appointed for eternal life believed* (Acts 13:44-48).

Like Paul, we are called to be a light to the nations. Our ambition should be the same as Paul's, *to preach the Gospel where Christ was not known, so that I would not be building on someone else's foundation* (Romans 15:20).

The point of all these passages is that we do not need to let our fear of losing a great incentive to missions drive our interpretation of Matthew 24. There is ample support for the need to bring the Gospel to the nations *without* forcing Matthew 24 to be part of that support.

The Abomination That Causes Desolation

Matthew 24:15 has fueled numerous flights of prophetic fantasy. *So when you see standing in the holy place 'the abomination that causes desolation,' spoken of through the prophet Daniel—let the reader understand—*. Once again, a simple reading of the text gives us the answer to what this abomination was. Jesus referred directly to the prophecy of Daniel as recorded in Daniel 9:27. That prophecy, given in the 6th century B.C., had to do with a time that was centuries in the future for Daniel and his initial readers.

Jesus used the presence of the "abomination" as a sign that Daniel's prophecy was about to be fulfilled. When those living at that time saw it, they should heed the words of Jenny in the film *Forrest Gump*: *"Run Christians, Run!"* He explained that if that event should occur in the winter, it would be all the more devastating for His disciples. The presence of the abomination would signal a season of unparalleled suffering for Jerusalem and its inhabitants. Even so, God's merciful proclivities would shorten that period. Regardless of the timing of this event, Jesus urged His followers to literally drop everything and run when they saw it. So what could it be?

If you have your Bible open to Matthew 24, put a bookmark there and turn to Luke's account of the same conversation in Luke 21. Beginning at verse 20, Luke gave his version of what Jesus said. Because Luke's readers were primarily Gentile, he passed over the specific reference to Daniel's prophecy (a non-issue for non-Jews), and he simply used the word "desolation" to describe the event that would signal the flight of God's people. The flight language is virtually identical to what appears in Matthew. Because of these parallel references, we can be completely confident that what Luke described in 21:20-24 is the same thing that Matthew recorded in verses 15 and following. Again, for a Gentile, the profaning of the Temple would be of little significance. But the **consequences** of the "abomination that causes desolation" would be the same.

Luke wrote *"When you see Jerusalem being surrounded by armies, you will know that its desolation is near"* (v. 20). The "abomination that causes desolation" was nothing less than the arrival of the Roman legions. As they overran the city of Jerusalem and finally overtook the Temple, these legions, with their Romans standards and idolatrous images, stood triumphantly on the Temple mount. Josephus recorded how the worship of "ensigns" and the setting up of an altar to Titus occurred on the Temple mount, on the very sight of the just-destroyed Temple.[19] Drawing upon Josephus' account, Biblical historian and theologian F.F. Bruce summed up what happened that day. *"When the Temple area was taken by the Romans, and the sanctuary itself was still burning, the soldiers brought their legionary standards into the sacred precincts, set them up opposite the eastern gate, and offered sacrifice to them there, acclaiming Titus as **imperator** (victorious commander) as they did so. The Roman custom of offering sacrifice to their standards had already been commented on by a Jewish writer as a symptom of their pagan arrogance, but the offering of such sacrifice in the Temple court was the supreme insult to the God of Israel. This action, following as it did the cessation of the daily sacrifice three*

---

[19] Josephus, *The War of the Jews*, 6.6.1, pp. 891-894.

weeks earlier, must have sensed to many Jews, as it evidently did to Josephus, a new and final fulfillment of Daniel's vision of a time when the continual burnt offering would be taken away and the abomination of desolation set up."[20]

FLEE TO THE MOUNTAINS

If our interpretation of Matthew 24 is correct, then Jesus' disciples (not just the 12) would have understood his words to mean than when they saw the Roman armies approaching, they should run.

> *Then let those who are in Judea flee to the mountains. Let no one on the housetop go down to take anything out of the house. Let no one in the field go back to get their cloak. How dreadful it will be in those days for pregnant women and nursing mothers! Pray that your flight will not take place in winter or on the Sabbath* (Matthew 24:16-20).

It is significant that Jesus words actually flew in the face of conventional thought. At the first sign of trouble, people of the first century headed *into* the city. It was believed (in most cases, rightly so) that greater safety lay within the city walls rather than outside them. Add to this the popular notion that God would never let His Temple be destroyed, and it is easy to see why Jesus' words might have gone unheeded. But history shows that this is precisely what first-century believers did. They fled.

Josephus gave one such account. *"As Josephus was speaking thus with a loud voice, the seditious would neither yield to what he said, nor did they deem it safe for them to alter*

---

[20] FF Bruce, *Israel and the Nations* (Downers Grove, IL: InterVarsity Press, 1997), p224.

their conduct; but as for the people, they had a great inclination to desert to the Romans; accordingly, some of them sold what they had, and even the most precious things that had been laid up as treasures by them, for every small matter, and swallowed down pieces of gold, that they might not be found out by the robbers; and when they had escaped to the Romans, went to stool, and had wherewithal to provide plentifully for themselves; for Titus let a great number of them go away into the country, whither they pleased."[21]

Christian historian and apologist, Eusebius, writing in the early fourth century sheds more light on the flight of believers. *"The whole body, however, of the church at Jerusalem, having been commanded by a divine revelation, given to men of approved piety there before the war, removed from the city, and dwelt at a certain town beyond the Jordan, called Pella. Here those that believed in Christ, having removed from Jerusalem, as if holy men had entirely abandoned the royal city itself, and the whole land of Judea; the divine justice, for their crimes against Christ and his apostles finally overtook them, totally destroying the whole generation of these evildoers from the earth.*[22]

The occasion for this great escape was that the siege of Jerusalem was unexpectedly and inexplicably terminated for a brief period. In his excellent commentary on Revelation, Foy Wallace explained: *"It is a remarkable but historical fact that Cestius Gallus, the Roman general, for some unknown reason, retired when they first marched against the city, suspended the siege, ceased the attack and withdrew his armies for an interval of time after the Romans had occupied the*

---

[21] Josephus, *Wars of the Jews*, 5, 10, 1. p. 861

[22] Eusebius, Translated by Arthur Cushman McGiffert. *From Nicene and Post-Nicene Fathers, Second Series*, Vol. 1. Edited by Philip Schaff and Henry Wace. (Buffalo, NY: Christian Literature Publishing Co., 1890.) E-Version *Church History*, 3.5.3.

Temple, thus giving every believing Jew the opportunity to obey the Lord's instruction to flee the city. Josephus the eyewitness, himself an unbeliever, chronicles this fact, and admitted his inability to account for the cessation of the fighting at this time, after a siege had begun. Can we account for it? We can. The Lord was fighting against Jerusalem Zechariah 14:2: 'For I will gather all nations against Jerusalem to battle; and the city shall be taken, and the houses rifled, and the women ravished; and half of the city shall go forth into captivity, and the residue of the people shall not be cut off from the city: The Lord was besieging that city. God was bringing these things to pass against the Jewish state and nation. Therefore, the opportunity was offered for the disciples to escape the siege, as Jesus had forewarned, and the disciples took it. So said Daniel; so said Jesus; so said Luke, so said Josephus"[23]

A final observation: why would Jesus be concerned with the *weather* and *when* this flight would occur if He was describing His second coming? What possible difference could it make if Jesus returned on a Saturday or a Sunday? Why would the temperature or the presence/absence of snow make any difference relative to His second coming? On the other hand, if Christ was referring to escaping from invading armies in first-century Palestine, then His words make supreme sense. The topography of the land made winter travel difficult. Some fugitives from Jerusalem did in fact try to escape in the winter, and, delayed by flooded wadis, were captured and killed. Travel restrictions on the Sabbath, coupled with the fact that the city gates were closed on the Sabbath made flight on that day virtually impossible. It is a testimony to both the grace of God and the common sense of Jesus' first-century disciples that so many of them escaped.

---

[23] Foy E. Wallace, *The Book of Revelation* (Nashville: Foy E. Wallace Jr. Publications, 1966), p. 352.

The Great Tribulation

> *For then there will be great distress, unequaled from the beginning of the world until now—and never to be equaled again. If those days had not been cut short, no one would survive, but for the sake of the elect those days will be shortened* (Matthew 24:21-22).

As Jesus unpacked the horrific events surrounding the Temple's destruction, he landed on a phrase that has fueled an entire cottage industry. Tribulation, Incorporated, is alive and well. A host of commentators and end-times experts argue that a time is coming when we will see unrivaled suffering in human history. The NIV translates Jesus' words as "great distress," while the KJV calls it a "great tribulation." The argument goes that Jesus must be speaking of some distant future event because He explained that the suffering of that time would be "unequaled from the beginning of the world until now—and never to be equaled again." Does that NECESSARILY mean that these events must be future?

It is impossible for those of us living in the 21st century to imagine how horrible the events were surrounding the destruction of Jerusalem. The great Baptist preacher C. H. Spurgeon attempted to impress his 19th century parishioners with just that. *"Read the record written by Josephus of the destruction of Jerusalem, and see how truly our Lord's words were fulfilled. The Jews impiously said, concerning the death of Christ, "His blood be on us, and on our children." Never did any other people invoke such an awful curse upon themselves, and upon no other nation did such a judgment ever fall. We read of Jews crucified till there was no more wood for making crosses; of thousands of the people slaying one another in their fierce faction fights within the city; of so many of them being sold for slaves that they became a drug in the market, and all but valueless; and of the fearful carnage when the Romans at length entered the doomed capital; and the blood-curdling story exactly bears out the Savior's statement uttered nearly forty years before the terrible events occurred."*[24]

It's also important to keep in mind that more is happening here than just physical suffering. The destruction of Jerusalem signaled the end of an era. The passing of the Kingdom from one people to another was not seamless or painless. The spiritual anguish of seeing the entire Jewish faith destroyed was beyond dreadful. The dwelling place of God was razed. This, coupled with unimaginable atrocities, proved to be a time of suffering the likes of which we will never see again. Could Jesus have been referring to an event that was still millennia away?

Possibly. But the context of Jesus words and the clear time-frame references make this most unlikely. Although one could argue that Jesus engaged in prophetic hyperbole here, the actual accounts of what went on in Jerusalem from 66-71 AD make Jesus' words completely believable. For the Jewish people, and for the early church, this was a time of suffering that remains unparalleled to this day.

Look, Here Is The Christ

> *At that time if anyone says to you, 'Look, here is the Messiah!' or, 'There he is!' do not believe it. For false messiahs and false prophets will appear and perform great signs and wonders to deceive, if*

---

[24] C.H. Spurgeon, *Commentary on Matthew: The Gospel of the Kingdom* (London: Passmore and Alabaster, 1893), pp. 412-413

> *possible, even the elect. See, I have told you ahead of time. "So if anyone tells you, 'There he is, out in the wilderness,' do not go out; or, 'Here he is, in the inner rooms,' do not believe it. For as lightning that comes from the east is visible even in the west, so will be the coming of the Son of Man. Wherever there is a carcass, there the vultures will gather* (Matthew 24:23-28).

Again, Christ warned of the coming of false Messiahs. His words here closely parallel the teaching recorded in Luke 17:20-37. Jesus was being quizzed as to the nature of the Kingdom. Like the disciples, the Pharisees asked "when?" "When (would) the Kingdom of God come?" Unlike the destruction of the Temple which would come after clearly observable signs, the Pharisees were told that the Kingdom "*does **not** come with your careful observation. Nor will people say, 'Here it is,' or 'There it is,' because the Kingdom of God is within you*" (Luke 17:20-21).

With strikingly similar language, Jesus continued in Luke 17:

> *Then he said to his disciples, "The time is coming when you will long to see one of the days of the Son of Man, but you will not see it. People will tell you, 'There he is!' or 'Here he is!' Do not go running off after them. For the Son of Man, in his day will be like the lightning, which flashes and lights up the sky from one end to the other. But first he must suffer many things and be rejected by this generation* (Luke 17:22-25).

Christ suggested that things would become so bad that the disciples will long to see "the days of the Son of Man" but they will have to wait. So intense would their longing be that they may become susceptible to false Christs. "Don't fall for it--He will come!" But first He must suffer and be rejected by "this generation." Then Jesus invoked two Old Testament examples: Noah and Lot (Luke 17:26-29). "It will be just like this on the day the Son of God is revealed (Luke 17:30). Just like what? Just like the sudden destruction that occurred in the lives of those two Old Testament characters.

The disciples then ask, "Where?" Where will all this happen? Where will this great day occur and where will this generation be subject to the same kind of cataclysm as Noah and Lot? "Where there is a dead body, there the vultures will gather" (Luke 17:37). Cryptic? No doubt. But when we tie these words to Jesus' words in Matthew 24 (as we should) it begins to make sense. Jesus is not telling His disciples to prepare for His Second Appearing. What sense would it make to tell them to run? Why would He urge them to flee without regard to personal belongings? What sense would it make to tell them to look for dead bodies as an indication of where this will occur? Virtually every Biblical commentator acknowledges that Jesus is referring to the destruction of Jerusalem in Luke 17. By using the exact same words and imagery as He does in Matthew 24, we should conclude that He is referring to the same event in both. As Jesus concluded this section in Matthew 24, he explained, *"see, I have told you this ahead of time."* The reason this is good news is that the disciples, if they heeded their Master's warning, would be able to escape the coming conflagration.

The Sun Will Be Darkened

> *Immediately after the distress of those days "'the sun will be darkened, and the moon will not give its light; the stars will fall from the sky, and the heavenly bodies will be shaken* (Matthew 24:29).

Aha! Gotcha! "This can't possibly be happening in 70 AD. Things like this have never happened!" Yes, they have. In fact they have happened many times. Do you remember at the outset, we said that we should apply the "literal" hermeneutic (in its classic, historic sense) when interpreting Scripture? We said that "unless there is good *Biblical* reason" we should understand things in their normal and customary way. So, is there any good *Biblical* reason to believe that we are intended to take these words figuratively? Are there examples of the Bible using this kind of language and imagery to describe things figuratively?

The very things described in Matthew 24 happened to Babylon, more than 2,000 years earlier.

> *See, the day of the LORD is coming —a cruel day, with wrath and fierce anger— to make the land desolate and destroy the sinners within it.* **The stars of heaven and their constellations will not show their light. The rising sun will be darkened and the moon will not give its light** (Isaiah 13:9-10 emphasis added).

The Kingdom of Edom suffered a similar fate.

> *Their slain will be thrown out, their dead bodies will stink; the mountains will be soaked with their blood.* **All the stars in the sky will be dissolved and the heavens rolled up like a scroll; all the starry host will fall like withered leaves from the vine, like shriveled figs from the fig tree** (Isaiah 34:3-4 emphasis added).

The judgment of Pharaoh, king of Egypt is described similarly:

> *When I snuff you out,* **I will cover the heavens and darken their stars; I will cover the sun with a cloud, and the moon will not give its light. All the shining lights in the heavens I will darken over you;** *I will bring darkness over your land, declares the Sovereign LORD* (Ezekiel 32:7-8 emphasis added).

Even the nation of Israel experienced the same kind of judgment earlier in her history, as the prophet Joel described:

> *Blow the trumpet in Zion; sound the alarm on my holy hill. Let all who live in the land tremble, for the day of the LORD is coming. It is close at hand—* **a day of darkness and gloom, a day of clouds and blackness. Before them the earth shakes, the heavens tremble, the sun and moon are darkened, and the stars no longer shine** (Joel 2:1-2, 10 emphasis added).

We could go on. The point is simply that this kind of "shaking" language is not intended to be understood in the customary way. It is figurative language, intended to convey the idea of judgment and cosmic upheaval. "But aren't you just 'picking and choosing,' interpreting things literally, but when things don't suit your purposes, suddenly they are 'figurative?'". No. As we said at the outset, the Bible is filled with various genres of literature. Often, different genres appear in the same passage. Good interpretation demands that we learn to distinguish one from the other. Some of Jesus' words mean precisely what they look like they mean, because there is no reason to think otherwise. But some of His words are drawn directly from other places in Scripture (Jesus' words in Matthew 24 are taken *directly* from the Isaiah 13 and 34 passages), compelling us to look at those words in their original context in order to understand. Jesus is doing more here than merely searching for colorful language to make His point. The religious leaders of Jesus day would certainly have run across Isaiah's words in their personal devotions. It is likely that the disciples recognized them as well. **Jesus' words were intended to be offensive!** To think that God would judge His own people in the same way that He judged their enemies, Babylon and Edom, was like nails on a chalkboard to their ears. The "great tribulation" of which Jesus spoke occurred in the years leading up to and including the destruction of Jerusalem/The Temple. Those waiting for another "great tribulation" will be waiting indefinitely.

THE SIGN OF THE SON OF MAN

At that time the sign of the Son of Man will appear in the sky, and all the nations of the earth will mourn... (Matthew 24:30a). A better translation of this verse is found in the English Standard Version (ESV): *Then will appear in heaven the sign of the Son of Man, and then all the tribes of the earth will mourn...* It is better because the word translated "sky" in

JESUS' GREAT "WINTERVENTION"

the NIV is more commonly translated "heaven," and the word for "nations" does not actually appear in the original. For example, the word for "nation," ἔθνος, is properly rendered in 24:7 as "ἔθνος" will rise against ἔθνος." But here in verse 30 the word used is φυλέ as in Matthew 19:28, "judging the twelve φυλες of Israel." Why is this significant? Because Jesus is *not* describing a universal event, He is describing events that are particular to the land of Israel. One could mistakenly conclude that Jesus is saying that He will be appearing in the sky. That is clearly *not* what He is saying. It is not Jesus that is appearing in the "sky;" it is *the sign* that is appearing in *Heaven*. That sign will not cause the "nations" to mourn, but it will cause the "tribes," as in "tribes of Israel" to mourn. What Jesus is saying is that as God's judgment is unfolding ("at that time") there will be a "sign" in Heaven—The Son of Man, sitting at the right hand of the Father—that will signal the time for Israel to mourn. They will mourn because they will realize that they had missed the hour of their visitation; that the Messiah had come and gone, and now He was coming again in final judgment upon the people of Israel. This interpretation is completely consistent with the other things that Jesus and His disciples taught.

As Jesus was being tried by the Sanhedrin, they demanded to know if He was the Christ. His answer?

> *"You have said so," Jesus replied. "But I say to all of you: **From now on you will see the Son of Man sitting at the right hand of the Mighty One and coming on the clouds of heaven**"* (Matthew 26:64 emphasis added).

They would see Him, sitting at the right hand of the Mighty One. Is this good news or bad news for them? It is most assuredly bad news. Jesus' presence in Heaven would confirm that He was who He said He was and that the Father had accepted His sacrifice as sufficient. At Jesus' ascension we are told that He was, in fact, taken "into heaven" (Acts 1:11). When Stephen was martyred, he saw a vision of Jesus in Heaven at the right hand of God (Acts 7:55-56). This picture of Jesus reigning from Heaven as a sign of bad news for the objects of His wrath is rounded out when we consider that Jesus' words in Matthew 24 are taken directly from the prophet Daniel.

> *In my vision at night I looked, and there before me was one like a son of man, coming with the clouds of heaven. He approached the Ancient of Days and was led into his presence. He was given authority, glory and sovereign power; all nations and peoples of every language worshiped him. His dominion is an everlasting dominion that will not pass away, and his Kingdom is one that will never be destroyed* (Daniel 7:13-14).

Jesus confirmed that what Daniel saw was about to happen. Jesus, now in a position of supreme authority, occupies the throne in Heaven, from which He will judge the nation of Israel and establish a Kingdom that will last forever.

The Son of Man, Coming On The Clouds

Matthew 24:30-31 has caused a great many commentators to follow a rabbit trail, due in large part to the words "coming on the clouds of the sky..." When Jesus ascended, a cloud hid Him from the stunned gaze of the disciples. The angels who appeared as Jesus passed out of sight remarked that Jesus would return "in the same way" they had seen Him go. As a result, clouds have become embedded in the Christian psyche as a necessary

JESUS' GREAT "WINTERVENTION"

accoutrement to Christ's return. Here is what Jesus actually said:

> *They will see the Son of Man coming on the clouds of the sky, with power and great glory. And he will send his angels with a loud trumpet call, and they will gather his elect from the four winds, from one end of the heavens to the other* (Matthew 24:30-31).

To understand these words, we need to turn once again to the Old Testament. The entire tone of the Olivet Discourse is one of judgment. Jesus is announcing, without equivocation, that He will return as Judge, culminating in the destruction of the greatest symbol of Israel's failure, the Temple. The reference to Jesus as "coming on the clouds" continues this judgment theme. As we have seen, Jesus' words explain the fulfillment of Daniel's prophecy by using the same imagery (Daniel 7:13). Daniel described seeing "one like a son of man coming with the clouds of heaven..." Both Daniel and Jesus are describing A return of Christ. This is what the cloud imagery is intended to convey; salvation for the elect, and the judgment of His enemies. For example,

> Deuteronomy 33:26 reads *there is no one like the God of Jeshurun,* **who rides on the heavens to help you and on the clouds in his majesty.** Or 2 Samuel 22:8-10; *The earth trembled and quaked, the foundations of the heavens shook; they trembled because he was angry. Smoke rose from his nostrils; consuming fire came from his mouth, burning coals blazed out of it. He parted the heavens and came down;* **dark clouds were under his feet.** The Psalms often employ this kind of imagery. *Sing to God, sing praise to his name, extol him who rides on the clouds—his name is the LORD— and rejoice*

> *before him* (Psalm 68:4). Again in Psalm 104:2-3 David wrote *He wraps himself in light as with a garment; he stretches out the heavens like a tent and lays the beams of his upper chambers on their waters.* ***He makes the clouds his chariot and rides on the wings of the wind.*** Ezekiel 30:2-3 makes a clear connection between judgment and clouds: *"'Wail and say, "Alas for that day!" For the day is near, the day of the LORD is near—* ***a day of clouds,*** *a time of doom for the nations.*

These and other passages[25] suggest that when God comes in power to judge and to save, He comes with the clouds. It is not the Second Appearing of Christ that Jesus is describing here, but the final break with the Old Covenant people of Israel, culminating in the judgment of those same people with the destruction of the greatest symbol of God's presence among them.

Two other things accompany this return of Jesus on the clouds. First, He would send His angels out *"with a loud trumpet call."* This trumpet was the *shofar* horn, used by Israel to signal important events. In this case, Jesus was signaling that the ethnocentric and nationalistic understanding of who God's people are was coming to an end. The word translated "angels," $\alpha\gamma\gamma\epsilon\lambda\lambda oo$ can also mean "messenger" and is often used to describe those who bring the Gospel of the Kingdom. John the Baptist is an $\alpha\gamma\gamma\epsilon\lambda\lambda oo$ (Matthew 11:10; Mark 1:2; Luke 7:27) as are the disciples (Luke 9:52). Regardless of the referent here, the point is the same. The original command to God's Old Covenant people to be a blessing to all nations had been judged an utter failure.

---

[25] "Cloud" references are numerous, especially among the prophets as they warned of God's coming judgment. Cf. Jeremiah 4:13-14; Nahum 1:3; Zephaniah 1:15-17.

As Jesus came to judge *one* people, He also extended an invitation to a New People.

This is the second thing that accompanied Jesus return on the clouds. The ethnic composition of God's chosen People moved from one nation to all nations, from one people, to many peoples. This is why the same $\alpha\gamma\gamma\epsilon\lambda\lambda o\sigma$ whose work was signaled by the *shofar* blast are now gathering people from all over the globe. The references to "the four winds" and "one end of the heavens to the other" are intended to convey the broad pool from which God would draw His new People. With these words, Jesus put the finishing touches on His work as Judge. While His special relationship to one people was ending, a new relationship to a New People was beginning.

Don't Be Fooled

So then, Jesus is referring in these verses to the ultimate destruction of the Temple in 70 AD. He is NOT referring to His Second Appearing. Jesus' warnings to His disciples to NOT be fooled by announcements of His coming can hardly refer to His final Appearing. There will be no need for someone to announce to us that Jesus might have come back and He is hanging out in the desert, or He is staying at the local Holiday Inn Express (the "inner rooms" of v. 26). His final coming will be unmistakable and visible to all. Clearly, Jesus has a different "coming" in mind here in Matthew 24 than His final return on the Last Day.

This Generation

> *Now learn this lesson from the fig tree: As soon as its twigs get tender and its leaves come out, you know that summer is near. Even so, when you see all these things, you know that it is near, right at the door. I tell you the truth, this generation will certainly not pass away until all these things have happened. Heaven and earth will pass away, but my words will never pass away* (Matthew 24:32-35).

Jesus finally answered the first question the disciples asked: "When?" In doing so He made an appeal to common sense. His first century readers knew how to tell one season from another. Fig trees provided great clues. "If you have enough sense to know when Summer is approaching, I've given you plenty of clues to know when the end is coming at the hands of Imperial Rome!" "In fact, when you see these things happening, that would be a great time to get out of town—with clouds as my chariots, I'm on my way…"

So as to leave no doubt, Jesus gave the ultimate "clue" as to the timeline of the events he had just unrolled. Again, a paraphrase: "You can bet that heaven and earth will not be here forever—but be sure of this—whatever I say WILL last forever, and I'm telling you that everything I've just told you will happen within the next 40 years." It takes no imagination whatever to see virtually every reference Jesus made in this chapter as having its historical fulfillment in the events surrounding the siege of Jerusalem from 66 to 70 AD.

JESUS' GREAT "WINTERVENTION"

HE SHALL REIGN FOREVER AND EVER

Perhaps you saw it during the Christmas season of 2010. On Saturday, October 30, the Opera Company of Philadelphia brought together over 650 choristers from 28 participating organizations to perform at Macy's in Center City Philadelphia. Accompanied by the Wanamaker Organ - the world's largest pipe organ - the OCP Chorus and throngs of singers from the community infiltrated the store as shoppers, and burst into a pop-up rendition of the Hallelujah Chorus from Handel's "Messiah" at 12 noon. This event was one of 1,000 "Random Acts of Culture" funded by the John S. and James L. Knight Foundation over the next three years.[26] It was positively stirring.

What most people don't know is that this most famous of Handel's works was not written for Christmas, but for Lent.[27] The "Hallelujah" chorus was written not to honor the birth or resurrection of Jesus but to celebrate the destruction of Jerusalem and the Second Temple in A.D. 70. To create the "Messiah" text, Charles Jennens, a formidable scholar and a friend of Handel's, put together a series of Scriptures adapted from the Book of Common Prayer and the King James Bible. Drawing extensively from Psalm 2, Handel, with Jennens lyrics, created a chorus that was designed to answer the question, "How should we view the definitive break with Judaism that the destruction of the

---

[26] The video can be seen at http://www.youtube.com/watch?v=wp_RHnQ-jgU.

[27] Michael Marissen, "*Unsettling History of That Joyous 'Hallelujah*,'" The New York Times, April 8, 2007. Marissen's article attempts to make a case for anti-Semitism being at the root of Handel's and Jennens' work. The fact is that Handel was openly "pro-Jewish" and acknowledged the great indebtedness of Christianity to its Jewish roots. But both Handel and Jennens also saw the significance of 70 A.D. as representing the definitive break with the Old Covenant.

Temple represented?" *"Hallelujah! For the Lord God omnipotent reigneth; the Kingdom of this world is become the Kingdom of our Lord and of his Christ"* (Revelation 19:6, and 11:5). We are right to feel ambivalent. The suffering experienced by fellow image-bearers of God was profound. But in terms of the significance of this event in the history of the Kingdom, there is no more appropriate response. "Hallelujah! For the Lord God omnipotent reigneth."

Chapter Summary

The event that Jesus warned was coming soon was the same event that New Testament writers often referred to as "the end of the age" or "the day of the Lord." That day, that event was the destruction of Jerusalem and the Temple in 70 A.D.

In the Olivet Discourse, Jesus laid out with laser-like precision the events that would precede that day. One by one His prophetic pronouncements came to pass, and within a single generation of when he said those things, Jerusalem and the Temple were razed.

It is impossible for 21st century Westerners to hear the collective gasp of that generation as they watched the Temple be dismantled stone by stone and the fires of invading Roman armies engulf the city.

Why was such an event so significant and so necessary? Up until 70 A.D., Christianity was largely viewed as a Jewish sect. In fact, the greatest tension in the early Church was generated by trying to integrate non-Jewish converts into the Body of Christ. With the destruction of the Temple, there could be no doubt that, if Christianity survived, it was not inextricably tied to the Rabbinic Judaism of the first-century. And survive it did—in fact it flourished. The implications for us are profound.

We cannot afford to lose sight of our calling as winsome warriors. As the true Israel, we must herald the coming of the Kingdom with abandon. Our mandate is to make disciples of ALL nations, teaching them to observe everything that Christ commanded us, both in word and deed. The consequences of our failure to do so will be as acute and as uncompromising as it was for first-century Judaism.

CHAPTER 6

THE GREAT REIGN ROBBERY [28]

AIR TO THE THRONE?

The God of heaven will set up a Kingdom that will never be destroyed..."
DANIEL 2:44

"The Last Days" is the time of the great harvest, of Christ's incrementally trampling down His enemies by the power of the Gospel. The definitive victory on the Cross gives way to the final "mop-up operation" that will conclude at Christ's Second Coming. "The Last Days" is a time of excitement and ecstasy, of trial and hardship, of temporary defeat and permanent victory, of the worldwide expansion of the Kingdom of God. It is a time of the "already/not yet" — the "already" of Christ's universal mediatorial reign within time and history, the "not yet" of remnants of the Second Adam and the sin that war against the incursion of the Kingdom of God and the new age (*Rom. 7*).We are called in "The Last Days" to faithfulness — and to victory in every area of thought, life, and society.
THOSE LONG-LIVED LAST DAYS, BY ANDREW SANDLIN

As for you, you were dead in your transgressions and sins, in which you used to live when you followed the ways of this world and of the ruler of the Kingdom of the air, the spirit who is now at work in those who are disobedient.
EPHESIANS 2:1-2

---

[28] R.B. Yerby, *Up, Up, And Away* (Sengel, PA: Reiner Publications, 1976), p. 73.

I was captivated by J.R.R. Tolkien's *Lord of the Rings* trilogy. I remember finishing *The Hobbit* and literally crying as Bilbo sailed off. I felt as if I had lost a friend. As I pored over *The Fellowship of the Ring* and the other two books, I was transported to Middle Earth. The emotional power of the exploits of Aragorn is palpable. The narrative crescendo of the story comes as Aragorn enters Mina Tirith. Our hero has labored in obscurity. He has forgone the comforts of family and home. He is a warrior, fighting for people who have no idea who he truly is. As he enters the fortified city, the steward announces his true pedigree. *"Here is Aragorn son of Arathorn, chieftain of the Dunedain of Arnor, Captain of the Host of the West, bearer of the Star of the North, wielder of the Sword Reforged, victorious in battle, whose hands bring healing, the Elfstone, Elessar of the line of Valandil, Isildur's son, Elendil's son of Numenor. Shall he be king and enter into the City and dwell there?* Finally, the true King, Aragorn, receives his due. There are battles to be fought and sacrifices to be made, but one thing is certain: The King has come. Shall he enter into the City and dwell there?

We know that one of the most prevalent themes in the Bible is the Kingdom of God. Both Old and New Testament speak of it constantly. It is THE central focus of the teachings of Jesus. God's desire is to display His sovereignty by establishing an everlasting Kingdom where He is glorified and enjoyed by all His subjects.

The fall into sin by mankind was our statement of rebellion—a declaration that we wished to secede from God's Kingdom and establish our own. Since the beginning, God has set about restoring himself as King, and all mankind as His subjects. There are those who suggest that the process of restoration is still primarily future. They argue that Jesus' first coming represented a failed attempt on God's part to usher in His everlasting Kingdom, and that for now, Satan calls the shots. He still functions within the permissive will of God, but He is the boss. Until Christ appears a second time, we must wait for His glory to be revealed until the 1,000 year millennial reign (Revelation 20:1-10). Ours is a woeful future until then. Dire predictions follow. Sensationalism is the order of the day. Christian fiction is passed off as Biblical truth, and countless end-time teachers assure us that "at any moment" Jesus will return to give it a second shot.[29] Is this what the Bible teaches regarding the Kingdom? Should we expect that things will only get worse? Shall the King enter the city and dwell there?

The Kingdom: What Is It?

As important an idea as it is, there is nowhere in Scripture where the Kingdom is defined. "For all his repeated mention of the Kingdom of God, Jesus never once paused to define it. Nor did any hearer ever interrupt Him to ask, 'Master, what do these word 'Kingdom of God,' which you use so often, mean?' On the contrary, Jesus used the term as if assured it would be understood, and indeed it was…To us, on the contrary, it is a strange term, and it is necessary that

---

[29] This notion that Christ's first appearing represented a failed attempt to establish His Kingdom is very popular. The "church" is God's Plan B. When He appears a second time He will get down to the real business of setting up an earthly Kingdom, headquartered in Jerusalem, with the now politically resurgent state of Israel as the epicenter of that reign. Cf. the writings of Hal Lindsey, J. Dwight Pentecost, and John Walvoord.

we give it content if we are to comprehend it."[30] In the most general sense, the Kingdom is both the authority TO rule, and the "territory" over which that rule is exercised. The Kingdom of God or the Kingdom of Heaven is wherever God reigns; His ever expanding rule whereby He brings everything under His authority, to the glory of God. Then He will hand the Kingdom over to the Father, and all things, Himself included, will be subject to the Father, *"so that He might be all in all"* (1 Corinthians 15:24-28). In one sense, that Kingdom includes everyone and everything. The problem is that not everyone ACKNOWLEDGES that rule. It is one thing to be King, and quite another to be recognized by your subjects.

It is the "unfolding" of God's reign that is detailed in the pages of Scripture. The Kingdom, rather than a concept, is a story. What follows is a (very) brief summary of that story.

Originally, God took a place that was largely uninhabitable, and He created a Paradise. It was to be the center of His sovereign reign over the universe, populated with joyful, God-glorifying subjects. The crowning achievement of God's creative passion was mankind. Humans, through Adam/Eve, were given authority over the earth—mankind ruled, as a steward, subject only to God Himself. But humanity chose to subject itself to another ruler, Satan. The earth, which man was destined to rule, now fell under the rule of another. The effects of the fall were immediate and widespread. One outcome often goes

---

[30] John Bright, *The Kingdom of God*, Location 103 of 4274, Kindle Ebook.

overlooked. With the fall into sin, the "earth" was handed over to Satan, and he was given authority over the nations that would ultimately arise (Luke 4:6). In other words, Satan was given the ability to deceive more than just individuals. He was given the authority to deceive entire nations, and keep them from salvation (Luke 8:10-12). He became a "usurper," a "thief." Under the watchful eye of the one True King, Satan's "rule" was PERMITTED, LIMITED, AND TEMPORARY.

Permitted

Regardless of the repercussions of the Fall into sin, Satan never "wrested" control of the nations from God. He was *given* that control. It is always dangerous to presume to know the mind of God, but one thing is certain. God exists to bring glory to Himself. Whatever His actions might be, His motives are undeniable.

> *And I will harden Pharaoh's heart, and he will pursue them. But I will gain **glory** for myself through Pharaoh and all his army, and the Egyptians will know that I am the LORD"* (Exodus 14:4).
>
> *Ascribe to the LORD the **glory** due his name. Bring an offering and come before him; worship the LORD in the splendor of his holiness* (1 Chronicles. 16:29).
>
> *Help us, O God our Savior, for the **glory** of your name; deliver us and forgive our sins for your name's sake* (Psalm 79:9).
>
> *You have enlarged the nation, O LORD; you have enlarged the nation. You have gained **glory** for yourself; you have extended all the borders of the land* (Isaiah 26:15).

> *"I am the LORD; that is my name! I will not give my glory to another or my praise to idols"* (Isaiah 42:8).

It would seem that God gained greater glory for Himself by freely giving Satan this control over the nations, and then winning it back through the apparent defeat at Calvary. Think of it! God could have wiped out the earth and started from scratch. God could have created beings that only "appeared" to be made in His image, but were really nothing more than automatons. God could have instantly destroyed Satan. Instead, God chose a path that included a rebellion in heaven, followed by a rebellion on earth. Both rebellions have always been under the permissive sovereignty of God.

Limited

The "rule" of Satan was never boundless. Nor was it ultimate. Satan never has, nor will he ever move one inch beyond what the Father allows. The story of Job powerfully illustrates this (Job 1:8-12; 2:3-6). Although limited, there *was* a unique expression of Satan's "rule" that God did permit, and that was Satan's ability to deceive entire nations. Prior to the call of Abraham, every nation was under the spell of the Evil One. This is why God began His great redemptive work by establishing one nation as the "headquarters" of the ever-expanding Kingdom that would someday subsume all other nations. The marching orders of God's people were to bring to all nations the message of forgiveness and righteousness that could only be found in the God of Israel. Up until the Incarnation, that work remained largely undone. Still, the scope of Satan's authority was not boundless. Beginning with the nation of Israel, God began the great reclamation project that is the Kingdom.

TEMPORARY

Obviously, this arrangement was only temporary. THE critical turning point in this arrangement with Satan came with the first coming of Jesus. When Jesus' disciples returned from bearing witness to the coming of the Kingdom, they were ebullient. *"Even the demons submit to us"* they declared. Their words were as much a question as a statement. Jesus answered the implied "How can this be...?" with *"I saw Satan fall like lightning from heaven"* (a place of authority) (Luke 10:17-18). As Jesus rode into Jerusalem to the cheers of His misguided people, He announced *"Now is the time for judgment on this world; now the prince of this world is driven out. But I, when I am lifted up from the earth, will draw all men to myself"* (John 12:31-32). The Faux-King or Prince of the nations was unceremoniously being shown the door. The Kingdom was now in the hands of its rightful Heir. Up until that time, Satan did enjoy some authority under the permissive will of the Father, but again, that authority was limited to Satan's ability to deceive the nations, a prerogative that was as temporary as it was limited.

So then, we see an amazing "template" placed over all of history. With mankind's initial rebellion, the abiding principle of REDEMPTION came into play. God *permitted* so that He might ultimately be *praised.* He "gave up" so that He might gain greater glory by redeeming the very world that was subjected to the Evil One. He *relinquished* so that He might *redeem.* Of course, what we have described here in a few sentences has been the overriding theme of all history since that initial taste of the forbidden fruit.

The "Prince of this World"

Satan wasted little time in exercising his authority to deceive. The fruit of his work is succinctly captured in the words of Genesis 6:5— *"every inclination of the thoughts of his (mankind's) heart was only evil, all the time."* Entire civilizations were blinded to the truth of who God was. In Noah's day, only one family was saved. Only one man, Abraham, was found to be faithful amidst Satan's tyrannical reign. The cities of Sodom and Gomorrah would have been spared if there had been even 10 righteous people there. Of all the peoples of the earth, only one could legitimately be called the people of God. Again and again, Satan blinded entire peoples, entire nations to the truth. Lesson learned? Satan is the ultimate self-serving sovereign.

But the "June 6, 1944"[31] of Scripture is found just five chapters after the introduction of the Flood narrative. In Genesis 12, the assault on Satan began in earnest. Both a physical and a spiritual beachhead were established as God separated out one nation from all the nations on earth. It was a beginning—One nation, one land where Satan's capacity to deceive would be compromised. Like yeast in a lump of dough, the truth of God's redemptive reign would begin to work its way throughout the whole earth. At least, that was the plan. With Israel as the epicenter, a great spiritual quake would rock the Kingdom of darkness and restore the One, True King to His throne. *"All peoples on earth will be blessed"* through this new People, Israel (Genesis 12:3).

---

[31] The date of the historic allied invasion of Europe in World War 2, often referred to as "D-Day."

Now, grab your Biblical remote and skip forward several "chapters" on the Kingdom DVD to Matthew 4 (or Mark 1, or Luke 4). The King is confronted by the Usurper. It is critical that we understand what Satan is up to here. He has an idea why Jesus is there. He (the Christ) had come to take His rightful place, and to complete the mission that the people of Israel had failed to finish. After several abortive attempts at derailing the coming of the Kingdom as God originally intended, Satan played his trump card. *...The Devil took Him to a very high mountain and showed Him all the Kingdoms of the world and their splendor. "All this I will **give you** if you will bow down and worship me"* (Matthew 4:8-9 emphasis mine). We tend to think that Satan's offer is a vain boast. The Kingdoms he shows Jesus are not his to give, are they? YES! (Luke 4:6). And that was precisely the problem. At that time, all these nations were still under the evil rule of the Usurper. The troops of the Almighty were still languishing on the shores of France, or Israel, as the case may be. Jesus came to wrest control from Satan. **But there would be no crown without the cross.** Jesus knew it. The temptation must have been truly great for Him to simply be "given" these Kingdoms. We know that there were times when Jesus entertained the possibility of finding another way to complete the will of the Father. *"If possible, let this cup pass from me"* (Matthew 26:39). In other words, "is there another way?" But with the same steely determination Jesus exhibited at Gethsemane, Jesus commanded, "Away from me, Satan." A defeated Pretender to the Throne could only sigh, "On to plan B."

It is precisely this kind of exchange that must have gone on again and again in the life of Jesus. While the "Showdown in the Desert" was obvious, the "Throw Down for the Throne" was an ongoing battle. Ultimately, the Kingdom ended up where it belonged; in the hands of the Christ. Keep in mind: It was not that the Kingdom had not been present prior to that. The Kingdom had always been present. Prior to the Incarnation, it existed, against God's express command, as the unique possession of one people, one ethnic group. Their mission was nothing less than to spread the fame of the God of Israel throughout the whole earth, and to make the Kingdom accessible to all peoples.

> *Sing to the LORD, all the earth; proclaim his salvation day after day. Declare his glory among the nations, his marvelous deeds among all peoples. For great is the LORD and most worthy of praise; he is to be feared above all gods* (1 Chronicles 16:23-25).

The failure of God's people to do this was precisely what made the Kingdom the central feature of what Jesus taught while on earth.

We need to skip ahead one more time, so grab that Biblical remote and move to the last chapter on the "Kingdom DVD." It is found in Revelation, chapter 20. While we will look at the entire book of Revelation in greater detail later, chapter 20 is particularly germane to this discussion. Although we still need to determine "when" the Kingdom is, I'll tip my hand a bit—The Kingdom of which Jesus spoke and of which Revelation refers to as "a thousand years" is NOW. We are currently living in the thousand year reign of Christ. Obviously there is much more explaining to do. But as it relates to the defeat of Satan and the spread of the Kingdom to the nations, Revelation 20 gives us another clue.

If, as we are arguing, the thousand year reign of Christ (The Kingdom) is now, then how can the following be true?

> *"And I saw an angel coming down out of heaven having the key to the Abyss and holding in his hand a great chain. He seized the dragon, that ancient serpent, who is the devil, or Satan, and bound him for a thousand years. He threw him into the Abyss, and locked and sealed it over him,* **to keep him from deceiving the nations anymore until the thousand years were ended.** *After that, he must be set free for a short time." "When the thousand years are over, Satan will be released from his prison and will go out to deceive the nations in the four corners of the earth..."* (Revelation 20:1-3; 7-8 emphasis added).

Some have interpreted these words to indicate a future golden age, a time when God's people will reign and Satan will be incapacitated.

But what EXACTLY do the Scriptures say about the limitations of Satan during these thousand years? It does **not** say that Satan will be powerless. It does **not** say that Satan will have no authority. It does **not** say that Satan will not be able to direct a host of activities from inside his prison. It **DOES** say that he will be limited in only ONE way, and that his incarceration is for ONE specific purpose—*"to keep him from deceiving the nations anymore."* The very prerogative that Satan was granted at the Fall is now taken from him. He can no longer put blinders over the spiritual eyes of entire people groups. People from every tribe and nation will now begin flocking to King Jesus, laying down their own Kingdoms in favor of The Everlasting Kingdom.

I watched with great interest a TV special that was aired recently on the *National Geographic Channel.* It documented the rise of a gang called The Aryan Brotherhood. What was most intriguing was that the power and control of the gang actually *increased* once its leaders were imprisoned. They were able to efficiently run what had become a large, international empire *from inside the prison.* They exercised complete control over activities outside the prison, including the sale of drugs, extortion, prostitution, even murders, from their prison cells. They devised ingenious and complicated "codes" for passing information both inside and outside of prison. I would imagine that, as diabolical and ingenious as these gang leaders are, that Satan is every bit their equal. While many of the particulars of Revelation 20 are up for debate, one thing is certain; Satan's "binding" is completely consistent with everything else we have learned. He is limited at precisely the point where he once flourished— the deceiving of the nations. Despite this limitation, he still maintains significant influence in the world.

To summarize: The Kingdom is the rule of God. Once compromised by the permitted, limited, and temporary rule of Satan, that Kingdom was initially "offered" to one people, the nation of Israel. Their mission was to serve as heralds of the coming of that Kingdom, both in word and deed. God's people failed. In spite of their failure more and more people groups today are acknowledging what has always been true—there is only one King, and His name is Jesus Christ. What began at Pentecost will someday be the reality for the world. The time is coming when every knee will bow, and every tongue will confess that *"Jesus is Lord"* (Phil. 2:10). In the words of CS Lewis, "Aslan is on the move!" There will be Hell to pay for anyone who gets in His way.

The Kingdom: When Is It?

Is the Kingdom, the universally recognized reign of Christ, a future event or a present reality? The Answer? Yes! There have been a number of books written on this topic, many of which are now Christian classics. Gerhardus Vos, John Bright, and Herman Riderboss, to name a few, have clearly articulated what has come to be known as the "already/not yet" feature of the Kingdom. In other words, the Kingdom is a present reality. It is here now. How else could we understand the words of Jesus—"Repent, the Kingdom is here."

On the other hand, the Kingdom has not been fully realized. If the Kingdom is the recognized reign of the One True King, then clearly not everyone recognizes that yet. The consummation of the Kingdom, which will come when Jesus appears a second time, has yet to occur. As we have noted, Satan still has much authority, and the battle continues to rage between The Kingdom and the anti-Kingdom, also known as the World, sin, and Satan himself. The same Jesus who declared that the Kingdom was here, also urged us to pray to the Father, *"Let Your Kingdom come, on earth as it is in Heaven."*

Think of it this way. Imagine that you are traveling from Detroit, Michigan, to Key West, Florida, sometime in

January. As you wend your way to the Keys you periodically see sign posts: "Key West-968 miles," "Key West-746 miles." The closer you get, the less far you have to go. You also notice that the temperature is growing increasingly warm. Things begin to appear in a mysterious color that you haven't seen in Michigan for several months: Green! A strange yellow hue begins covering everything you see: Sun! You travel on, and although you haven't yet arrived, you continue getting closer and closer, and there are signs all around you that indicate you're headed in the right direction. That is how the timeline of history is unfolding relative to the Kingdom. Key West exists! It is already there, but you haven't yet arrived. The Kingdom exists! It is here, among us, but we have not yet fully "arrived."

Obviously, that analogy breaks down at several key points. Movement toward the consummation of the Kingdom is not a leisurely drive—it is a war, being waged at every conceivable level. And the Kingdom is not a destination, it is an unfolding reality. The point is this: The Kingdom is here, now. Jesus Christ is on the throne. He is currently bringing everything under His sovereign control. He is currently populating His Kingdom with subjects from every tribe, nation, and tongue in the world. Every spiritual ruler and authority is being vanquished. Even death itself is on the ropes, and will one day be forever done away with. As followers of the King, our mission is to be heralds of this ever-growing, ever-advancing Kingdom. Our ambition is to surrender our lives and our wills to the ethic of the Kingdom as outlined in Matthew 5-7. Our calling is to teach future and existing citizens of this Kingdom everything that Jesus has taught us. In short, we are to fight against anyone and anything that fails to recognize Christ as King, and teach people from all nations how to live as joy-filled citizens of the only Kingdom that will last forever.

Conclusion

As we will see in later chapters, the implications of the presence of the Kingdom are profound. For now, suffice it to say that the Kingdom of God is His rule and authority which extends over every aspect of creation. The coming of Christ to earth inaugurated a new era for the presence of the Kingdom—an era in which the blessings and benefits of Kingdom citizenship were opened to all people in the same way it had been uniquely opened to the people of Israel. The Kingdom of God is growing, increasing in power and expression, until the day when Christ appears a second time, at which time the consummated Kingdom will be turned over to God the Father. As we labor together as winsome warriors, we do so with the confidence that the decisive battle has already been fought, and the victory is ours. If Christ reigns, we reign with Him. We are still at war. The "hedgerows" of "God-haters" must still be fought through. But the King has come, and He sits on the Throne. He invites us to acknowledge that we reign with Him.

It is as if the Great Steward of Heaven is announcing: "Here is Jesus: Advocate (1 John 2:1), Almighty (Rev. 1:8; Mt. 28:18), Alpha and Omega (Rev. 1:8; 22:13), Amen (Rev. 3:14), Atoning Sacrifice for our Sins (1 John 2:2), Author of Life (Acts 3:15), Blessed and only Ruler (1 Tim. 6:15), Bread of Life (John 6:35; 6:48), Chief Cornerstone (Eph. 2:20), Creator (John 1:3), Deliverer (Rom. 11:26), Everlasting Father (Isa. 9:6), Faithful and True (Rev. 19:11), Firstborn From the Dead (Rev. 1:5), Great High Priest (Heb. 4:14),Heir of all things (Heb. 1:2), Horn of

Salvation (Luke 1:69), King Eternal (1 Tim. 1:17), King of Israel (John 1:49), King of kings (1 Tim 6:15; Rev. 19:16), King of the Ages (Rev. 15:3), Lamb of God (John 1:29), Light of the World (John 8:12), Lion of the Tribe of Judah (Rev. 5:5), Lord of All (Acts 10:36), Lord of Glory (1 Cor. 2:8), Mediator of the New Covenant (Heb. 9:15), Mighty God (Isa. 9:6) Morning Star (Rev. 22:16) Power of God (1 Cor. 1:24), Righteous One (Acts 7:52; 1 John 2:1), Ruler of the Kings of the Earth (Rev. 1:5), Savior (Eph. 5:23; Titus 1:4; 3:6; 2 Pet. 2:20), Son of Man (Mt. 8:20), Son of the Most High God (Lk. 1:32), The Way (John 14:6), Wonderful Counselor (Isa. 9:6) Word of God (Rev. 19:13); Shall He enter the cities of our world, the strongholds of the principalities and powers and authorities that vainly try to fight against Him?" Saying "yes" doesn't *make* it so, it only confirms that it *is* so. "Come, Lord Jesus." Enter the strongholds of our hearts. Let your reign extend to the nations! "Your Kingdom come, Your will be done, on earth as it is in Heaven."

Chapter Summary

The Kingdom is one of the unifying themes of Scripture. It is THE central feature of the teachings of Jesus Christ. The story of the Kingdom began in the Garden of Eden, and it will end in the same kind of place (Revelation 22). In the meantime, the one-time ruler of the nations, Satan, has been defeated and is now restricted in his ability to deceive entire nations.

Instead, the True King, Christ Jesus, reigns over the earth. He is busy expanding His rule and authority over every nation, every authority, every principality and power, and every person on earth. We are currently living during that ever-expanding rule of Christ, most often referred to as the Kingdom, and in one instance, in Revelation 20, as "1,000 years." The latter is a symbolic term that describes an ideal period of time.

The implications for the Church are as startling as they are tantalizing. As Christ, who is seated at the right-hand of the Father, *"far above all rule and authority,"* continues to advance the Kingdom, He does so *"for the Church, which is His body, the fullness of Him who fills everything in every way"* (Ephesians 1:22-23). From the beginning of the great Kingdom narrative, it was God's intent to use the Church to make His "manifold wisdom" known to the "rulers and authorities in the heavenly realms" (Ephesians 3:10-11). That "wisdom" was that *"through the gospel the Gentiles are heirs together with Israel, members together of one body, and sharers together in the promise in Christ Jesus"* (Ephesians 3:6). This truth is at the center of the Kingdom. Satan can no longer stop it! Christ will complete it! The Church will share in it! "Your Kingdom come, Your will be done, ON EARTH as it is in Heaven..."

CHAPTER 7

Is Jesus A Fan Of Big Love?

THE ONE PEOPLE OF GOD

The God of heaven will set up a Kingdom that will never be destroyed..."
DANIEL 2:44

Jesus said to them, "Have you never read in the Scriptures:
"'The stone the builders rejected has become the cornerstone;
the Lord has done this, and it is marvelous in our eyes'?
"Therefore I tell you that the Kingdom of God will be taken away from you and given to a people who will produce its fruit. Anyone who falls on this stone will be broken to pieces; anyone on whom it falls will be crushed.
MATTHEW 21:42-44

Bishop Krister Stendahl was one of the first scholars to argue for it, namely that there are two different salvation "tracks"— the Christian track for the believing remnant and believing Gentiles, and the track for historical Israel which relies on God's covenant with them. Romans 11 stands in clear opposition to this trend because of its insistence on the fact that there is only one olive tree, to which Jews and Gentile believers both belong. . . "The irony of this," writes Tom Wright, "is that the late twentieth century, in order to avoid anti-Semitism, has advocated a position (the non-evangelization of the Jews) which Paul regards precisely as anti-Semitic.
JOHN STOTT, *ROMANS: GOD'S GOOD NEWS FOR THE WORLD*

WINSOME WARRIORS

At the time of this writing, the cable network HBO is airing a series called *"Big Love."* The series chronicles the life of Bill Henrickson, played by actor Bill Paxton, and his three wives. The Emmy and Golden Globe nominated series has generated more than just a little controversy, given its theme of modern day polygamy.

According to many contemporary Christian writers and thinkers, Bill is not the only polygamist we ought to concern ourselves with—Jesus Christ is another. The metaphor of marriage, used to describe Jesus' relationship to the Church, is a Biblical one. The Church IS the "bride of Christ" (Revelation 21:9). According to some, this would be the "second" bride of Jesus, as He is, in fact, still married to his first wife, the people of Israel, who are also referred to as the bride of Christ (Isa. 62:5). So which is it? Does Jesus have two brides, an Old Testament one and a New Testament one? As we will see (See also Appendix #2), it is no accident that PRECISELY the same metaphor that was used to describe God's relationship to ethnic Israel is now applied to the Church. For some, this is not that significant. For them, ethnic Israel and the current political state of Israel are still, and have always been, at the heart of God's Kingdom agenda. Failure to support the modern state of Israel is tantamount to opposing the will of God.

Not only does this idea confuse our understanding of the Kingdom, but it greatly compromises our role as Winsome Warriors in the world today. But if the Old Covenant People of God, Israel, has naturally expanded to include Gentiles and create a new People of God, the Church, then *our* marching orders have everything to do with *their* marching orders. God never intended to create a People composed of ONE ethnicity. Although He began with one group, His desire was always to see that group expand to include peoples from EVERY nation. Alas, a brief sampling of contemporary evangelical thought makes clear that for many, that idea is nonsense.

The Popular View—A Love Affair With Israel

"...Several overriding truths manifest themselves over and over. The first is God's unfathomable love for the nation of Israel—a sovereign and gracious love that extends undiminished from eternity past to eternity future; an omnipotent love that will unfailingly bring ultimate redemption to those of the natural line of Abraham...Apart from that momentous truth, the end times can be nothing but an enigma that baffles every attempt to comprehend it."
Robert Van Kampen, The Sign

"All the events that surround the coming of Jesus to the earth and the end of the world require that Israel exist as a nation in the land of Palestine...the geopolitical situation during the end times requires the existence of Israel as a nation..."
Ed Dobson, *The End*

"God will keep his original promises to the fathers and will one day convert and place Israel as the head of the nations."
(House and Ice, *Dominion Theology*, p. 175.)

"Theologically, any Christian has to support Israel...If we fail to protect Israel, we will cease to be important to God."
Rev. Jerry Falwell

"Over the centuries, Christians have been quick to condemn the Jews for failing to recognize Jesus as Messiah. This approach led to replacement theology and the viewpoint of some that God has rejected and broken covenant with the Jewish people. These ideas, in turn, opened the door to a vicious Christian anti-

Semitism that led to the Crusades, the Inquisition and countless pogroms."
John Hagee, A Special Message from Pastor John Hagee Regarding His Book In Defense of Israel, www.cufi.org (Christian united for Israel)

"There remains only one unchanging and sufficient reason for nations to align themselves with Israel; God has revealed clearly in his word that he intends to restore Israel and that he requires all other nations to cooperate with His purpose. Any nation that rejects this revelation of God's word, has in effect, rejected God himself, and therefore, must suffer the consequences."
John Hagee, Overview of "Jerusalem Countdown" from www.cufi.org.

"To be apathetic toward God's Divine plan or Eternal purpose, and our role as Christians in it, means to reject Our Lord's Divine Assignment to the Church and heavenly opportunity. God's prophetic time clock has been set on Jerusalem time! And the spotlight of Heaven is still on the Jews. It all began with them, and it will all end with them. God's plan is an eternal one! If what we do as Christians does not matter in the light of eternity, then we had better stop doing it. As Christians, we can no more neglect our responsibility to stand with the House of Israel then we can neglect believing in the promises of God... To summarize the 66 books of the Bible in one word, you only have to say the word "Israel." The Bible begins with and ends with Israel."

"There is a doctrine in vogue at the present time, spawned by Hell, which teaches that the Church has replaced Israel in the plan and heart of God. This doctrine is known alternately as replacement theology, progressive dispensationalism or supersessionism."
Michael Evans, "Why Christians Should Support Israel"

"The God of Israel has sworn in the prophecies that He will not forsake the Israelis, nor let them be destroyed. To Israel as a nation were made unique promises... All other nations received blessings only through Israel. They were the only nation that was promised a specific plot of land, a city, and a Kingdom on an earth from which the original curse would be removed. Unless one goes off into allegorical la-la land, these prophecies literally demand a National restoration of Israel as a distinct and unique believing Nation in the future Kingdom."
Hal Lindsey, "The 1980's; Countdown to Armageddon; The Road to Holocaust

"The Regenerate Israelite has always been the True Israelite. This group combines together both the racial and spiritual factors that the Bible describes as 'the remnant of Israel.'... The Bible reveals the insufficiency of being only a racial and religious Jew... The Bible has always taught that only the racial Jew who is born spiritually is a true Israelite and heir to the eternal promises... And that they continue to be God's special people."
Hal Lindsey, "The Road to Holocaust"

"...at some point in history - very soon, I believe - God's special focus and blessing is going to shift back to the Jews. At that moment, the Jews will once again be responsible, as God's representatives, to take His message to the whole world. This mission - incomplete and seemingly impossible for the last 2,000 years - will be accomplished by the 144,000 Jewish Billy Graham's in seven years."
Hal Lindsey, "The Apocalypse Code"

"God does not look on all of His children the same way. He sees us divided into categories, the Jews and the Gentiles. God has one plan, an earthly plan, for the Jews. And He has a second

plan, a heavenly plan, for the born-again Christians. The other peoples of the world – Muslims, Buddhists, and those of other faiths as well as those Christians not born again – do not concern Him. As for destroying planet earth, we can do nothing."

Dr. John Walvoord, Southwestern School of the Bible Professor

Exhausted yet? Statements like these represent the "majority report" among evangelicals. They are only the tip of the iceberg. Entire ministries, radio and television broadcasts, and a growing number of churches are dedicated to promoting the idea that the Jewish people were and still are, God's chosen people, and that the Jewish state will someday be restored to international prominence. Their argument continues that the Church represents a kind of "parenthesis" in God's plan—a "plan B" if you will. God's unique love affair with the state of Israel will be consummated in a literal 1,000-year rule of Christ from Jerusalem in the rebuilt Temple at some point in the future.

The Bigger Picture: God's Love Affair With Himself

The focus of God's affections has never been a people—Israel or any other nation. At the core of all God's motivations is a desire to protect and promote His own great name.

> *See, I have refined you, though not as silver; I have tested you in the furnace of affliction.* ***For my own sake****, for my own sake, I do this. How can I let myself be defamed?* ***I will not yield my glory to another*** *(Isaiah 48:10-11).*

The reason He chose Israel was the same reason He does everything—to bring glory to His name.

> *I have swept away your offenses like a cloud, your sins like the morning mist. Return to me, for I have redeemed you." Sing for joy, O heavens, for the LORD has done this; shout aloud, O earth beneath. Burst into song, you mountains, you forests and all your trees,* **for the LORD has redeemed Jacob, he displays his glory in Israel** *(Isaiah 44:22-23).*

Even God's commitment to restore the fortunes of Israel after the Babylonian Exile (587–538 B.C.) was rooted in His concern for His own glory.

> *Therefore say to the house of Israel, 'This is what the Sovereign LORD says: It is not for your sake, O house of Israel, that I am going to do these things,* **but for the sake of my holy name,** *which you have profaned among the nations where you have gone.* **I will show the holiness of my great name,** *which has been profaned among the nations, the name you have profaned among them. Then the nations will know that I am the LORD, declares the Sovereign LORD, when I show myself holy through you before their eyes. Then you will remember your evil ways and wicked deeds, and you will loathe yourselves for your sins and detestable practices.* **I want you to know that I am not doing this for your sake,** *declares the Sovereign LORD. Be ashamed and disgraced for your conduct, O house of Israel!* (Ezekiel 36:22-23, 31-32 emphasis added).

God always puts His own reputation and His own name before any other consideration. Uppermost in the affections of God, is God.

It is hard for us to imagine such a being. The only exposure we have to beings like that are tyrants and egotists, fascists or totalitarian dictators. But in pursuing His own glory, God never gives in to the kind of self-absorption or narcissism that sinful humans are prone to. In the pursuit of His own glory, God also accomplishes the greatest good for those He has created. By putting His own glory first, God insists that everything He made should live to reflect back to Him the glory that He is due. The reason this is such good news for us is because when we do this, when we live to glorify God, we are most happy.[32] The very thing that God demands, acknowledging His greater glory, is the very thing that accounts for our greatest good! Unlike egomaniacs and pathological narcissists, when God pursues His own glory it is for OUR good.

The fundamental problem we all face is that we fail to give God His due. We fail to glorify Him as God. This is the meaning of Romans 3:23 when it says that we have all sinned and *"fall short of the glory of God."* Instead, we are all committed to exchanging God's glory for something else. We treat other things as ultimate. We pursue our ultimate satisfaction in things that cannot truly satisfy (Romans 1:20-25). In short, we go about our lives building mini-kingdoms, worshipping other kings, and building entire cultures around

---

[32] For those familiar with the work of John Piper, you will immediately see his influence here. For those unfamiliar with John Piper, please visit *desiringgod.org*, or run to your local bookstore and pick up anything he has written. You won't be sorry!

those vain pursuits. By embracing the "righteousness of God" in Jesus Christ, we are set free from the bondage of sin and made free to honor God as God. Any person who surrenders their "Kingdom" and their commitment to their own glory, and joins God in promoting His glory, is a part of God's family. Anyone who, by faith, through grace, commits their life to Jesus Christ is a part of God's family. This has been God's plan from the beginning, to show the world how to be truly satisfied in making much of God. To do that, God began with a person, and then a people. Using the metaphor of a marriage, it's not hard to see how this plan unfolded.

The Unfolding of God's Plan For His Own Glory

I remember it with crystal clarity (at least that's what I'd like my wife to believe). I had chosen one of our favorite restaurants, a "fancy" place by college student standards. She later recounted how she sensed that something was afoot that night. "I thought he was going to break up with me. He was so serious!"

After we had eaten and we were both picking at our dessert, I reached into my pocket and grabbed the felt-covered box that was there. I remember that I probably checked more than a dozen times during the meal to make certain it was still there! As I produced the box, I slid out of my seat and onto one knee. I pushed the now open container over to her and asked the question that would change my life forever—"Will you marry me?"

As carefully planned and romantic as my proposal was, it pales by comparison to God's popping of the question.

His proposal to His bride is recorded in Genesis 12:1-3, and then elaborated on in Genesis 17. As we look carefully at the words of that proposal, we begin to catch a glimpse of what God intended from the start.

> *The LORD had said to Abram, "Leave your country, your people and your father's household and go to the land I will show you. I will make you into a great nation and I will bless you; I will make your name great, and you will be a blessing. I will bless those Who bless you, and whoever curses you I will curse; and all peoples on earth will be blessed through you"* (Genesis 12:1-3).

And then again in Genesis 17, we read:

> *When Abram was ninety-nine years old, the LORD appeared to him and said, "I am God Almighty; walk before me faithfully and be blameless. Then I will make my covenant between me and you and will greatly increase your numbers."*
>
> *Abram fell facedown, and God said to him, "As for me, this is my covenant with you: You will be the father of many nations. No longer will you be called Abram; your name will be Abraham, for I have made you a father of many nations. I will make you very fruitful; I will make nations of you, and kings will come from you. I will establish my covenant as an everlasting covenant between me and you and your descendants after you for the generations to come, to be your God and the God of your descendants after you. The whole land of Canaan, where you now reside as a foreigner, I will give as an everlasting possession to you and your descendants after you; and I will be their God." Then God said to Abraham,*

> *"As for you, you must keep my covenant, you and your descendants after you for the generations to come... Any uncircumcised male, who has not been circumcised in the flesh, will be cut off from his people; he has broken my covenant"* (Genesis 17:1-9, 14).

These verses form the foundation for the Christian Zionist movement that was captured in the quotations at the beginning of this chapter. God's love, the argument goes, is directed toward those people who are ethnic Jews, descended from Abraham. To be part of Israel is a matter of blood. Further, this covenant that God made with Israel was irrevocable and unconditional. As long as there are people walking this earth who can trace their bloodline back to Abraham, those people have "favored nation status" in God's eyes. Is that really what these and other verses are saying?

ABRAHAM AND THE NATIONS

The Apostle Paul would strenuously object. In his commentary on these verses in Romans 4:16-17, Paul wrote,

> *Therefore, the promise comes by faith, so that it may be by grace and may be guaranteed to all* **Abraham's offspring—not only to those who are of the law but also to those who have the faith of Abraham.** *He is the father of us all. As it is written: "I have made you a father of many nations." He is our father in the sight of God, in whom he believed—the God who gives life to the dead and calls into being things that were not* (Romans 4:16-17).

Or again in Romans 2, Paul affirms:

> *A person is not a Jew who is one only outwardly, nor is circumcision merely outward and physical.* **No, a person is a Jew who is one inwardly;** *and circumcision is circumcision of the heart, by the Spirit, not by the written code. Such a person's praise is not from other people, but from God* (Romans 2:28-29).

The Conditional Nature of the Covenant

No less an authority than the Apostle Paul sees the scope of God's covenant promise as including both Jews and Gentiles. To argue that Abraham became the father of many nations through his offspring, Isaac AND Ishmael, is to argue against Paul. From the very start, it was God's intention to have one wife—a bride made up of all those who came to him by faith, regardless of their ethnicity. Any one of us, regardless of ethnicity, can become "Abraham's offspring" and an heir to God's promises. This is why the Apostle Paul is able to say so unequivocally, *If you belong to Christ, then you are Abraham's seed, and heirs according to the promise* (Galatians 3:29).

So if faith is the means of becoming part of the Bride, regardless of your ethnicity, is there anything that can nullify or preclude our joining this family? Yes. Again and again, God made it clear that unrepentant rebellion would exclude a person from the blessings of the covenant, regardless of their bloodline. A failure to keep covenant with God, be it an everlasting covenant or not, would result in the loss of the status of "people of God." John Bright, in commenting on Amos' contribution to our understanding of the Kingdom, remarked "The bond between Israel and God has been broken; idolatry, gross immorality, and unbrotherly greed on a nationwide scale have broken it...And since Israel has parted company with God, is truly no longer His people, all her exuberant confidence in the future is a false confidence. She has no future but utter and inescapable ruin."[33] Again and again the Scriptures bear this out. In Exodus 19, we read

> Then Moses went up to God, and the LORD called to him from the mountain and said, "This is what you are to say to the descendants of Jacob and what you are to tell the people of Israel: 'You yourselves have seen what I did to Egypt, and how I carried you on eagles' wings and brought you to myself. **Now if you obey me fully and keep my covenant, then out of all nations you will be my treasured possession.** Although the whole earth is mine, you will be for me a kingdom of priests and a holy nation.' These are the words you are to speak to the Israelites" (Exodus 19:3-6).

"IF you obey me fully and keep my covenant" is the message that Moses brought to God's people. This was the one and only requirement that had to be met for Israel to maintain its position as "treasured possession" out of all other nations. The clearest expression of the provisional nature of God's relationship to Israel is found in Deuteronomy 28.

The fact that certain criteria must be met is clear from the first word of this chapter: "*if.*"

---

[33] John Bright, *The Kingdom of God*, location 700 of 4274, Kindle Ebook.

> *If you fully obey the LORD your God and carefully follow all his commands I give you today, the LORD your God will set you high above all the nations on earth. All these blessings will come upon you and accompany you if you obey the LORD your God* (Deuteronomy 28:1-2).

The logical corollary to "if" is found in verses 15 and following: "however."

> *However, if you do not obey the LORD your God and do not carefully follow all his commands and decrees I am giving you today, all these curses will come upon you and overtake you* (Deuteronomy 28:15).

It is precisely the fulfillment of the curses in Deuteronomy 28 that we see in the first half of the book of Revelation.[34] Moses then told Israel that a time would come when they would be brought back to the land after they repented, a promise that was fulfilled in the return from exile under the Persian kings Darius and Artaxerxes. The final word was then given in Deuteronomy 30. There was no promise of national restoration. There was no hope of **another** "return," or re-establishment of rule.

> *But if your heart turns away and you are not obedient, and if you are drawn away to bow down to other gods and worship them, I declare to you this day that you will certainly be destroyed. You will not live long in the land you are crossing the Jordan to enter and possess* (Deuteronomy 30:17-18).

---

[34] Although we will look at this in detail later, it may be helpful to go through Deuteronomy 28 and circle or underline every curse that is pronounced from verse 15-68. The parallels between what we read in Deuteronomy 28 and Revelation 4-11 are striking.

Even faithfulness and obedience like that of King David could not rescue Israel from the Lord's rejection. Asaph, in Psalm 78 wrote

> *And so he brought them to the border of his holy land, to the hill country his right hand had taken. He drove out nations before them and allotted their lands to them as an inheritance; he settled the tribes of Israel in their homes. But they put God to the test and rebelled against the Most High; they did not keep his statutes. Like their ancestors they were disloyal and faithless, as unreliable as a faulty bow. They angered him with their high places; they aroused his jealousy with their idols.* **When God heard them, he was furious; he rejected Israel completely.** *He abandoned the tabernacle of Shiloh, the tent he had set up among humans. He sent the ark of his might into captivity, his splendor into the hands of the enemy* (Psalm 78:54-61).

Several hundred years later, Daniel recounted how a similar fate would befall the chosen people of Israel. In the last four chapters of his prophecy, Daniel chronicled how the people of Israel had rebelled against God and failed to keep covenant with Him (chapter 9). What followed in chapters 10-12 was the prophecy concerning the ultimate destruction of the Temple and the judgment of Israel in 70 AD.[35] Commenting on the work of a contemporary of Daniel, the prophet Ezekiel, Bright explains: "Ezekiel had exactly the same conviction. In one of those bizarre visions to which this

---

[35] Later on, we will look in much greater detail at the prophecies of Daniel. As we saw in chapter 3, the reason Daniel was told to "seal up" the words of his prophecy was because much of it had to do with the events surrounding the destruction of Jerusalem in 70 AD.

strange prophet was subjected (Ezekiel 10-11), it seemed to him that he saw the very Glory of Yahweh—conceived in Hebrew theology as enthroned in the awful darkness of the Holy of Holies and symbolizing the living Presence of Yahweh among his people—come out of the Temple, hover over it, and then depart. Yahweh is no longer with this people and this city!"[36] The prophets foretold that a Day was coming when God would break covenant with His people, and leave them. That day came in 70 A.D. with the destruction of the Temple.

Paul And His People

The most compelling and complete explanation of the conditional nature of God's covenant promises and God's relationship to ethnic Israel is provided by the Apostle Paul in Romans 9-11. In order to really understand the true Bride of Christ and the conditional nature of God's relationship to ethnic Israel, we have to understand these chapters.

Romans 9

If you don't feel the anguish and the pathos of these chapters (Romans 9-11), then you may want to check your pulse. This is not some academic exercise for Paul, and it shouldn't be for us either. Paul can hardly choke back the tears. His own people, the nation of Israel, are lost. Most of its citizens are "cut off from Christ." Paul doesn't offer this up for debate. It is a simple fact. Most Jews are not saved, either in Paul's day or our own. Paul is able to see beyond the personal pain that this fact brings him, and see the much bigger problem that this presents us with. If most Jews are lost, and if most of the people of Israel are cut off from Christ

---

[36] John Bright, *The Kingdom of God*, Location 1310 of 4274, Kindle Ebook.

for eternity, then what of God's covenant promise to never leave or abandon His chosen People? Don't God's covenants with Noah and Abraham and David obligate God to save His chosen people regardless of their behavior? Isn't His promise to His chosen People unconditional?

The much bigger question is, "what of the nature of God's word in general?" If God broke His promise to Israel, what other promises might He break? If God is not faithful to His word, then how certain can any of us be that nothing can separate us from His love, or that all things in our lives will work together for our good? Again, this is no academic exercise or some obscure argument regarding the end times—this is foundational to who God is and how He acts.

It is this very question, "has God's word failed," that launches Paul into the most extensive discussion of God's relationship to His covenant people, Israel, in all the Bible.

Paul begins with the foundational conviction that God has *not* failed. *But it is not as though the word of God has failed* (Romans 9:6). In other words, God's promise to persevere in His love for His people might **appear** to have failed, since so many of ethnic Israel have rejected God's covenant promises and covenant responsibilities, and are now "cut off from Christ." Paul spends the next three chapters building his case that God's word has NOT failed.

In verses 7ff, Paul gives the first reason why we can trust that God's Word has not failed—because His promise is to those who are true Israelites by election, not Israelites by blood. GOD NEVER DECREED THAT EVERY INDIVIDUAL WHO TRACED THEIR ETHNICITY BACK

TO ABRAHAM WOULD BE SAVED. *"It is not the children of the flesh who are the children of God, but the children of the promise are counted as offspring."* (v. 8) In other words, God is not obligated to save someone because of ancestry or parents, regardless of their family tree. In essence, Paul is urging all of us to be careful in our assessment of who qualifies as a "descendent of Abraham." There are "true" descendents and then there are descendents by blood. Some of those in the last category (descendents by blood) are also in the first category (true descendents), but many in the first group (true descendents) are not part of the second group (descendents by blood)! This, explains Paul, is why God's promise to the "true" Israel has not failed. God HAS fulfilled His promise to Israel by saving whomever He chooses, so that, as Romans 9:11 says, *"God's purpose of election might continue, not because of works but because of his call."* **So the first point in Paul's argument that the word of God has not failed is that there is a major distinction between physical Israel and spiritual Israel. The covenant promises apply to those who are spiritual Israel by virtue of God's electing love, extended to all who are "true Israelites."** God's initial covenant commitment to His people was ALWAYS a commitment to "true" Israel, *not* ethnic Israel.

Paul summarizes his point in Romans 9:8. Here, he makes the distinction between "natural children" and "children of promise." It is the latter who are truly Abraham's offspring. In other words, there are a people within a people. God's "chosen" people are not the natural people, the Jewish people, but the "children of promise," or those who have been chosen by God's electing love. God never intended to have a "chosen" people from one nation. There was never a "plan B," never an alternative if things did not go well with the offspring of Abraham. **From the beginning, God intended that His chosen people would be composed of people from all nations, and be called the "true Israel," regardless of their ethnic heritage.**

Paul then anticipates a counter argument. "Where are you getting these ideas, Paul?" Is this really how God acted in the Old Testament, or is this just some new-fangled idea you dreamed up?" "Where do you get this notion of a people within a people, natural children and children of promise, true Israelites and Israelites that are cut-off?" Remember, Paul is trying to support one key argument—that, appearances notwithstanding, God's promise to Israel has NOT failed. To support his teaching, Paul turns to the Old Testament. He uses three stories to illustrate: Isaac and Ishmael, Jacob and Esau, and Moses and Pharaoh.

Isaac & Ishmael

If you don't remember the story of Isaac and Ishmael, now might be a good time to reread Genesis 12-21. The Reader's Digest version goes something like this. God made a promise to Abraham, that he would be blessed with many descendents, become the father of many nations, and bless the world through his offspring. This was not wishful thinking on God's part. God did not rely on human cooperation or human effort. He decided. He directed. He determined. The fulfillment of these promises to Abraham would be wholly and completely a work of God. But Abraham felt the need to get God out of a jam. As the writer of Hebrews put it, Abraham, at the time of the promise, was "as good as dead." Sarah was no spring chicken either. Their nuptials failed to produce any children, so both Abraham and

Sarah took matters into their own hands, had Abe sleep with Sarah's personal secretary and voila! A son was born. They named him Ishmael. Problem solved? Not so fast.

In Romans chapter 7, Paul quoted Genesis 21:12 in verse 7: *"It is through Isaac that your offspring will be reckoned."* In other words, being the actual "fruit of Abraham's loins," and being the oldest at that (very big deal in Abraham's culture) did not necessarily count for anything! Two verses later in Romans 7 Paul quoted Genesis 18:10, 14. He did this to illustrate precisely the *wrong* way to go about becoming a child of promise. When God made the original promise to Abraham, He followed that up with some corroborative details—within a few months of the brunch described in Genesis 18, Sarah did in fact have a son, from whom many descendants would follow. But Abraham, doing no more than any mere human could do, took matters in his own hands and even suggested to God that perhaps Ishmael could fulfill the promise (Genesis 17:18). But one does not become a child of promise through human effort. We become part of the "chosen" people through the sovereign grace of God, not through our ethnicity or bloodline or family tree.

Abraham then had a son with Sarah. It was a miracle! When all seemed lost, God opened the womb of Sarah and Isaac was born. No back room deals, no bedroom shenanigans—this child was born in a way that no one but God could pull off. And that was precisely the point. **No one becomes part of the chosen people through anything other than the efforts of God**. It was Isaac, not Ishmael, who was the child of promise. It was the fruit of God's sovereign grace, not human effort that achieved "chosen people" status. Paul then pulls us much further into the deep end of the pool with his next illustration.

Jacob & Esau

Again, if it's hard to recall those gripping forays into flannel-graph-OT-history, or if you just never went to Sunday school, you really should reread Genesis 25-33. Jacob & Esau were the children of the long-awaited "child of promise" Isaac and his wife Rebekah. They were twins. They were from the same womb, born into the same home, and, unlike Isaac and Ishmael, they were the issue of the same two parents. This is critical—they both had the same blood flowing in their veins that made them "sons of Abraham." They were both "Israel." If ethnicity or bloodlines were the determining factor, then there would be no difference in God's Covenantal commitment to both boys! But there is a difference, because being part of God's "chosen people" had nothing to do then, or now, with who your parents are. In Romans 9:11-13, Paul muddies the already unclear waters by introducing another key concept, and the answer to the question, "so what *does* qualify someone as God's chosen people?" The answer is, God's electing love.

Before Ishmael and Isaac had done anything good or bad, God's electing grace was in full operation. Paul quoted Genesis 25:23 to make it clear that the destiny of these boys was sealed before Rebekah was effaced or anything close to 10 centimeters. And why did God choose Jacob over Esau? *"...In order that God's purpose in election might stand."* In other words, what matters is God's electing grace, not our behavior. God makes His choices based solely on His divine prerogatives.

How does this relate to our original question—"has God's word failed?"—given that so many of the "chosen people" are now "cut off from Christ?" How does this magnify the glory of God, the very thing that He lives for? What Paul is illustrating is that God is infinitely free and unfettered in His decision making. He does not need to consider works done in the past, present or future. He is dependent on no one and nothing to make His choices. God can choose to create a "true Israel" within a larger "Israel." **God is free to have a people within a people if He so chooses. His people are chosen without regard to anything about them—neither their behavior, their ethnicity, their parents, nor their religious proclivities. God is gloriously free!** He cannot be bought, manipulated, or cajoled. He is beholding to no one. This is why the word of God has not failed. It cannot fail. The judgment regarding the efficacy of God's word is wholly and completely up to God. This is precisely what made Temple practice in Jesus' day so egregious. Like Abraham and Jacob, people were trying to force God's hand. They were trying to coerce a blessing or manipulate their status as God's "chosen people."

Just to make certain that we don't miss the point, Paul reiterates in Romans 9:12, *"Not by works but by Him who calls—she (mother Rebekah) was told, 'the older will serve the younger.'"* The final brushstroke in Paul's picture of Jacob and Esau is a quotation from Malachi 1:2-3: *"Jacob I loved, but Esau I hated."* Paul makes an interesting choice of words here. When you read the words, "not by works…," what would you expect to follow? "Not by works…but by faith," right? Paul intentionally avoids the word faith here because faith is a condition. We cannot believe on Jesus Christ without faith. We cannot become part of God's "chosen" people without putting our faith in Christ. Paul's point is that God did not (does not) look ahead to see who is most likely to respond in faith to Him, and on the basis of that, make His choice. God does not choose His people **because** they will believe; He chooses them so that they are **able** to believe!

What are we to make of the fact that God "hates" Esau? God is not capricious. He is not mean. God punishes Esau precisely because he does not believe. He is destined to receive exactly what he deserves. The glory of God is on display in that He chooses to love Jacob, and give him precisely what he does *not* deserve. God needs no more justification in behaving in this way than the fact that He is God. Because this is so, God is completely and infinitely free in exercising His sovereign grace, and nothing can influence that choice. *This is why God's Word can never fail.* This is why He is glorious. This is why we are invited to herald His glory to all the nations. This is a hard teaching. Rather than leave this teaching alone, Paul pulls us even further into the deep end of the pool.

Moses & Pharaoh

We are still dealing with the question of how so many of the "chosen people" appear to *not* be chosen and living in rebellion against God. Didn't God promise that they would always be His chosen people? *Thus far, Paul has argued that the problem is not with God's word, but our understanding of how God makes His choices, and who God has actually chosen.* God chooses on the basis of being God. His everlasting commitment to His people remains constant. This "people" is not limited to the ethnic descendents of Abraham or the political state of Israel. It seems that God is not primarily interested in who we are, but in who He is. The natural objection is, "that's not fair." It is this very objection that Paul now addresses.

Since God is doing all the choosing, and since He doesn't appear to make His choices according to any discernible pattern and since His choices are absolute, the obvious question that needs answering is, "Is God unjust?" In a word, No! Paul again quotes from the Old Testament—Exodus 33:19. *"I will have mercy on whom I have mercy, and I will have compassion on whom I have compassion."* These words come in the context of Moses' demand that the chosen people be released from slavery in Egypt. It's critical to understand these words in that context.

In Exodus 33, Moses is "debating" with God. Moses is looking for some affirmation that God is truly with him and with Israel. He wants to be certain that if he makes a move, God will move with him. Since Moses had only recently been introduced to God, he asks to know God more fully. As the leader of God's people, Moses feels the pressure of that position. Moses asks for God to make His presence known. He implores God—"show me your glory." What is God's response? How does God show Moses His glory? He promises to pass in front of Moses, declaring that He will have mercy on whom He has mercy, and compassion on whom He will have compassion. What God is saying is that His glory is expressed in the fact that He is free to choose whomever He wills to experience His mercy and compassion. **At the heart of God's glory is His unfettered freedom of choice!**

Mercy and compassion will come to whomever God chooses, regardless of our desire or effort. But there is more to God's glory than just His mercy and compassion. In Romans 9:17, Paul reminds us of Pharaoh's destiny. Before Pharaoh was born, or before he had done anything good or bad, God had determined that His glory would best be achieved by raising up a rebel, a man who would be "cut off" from Christ. God has a point to make, and He makes it to the whole world. That point is that God is gloriously free to do whatever pleases Him. This is the clear meaning of Paul's use of Exodus 9:16 in Romans 9:17. Paul then repeats the quotation from Exodus with a critical elaboration. What is the opposite of God's mercy and compassion? "Hardening."

When did God harden Pharaoh's heart? Only after Pharaoh showed signs of resistance? Only after Pharaoh had decided to rebel against the God of Israel? If this were true, then everything Paul has said up to this point would fall apart. This is why the answer is, "before Pharaoh was ever born—before Moses ever had any contact with Pharaoh." We know this from at least two Scriptures—Exodus 4:21 and 7:3. This is critical to understanding that God's choices are not a matter of reacting to our self-determination, but rather the outworking of His unconditional election. To say this is a mystery (and beyond the scope of this book) is an understatement. It is abundantly clear from what has gone before, that God is not hardening the heart of Pharaoh based on God's knowing ahead of time that Pharaoh would be stubborn and rebellious. That is exactly the OPPOSITE of what Paul has been arguing thus far. We also know that each of us is responsible before God for the choices we make. When we are punished, we receive the deserved sentence of judgment for our willful disobedience. When we are saved, we receive the undeserved gift of salvation. In both cases, it is God who chooses. When it comes to our response to God's electing grace, God so constrains us that we are unable to resist His will, but He does so in such a way that we remain fully responsible for our choices. Is your head spinning like a top yet? All the more reason to sing the praises of God's glorious, sovereign grace. What for us is an irreconcilable paradox is child's play for God.

But That's Not Fair!

The inevitable follow-up question to "Is God unjust" is voiced in verse 19 of Romans 9. "OK Paul, you argue that God is just because He upholds His free and sovereign choice, which is at the heart of what makes Him glorious." "No one can resist His mercy or His hardening." "Then how in the world can God still say that we are accountable for our choices!?" "That is complete non-sense." Paul proceeds to give at least two reasons for why it makes perfect God-sense.

The first reason conjures up a humorous mental image—talking clay. Imagine, suggests Paul, that a potter slaps down a moist lump of clay on the spinning wheel. As he muses over the clay, wondering whether to make an ash tray or a dining table centerpiece, the clay pipes up—"Make me something beautiful!" "I don't wanna be an ash tray, I wanna be a princess!" The text actually says "common" and "noble" purposes, but you get the idea. We can't imagine such a scene apart from an animated Disney film. Paul's meaning is even deeper. It is not just that clay *cannot* talk; it is that clay *should not* talk. Clay has no authority to tell the Potter how to use His freedom of choice. We, as the creature, are in no position to say to the Creator, "You are using your sovereignty badly." We are not invited to admonish God, suggesting that His electing love and unconditional grace is misplaced or misguided. And we are certainly in no position to tell God what does or does not make Him glorious. God can still hold us accountable for our choices because He made us. He decides what constitutes accountability. The second reason why this arrangement makes perfect "God-sense" is found in 9:22 and following.

Paul leaves no doubt as to why God does not consult the clay—*"...to make the riches of His glory known..."* As we indicated at the start, God's glory is what He is about. How does acting in this way make God's glory known? How does not consulting with the clay reveal something about the glory of God? First, it illustrates "His wrath" (9:22). God does not coddle or permit sin. He destroys it. People, destined for destruction, will bear the just and deserved wrath of God against sin. Second, acting in this way shows God's power. God is the final arbiter. God is the judge. There is no higher court of appeal. Ultimate power rests with Him, and His verdict is final. Finally, acting this way is designed to illustrate to the "objects of His mercy" just how glorious and deserving of praise God is. Rather than debating with God over whether or not He is fair, we ought to fall on our faces and worship this God, who, although He has every right to punish us, has instead ordained that we be recipients of His free, electing grace and love.

Let's Review What We Have Learned Thus Far

Problem #1: Most of God's chosen people, the people of Israel, have been cut off from Christ. They will forever bear the just punishment of those who are not part of God's people. God made a covenant, in which He promised to love His Chosen People unconditionally, to persevere in His love for them forever. It appears that God is going back on His word, since so many Israelites will be lost for eternity.

The Question: Has God's Word, His promise to love His People, forever failed? (Romans 9:6).

The Answer: No. There are a people within a People. The People God had promised to love unconditionally are not necessarily Jews. Citizens of the True Israel are those who have been elected to salvation by God's sovereign and completely free will. They will be saved, just as God had promised.

Problem #2: God does not appear to be righteous. He chooses His people based solely on His divine prerogatives, not on the basis of ethnicity, or behavior, or potential "usefulness." For no apparent reason, some people get chosen, and others do not.

The Question: Is God unjust? (Romans 9:14).

The Answer: No. God is perfectly just. But He has a bigger agenda—to be acknowledged as the only true God, and to cause His glory to be praised throughout the whole earth. That glory is centered in His completely free and unconditional election. The very fact that He is completely free to choose whomever He wills is reason enough to praise the riches of His glorious grace. Let it be known to all—salvation is the fruit of the free, sovereign call of God, not the fruit of anything we are or do.

Problem #3: When God's extends his electing grace to someone, He also withholds that grace from others. In both cases, God's will cannot be resisted. His choices are ultimate and final.

The Question: How can God hold us accountable for the choices we make? If no one can resist His will, how can we be held responsible for our decisions? (Romans 9:19).

The Answer: Only a being as glorious as God can embrace both His sovereignty and our responsibility in a way that is consistent. God acts in this way to put the riches of His glory on display. That glory is perfectly expressed in His wrath, His power, and His mercy. We, the objects of both His mercy and wrath, are in no position to question His authority or the use of His power. Hush! No talking clay permitted!

Enter The Goyim

So, what does all this have to do with the conditional nature of God's promise to Abraham and his descendents? Everything. By now we should have a pretty clear picture of a God who is not bound by our standards and our expectations. Having established that God is free to do whatever He chooses, Paul now turns to the bigger story that is unfolding with regard to His chosen People.

For the first time in these three chapters, Paul mentions Gentiles. He has been gently leading his readers down the path of inevitable and inescapable conclusions. **If ethnic Israel is not God's chosen people, then who is?** In verse 24, the feline is released from the sack. **God's chosen people are all those *"whom He has also called, not only from the Jews but also from the Gentiles."***

WINSOME WARRIORS

As he has consistently done throughout, Paul turns to the Old Testament for support. Quoting from Hosea 2:23, Hosea 1:10, Isaiah 10:22-23, and Isaiah 1:9, Paul unloads a *Tanach*[37] *torrent*, leaving little doubt as to where he is getting his ideas from. God has, from the beginning, destined that His People would be composed of individuals from every nation on earth, not just the Jews.

There is little doubt that Paul's words here were a shock to *all* his readers. Jewish readers thought they were included as God's people *because* they were Jewish, only to discover that race is no "get out of jail free" card. As numerous as the Jews are, only a "remnant" will actually be saved. Gentile readers were shocked to learn that they could move from "not my people" status to "my people" status with nothing more than a nod from the sovereign head of God.

It would appear that God, ever the iconoclast, is determined to smash any pretense surrounding ethnic or racial superiority. On the one hand, we should be humbled. Racial roots don't cut it with God, either for or against. On the other hand, we Gentiles should be filled with gratitude and awe. We are part of God's people. We are God's loved one. Imagine how this expands our own personal history, how the narrative of our lives becomes so much broader and deeper. The very things that Paul described in verses 4 and 5 of chapter 9 now become our reality, part of our story, part of our history. Ours is the adoption, the divine glory, the covenants, the receiving of the law, the Temple worship and the promises. Ours is the patriarchs, and from our ancestors can be traced the direct line to the Messiah!

---

[37] Tanach is the Hebrew word used to describe the Old Testament.

To argue, as so many have, that the nation of Israel, the Jewish race is front and center in the plan of God, seems to fly in the face of what Paul has taught thus far. Who is the apple of God's eye? His chosen People. Who is God's chosen People? All who are called by God, both Jews and Gentiles. As God unfolds history for the sake of His glory, His focus has always been, and will always be, His chosen People, both Jews and Gentiles.

So Where Did Israel Go Wrong?

"What then shall we say?" (9:30). It's a fair question. Paul has been repeatedly dragging us into the deep end of the pool demanding that we swim. Finally, he throws us a life ring. Without equivocation, he explains what went wrong with Israel and right with the Gentiles.

Thus far, Paul has made no bones about declaring that the first thing someone needs to be right with God is to be called by God in the first place. Without the touch of His electing grace, there is no hope for salvation. Now Paul speaks to the second thing needed to be saved— "righteousness."

Paul has already spent the better portion of the book of Romans explaining this very thing. *"No one is righteous, not even one..."* (3:10). *"Apart from the righteousness that God offers through faith in Jesus Christ, no one can be saved"* (3:21-24). And *"no one will be declared righteous in God's sight by observing the law"* (3:20).

The great irony is that the very people who ***should have*** known better, the Jews, did not obtain this righteousness, and the very people who were ***not*** exposed to the God of Israel, did obtain this righteousness. Why? Because the people of Israel *"pursued the law as the way of righteousness....they pursued it not by faith but as if it were by works"* (9:31-32). The very thing the law was intended to do, namely, to impress upon us that we cannot obtain this righteousness by observing the law, the Jews ignored. And people who were never exposed to the law in the first place, have obtained the righteousness needed for salvation because they have put their faith in Jesus as the Messiah. The people of Israel saw Jesus Christ as an interloper. He declared the finely tuned system of "righteousness by works," centered in the Temple, to be invalid. It had to be destroyed, not developed, replaced not refined. As a result, Israel rejected their Messiah. This tragedy of missed opportunities broke Paul's heart.

Romans 10

Can you hear the mournful cry of the apostle? Paul's own people *"sought to establish their own (righteousness), (and they) did not submit to God's righteousness"* (10:3). This is why the Apostle declares that his heart's desire and prayer to God is that Israel might be saved. But as it stands now, most of them are lost.

They are lost because they have not obtained the second criteria for salvation, righteousness in Christ. Beginning in verse 5 of chapter 10, Paul elaborates on the critical distinction between approaching the law by faith, and approaching it as if it is by works. PAUL IS STILL ADDRESSING THE ISSUE OF WHETHER OR NOT ETHNIC ISRAEL IS GOD'S CHOSEN PEOPLE, AND IF NOT, WHY NOT?

The answer to that question has been a consistent "no." There are bigger goings on to consider, namely that *"Christ is the culmination of the law so that there may be righteousness for everyone who believe"* (10:4).

This is not some new teaching. Moses already wrote about this ages ago when he brought down the law from Sinai. On the one hand, there was a righteousness that was "by the law" or by works, and a righteousness that was by faith—and the latter did not require any Herculean efforts on our part to obtain—no going up to heaven or down to the place of the dead (10:6-7). No, this righteousness is right here with us, in our hearts. It is here for everyone who believes, not just Israel (10:8). The question is not, "can I keep the law," but rather, "will I trust in One who can?"

Access to this righteousness was readily available because God had placed it in the heart of every person, waiting to be awakened by the vivifying work of God's Spirit. Once our dead hearts are reanimated, we are able to "declare" and "believe" (10:9-10). Both our mouths and our hearts bear witness that we have in fact obtained the righteousness that saves. For whom does this opportunity present itself? The shocking dénouement: EVERYONE*!* *"For there is no difference between Jew and Gentile—the same Lord is Lord of all and richly blesses all who call on him, for "everyone who calls on the name of the Lord shall be saved"* (10:12-13). What has been implicit thus far is now made explicit—Jew or Gentile is irrelevant, only calling on the Lord matters.

Que Sera, Sera?

"So let me get this straight...." "God's electing grace is the first requirement for becoming part of His chosen people." "This electing grace is extended to some and not to others, regardless of their ethnicity, their behavior, their potential usefulness to God, etc." "The second requirement for becoming part of God's chosen People is to embrace the righteousness that comes from faith in Christ, not from works of the law." "Most of ethnic Israel rejected Christ and continues to put their faith in their own righteousness." "THEN WHY BOTHER TO TELL ANYBODY, JEW OR GENTILE ABOUT JESUS IF IT IS ULTIMATELY GOD WHO DECIDES?" Once again, I am astounded at how profound God's word is, and how brilliant the Apostle is. Before I even realize there is an objection rattling around in my head, it is articulated for me! "Yeah! Why should we bother to engage in missions if all this is true?"

For Paul, there is no dilemma. Obviously, he is aware of the problems his teaching raises—just look at the bulk of chapter 9! Despite Paul's glad and humble submission to the sovereign election of God, Paul continues to: 1. Have great sorrow and unceasing anguish for his Jewish countrymen (9:2). 2. Offer his own salvation in exchange for the salvation of His people (9:3). 3. Express that his heart's desire is that Israel might be saved (10:1). 4. Indicate that he prays faithfully for the salvation of his kinsmen (10:1). 5. Urge others to preach the Gospel to people from every nation. (10:14-15).

Oh that we would all follow Paul's lead! We must, without reservation, preach the truth of the glorious riches of God's grace. We must be willing to concede that there are things about God's sovereignty that puzzle and even frustrate us. We must humbly concede that salvation is wholly and completely a work of God. At the same time *we must invite*

God's Spirit to break our hearts for the plight of the lost. And that will only happen if we are first stunned by the greatness and goodness and glory of God!

As a boy, I remember attending a college bowl game at the Orange Bowl in my boyhood home of Miami, Florida. My father, a family friend and I went to watch teams I have long since forgotten. What I do remember is the rush of excitement as I walked through the breezeway from inside the bowels of the stadium into the open air of the stadium seats. I remember being awed by the panoramic view of tens of thousands of people that spread out before me. I remember how vivid the green of the field looked and how brilliant and white the lines looked that had been painted on the field. I remember the cacophony of bands and cheerleaders and PA systems and beer vendors. As vivid as those memories are, I would forever be marked by another memory from that night.

After the game, we gathered our things and began making our way toward the exits. As I walked next to my father, both of us, at almost the same time, realized that our friend was no longer walking with us. I remember looking back to see him standing at the opening of the breezeway that looked out over the stadium, his backed turned towards

A popular tract by Chic Publications which boldly details the fact that all nations that have opposed the Jewish State have suffered terribly, and those who support her have been blessed.

us, facing the ever-thinning crowd. As my dad and I walked back to him I will never forget what I saw—my father's friend, an adult whom I only knew in relationship to my dad, was standing at the mouth of that stadium exit with tears streaming down his face. I remember like it was yesterday how he answered my dad's question as to what he was doing. It was as if the din of the restless crowd suddenly faded to the background, and all I could hear was my father's friend say, "Bob, thousands of these people will spend a Christless eternity."

This man, I would later discover was an elder in the Orthodox Presbyterian Church, the same denomination in which I was raised. A staunch Calvinist, (is there any other kind!), at no time did my dad's friend make a reference to God's electing grace, which he most certainly believed in. At no point did my father's friend suggest that since no one can resist God's will there was no need to evangelize. I don't remember my dad's friend ever sighing and suggesting that since God hardens whomever He will and shows mercy to whomever He wills, it really shouldn't concern us who will or will not spend an eternity apart from Jesus. Like Paul, the heart of my father's friend broke. Like Paul, my father's friend longed to see people of all races come to Jesus. Like Paul, my father's friend acknowledged that no feet are as beautiful as the feet of those who bring the good news of the righteousness that can only be found by grace through faith in Jesus Christ. And like Paul, my father's friend was a man who was overwhelmed by the fact God is more glorious than any of us could possibly imagine.

It's All In The Feet!

"So that's it? That's why so many Jews are cut off from Christ—because they never heard the Gospel?" "The beautiful feet of those bringing the Gospel have apparently never reached the majority of the Jewish race?!" As always, Paul anticipates the mind of his readers. *"But I ask: Did they not hear? Of course they did..."* (10:18). Then perhaps the problem is that they didn't understand the message (10:19). No. Their "hardness" of heart was all part of God's plan. It was God's intention to make the Jews "jealous" by offering citizenship in His Kingdom to another people, the Gentiles. Even as God extended His covenant love to Abraham, God began to cover the ears of one people, and open His hands to another people.

As Isaiah foretold, *"All day long I (God) have held out my hands to a disobedient and obstinate people"* (Isaiah 65:2). At this point Paul's extended discussion of the salvation of His Jewish kinsmen reaches a crescendo. Given the reality of how lost the Jewish people were in Paul's day (and ours!), the only logical conclusion is that God has completely rejected His people, the Jews, right? Not so fast! Ultimately, "all Israel will be saved." Are you thoroughly confused yet?

Romans 11

In classic rabbinic style, Paul continues to answer questions with questions. *"I ask you then, did God reject His people"* (11:1)? There are several very good reasons why the answer is "no!"

Reason #1: "Look at me!" "If God rejected His people, how do you explain me?" Paul asks. Paul is clearly talking about ethnic Israel at this point, not the "true Israel" of chapter 9. He makes a point of tracing his own ethnic pedigree back to Benjamin and then Abraham.

Reason #2: God "foreknew" ethnic Israel. Be careful not to read English meanings back into the languages of the Bible. It's easy to see the word "foreknew" and understand it to mean that God "knew" ahead of time: and, on the basis of what He saw would happen, He made His choices. We know from the Bible that that is NOT how God foreknows. When God "knows" someone or something, it is tantamount to His making a choice. If God determines to know you, He determines your destiny beforehand. When we look at Scripture, we see no hint of self-determination on the part of those whom God "knows" beforehand. When God knows you, it is the same as saying that He chose you or He has determined to favor you in some way. Here are just a few examples from the Bible of this kind of divine knowing: Romans 11:1-2; Amos 3:1-2; Genesis 18:17-19; Hosea 13:4-5; Psalm 1:6; Matt. 7:23; 1 Cor. 8:3; Gal. 4:8-9; 2 Tim. 2:16-19. Go ahead and look them up, and then ask yourself, "When it says God 'knows' someone in these passages, how does that impact the destiny of those same people?"

Reason #3: There is historical precedent to what Paul (and we) observed. In the days of Elijah the prophet, it also appeared as if God had rejected His people. All of them, at least by Elijah's reckoning, had turned from God and were lost. How did God answer Elijah's lament? *"I have reserved for myself seven thousand who have not bowed the knee to Baal"* (Romans 11:4). "It is the same in our day" suggested Paul. Despite appearances, God always preserves at least *a few ethnic Jews* who remain faithful to the God of Israel.

Reason #4: God's reputation is at stake. Imagine the "embarrassment" if God were to call to Himself a people, only to have the whole bunch thumb their noses at Him and say, "no thanks, we've found a better offer." Do you see how consistent the themes are that Paul has raised in these chapters? God's glory is at stake! His fame is at risk! But God will have none of it. This is why He reserved 7,000 faithful followers in Elijah's day, just as He does in every age. Why does God do this—"For myself..." he tells Elijah in 1 Kings 19:18. It was the same in Paul's day, just as it is in our day.

Reason #5: To illustrate the all surpassing glory of God's grace! *"So too, at the present time, there is a remnant chosen by grace. And if by grace, then it cannot be based on works; if it were, grace would no longer be grace"* (11:5-6). Don't ever be confused. God chooses whomever He wills on the basis of His grace, not good or bad behavior, not ethnicity, not potential usefulness—nothing, but God's perfectly free and glorious grace.

And Your Point Would Be...?

There is no need for Paul to make the case for God's electing grace. He spent the better part of chapter 9 doing just that. The conclusions reached on the basis of the preceding 5 points are inescapable: *While God may not have rejected all people who trace their ethnic roots back to Abraham, many of them will be lost forever because God hardened their hearts. Like Pharaoh, some were created as vessels of destruction, while others as vessels of mercy.* ***The determining factor is God's election, not their ethnicity. Such was the plan from the start.***

Three Old Testament superstars, Moses, Isaiah and David bear witness to this. As a people, Old Testament Israel sought after God, but only some found what they were looking for, while others "were hardened." Just as in the days of Jesus (Matthew 13:11-17), many of Israel were incapable of hearing and understanding, **unable** to receive the grace of God. This is the only way to make sense of Jesus' words in John 8:

> *Jesus said to them, "If God were your Father, you would love me, for I came from God and now am here. I have not come on my own; but he sent me. Why is my language not clear to you?* ***Because you are unable to hear what I say.*** *You belong to your father, the devil, and you want to carry out your father's desire. He was a murderer from the beginning, not holding to the truth, for there is no truth in him. When he lies, he speaks his native language, for he is a liar and the father of lies. Yet because I tell the truth, you do not believe me! Can any of you prove me guilty of sin? If I am telling the truth, why don't you believe me? He who belongs to God hears what God says.* ***The reason you do not hear is that you do not belong to God***" (John 8:42-47).

Listen again to the teaching of Jesus:

> *The disciples came to him and asked, "Why do you speak to the people in parables?" He replied, "The knowledge of the secrets of the Kingdom of heaven has been given to you, but not to them. Whoever has will be given more, and he will have an abundance. Whoever does not have, even what he has will be taken from him.* ***This is why I speak to them in parables:*** *"Though seeing, they do not see; though*

> ***hearing, they do not hear or understand.*** *In them is fulfilled the prophecy of Isaiah: "'You will be ever hearing but never understanding; you will be ever seeing but never perceiving. For this people's heart has become calloused; they hardly hear with their ears, and they have closed their eyes.* ***Otherwise they might see with their eyes, hear with their ears, understand with their hearts and turn, and I would heal them'*** (Matthew 13:10-15 emphasis added).

The "Israel" of Jesus day had corrupted true religion and turned it into Judaism, rooted in the law and centered in the practices surrounding the Temple. They had scorned the ethical and moral requirements of the Kingdom. They had built a religion centered in outward show designed to manipulate God and curry His favor. As long as there had been prophets in Israel, God's assessment of this kind of religion was clear:

> *They sow the wind and reap the whirlwind. The stalk has no head; it will produce no flour. Were it to yield grain, foreigners would swallow it up. Israel is swallowed up; now she is among the nations like a worthless thing* (Hosea 8:7-8).

For Jesus' contemporaries, the cost of grace was too high, precisely because it cost nothing and no price could be higher for arrogant, Godless people to pay. From their perspective, if there was nothing that they could contribute by keeping the law, then the teachings of Jesus could not be from God.

In all cases either for or against God, the decisive factor is grace. When God offers it, it cannot be resisted; and when God withholds it, it cannot be earned. If God chose to elect seven thousand in the days of Elijah for His own name's sake, He will do the same in Paul's day, and in ours. Whether seven thousand or 70 million, God's grace is freely offered to whomever He chooses. His own glory demands that there will always be some blood relatives of Abraham who are saved.

It's Time to Mix Some Metaphors

"Come on Paul, throw me a bone! Did God reject His people, ethnic Israel, or not?" "You started this discussion with an unequivocal 'no,' but now I'm not so sure!" "You just got through quoting all these Old Testament heavyweights who seemed to be predicting that a day would come when Israel would be lost forever." "So which is it—are they beyond hope or not?"

Do you remember, way back at the beginning of this chapter we used a metaphor to describe God's relationship to His people? That's it...*marriage*. God had entered into a passionate love relationship with His people that could only be captured by the word "marriage." That relationship did not include two wives, or one wife and a mistress. She is all the same bride, the Chosen People, the True Israel, the People of God. Paul gives the definitive answer to the question, "did God reject His people" by introducing us to a different metaphor, that of a tree. How many trees? One. How many root systems? One. How many trunks? One. How many branches? A multitude.

The Power of Personal Pronouns

Paul begins the "tree" section of his argument with another question: *"Did they stumble so as to fall beyond recovery?"* (Romans 11:11). Who is the "they" Paul refers to? Paul is referring to ethnic Israel as a whole, the blood relatives of Abraham. Paul is pointing us back to 11:1, where he asked "Did God reject His people." "They" are "His people." Paul is asking, "Is there any hope for the original Chosen people, the nation of Israel?" The answer is, "yes." There is hope, but it is hope deferred. There are at least two good reasons why God has chosen to shut the spiritual eyes of ethnic Israel, for now.

The Good News: *"Because of their transgression, salvation has come to the Gentiles..."* (Romans 11:11). That is reason number one—God has purposefully chosen to blind the eyes of the Jews in order that the Gospel might be more readily available to us (assuming that you are a Gentile.) *"Their (the Jews) rejection brought reconciliation to the world (of Gentiles)"* (11:15). Like a grain offering as part of the Jewish Feast of Firstfruits, ethnic Israel as a whole was the first to feel the loving embrace of God. They were the first to be wooed as a lover, the first to feel the white hot affection of the God of creation (11:16). From the start, they were called to share the blessings of God's covenant love with the Gentiles, but they chose not to. From the start they were called to embrace an ethic that set them apart from every other nation, but they chose not to. As a result, God pulled the veil of blindness over their spiritual eyes.

The Good News Part Deux: The current "stumbling" of ethnic Israel is good news for Gentiles. But it is also good news for future generations of Jews. This is the second reason why God has temporarily blinded the Jewish people. How amazing is God, that even as He hardens some, He does so with the end in mind that ethnic Israel will one day come to its senses and seek the God of Israel once more. And so they will! The election of only a remnant will give way to a great surge of salvation among Israel as they become jealous of what they see happening among the Gentiles! (11:11, 14). Paul is keenly aware of the role he is playing as a missionary to the Gentiles. *Imagine the thrill he experienced as it was revealed to him that his work among the Gentiles was accomplishing the very thing he longed for—"...I make much of my ministry (to the Gentiles) in the hope that I may somehow arouse my own people to envy and save some of them..."* (Romans 11:14).

The Great Tree

With this as the foundation, Paul now launches into an extended discussion using the tree metaphor. He paints a picture of a great tree, the roots and trunk of which are ethnic Israel as a whole. It is a cultivated olive tree, one specifically nurtured for optimal fruit production. All the realities he spoke of in Romans 9:4-5 form the roots and the trunk of this great tree. The branches are individuals and families from ethnic Israel, blood relatives of Abraham. Most of those branches, in Paul's day and our own, have been "broken off." This is another way of saying that they have been "hardened" and that they have "persisted in unbelief." (Don't miss the paradox! They are hardened *and* held responsible for their unbelief.) Growing up around this glorious tree are many other "wild" trees that represent all the other nations and peoples of the earth. And it had been God's intention from the beginning that they all be part of the same tree!

Over time, as God has broken off branches from the cultivated tree, He has taken branches from the wild trees and "grafted them in." These wild branches are now nourished and fed by the very same root and trunk that the original branches enjoyed. Imagine! As a Gentile, I enjoy "adoption...divine glory, the covenants, the receiving of the law, the Temple worship and the promises...the patriarchs, from whom the human ancestry of the Messiah is traced!! Praise God! What a history! What a heritage! What a tree! Move over Jews, there's a new branch in town!

Easy, Gentile-boy. Ease up on the gas just a bit. Lest we Gentiles get too uppity (Romans 11:18), Paul adds a sobering thought and a glorious promise. The sobering thought is that we got to be part of this great tree in exactly the same way the tree was planted and cultivated in the first place—as a result of God's electing grace. Just as Israel was chosen for no other reason than to magnify the glorious riches of God's grace, so we too were chosen. And let's not forget who is supporting whom. Branches don't support the trunk, it's the other way around (11:18). It is essential that we Gentiles not fall prey to the same kind of thinking that got Israel in trouble in the first place. What thinking? The thinking that there is anything about us (ethnicity, bloodlines, religion, usefulness) that forces God to work with us!

Remember, God operates in this way, in part, to illustrate "His wrath and make His power known..." (9:22). Being grafted in is the fruit of electing love, not works. Rather than posturing like peacocks we would be better served to "tremble" (11:20). In treating God like their own prized possession, Israel had the Kingdom taken from them and given to a people who would produce its fruit (Matt.

21:43). Imagine the grief that must have washed over Paul as he recounted the words of Jesus to the original twelve:

> *"I tell you, many will come from the East and the West (Gentiles) and recline at table with Abraham, Isaac and Jacob in the Kingdom of Heaven, while the sons of the Kingdom (Israel) will be thrown into the outer darkness. In that place there will be weeping and gnashing of teeth"* (Matt. 8:11-12).

If they could be cut off, natural branches that they were, imagine how easy it would be for us "wild" branches to also be cut off. This highlights the inescapable truth that "everlasting covenants" CAN be broken. This is the point of the book of Hosea. *After she had weaned Lo-Ruhamah, Gomer had another son. Then the LORD said, "Call him Lo-Ammi, for you are not my people, and I am not your God"* (Hosea 1:8-9). What Paul is saying in Romans 11:21 is "Be careful! Just because you appear to be part of God's people, that does not mean that you might not be cut-off too." How can we live without that fear? What is it that guarantees our connection to the tree? Our ethnicity? Our religion? Our "good works?" No. "The kindness of God" (11:22).

In the midst of this sobering warning, there is also a marvelous promise. Just as surely as many of the natural branches are being broken off, a day is coming when many will be grafted back in (Romans 11:23). Wild olive branches might struggle to receive the nourishing sap of our Jewish heritage, but not so the natural branches. They will "take" to the tree as naturally as one might expect. In fact, a day is coming when we will see an incredible movement of God's Spirit among ethnic Israel. The Divine Husbandman will be busy, furiously grafting natural branches back into the tree. Paul has saved this, the greatest mystery of all, for last.

All Israel Will Be Saved

Paul calls it a "mystery." He has chosen to share this mystery with us for one reason: to keep us (Gentiles) from being "conceited." There is something in all of us that wants to believe that at least some part of our salvation was the fruit of our own efforts. As Paul has built his case throughout these chapters, the inescapable conclusion is that *grace, not works, has accounted for our being part of the Kingdom Tree.*

God has predestined a certain number of Gentiles who will be saved, at which point God will lift the veil of hardening that covers most of Israel to this day (11:25). When that happens, there will be a great "people movement" among the Jews. A tsunami of conversion will sweep over ethnic Israel, and "so all Israel will be saved." How will this happen? While the details of this great future day remain a mystery, we know several things for certain.

First, they will be saved in the same way that all humanity is made right with God, through repentance and faith in Jesus Christ. *"The deliverer will come from Zion; He will turn godlessness away from Jacob"* (11:26). Who is this "deliverer?" He is the Christ, the Son of the Living God, the same deliverer of which Paul spoke in Colossians 1:10 and 1 Thessalonians 1:13.

Why state the patently obvious, that salvation will come again to ethnic Israel through faith in Jesus Christ? Because there are many in the Jewish community and an increasing number in the Christian community who believe that there are two different and separate ways for Gentiles and Jews to be saved. The most outspoken of these Christian teachers, John Hagee, is also one of the most influential. He is the co-founder of Christians United for Israel, the fastest growing grass roots organization that is committed to the protection and promotion of the State of Israel. Hagee's television broadcasts regularly draw close to 100 million viewers. Hagee believes and teaches that "... trying to convert Jews is a 'waste of time.' The Jewish person who has his roots in Judaism is not going to convert to Christianity. There is no form of Christian evangelism that has failed so miserably as evangelizing the Jewish people. They (already) have a faith structure... Everyone else, whether Buddhist or Baha'i, needs to believe in Jesus... But not Jews. Jews already have a covenant with God that has never been replaced by Christianity."[38]

In a letter responding to criticism regarding his teaching that a non-Christocentric means of salvation was available to Jews, Hagee cited the very chapters under discussion—Romans 9-11. "There are Jewish people who have a relationship with God right now according to the election of grace. (Romans 11:5) ...The Jewish people are judicially blinded to the identity of Messiah...Question: If God blinded the Jewish people to the identity of Jesus as Messiah, how could He send them to hell for not seeing what he had forbidden them to see? ... Inasmuch as God has

---

[38] "San Antonio fundamentalist battles anti-Semitism," *Houston Chronicle*, April 30, 1988, sec. 6, pg. 1

blinded them to the identity of Messiah, *targeting the Jewish people for mass evangelism is fruitless."*[39]

Hagee's argument is PRECISELY the argument Paul addressed in Romans 9. If God has hardened the heart of some, how can He hold them responsible for their choices? The implied answer that Hagee gives is "He cannot." Therefore, Hagee assumes, God must refer back to His original covenant with Israel to save them. His argument continues that it is pointless to try and evangelize the Jewish people under the umbrella of the Great Commission. Is this the answer Paul gives? No! *God can and does elect some to salvation while He hardens the hearts of others. At the same time, God holds each of us responsible for the choices we make. This is not a game for God. This is not Biblical double-talk. It is at the very heart of what makes God so glorious. For Him, there is no contradiction.*

We are not at liberty to discard Biblical teachings that we find inconvenient or difficult. Instead, we are urged by Paul to imagine ourselves as putty in God's hands. We are the clay, He is the Potter. He does harden the hearts of some. He does elect others to salvation by grace alone. He does offer salvation to all who believe in Jesus Christ. *"Salvation is found in no one else, for there is no other name under heaven given to men by which we must be saved"* (Acts 4:12). This is the first and most critical conclusion that we must come to as we consider what Paul means by "all Israel will be saved." The coming salvation of the Jewish people will come by putting their faith in Jesus Christ. There will be no Plan B, no

---

[39] John Hagee letter (on Cornerstone Church letterhead) to Erwin M. de Castro of the Christian Research Institute, October 18, 1994, pg. 3

"salvation Jewish-style," no return to old-covenant redemption.

Second, we cannot help but conclude that Paul has the ethnic people of Israel in mind in Romans 11:26. "All Israel" must mean all "ethnic Israel." The entire discussion in chapters 9-11 of Romans has focused on the distinction between Gentiles and ethnic Israel. Beginning in chapter 9, Paul references "those of my own race," and he ends in chapter 11 by referring to God's "people" as those who, like himself, were blood relatives of Abraham. In Romans 11:25, Paul is clearly referring to ethnic Israel which, as we have already seen, is currently experiencing a "hardening." It would be quite an expositional leap to think that the Israel of verse 11:26 could mean anything other than the same thing it meant in verse 11:25. The "enemies of God" in the first half of 11:28 are the same "cut-off" people Paul has been referring to throughout these chapters, the nation of Israel. The election spoken of in the last half of the verse must refer to the same people.

Equally clear is that at no point does Paul suggest that a second or separate tree will be planted or nurtured from this group. There is no "narrowing" of the "true" People of God, only a broadening which includes the Jewish people. **The mystery of which Paul speaks in Romans 11 is that at some point in the future, there will be a great movement of God's Spirit among ethnic Israel, and they will be added to the number of the elect.** This does not mean that every person who has ever been or ever will be of Jewish descent will be saved. Why not? *Because Paul has just spent the last three chapters making the case that salvation is not tied to ethnicity!* To argue that all Israel will be saved for no other reason than that they are Israel is to nullify the very point that Paul has painstakingly made thus far.

What it does mean is that there will be such a surge of evangelism among a single people group, in this case ethnic Jews, that we can rightly say they are "all" saved. A marvelous and glorious national conversion of ethnic Israel will someday come to pass. Contemporary missiology has both observed and defined this very phenomenon. One of the leading contributors to current world missions is the late Donald McGavran. He wrote: "People become Christian as a wave of decision for Christ sweeps through the group mind, involving many individual decisions but being far more than merely their sum. This may be called a chain reaction. Each decision sets off others and the sum total powerfully affects every individual. When conditions are right, not merely each sub-group, but the entire group concerned decides together."[40]

There are many examples of this phenomenon that are readily observable.[41] This passage gives us every reason to believe that someday a "wave of decision for Christ" will sweep over the Jewish people. This future generation of Jews will be grafted in again to the great salvation tree.

The use of the word "all" in describing the salvation of Israel is identical to Paul's use of "all" in verse 32: *"For God has bound all men* (Gentiles first, then Jews*) over to*

---

[40] Donald McGavran, "The Bridges of God" *in Perspectives on The World Christian Movement: A Reader*, ed. Ralph D. Winter & Steven C. Hawthorne (Pasadena, CA: William Carey Library, 1999), p. 322.

[41] Ibid., Pp. 332-336.

disobedience so that he may have mercy on them all (Jews first, then Gentiles, then Jews again)." Paul states emphatically in verses 30-31 that God is determined to put His mercy on display! He did this first by "binding" the Gentiles over to disobedience (11:32). The word Paul uses suggests that God has gathered the nations in a net and hemmed them in, keeping them from reaching His mercy.[42] This is strong language! Paul himself gives us a clue as to what he means by this in the sermon he preached in Lystre/Derbe. It is recorded in Acts 14. In verse 6 he tells his listeners that *"in the past, He (God) let nations go their own way..."* In other words, God purposefully permitted Gentile nations to continue in their disobedience and then kept them from finding Him for a very specific purpose—in order that they might receive mercy. As we have seen, He accomplished this by giving Satan authority over those nations. Now, God has "bound" Israel over to disobedience for the very same reason—to show them mercy at some point in the future. From the beginning of time to the end of time, God has purposed to put His mercy on display as a means of magnifying the glorious riches of His sovereign will!

It is obvious that Paul is using the term "all" in the broadest sense. Paul is not preaching a kind of universalism which declares that all human individuals are saved from the wrath of judgment. We know from the Old and New Testament that there were many Gentiles who believed during the first phase of God's redemptive plan, when "all" Gentiles were bound over to disobedience, just as there were and are some Jews who believe now. By "all" Paul means

---

[42] The Greek word is συνεκλεισεν, which means to shut up or consign, to enclose or shut up on all sides—to shut up completely.

that as a group, Gentiles first and Jews now, are in a state of disobedience. Someday, Jews as a group will experience a great repentance and turn to Christ; although not every single individual that is part of that group will repent.

One final point of clarification: at no point does Paul or any other Biblical writer equate "Israel" with the current state of Israel. When Paul says that "all Israel will be saved" he is not suggesting that everyone within the borders of the current state of Israel will be saved. Without serious Biblical consideration, it is easy to fall into the trap of equating the two. To reiterate—the current state of Israel is NOT to be confused with the people of Israel.

Now What?

We've identified two metaphors that capture God's relationship to His people—the marriage metaphor and the tree metaphor. What both make clear is that there are not two brides or two trees, only one. The True Israel that is God's prized possession is people from *all* the nations, not the *one* nation of Israel. Although this One People includes many Jews, and will someday see a great influx of Jews, does not change the fact that there has only ever been ONE people of God. Nothing Paul has taught in Romans 9-11 would lead us to believe that this will change. When the Old Testament spoke of the future of Israel, it meant the "true Israel," not the "state" of Israel or an ethnic group called "Jews." Ethnicity does not enter the picture. Isaac and Ishmael proved this. Jacob and Esau proved this. Abraham and Moses and David all confirmed this. From start to finish, God's people have only ever been those who enter His family by faith.

If this is true, then we should expect to find a great deal of "crossover" in the names and appellations that are used to describe "Israel" in the Old Testament and those used to describe the Church or the True Israel in the New Testament. The evidence is overwhelming.[43] In the OT, Israel is called "the beloved of God" (Deuteronomy 33:3; Ezra 3:11) as are Christ-followers (Romans 9:25; Colossians 3:12). Israel is called the "children of God" (Deuteronomy 14:1; Isaiah 1:2, 4; Hosea 11:1) as is The Church (John 1:12; Philippians 2:15; 1 John 3:1). Israel is called the "field of God" (Jeremiah 12:10) as is the Church (1 Corinthians 3:9). Israel is described as the "flock of God" (Psalm 78:52; Micah 5:4; Zechariah 10:3) as are Christ-followers (John 10:14; 1 Peter 5:2-3). Israel is called the "house of God" (Numbers 12:7) as are Christ-followers (1 Timothy 3:15; Hebrews 10:21). Israel is the "people of God" (Exodus 6:7; 2 Samuel 7:23) as is the Church (Romans 9:25; Ephesians 4:12; 2 Thessalonians 1:10). Israel is the "priests of God" (Exodus 19:6) as is the Church (1 Peter 2:5, 9; Revelation 1:6). Israel is God's "wife" (Isaiah 5:3-7; 54:5-6; Jeremiah 2:2) and so are Christ-followers (Ephesians 5:31-32). The Israelites are "children of Abraham" (2 Chronicles 20:7) and so is the Church (Romans 4:11, 16; Galatians 4:23, 28, 31). Israel is a "chosen people" (Deuteronomy 7:7; Isaiah 43:20-21) as are Christ-followers (Colossians 3:12; 1 Peter 2:9). The Church is often referred to as "Israel" (John 11:50-52; 1 Corinthians 10:1; Galatians 6:15-16; Ephesians 2:12, 19). God is said to "walk among" Israel, (Leviticus 26:11-12) and He walks with those who are in Christ (2 Corinthians 6:16). In Deuteronomy 32:36 God

---

[43] For an excellent list of all these types of comparisons between Israel and the Church, Cf. Appendix #2, based on notes from Charles D. Provan, "*The Church is Israel Now*." The book can be ordered from Ross House Books..

promises to "judge" His people Israel, and He promises to judge His Church (Hebrews 10:30). God promised to "lay a stone in Zion, a tested stone, a precious cornerstone for a sure foundation" (Isaiah 28:16) for Israel, and He applies the same promise to the Church (Romans 10:11; 1 Peter 2:6). Again and again we see the Church and Israel portrayed as one and the same. *The Church does not "replace" Israel, it completes Israel.*

All of these passages confirm what Paul has labored hard to teach in Romans 9-11. God has always purposed to have One People, not two. God has not "replaced" Israel with the Church; He has simply revealed the nature of the True Israel that He intended from the beginning. The Old Covenant, *which was deemed obsolete from the start*, has given way to the New Covenant in Christ. Judaism was a corruption of the faith of Abraham. Early on, Christianity was viewed as an offshoot of Judaism. From God's perspective, this simply would not do. A definitive break with Judaism was needed. July 30, 70 AD was that date. The Kingdom of God dawned on that date as never before. The People of God were forever redefined on that day.

Radical Christian feminists will often refer to Galatians 3 as the "cornerstone" of their teaching that every office in the Church should be open to women. I am hard pressed to imagine a worse application of a Scripture. The point of Galatians 3 is this: There is only one "seed of Abraham," and it is all those who are "in Christ Jesus."

You are all sons of God through faith in Christ Jesus, for all of you who were baptized into Christ have clothed yourselves with Christ. There is neither Jew nor Greek,

> *slave nor free, male nor female, for you are all one in Christ Jesus. If you belong to Christ, then you are Abraham's seed, and heirs according to the promise* (Galatians 3:26-29).

For every follower of Jesus Christ, the moment of our conversion is also the moment when we become "Abraham's seed." As the weight of that sinks in, I am drawn back to Sunday school. Sunday school songs have a way of sticking with you. One in particular has stayed with me for years, mainly I think because it was one of the few songs where we could move around during class without being scolded. At the time, I had no idea that I was learning great Biblical theology. The song goes like this: *"Father Abraham had many sons, many sons had Father Abraham. I am one of them and so are you. So let's all praise the Lord. Right arm, left arm, right foot, left foot, Chin up, turn around, sit down!"* Amen.

Chapter Summary

There is only one People of God. Building on the metaphors of marriage and gardening, the Scriptures declare that God's intent was always to have ONE bride, and to nurture and grow ONE tree, both consisting of people from many nations. It was the particular mandate of Abraham and his seed to bring that truth to the nations. God's abiding favor over the people of Israel was contingent upon their fulfilling that covenant destiny. They failed to do so. The many promises of a "return" to the land of Israel included in both the major and minor prophets were fulfilled in the return from exile recorded for us in the books of Ezra and Nehemiah. Any hope of a future return, or a return to the land that began with the establishment of the state of Israel in 1948 is misguided.

Perhaps the clearest explanation of the current and future relationship of God to the people of Israel is found in Romans 9-11. Those chapters are built on the foundation of Paul's explanation of what makes a person a true "Jew." *A person is not a Jew who is one only outwardly, nor is circumcision merely outward and physical. No, a person is a Jew who is one inwardly; and circumcision is circumcision of the heart, by the Spirit, not by the written code. Such a person's praise is not from other people, but from God* (Romans 2:28-29).

In Romans 9-11 Paul proceeded to explain in breathtaking detail that the sovereign good pleasure of God is beyond our comprehension. God is completely free to choose whatever and whomever He wants. Beginning with one people, Israel, God has chosen to include Gentiles as part of His people, the intended outcome of His calling Abraham in the first place. There is no hint in Paul's writing that God intends something special for the current **State** of Israel. There is no suggestion that someday, Jesus will restore the fortunes of national Israel in order to rule the earth from Jerusalem.

Instead, Paul envisioned a day when there would be a great outpouring of God's Spirit upon ethnic Jews. Being first among the nations that God called to Himself still counts for something! Israel was the first to receive the covenant, the first to receive the law, the first to send out prophets to proclaim the truth. As such, there is still a special place in God's heart for this people, and someday in the future, we will witness a wave of conversion among the Jews. This wave of conversion will not create a new Israel, but will only serve to expand the true Israel.

CHAPTER 8

Will The Real Antichrist Please Stand Up?

COME AND GONE

Dear children, this is the last hour; and as you have heard that the antichrist is coming, even now many antichrists have come. This is how we know it is the last hour. They went out from us, but they did not really belong to us. For if they had belonged to us, they would have remained with us; but their going showed that none of them belonged to us.
1 JOHN 2:18-19

Somewhere, at this very moment, on planet Earth, the antichrist is almost certainly alive—biding his time, awaiting his cue...That likelihood is based upon a sober evaluation of current events in relation to Bible prophecy...he is probably active in politics, perhaps even an admired world leader whose name is almost daily on everyone's lips.
DAVID HUNT *GLOBAL PEACE AND THE RISE OF ANTICHRIST*

It is unBiblical to use the term 'antichrist' for a present-day or future political ruler. The proper context is theological and pre-a.d. 70.
GARY DEMAR, *LAST DAYS MADNESS*

If you would like to have some fun and you have oodles of spare time, sit down at your computer and Google "antichrist." Yowza! If half of what you read is true, there's an antichrist under every bush. Apparently the only criteria for weighing in on this issue is the ability to hunt and peck at a keyboard, a very fertile imagination, and access to a calculator.

Like Baskin-Robbins "flavor of the week," the title Antichrist is regularly assigned to someone new—everyone from David Hasselhoff, to Barak Obama, to the Pope, to Warren Buffet and George W. Bush. Trying to identify this mystery man is not unlike a game show I watched as a child called *To Tell the Truth*. If you are over 40 and you recognize the names Orson Bean or Kitty Carlisle, you know what I'm talking about. For the uninitiated, the show featured a panel of four celebrities attempting to correctly identify a described contestant who typically had an unusual occupation or experience.

There were three "players," each trying to convince the panelists that they were whomever the central character was for that episode. The climax of the show came when the host (played by Mike Wallace of *60 Minutes* fame in the original pilot) would opine, "Will the real (central character) please stand up?" The three contestants would then do their best impersonation of the ground hogs in that arcade game where they pop up from openings and you have to smash them on the head with a mallet. Once each of them was finished feigning standing up, the real character would ascend. It is the longest running game show in the history of television. Who knew?

So, let's play *To Tell the Truth*, shall we? You are the celebrity panelist, and together we are going to ask questions about: The Antichrist—the "man of lawlessness" in the writings of Paul—and John's discussion of the Beast in Revelation—and then we will ask, "Will the real Antichrist please stand up?" I know. I'm all aquiver too.

The Antichrist In General

Like so many end-times related topics, the term "antichrist" is actually quite obscure. It appears a grand total of four times in all of Scripture, all of them in the epistles of John (1 John 2:18-22 [twice]; 1 John 4:2-3; 2 John 7). John was very intentional in his use of the word *antichrist*, (αντιχριστος) rather than *pseudo Christ* (ψευδοχριστοσ), the latter being the prophets that Jesus warned of in the Olivet discourse. John did use the term for "false" prophet in 1 John 4, so he was obviously familiar with the word. A false-Christ would be someone who claimed to be the Christ, or someone who tried to gather a following as The Messiah. But John used the term "antichrist" to convey overt opposition to the teachings, claims and Kingdom agenda of Jesus Christ. *He used the term to describe both the heretical worldview that opposed Christ, as well as the people/persons who embraced such a view.*

The Antichrist In John

All right—you got me. If the term "anti-Christ" *only* appears in John, then having a section titled "The Antichrist in General" and another one titled "The Antichrist in John" is redundant—or unnecessary—or repetitive—or repeatedly, unnecessarily redundant. Regardless, here we are.

1 John 2:18-27

As we have done throughout, we need to take time-frame references seriously. John introduced his discussion of "antichrist" with an ominous sounding warning; *"Dear children, this is the last hour..."* (2:18). Expressions like "This is the last quarter," or "this is the last skate," or "this is your last chance" leave little doubt as to their meaning. Why not interpret God's word in the same way? There is nothing in the original language that suggests some hidden or secret meaning to his words. They need to be taken at face value: "I am writing to you about something that is imminent. Listen up! What follows is material that will impact you and your immediate family."

Last Days Rabbit Trail

"Not so fast!' you may say. That may describe our *English* usage of the phrase "last hour" but is that how it is used in Greek (the language John originally wrote in)? Fair enough. The phrase "last days/last hour" appears nine times in the New Testament. Taking each one chronologically as they appear in our English Bibles, the first is found in 1 Timothy 4:1. Paul is telling Timothy to be on the lookout for false teaching. He warned,

> *The Spirit clearly says that in **later times**(last days) some will abandon the faith and follow deceiving spirits and things taught by demons. Such teachings*

> come through hypocritical liars, whose consciences have been seared as with a hot iron. They forbid people to marry and order them to abstain from certain foods, which God created to be received with thanksgiving by those who believe and who know the truth. For everything God created is good, and nothing is to be rejected if it is received with thanksgiving, because it is consecrated by the word of God and prayer. If you point these things out to the brothers, you will be a good minister of Christ Jesus (1 Timothy 4:1-6).

Why does Timothy need to point these things out? If the "later times" were still thousands of years off why be concerned? The Spirit clearly says that these things will happen in the "later times"—unless of course, Paul was saying that *they* were living in the later times, requiring the exposure of these false teachers. That clearly seems to be the case.

Some have argued that Paul meant that the entire time period between Christ's first and second appearing was the "later times." Ever since Christ came the first time, the argument goes, we have been living in an age of apostasy. Is that what the record shows? The history of the Church and the flourishing of the Gospel would make such an argument ludicrous. However, the history of the *first-century Church* is filled with examples of and warnings against people turning from the faith. Due to the great persecution the Church experienced, this was a major problem *at that time*. Besides, the use of the phrase as a preface to a warning that would directly impact

Timothy's ministry suggests a specific and short time period.

The next use of this phrase is found in 2 Timothy 3:1. Again, Paul is addressing Timothy.

> *And the Lord's servant must not quarrel; instead, he must be kind to everyone, able to teach, not resentful. Those who oppose him he must gently instruct, in the hope that God will grant them repentance leading them to a knowledge of the truth, and that they will come to their senses and escape from the trap of the devil, who has taken them captive to do his will. But mark this: There will be terrible times in the **last days**. People will be lovers of themselves, lovers of money, boastful, proud, abusive, disobedient to their parents, ungrateful, unholy, without love, unforgiving, slanderous, without self-control, brutal, not lovers of the good, treacherous, rash, conceited, lovers of pleasure rather than lovers of God—having a form of godliness but denying its power. Have nothing to do with them* (2 Timothy 2:24-3:5).

Paul encouraged Timothy to "gently instruct" those who opposed him. This opposition was inspired by the Devil. He had "taken them captive to do his will." Paul seems to suggest, "as harsh as that may sound, Timothy, mark my words: there will be terrible times in the last days... People will engage in all manner of despicable behavior. Avoid people like that." The obvious question is, "Why avoid these people if they would be living thousands of years in the future?" This cannot be Paul's meaning. He warned Timothy to avoid such people precisely because they would appear in the "last days," or the very days that Timothy was living in.

Hebrews 1:1-2 is clear:

> *In the past God spoke to our forefathers through the prophets at many times and in various ways, but in these **last days** he has spoken to us by his Son, whom he appointed heir of all things, and through whom he made the universe.*

There *was* a time when God chose to speak to us through prophets and other mediums. But *now*, God speaks through His Son. How does the writer of Hebrews describe the "now" during which the readers of Hebrews were living? *"These last days."*

James, the half-brother of Jesus warned of coming judgment. The "rich" were on particularly thin ice. James wrote

> *Now listen, you rich people, weep and wail because of the misery that is coming upon you. Your wealth has rotted, and moths have eaten your clothes. Your gold and silver are corroded. Their corrosion will testify against you and eat your flesh like fire. You have hoarded wealth in the **last days*** (James 5:1-3).

How should we understand James' reference to the "last days?" The plain and clear meaning of his words is exactly what we would expect. "You rich people are storing up wealth for someone else! "Fire" is coming, because you have hoarded your wealth now, or "in the last days."

The Apostle Peter echoed the warning that Jesus gave in Matthew 24. If Jesus' disciples understood His words correctly, which they did, they had an opportunity to "escape" the coming judgment at the hands of the Roman Empire. Peter said

> *Praise be to the God and Father of our Lord Jesus Christ! In his great mercy he has given us new birth into a living hope through the resurrection of Jesus Christ from the dead, and into an inheritance that can never perish, spoil or fade—kept in heaven for you, who through faith are shielded by God's power until the coming of the salvation that is ready to be revealed in the **last time*** (1 Peter 1:3-5).

There is nothing in this text that *demands* a first-century application. But Peter alluded to a salvation that was "ready to be revealed." He suggested God would "shield" His children from something. This "shielding" was described as "salvation that is ready to be revealed in the last time." It is possible that Peter was speaking to a hope that did not exist for his first-century readers, but only for those living thousands of years in the future. That seems unlikely. Given the context of Jesus' teaching regarding the imminent destruction of Jerusalem and the possibility that some could escape that holocaust, it seems more likely that Peter had the same event in mind. That event would occur in the "last time" or their time.

> *But, dear friends, remember what the apostles of our Lord Jesus Christ foretold. They said to you, "In the **last times** there will be scoffers who will follow their own ungodly desires." These are the men who divide you, who follow mere natural instincts and do not have the Spirit. But you, dear friends, build yourselves up in your most holy faith and pray in the Holy Spirit. Keep yourselves in God's love as you*

> *wait for the mercy of our Lord Jesus Christ to bring you to eternal life* (Jude 17-21).

Jude is directly quoting the apostles. Their teaching had been explicit, and it applied directly to the first-century Church. On the authority of the apostles, Jude was saying "Watch out! Churches are going to be filled with people who will try to lead you astray. Don't listen. Hold to the teaching of the apostles, pray, and keep loving others. You are living at precisely the times that the apostles spoke of—the last times." An admonition to that generation to keep the faith in spite of "scoffers" who would come thousands of years after they were dead and gone is unlikely. **The plain meaning of Jude's words, just like every other use of this phrase in Scripture, indicate that the time between Jesus' ascension and the destruction of Jerusalem in 70 A.D. were the "last times."** While we may face dire circumstances and grim situations now, we should not expect that we will face the daunting challenges that Christ's first-century followers faced in the "last days." Those days are done! We live on the other side of the last days, the days of Christ's expanding rule, the days of greater victories, the days of Satan's final defeat, and the days of reigning with Christ!

The Last Hour

Meanwhile, back at 1 John 2...John actually *ramps up* the prophetic timetable. In speaking of the antichrist, John suggested that it was not only the "last days," it was the "last hour!" John meant his original readers to understand that the time of the antichrist was even closer than they thought.

Not long ago, I was stunned by a Christian talk-radio program that featured "the leading expert on the Antichrist." The host asked this "expert" to summarize the Biblical teaching on the Antichrist. He quoted 1 John 2:18-27, and then launched into a discussion of who this Antichrist might be as we look at the current political landscape. He did not even stop to address the very words he read! He blithely shot past John's introduction to the entire topic of antichrist, *"Dear children, this is the last hour..."* and moved on to harrowing stories of potential candidates for the title "Antichrist." Once again we see how our preconceptions blind us to things that are clearly in the texts before us. Would it not make sense to try and understand what John meant by "this is the last hour" before moving on? Most end-times teachers answer that question with a resounding "no!" Sound interpretation demands that we not make the same mistake. With this clear time-frame reference in mind, John addressed the issue of "the antichrist" or more particularly "antichrists." From John's perspective, the very presence of the latter confirmed that John's readers were living in the last hour.

It is these "antichrists," not "*the* Antichrist" that is the *primary* focus of John's letters—"antichrists" and the "spirit of the antichrist." THE IDENTITY OF THESE ANTICHRISTS WAS NO MYSTERY. Apparently, there was a burgeoning heresy that was arising in the church in the first century. This heresy focused on the nature of Jesus Christ and included two key arguments: That Jesus was not The Christ, and that Jesus had not actually come "in the flesh." As we sift through the scant data that John provided, we can come to at least four additional conclusions regarding antichrists, or "the spirit of antichrist."

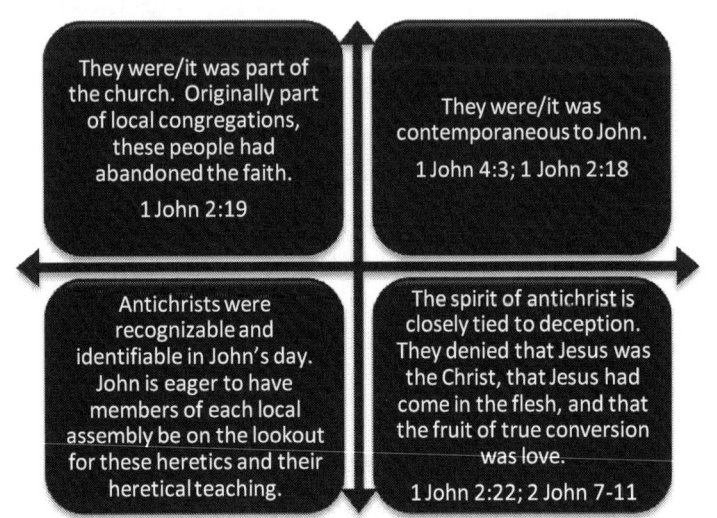

> **They were/it was part of the church.** Originally part of local congregations, these people had abandoned the faith.
> 1 John 2:19

> **They were/it was contemporaneous to John.**
> 1 John 4:3; 1 John 2:18

> **Antichrists were recognizable and identifiable in John's day.** John is eager to have members of each local assembly be on the lookout for these heretics and their heretical teaching.

> **The spirit of antichrist is closely tied to deception.** They denied that Jesus was the Christ, that Jesus had come in the flesh, and that the fruit of true conversion was love.
> 1 John 2:22; 2 John 7-11

As we begin to flesh out the nature of the antichrist spirit and the teachings of these antichrists, it is more than just "coincidence" that history records just such a heretical movement around the time of John. I cannot stress enough the fact that John indicated that the spirit of antichrist WAS ALREADY PRESENT AT THE TIME OF HIS WRITING. In the first century, members of the early church began to embrace a set of heretical teachings that later came to be known as Gnosticism.

At the heart of these teachings was the notion that the material/physical world was bad, while the spiritual was good. Anything material must be rejected as evil. The "flesh" in particular was the repository of evil. As an article of faith, early Gnostics rejected the notion that Jesus had come "in the flesh." As part of their attempt to honor Jesus, they could not reconcile the incarnation with this central teaching of theirs.

In addition, they taught that the true path to salvation was through increased knowledge, often a "secret" knowledge that (you guessed it!) only they possessed. The Greek word "gnosis" means "knowledge," hence the name "Gnostics" or "Gnosticism."

As we look at John's brief description of what these early antichrist heretics believed we see a perfect description of pre-Gnostic teachings. Although full-blown Gnosticism was still some time off, its roots were unmistakably present in the first century. That John was responding to this heresy is borne out by how much attention he gives to Christ's human nature. The heart of 1 John is a proclamation that Jesus had come and that John had seen and heard and touched that same Jesus (1 John 1:1-3). John urged his readers to "test the spirits" of those who taught in the church, and to reject the teaching of those false prophets that failed to acknowledge that Christ had come "in the flesh" (1 John 4:2). It was precisely the deceiving spirit of antichrist that accounted for this new teaching that Christ was only a "spirit" and not also a flesh and blood man (2 John 7).

To counter the other core teaching of pre-Gnostic heretics, that salvation was found in knowledge rather than faith in Christ, John went to great lengths to assure his readers that salvation could *only* be found in Christ (1 John 1:7; 2:2; 12, 22, 24-25; 3:23; 4:13-15; 5:1-5, 10-13). So the "spirit of antichrist" was alive and kicking in John's day. The presence of antichrists was a clear signal that *The* Antichrist could not be far behind. That John had a specific individual in mind is clear from his use of the definite article in describing this person. He was not "a" antichrist, but "The

Antichrist." Who, then, was the Antichrist of which John warned?

It is safe to assume that the characteristics of earlier antichrists would be more pronounced and more clearly defined in THE ANTICHRIST. Based on that assumption we would expect the Antichrist to:

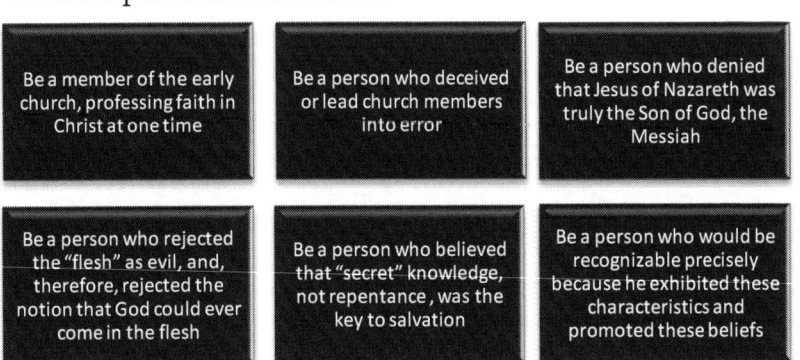

Be a member of the early church, professing faith in Christ at one time	Be a person who deceived or lead church members into error	Be a person who denied that Jesus of Nazareth was truly the Son of God, the Messiah
Be a person who rejected the "flesh" as evil, and, therefore, rejected the notion that God could ever come in the flesh	Be a person who believed that "secret" knowledge, not repentance, was the key to salvation	Be a person who would be recognizable precisely because he exhibited these characteristics and promoted these beliefs

How can anyone who offers prognostications as to the identity of The Antichrist do so without taking into account the clear parameters that John gave us? Again, the answer is that only people who have already decided that he must be a future figure can offer guesses to his identity that fall outside the first century. *On the other hand, if we take John's words at face value, there are a number of individuals who fit the bill,* some of whom the Apostle John actually had contact with in the latter years of his life. The three most likely candidates for The Antichrist are Cerinthus, Simon Magus, and the early deacon Nicolas.

Please Stand Up

As we have already noted, Gnosticism did not fully develop until the latter second and early third century. But we see the seeds of this heresy already being sown in the first century. Although no known writings of Cerinthus survive today, he is often identified by later church fathers as a key figure in the developing Gnostic heresy of the first century. The peak of his popularity came around 100 A.D. Based on the early church fathers' denunciations of Cerinthus, we can piece together key elements of his teachings.[44]

A Jewish convert from Egypt, Cerinthus was part of the church in Ephesus. As his popularity grew, so did his unorthodox teachings. He boasted that he was in regular communication with angels, and that his teachings were inspired by these spirits. He believed that the world was created by a "lesser god" and not the God of Israel. Salvation came through a "mystical" interaction with the law, guided by secret information that he alone had received from his angelic visitors. The law was originally given by angels, so the latter played an important role in the theology of Cerinthus. It is very likely that Paul's admonition to the church in Colossae was a direct reference to the teachings of men like Cerinthus.

> *Do not let anyone who delights in false humility and the worship of angels disqualify you from the prize. Such a person goes into great detail about what he has seen, and his unspiritual mind puffs him up with idle notions (Colossians 2:18).*

At the heart of Cerinthus' teaching was his view that physical matter was inherently evil. He taught that Jesus THE MAN would someday be raised from the dead and establish a thousand year reign on earth characterized by

---

[44] Cerinthus is singled out as an early heretic in the writing of Irenaeus in *Against Heresies*, and the writings of Epiphanius of Salamis in *Panarion*.

sensual pleasure and physical indulgence. Since the body is evil and will someday be done away with, it doesn't matter how we indulge or deny it.

Regarding Jesus of Nazareth, Cerinthus taught that He was born of the union between Joseph and Mary. At His baptism, the "spirit" of "The Christ" descended upon Him. For the next three years, Jesus the man was inhabited by the Christ spirit, which left Him at the crucifixion. What is remarkable about the teachings of men like Cerinthus is that their ideas survive to this day and are actually becoming more and more popular.[45]

Cerinthus was a staunch legalist. He taught that salvation could only be had through strict observance of the law. Circumcision and Sabbath observance were at the heart of true righteousness. Paul's letter to the Galatians is regarded by many as a direct refutation of the teachings of Cerinthus. He may well have had Cerinthus in mind when he wrote,

> *You were running a good race. Who cut in on you to keep you from obeying the truth? That kind of persuasion does not come from the one who calls you. "A little yeast works through the whole batch of dough." I am confident in the Lord that you will take no other view. The one who is throwing you into confusion, whoever that may be, will have to pay the penalty. Brothers and sisters, if I am still preaching circumcision, why am I still being persecuted? In that case the offense of the cross has been abolished. As for those agitators, I*

---

[45] Ekhart Tolle, for example, in *The Power of Now*, resurrects many of the teachings of proto-gnostics like Cerinthus, including the notion that Jesus of Nazareth was not 'The' Christ, but that the spirit of Christ descended upon Him for a time, just as It has a number of other prominent spiritual leaders throughout history.

> *wish they would go the whole way and emasculate themselves!* (Galatians 5:7-12).

Although the information is somewhat anecdotal, we have good reason to believe that the Apostle John actually knew of and in fact met Cerinthus. Irenaeus (2nd Century A.D.), quoting Polycarp (69-155 A.D.), told the story that John, nearing the end of his life, so detested Cerinthus that he once fled a bathhouse when he found out Cerinthus was inside, yelling "Let us flee, lest the building fall down; for Cerinthus, the enemy of the truth, is inside!"[46]

The great church father Tertullian (A.D. 160-220) wrote this of Cerinthus: "After him (Carpocrates) broke out the heretic Cerinthus, teaching similarly. For he, too, says that the world was originated by those angels; and sets forth Christ as born of the seed of Joseph, contending that He was merely human, without divinity; affirming also that the Law was given by angels; representing the God of the Jews as not the Lord, but an angel."[47] Cerinthus' fascination with angels included his contention that an angel had personally delivered to him the truth regarding the Millennium. Paul clearly has someone like Cerinthus in mind as he penned Galatians.

> *I am astonished that you are so quickly deserting the one who called you to live in the grace of Christ and are turning to a different Gospel—which is really no Gospel at all. Evidently some people are throwing you into confusion and are trying to pervert the Gospel of Christ.*

---

[46] Irenaeus, *Againt Heresies*, III.3.4. *Ante-Nicene Fathers* Edited by Alexander Roberts, E Version, the Gnostic Society Library.

[47] Ibid.

But even if we or an angel from heaven should preach a Gospel other than the one we preached to you, let them be under God's curse! (Galatians 1:6-8).

The second contestant on the Antichrist episode of *"To Tell the Truth"* is Simon Magus. Also known as Simon the Sorcerer, he lived in the latter portion of the first century A.D. Part of his story is recorded in the Acts of the Apostles, chapter 8:9-24:

Now for some time a man named Simon had practiced sorcery in the city and amazed all the people of Samaria. He boasted that he was someone great, and all the people, both high and low, gave him their attention and exclaimed, "This man is rightly called the Great Power of God." They followed him because he had amazed them for a long time with his sorcery. But when they believed Philip as he proclaimed the good news of the Kingdom of God and the name of Jesus Christ, they were baptized, both men and women. Simon himself believed and was baptized. And he followed Philip everywhere, astonished by the great signs and miracles he saw.

When the apostles in Jerusalem heard that Samaria had accepted the word of God, they sent Peter and John to Samaria. When they arrived, they prayed for the new believers there that they might receive the Holy Spirit, because the Holy Spirit had not yet come on any of them; they had simply been baptized in the name of the Lord Jesus. Then Peter and John placed their hands on them, and they received the Holy Spirit. When Simon saw that the Spirit was given at the laying on of the apostles' hands, he offered them money and said, "Give me also this ability so that everyone on whom I lay my hands may receive the

> *Holy Spirit." Peter answered: "May your money perish with you, because you thought you could buy the gift of God with money! You have no part or share in this ministry, because your heart is not right before God. Repent of this wickedness and pray to the Lord in the hope that he may forgive you for having such a thought in your heart. For I see that you are full of bitterness and captive to sin." Then Simon answered, "Pray to the Lord for me so that nothing you have said may happen to me"* (Acts 8:9-24)

Despite the reference to the fact that Simon "believed and was baptized," it is clear from the conclusion of the story that his "conversion" was self-serving and not sincere.

We know from the writings of later Gnostics that they regarded Simon as the source of much of their theology, and the great church father Justin Martyr (103-165 A.D.) referred to him as "the source of all heresies." A Samaritan and a native of Gitta, Simon conferred upon himself the title "Standing One," hinting at the fact that he was greater even than God and that the spirit of the Christ, once passing from Jesus of Nazareth, had now descended upon himself. As the number of Simon's disciples grew, a full-blown sect grew up around him called the "Simonians." Simon's teachings are known to us primarily through the writings of his opponents. At the heart of his heretical teaching was the relationship between Simon and a woman named "Helen." Simon taught that in the beginning God had his "First Thought," his *Ennoia*, which was female. The actual fruit of this "thought" or Ennoia, was a spirit who was the embodiment of wisdom, and, like the Christ spirit, would descend upon different women at different times. Later to be identified in Gnostic thought as Sophia, this being's first act was to create the angels. But the angels rebelled against her out of jealousy and created the world as her prison, imprisoning her in a female body. Thereafter, she was reincarnated many times including Helen of Troy among others, and she finally was reincarnated as Helen, a slave and prostitute in the Phoenician city of Tyre. God then descended in the form of Simon Magus, to rescue his *Ennoia*, and to confer salvation upon men through knowledge of himself, now embodied in Simon. In the latter years of his life, Simon never travelled without Helen, who became his mistress and constant companion.

Like Cerinthus, Simon rejected all orthodox teaching regarding Jesus Christ, the authority of Scripture, the Atonement, and salvation through faith in Christ. Unlike Cerinthus, he seems to have gathered a larger following in the first century, and had a greater impact on the growth of Gnosticism in later centuries. History records that the legacy of Simon has continued to inspire writers and musicians. In Dante's classic "Inferno" Simon appears in the third ditch of the eighth circle of Hell, while Henry Wadsworth Longfellow immortalized Simon and Helen in two works, *Christus: A Mystery* and *Helen of Tyre*.

The 1954 film *The Silver Chalice*, starring Jack Palance and a young Paul Newman, featured a central character, Simon the Magician, patterned after his first century namesake. The 1997 film *The Saint*, starring Val Kilmer, introduced the main character, played by Kilmer, referring to himself as "Simon Magus the magician." Simon Magus is a villain in an early edition of DC Comics **Justice League of America.** In Robin Cook's bestseller *Intervention*, Simon Magus was a central character. As recently as 2010, alternative rock band **St. Sunday** released a concept album based on the teachings of Simon Magus. Magus' radical reworking of Christian orthodoxy, coupled with his charismatic personality and penchant for magic, made him a cult hero in the first century, and an ideal candidate for John's Antichrist. Many of the teachings of Simon and other proto-Gnostics have fueled works including Dan Brown's *The DaVinci Code*.

The third likely candidate for the Antichrist is one of the first deacons of the Church, Nicolas. He is mentioned in passing in Acts 6:5: *This proposal pleased the whole group. They chose Stephen, a man full of faith and of the Holy Spirit; also Philip, Procorus, Nicanor, Timon, Parmenas, and **Nicolas** from Antioch, a convert to Judaism.*

Like Simon, a casual reading of the text would indicate that he was a believer. But history records that over time Nicolas drifted from the orthodox faith, and in fact became the founder of a growing heresy that is referred to in Revelation 2:6, 15. In both Ephesus and Pergamon, the teachings of Nicolas had taken hold and were corrupting the Gospel and the lives of all those who held to his teachings. He is mentioned by a number of early church fathers (including Irenaeus, Epiphanius, and Theodoret) as being the founder of a destructive sect that drew many away from the teachings of the Apostles.

In addition to espousing similar teachings to Cerinthus and Simon, Nicolas' strain of pre-Gnosticism featured a licentiousness that was popular in pagan society. Because of the inherent evil of matter/the body, the latter should be indulged as insignificant and temporary. Irenaeus lamented that Nicolas and his disciples "lead lives of unrestrained indulgence." Polygamy, orgies, and "wife-swapping" were all elements of Nicolaitan practice. It is not surprising that Revelation reserved such scathing rebukes for those who practiced these things, and such high praise for those who "hated" this sect (Revelation 2:6).

While the "spirit of antichrist" is alive and well today, The Antichrist has in all likelihood, come and gone. All three of our candidates for The Antichrist fit perfectly with John's description of the spirit they represented. Each was originally a part of the Church. Each of them rejected the notion that Jesus was the Christ, and that He had come in the flesh. All three embraced a worldview that saw matter as evil, and fleshly indulgences as irrelevant. While we can't say with complete certainty that any of these men were the Antichrist of which John wrote, all three could easily pass as this enigmatic character. "Will the real Antichrist please stand up?"

The Antichrist In Paul

There is no Antichrist in Paul. He never used the term or mentioned anyone remotely connected to John's Antichrist. Who knew? Although Paul did speak of a "man of lawlessness," THE ANTICHRIST AND THE "MAN OF LAWLESSNESS ARE NOT THE SAME INDIVIDUAL! Again, a sloppy reading of the Bible coupled with popular teachings has kept us from answering a simple question: Where, in the entire corpus of Scripture, are we told that the Antichrist and "man of lawlessness" are one and the same? Nowhere. As we will see later, the Beast of Revelation and Paul's Man of Lawlessness in 2 Thessalonians 2 are described in very specific terms with very observable characteristics.

NONE OF THOSE CHARACTERISTICS ARE REMOTELY SIMILAR TO WHAT JOHN DESCRIBED AS THE SPIRIT OF ANTICHRIST OR THE ANTICHRIST.

The only possible reference in Paul's writings to the *spirit* of antichrist is found in 1 Timothy 4.

> *The Spirit clearly says that in later times some will* **abandon the faith and follow deceiving spirits and things taught by demons**. *Such teachings come through* **hypocritical liars**, *whose consciences have been seared as with a hot iron.* **They forbid people to marry and order them to abstain from certain foods**, *which God created to be received with thanksgiving by those who believe and who know the truth. For everything God created is good, and nothing is to be rejected if it is received with thanksgiving, because it is consecrated by the word of God and prayer. If you point these things out to the brothers and sisters, you will be a good minister of Christ Jesus, nourished on the truths of the faith and of the good teaching that you have followed.* **Have nothing to do with godless myths and old wives' tales;** *rather, train yourself to be godly. For physical training is of some value, but godliness has value for all things, holding promise for both the present life and the life to come. This is a trustworthy saying that deserves full acceptance. That is why we labor and strive, because we have put our hope in the living God, who is the Savior of all people, and especially of those who believe. Command and teach these things* (1 Timothy 4:1-11 emphasis added).

The connection between Paul's admonition to Timothy and the spirit of antichrist is not absolute. But Paul *does* suggest that these unorthodox teachings would come from those who were part of the church (they were *hypocrites*), and be built around godless myths and old wives tales. It sounds eerily similar to the kinds of things that pre-Gnostics like Cerinthus, Simon and Nicolas were teaching.

THE MAN OF LAWLESSNESS

According to Acts 17 and 18, Paul wrote to the Thessalonians from Corinth. In the early 50's (the best guess is in 52 A.D.) Paul shot off two back-to-back letters in the hopes of encouraging the fledgling believers in this Macedonian city. Paul's greatest opposition in Thessalonica came from Jews who came there to denounce the Gospel of the Kingdom (Acts 17:4-15). They even followed Paul to Berea, Athens and then Corinth, where they continued to instigate riots and civil unrest. Jewish resistance to Paul was so violent that he made a critical ministry decision at that point:

> *But when the Jews opposed Paul and became abusive, he shook out his clothes in protest and said to them, "Your blood be on your own heads! I am clear of my responsibility. From now on I will go to the Gentiles (Acts 18:6).*

This historical overview explains the passionate denunciation of the Jews included in both of Paul's letters to Thessalonica.

> *For you, brothers, became imitators of God's churches in Judea, which are in Christ Jesus: You suffered from your own countrymen the same things those churches suffered from the Jews, who killed the Lord Jesus and the prophets and also drove us out.*

> *They displease God and are hostile to all men in their effort to keep us from speaking to the Gentiles so that they may be saved. In this way they always heap up their sins to the limit. The wrath of God has come upon them at last* (1 Thessalonians 2:14-16 emphasis added).

Against this backdrop Paul penned some of his most pointed teaching regarding the "end times." In 2 Thessalonians Paul tried to comfort a church that was in the throes of persecution at the hands of the Jews. Rome still held to a policy of tolerance toward Christianity. Not so Judaism. Paul knew from personal experience in his life as "Saul" how the Jewish religious establishment felt about followers of Jesus of Nazareth. Paul bragged about how the Thessalonians were holding up under this persecution (2 Thessalonians 1:4). A large part of his comfort centered on the fact that God would not let those responsible for this persecution go unpunished. Those who remained faithful would be vindicated. That vindication would come in the form of God's judgment upon those who persecuted His Church, a judgment marked by the powerful and vengeful "day" of the Lord (2 Thessalonians 1:5-12). The persecution at the hands of the Jews was "proof" to Paul that this day was fast approaching.

> *All this is evidence that God's judgment is right, and as a result you will be counted worthy of the Kingdom of God, for which you are suffering. God is just: He will pay back trouble to those who trouble you and give relief to you who are troubled, and to us as well. This will happen when the Lord Jesus is* **revealed from heaven in blazing fire with his powerful angels.** *He will punish those who do not know God*

> *and do not obey the Gospel of our Lord Jesus. They will be punished with everlasting destruction and shut out **from the presence of the Lord and from the majesty of his power on the day he comes to be glorified in his holy people and to be marveled at among all those who have believed.** This includes you, because you believed our testimony to you* (2 Thessalonians 1:5-10 emphasis added).

It is easy to miss Paul's reference to who will share in the glory of that day—"this includes *you*." The Thessalonians would be vindicated, and they would share in Christ's glory, just as they would reflect Christ's glory. Unlike their persecutors, they had believed the testimony of Paul. Their belief guaranteed them a front row seat to Christ's marvelous display of both judgment and glory "when He comes."[48]

Paul's choice of words in verse 9 was taken directly from Isaiah 2. The expression "from the presence of the Lord and the majesty of his power" occured in only two places in Scripture—here and in Isaiah 2:10, 17-21.[49] On three

---

[48] The Greek here is difficult, making the English unclear. What group is it that the Thessalonians are "included" in--those who believed Paul's testimony, or those who will marvel on the "day he comes to be glorified in his holy people?" The Greek here favors the latter as Bruce and Stott argue. Neither Bruce nor Stott believe that Paul is speaking here of Christ's "judgment coming" in 70 A.D., but both agree that the original supports the idea that what the Thessalonians are being included in is the glory of that day. F.F. Bruce, *W.B.C. 1 & 2 Thessalonians* (Waco, TX: Word Books, 1982), pp. 152-155. John Stott, *The Gospel and the End of Time* (Downers Grove, IL: InterVaristy Press, 1991), pp. 147-150.

[49] Of course, the OT was written in Hebrew/Aramaic and the NT in Greek. But the OT was translated into Greek in a process that extended from the 3rd century B.C. to 132 B.C. NT writers and many of the early Church Fathers quoted directly from this translation of the OT.

different occassions, Isaiah used this phrase in describing the coming day of the Lord. The significance is that the Isaiah passage is referring specifically to the judgment of Judah and Jerusalem (Isaiah 2:1; 3:8). Paul's use of the very same and very rare expression is no accident. He understood that the day of the Lord spoken of in Isaiah was the same day that would see its fulfillment in Paul's lifetime. The great and terrible day of the Lord was almost upon them.

In 2 Thessalonians 2, Paul moved on to a specific problem—"the anxiety that the church in Thessalonica was feeling due to rumors that this "day of the Lord" had already come and gone (2 Thessalonians 2:1-2). That the Church feared such a possibility suggests that they felt such a thing was imminent. If they had been taught that "the day of the Lord" was still thousands of years off, they would hardly be rattled at suggestions that it had already come. In fact, many in the church were so confident that the day of the Lord was imminent that they had stopped working. "Why bother to work if our world will end within our lifetime?" Such a lackidasical attitude was just as troubling to Paul as the unfounded worries that the day of the Lord had already come. Paul urged those who were worrying to relax, and those who were idle to get to work (2 Thessalonians 3:6-15). In correcting both errors, Paul reminded the Thessalonians that he had already told them details regarding the day of the Lord (2 Thessalonians 2:5). What information was Paul referring to? How could Paul be so confident that if the Thessalonians would just think back to his earlier visit, they would easily be able to put the pieces together?

While the details of that earlier conversation are lost, *we can be quite certain that the earlier teaching that Paul was referring to was Paul's reiteration of Jesus' teaching in the Olivet Discourse.* As Paul summarized that earlier teaching in 2 Thessalonians 2, the language that he used and the topics he covered were strikingly similar to Jesus' words. As we have already shown, Matthew 24 was Jesus' explanation of the events preceding the eventual destruction of Jerusalem and Herod's Temple in 70 A.D. Paul was doing the same thing in 2 Thessalonians 2.

The immediate context of this epistle is the persecution of the saints. Christ specifically warned of this in Matthew 24: 9-11. Paul began 2 Thessalonians 2 by referring to the "coming" of the Lord and "our being gathered to Him…" Christ also explained that one of the features of His coming in judgment in 70 A.D. would be a great "gathering" of God's People (Matthew 24:31—Jesus and Paul use the identical Greek word; επισυναγω). This form of the word for "gather together" is only found in two places in all of Scripture; here and in the Olivet Discourse. In 2 Thessalonians 2:3, Paul mentioned a great "apostasy." In the same way Christ warned in Matthew 24:5 that many would be deceived and "apostosize." Jesus also warned that His disciples might be misled into thinking that Jesus had already returned (24:23-26). "Don't be fooled. Instead, look for the unmistakeable signs of My actual coming." This was precisely the same challenge that Paul was faced with—

> *Concerning the coming of our Lord Jesus Christ and our being gathered to him, we ask you, brothers,* **not to become easily unsettled or alarmed** *by some prophecy, report or letter supposed to have come from us, saying that* **the day of the Lord has already come** (2 Thessalonians 2:1-2, emphasis added).

Paul in 2 Thessaslonians, and Jesus in Matthew 24, Mark 13 and Luke 21, were describing the same event—the destruction of Jerusalem in 70 A.D.

In 2 Thessalonians 2:3, Paul spoke of the "man of lawlessness" and in 2:7 of the "power of lawlessness." In Matthew 24:12, Christ warned that there would be an increase in "lawlessness" in the last day (again, Christ and Paul used the identical Greek word). In 2 Thessalonians 2:4, Paul explained that this man would set himself up in God's Temple. Christ warned the disciples of the same thing in Matthew 24:15. Paul reminded the Thessalonians that the man of lawlessness would be overthrown at the glorious coming of the Lord which parallels Jesus' words in Matthew 24:30. Paul ended his "day of the Lord refresher course" by reminding the church that the coming of the Lawless One would be accompanied by "counterfeit miracles, signs and wonders..." In Matthew 24:23-24, Christ again used the identical Greek words to describe these "signs and wonders." Finally, Paul urged the Thessalonians to "stand firm" in 2:15, the very thing that Christ urged the disciples to do in Matthew 24:13.

It appears that Paul had a version of the Olivet Discourse in his hands as he initially taught the Thessalonians about that day. Even his brief review of that teaching in 2 Thessalonians 2 bears a striking resemblance to the words and teaching of Jesus in Matthew 24.

But what of this "man of lawlessness?" To whom is Paul referring. Apparently, this man already existed. He was "being held back" for now, but in the not too distant future, this restraint would be lifted and he would be revealed (2

Thessalonians 2:6). If the man of lawlessness was being restrained at the time Paul wrote this letter (51 to 52 A.D.), then Paul could not be referring to some person who would arise thousands of years later. AND THE THESSALONIANS ALREADY KNEW WHAT WAS HOLDING HIM BACK. *And now **you know what is holding him back**, so that he may be revealed at the proper time* (2 Thessalonians 2:6). Just like the "spirit of antichrist" which John indicated was at work during his own lifetime, Paul told them that "the secret power of lawlessness" was *already at work* (v.7). In addressing the concern that they might have missed the "coming of our Lord Jesus Christ" (2 Thessalonians 2:1), Paul does not respond by saying, "We know that the secret rapture must occur first, and we know that after that there must be a seven year period of tribulation, and *then* we will witness the coming of our Lord."

Instead, Paul assured the Thessalonians that they had not missed this coming of Jesus. He reminded them that two things had to happen before that event: first, the "rebellion" needed to occur, and second, the "man of lawlessness" had to be revealed (2 Thessalonians 2:3). Why would Paul remind them of what to look for if they would remain completely unaffected by those events? Why not just say "Relax. You didn't miss it because you will be dead and gone long before that happens?" It is more likely that Paul gave them specific instructions to be on the lookout for the great rebellion and the man of lawlessness because these events would occur in their lifetime and directly affect them.

The Great Rebellion

The NIV translates the word "$\alpha\pi o\sigma\tau\alpha\sigma\iota\alpha$" as "rebellion," pointing to the fact that the word can mean either a political or a religious uprising. Before the great day of the Lord, Paul explained that there would be just such a rebellion. He is referring to the great Jewish Revolt which precipitated the invasion of Israel by Rome beginning in 66 A.D. Josephus noted that the aspirations of the Jews in relation to Rome included hopes of a "revolt-$\alpha\pi o\sigma\tau\alpha\sigma\iota\alpha$." Later, some of the religious leaders in Jerusalem tried to dissuade dissidents and their followers from pursing a "revolt-$\alpha\pi o\sigma\tau\alpha\sigma\iota\alpha$" against Rome.[50] The New Jerusalem Bible translation actually uses the word, "Great Revolt." It was this rebellion against Rome that Paul had in mind. This rebellion would then set in motion the events that would reveal the "man of lawlessness." But what of the identity of this man? If he is not the same person as the Antichrist, who was he? There are very good reasons to believe that "the man of lawlessness" that Paul spoke of in 2 Thessalonians 2:1-12 was Titus, the general who destroyed Jerusalem and the Temple, and who later became the 11th emperor of Rome.

The Man Of Lawlessness Revealed

There are two possibilities why Paul did not simply say, "the man of lawlessness is Titus." It is possible that Paul did not want to unnecessarily incur the wrath of Rome. Titus was alive at the time Paul wrote. But at only 13 years of age, his future was still uncertain. The likelihood that Paul might have felt the fallout from "outing" the young Titus is unlikely. In addition, The Jewish Revolt was still fourteen years away. More probable is that Paul simply did not know the exact identity of the man of lawlessness. What he did know was made plain in *the text:*

---

[50] Kenneth L. Gentry Jr., *The Man of Lawlessness*, Covenant Media Foundation. http://www.cmfnow.com/articles/pt550.htm.

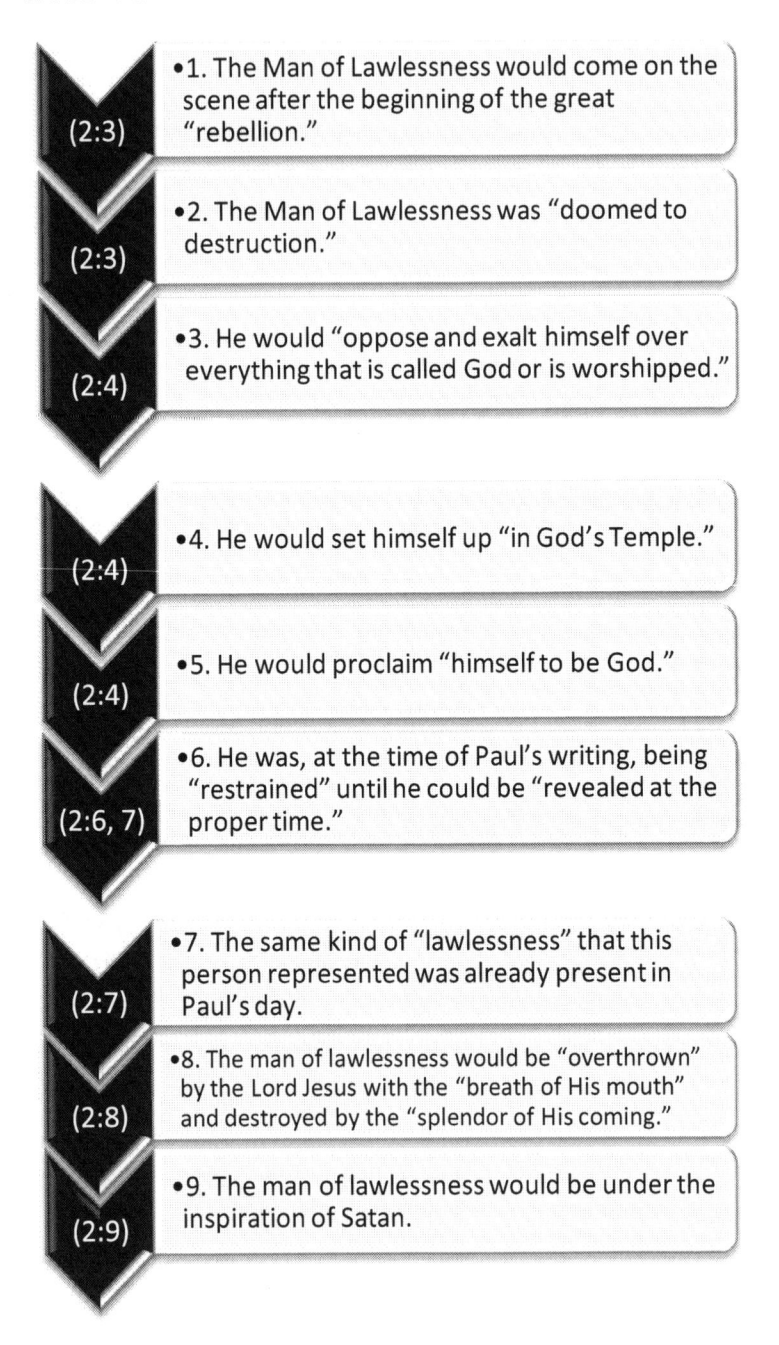

- (2:3) •1. The Man of Lawlessness would come on the scene after the beginning of the great "rebellion."
- (2:3) •2. The Man of Lawlessness was "doomed to destruction."
- (2:4) •3. He would "oppose and exalt himself over everything that is called God or is worshipped."
- (2:4) •4. He would set himself up "in God's Temple."
- (2:4) •5. He would proclaim "himself to be God."
- (2:6, 7) •6. He was, at the time of Paul's writing, being "restrained" until he could be "revealed at the proper time."
- (2:7) •7. The same kind of "lawlessness" that this person represented was already present in Paul's day.
- (2:8) •8. The man of lawlessness would be "overthrown" by the Lord Jesus with the "breath of His mouth" and destroyed by the "splendor of His coming."
- (2:9) •9. The man of lawlessness would be under the inspiration of Satan.

> **(2:9, 10)** • 10. The coming of the man of lawlessness would be accompanied by "all kinds of counterfeit miracles, signs and wonders, and in every sort of evil that deceives those who are perishing."

Does Titus fit the bill? Indeed, he does. We will examine each expectation in order.

1. The single event that vaulted Titus to both power and prominence was the Jewish "Rebellion" of 66 A.D. Vespasian, Titus' father was dispatched to Judea, where he was joined by his son who brought with him the 15th Legion to help put down the revolt.[51] Titus' political ascendency occurred in direct relationship to this Rebellion.

2. Titus' reign as emperor was short by any standard. He ruled from 79-81 A.D. when he was poisoned by his brother, Domitian. Titus could not have known that he was marked for "destruction" not long after his reign began.

3. Upon entering the soon to be destroyed Temple, The Babylonian Talmud records the following regarding Titus: "Vespasian sent Titus who said, 'Where is their God, the rock in whom they trusted?' This was the wicked Titus who blasphemed and insulted Heaven."[52] With words like these, Titus opposed and exalted himself above everything that is called God.

---

[51] Josephus, *War of the Jews*. 3.4.2., pp. 769-770.

[52] As quoted in Duncan McKenzie, *The Man of Lawlessness, Part Two: The Falling Away*, p. 13 http://planetpreterist.com/content/man-lawlessness-part-two

4. The only "leader" of note who actually entered the Temple was Titus himself. While the Roman troops were actually hesitant to enter the Temple for fear of angering the Jewish God, it was Titus who urged them on.[53]

5. The cult of Emperor Worship played a much more important role in the development of first-century Christianity than what was once believed. Titus, like the emperors before and after him, was not disinclined to be worshipped as god.[54] Josephus recorded "*and now the Romans, upon the flight of the seditious into the city, and upon the burning of the holy house itself, and of all the buildings round about it, brought their ensigns to the Temple, and set them over against its easter gate; and there did they offer sacrifices to them, and there did they make Titus imperator (sovereign).*"[55] In short, Titus declared himself to be God.

6. The restrainer of which Paul spoke may well have been the emperor Nero. The war against the Jews, which began in 66 A.D. was suspended for a season (during which many Christians, acting upon Jesus' encouragement to "flee" actually left Jerusalem) due to the suicide of Nero. His unexpected death threw the entire empire into a panic. Many believed that the empire would collapse, as the last of

---

[53] Dio Cassius, *Roman History*. 15.6.2. Loeb Classical Library, 9 volumes, Greek texts and facing English translation: Harvard University Press, 1914 thru 1927. Translation by Earnest Cary. E-Version.

[54] *Kykeon, Studies in Honour of H.S. Versnel*, Ed. H.F.J. Horstmanshoff, H.W. Singor, F.T. Van Straten & J.H.M. Strubbe (Leiden-Boston-Koln: Brill Publications, 2002) "*The Apocalypse of John and the Imperial Cult*" by Henk Jan De Jonge, pp. 127-141 provides an excellent rethinking of the significance of the cult, especially as it relates to Revelation.

[55] Josephus, *The Wars of the Jews*, 6.6.1. p. 891.

the Julio-Claudian line of emperors had passed. Civil wars erupted as numerous candidates vied for the throne. Nero's death opened the door to a new line of emperors, the Flavian Dynasty. After three short-lived attempts at rule (Galba, Otho and Vitellius), Vespasian took the throne, proclaiming his son, Titus, as the next emperor. Another possibility regarding the identity of the "restrainer" is that God Himself, through the operation of an angelic prince, was holding Titus back until the "proper time." Regardless of who the restrainer was, the point is that Titus could not fill his role as the man of lawlessness until God sovereignly engineered his ascendency.

7. History records that an earlier emperor, Caligula (31-41 A.D.) had made plans to erect a statue of himself in the Temple in 41 A.D. On January 24 of 41 A.D., Caligula was assassinated by a group of conspirators, thus halting his blasphemous efforts. This may well have been behind the meaning of Paul's suggestion that the "power" of lawlessness was already at work (2 Thessaslonians 2:7). If the "lawlessness" of which Paul spoke was the common practice of Emperor worship, this too would make sense. (Cf. # 5 above and corresponding footnote for details on the role the cult played in the Empire) The fact that Caligula's efforts were foiled is another clear sign of the sovereignty of God. Titus had been "ordained" as the "man doomed to destruction" (2 Thessalonians 2:3). Not even Caligula's vanity and the power of the Emperor were enough to alter God's reserving of that role for Titus.

8. How was Titus "destroyed" by Christ's judgment-coming in 70 A.D.? He clearly lived to September 13, 81 A.D. McKenzie has rightly observed that the word for "destroyed" suggests a loss of "well being" not a loss of being. "The

parousia (coming) of Jesus, 'the manifestation of His presence' (2 Thessalonians 2:8 YLT), did not kill Titus; rather, it rendered useless the demonic forces working through him. This is similar to how Jesus' death on the cross did not put an end to Satan's existence, it destroyed his power."[56] The same word for "destroyed" is used in Hebrews 2:14: *Since the children have flesh and blood, he too shared in their humanity so that by his death he might **destroy** him who holds the power of death—that is, the devil.* In a very real sense, the demonic forces that empowered Titus were "destroyed" in this sense at Jesus' 70 A.D. coming.

9. An observable difference came over Titus after the destruction of Jerusalem and his ascendency to the throne. Initially, his contemporaries feared the worst from him. To suggest that he was under the inspiration of Satan or some other demonic presence in the years surrounding the razing of Jerusalem is not far-fetched. *Besides cruelty, he was also suspected of riotous living, since he protracted his revels until the middle of the night with the most prodigal of his friends; likewise of unchastity because of his troops of catamites and eunuchs, and his notorious passion for queen Berenice, to whom it was even said that he promised marriage. He was suspected of greed as well; for it was well known that in cases which came before his father he put a price on his influence and accepted bribes. In short, people not only thought, but openly declared, that he would be a second Nero.*[57] In fact, Titus went on to become a well-loved and virtuous emperor, albeit for only a

---

[56] Duncan McKenzie, "The Man of Lawlessness, Part Three: The Destruction of the Antichrist." http://planetpreterist.com/content/man-lawlessness-part-three-destruction-antichrist.

[57] Suetonius, *The Lives of Twelve Caesars*, Life of Titus 7. P. 330. Loeb Classical Library edition, 1913-1914. University of Chicago, E-Version.

short time. This "change" came about *after* his triumphal return to Rome in 70 A.D. This supports the idea that the animating evil spirit that "posessed" him was "destroyed" in 70 A.D. at the coming of Christ.

10. The Roman historians Tacitus and Suetonius, as well as Josephus, recount numerous "miracles" performed by Titus' father, Vespasian.[58] In trying to convince his countrymen to surrender to Rome, Josephus appealed to the fact that Titus' presence was also attended by miracles.[59] The text of 2 Thessalonians does not demand that the man of lawlessness *himself* would perform miracles, only that his arrival would be attended by such counterfeit signs. There is no question that this was the case as it related to Titus.

In every way, the particulars of what Paul described as "the man of lawlessness" find their historical fulfillment in Titus Flavius Caesar Vespasianus Augustus, the eleventh emperor of Rome. The Antichrist that John described bears no resemblance to the man of lawlessness. As we will see, the Beast of Revelation, often conflated with the Antichrist, is actually a third person, distinct from both the man of lawlessness and the Antichrist.

The Beast Of Revelation

Everything that John had to say about "the Beast" is found in Revelation 13 and 17. As we parse these chapters, we discover several things about the Beast. First, the Beast is sometimes referred to generally as a place.

---

[58] Tacitus, *The Histories*, 1.10; Suetonius, The Twelve Caesars, Vespasian, 7.

[59] Josephus, *The Wars of the Jews*, 5.9.4. pp. 860-861.

> *Then the angel carried me away in the Spirit into a wilderness. There I saw a woman sitting on a scarlet beast that was covered with blasphemous names and had seven heads and ten horns... "This calls for a mind with wisdom. The seven heads are seven hills on which the woman sits* (Revelation 17:3,9).

Few places in the ancient world were as well known for their topographical distinctives as Rome. Forming the geographic heart of the city are seven hills: Aventine Hill, Caelian Hill, Capitoline Hill, Esquiline Hill, Palatine Hill, Quirinal Hill, and Viminal Hill. They have all figured prominently in Roman history, mythology, politics and religion. The annual festival *Septimonteum*, referenced by the Roman historians Seutonius and Plutarch, means feast of "the seven-hilled city." Both Christian and Roman authors referred to Rome as the city of seven hills, including Virgil, Horace, Ovid, Jerome and Tertullian. During the reign of Emperor Vespasian (69-79 A.D.), coins were minted depicting the goddess *Roma* as a woman seated on seven hills. Rome was universally recognized as the ancient city of seven hills, and there is no reason to believe that John intended his readers to think otherwise.

In addition to this general reference to the Beast as a city, John also made a general reference to the Beast as a Kingdom. In Revelation 17:9-10, John wrote:

> *This calls for a mind with wisdom. The seven heads are seven hills on which the woman sits. They are also seven kings. Five have fallen, one is, the other has not yet come; but when he does come, he must remain for only a little while.*

These "seven kings" represented a Kingdom, the capital city of which we can assume was the city "of seven hills." If the city was Rome, then surely the Kingdom of which John spoke was the Roman Empire. These seven kings or emperors appeared chronologically: five of them had already reigned, one was currently (at the time of John's writing) reigning, and the seventh was still coming, and he would reign for only a short time. But in the very same context that John identified the Beast as a city and a Kingdom, he also identified the Beast as a person. Who is this person? Here is a summary of what we can glean from Revelation 13 and 17.

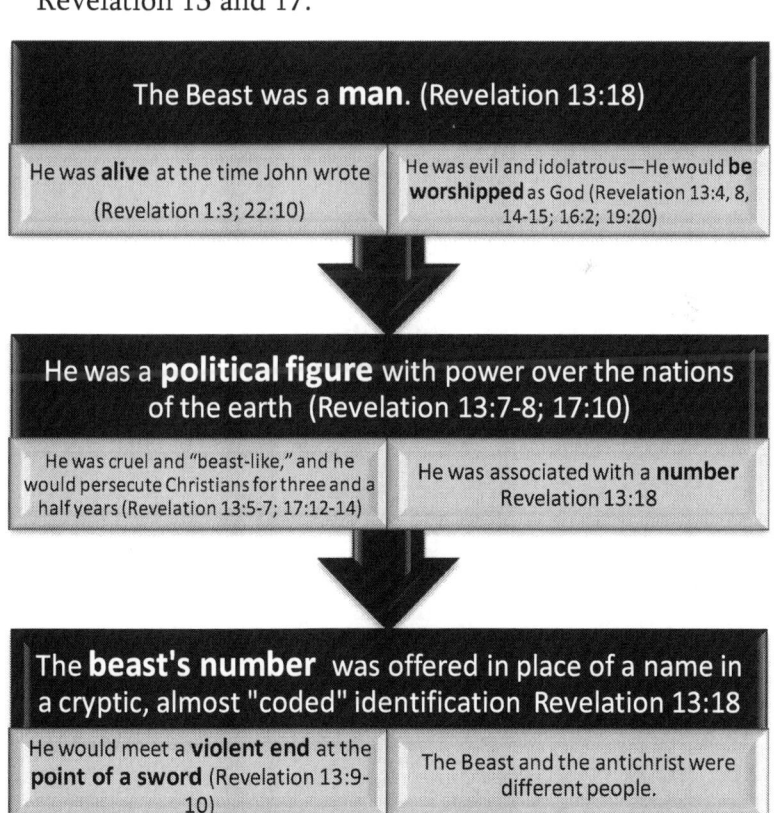

The Beast was a man. (Revelation 13:18)

| He was **alive** at the time John wrote (Revelation 1:3; 22:10) | He was evil and idolatrous—He would **be worshipped** as God (Revelation 13:4, 8, 14-15; 16:2; 19:20) |

⬇

He was a political figure with power over the nations of the earth (Revelation 13:7-8; 17:10)

| He was cruel and "beast-like," and he would persecute Christians for three and a half years (Revelation 13:5-7; 17:12-14) | He was associated with a **number** Revelation 13:18 |

⬇

The **beast's number** was offered in place of a name in a cryptic, almost "coded" identification Revelation 13:18

| He would meet a **violent end** at the **point of a sword** (Revelation 13:9-10) | The Beast and the antichrist were different people. |

Was there a first century candidate that met these criteria? There was, and he was none other than Nero Claudius Drusus Germanicus, more commonly known as the Roman Emperor Nero (A.D. 15-A.D. 68).

The Beast Was A Man

John was writing to a specific people (Revelation 1:4, 19-20) and he was writing timely encouragement to those suffering under severe persecution (Revelation 1:9; 2:3). John's message to every church was that they should persevere, and in so doing "overcome" the seemingly overwhelming odds against them (2:7, 11, 17, 26; 3: 5, 12, 21). The Revelation that he recorded was information that would directly affect their lives. He told them again and again that these things would happen soon, in their lifetime. With church members on the edge of their pews, John alerted his readers to the coming of "a man." *This calls for wisdom. Let the person who has insight calculate the number of the beast, for it is the number of **a man**. That number is 666* (Revelation 13:18 emphasis added).

John's conscious omission of a definite article is correctly translated in virtually every English translation. John was not speaking generically—he was not providing information that was intended to broaden possible interpretations, he was intentionally limiting speculation to a single individual. The Beast was "a man."

The Beast was Alive in John's Day

Given John's emphatic insistence that the contents of Revelation pertained to the immediate future, any attempt to identify the Beast as someone outside the first century is misguided. It simply defies a clear, straightforward reading of the text to suggest otherwise. What sense would it make for John to provide the seven churches with insight and encouragement that he intended only for people living thousands of years in the future?

In addition, John lists the "seven" heads or "kings" in Revelation 17:10. We already know that the Beast, identified generally, is Rome, and the Roman Empire. Although we will detail the meaning of this chronology in a later section, it is clear that John referred to the sixth king as one "who is." The use of the present tense makes it clear that, from John's perspective, the Beast was alive as John wrote Revelation.

The Beast Would Be Worshipped

The cult of emperor worship began with the very first emperor, Julius Caesar. He was given the title of "Jupiter," the highest honor that could be afforded a human. An image of Julius Caesar was placed in the Temple of Quirinius with the inscription "To the invincible God." Upon his death, the Roman Senate decreed that he be referred to as "divine Julius." Each successive emperor was accorded divine status, both by decree and by the will of the people. Archeologists have discovered Temples, inscriptions, statues, and coins, all deifying each emperor.[60] Of particular note is the strength of the cult of emperor worship in the very cities to which John addressed Revelation. There were Temples, priesthoods, ceremonies, and games for the emperor cult in

---

[60] Kurt Aland, *A History of Christianity* (Philadelphia: Fortress Press, 1985) 1:18-19

all seven of the cities addressed in Revelation 2 and 3. "Ephesus alone had at least five Temples and shrines for the imperial cult before the end of the first century CE. Pergamum had two famous Temples for the imperial cult. In 29 B.C.E it was the first city of Asia to receive authorization from Octavian to establish a provincial cult and Temple for Rome and the emperor."[61] Ephesus, Smyrna, Pergamum and Sardis were part of the rotation of cities where annual meetings were held by provincial councils which were tasked with organizing the imperial cult.[62]

It should come as no surprise that Nero engaged in the same practice. In fact, Nero's vanity and self-aggrandizement took the cult to a new high. Second only to Jupiter (Zeus), the greatest god in the Roman pantheon was Apollos. The Roman historian Seutonius noted that "since he (Nero) was acclaimed as the equal of Apollo in music and of the Sun in driving a chariot, he had planned to emulate the exploits of Hercules as well."[63] In Ancient Athens, an inscription was discovered describing him as "the all powerful Nero Ceasar Sebastos, a new Apollo."[64]

---

[61] Henk Jan De Jonge, *The Apocalypse of John and The Imperial Cult*, in *Kykeon: Studies in Honour of H.S. Versnel*, pp. 132-133.

[62] Ibid., p. 133.

[63] Suetonius, *The Lives of the 12 Caesars*, Nero, Trans. Alexander Thomson p. 53

[64] Mary E. Smallwood, *Documents Illustrating the Principates Gaius Claudius and Nero* (Cambridge University Press, 1967) p. 52

The Greeks went so far as to confer upon Nero the title: "Zeus, Our Liberator."[65]

Numerous coins were minted during Nero's reign depicting him as Apollos in a variety of poses, while on others, his crown radiated like the sun. A statue of Nero was erected in the Temple of Mars in Rome, which Tacitus noted was of equal size to the statue of Mars himself.[66] As Nero's narcissistic tendencies increased, he began to confer deity upon relatives, including ex-wives and children. Even foreign dignitaries were required to worship Nero, conferring upon him the titles of "my god," my Fate" and "my Fortune."[67] That Nero demanded and received worship as a god is beyond dispute.

The Beast Was A Political Figure

The Beast was identified as a king, with power over all the peoples of the earth. No king living in the first century could make such a boast, save one: The Roman Emperor. John gave us another clue as to the identity of the Beast by tracking his rise to power. We are told, *"This calls for a mind with wisdom. The seven heads are seven hills on which the woman sits. They are also seven kings. Five have fallen, one is, the other has not yet come; but when he does come, he must remain for only a little while"* (Revelation 17:9-10). Does Nero match John's chronology?

---

[65] Arthur Weigall, *Nero; Emperor of Rome* (London: Thornton Butterworth, 1933), p. 276

[66] Tacitus, *Annals*, 13:8:11

[67] Dio Cassius, *Roman History* 62:5:2.

WILL THE REAL ANTICHRIST PLEASE STAND UP

John's call for "wisdom" is a simple matter of mathematics. The line of Romans emperors was as follows:

Julius Caesar	49-44 B.C.
Augustus	31-14 B.C.
Tiberius	14 B.C.-37 A.D.
Caligula	37-41 A.D.
Claudius	41-54 A.D.
Nero	54-68 A.D.
Galba (11 Months)	68-69 A.D.

Artist's rendering of the Colossus of the Sun and the Flavian Amphitheater. Described by Nero as a "self-portrait," the image rose nearly 90 feet into the air. Of the image itself nothing survives, but it is known from illustrations on imperial coins minted by Alexander Severus and Gordianus III.

It is important to note that Nero was the last emperor from the Julio-Claudian line. Rome's ruling blood-line of the Caesars, the group that had birthed, bred and steadied the greatest empire on earth had been extinguished. The resulting political upheaval was unprecedented. The mad dash to fill this political vacuum resulted in horrific civil wars and catastrophic political unrest. This explains why the seventh emperor, Galba, remained "for only a little while." His reign lasted less than eleven months. As this simple chronology illustrates, Nero fell in line with exactly what John had predicted. This also gives great support to the idea that the Beast was already alive in John's lifetime. He was the king who "is." In fact, the Beast/Nero was the Roman emperor when John wrote the book of Revelation.[68]

THE BEAST: FIERCE PERSECUTOR OF CHRISTIANS FOR 42 MONTHS

John's choice of the word "beast" to describe Nero was apt. When used figuratively to describe persons, the Greek word *therion-θεριον* means a person with a "bestial nature, a beast or monster."[69] Drawing upon the imagery of Daniel (Daniel 7), John's Beast is a composite of several carnivores that stalk and devour their prey: *The beast I saw resembled a leopard, but had feet like those of a bear and a mouth like that of a lion* (Revelation 13:2a).

Both Nero's contemporaries and later historians assigned to him all the characteristics of a beast. Seutonius,

---

[68] The question of when the book of Revelation was written is enormously important. This debate will be taken up later in more detail.

[69] Arndt-Gingrich, *Lexicon*, p. 361.

one of Nero's biographers recorded that "*Although at first his acts of wantonness, lust, extravagance, avarice and cruelty were gradual and secret, and might be condoned as follies of youth, yet even then their nature was such that no one doubted that they were defects of his character and not due to his time of life. No sooner was twilight over than he would catch up a cap or a wig and go to the taverns or range about the streets playing pranks, which however were very far from harmless; for he used to beat men as they came home from dinner, stabbing any who resisted him and throwing them into the sewers. He would even break into shops and rob them, setting up a market in the Palace, where he divided the booty which he took, sold it at auction, and then squandered the proceeds.*"[70]

An unabashed bisexual, Nero engaged in every conceivable kind of sexual deviance. His excesses were again described by Seutonius: "*He so prostituted his own chastity that after defiling almost every part of his body, he at last devised a kind of game, in which, covered with the skin of some wild animal, he was let loose from a cage and attacked the private parts of men and women, who were bound to stakes, and when he had sated his mad lust, was dispatched by his freedman Doryphorus.*"[71]

That Nero was notorious for executing family and friends alike is a matter or record—his mother, aunt, brother, wife (kicked to death while pregnant because she had scolded him for coming home late from the chariot races), political

---

[70] Seutonius, Nero. p. 130

[71] Ibid, p. 134.

rivals, political allies, senators, servants, lovers, and more, all felt the wrath of Nero who *"showed neither discrimination nor moderation in putting to death whomsoever he pleased on any pretext whatever."*[72] Countless other Roman writers confirm the tyrannical evil of Nero, including Pliny the Elder and Tacitus. Little wonder that the well-traveled Apollonius of Tyana, who died in A.D. 96 wrote, *"I have seen many, many wild beasts of Arabia and India; but this beast, that is commonly called a Tyrant, I know not how many heads it has, nor if it be crooked of claw, and armed with horrible fangs...and of wild beasts you cannot say that they were ever known to eat their own mother, but Nero has gorged himself on this diet."*[73]

As violent and cruel as the excesses of Nero were, he reserved his greatest aggression for the Church. Clement of Rome, a contemporary of John, observed that Nero's persecution of Christians took the lives of "a vast number of the elect...through many indignities and tortures."[74] The church father Eusebius (A.D. 260-340) confirmed that Nero was *"the first of the emperors who showed himself an enemy of the divine religion"*[75] The early church historian Sulpicius Severas (A.D. 360-420) added that Nero was *"the basest of all men, and even of wild beasts...he showed himself in every way most abominable and cruel...he first attempted to*

---

[72] Ibid. p. 154.

[73] Philostratus, Life of Apollonius, p. 438. *Loeb Classical Library*, translation by F.C. Conybeare, 1912. E-Version, Livius.org.

[74] 1 Clement 6:1

[75] Eusebius, *Ecclesiastical History* 2:25: 3

abolish the name of Christian."[76] History is replete, from both Christian and non-Christian sources alike regarding the ferocity of the Neronic persecution of Christians.[77] The most devastating outcome of this persecution was the loss of two of the church's greatest leaders. *"He (Nero,) was the first at Rome to torture and inflict the penalty of death upon Christians, and he ordered them throughout all the provinces to be afflicted with like persecution; and in his attempt to wipe out the very name, he killed the most blessed apostles of Christ, Peter and Paul."*[78]

While Christianity had been tolerated from the reigns of Tiberius to Claudius, Nero embarked on a concerted campaign to stamp out this new religion. This stunning reversal of the empire's position must have shocked the early Church. In the context of this new wave of persecution, the message of Revelation was desperately needed for the first-century believers.

Perhaps the greatest argument for Nero being the Beast of Revelation is the length of the Neronic persecution. In John's vision we are told

> *The beast was given a mouth to utter proud words and blasphemies **and to exercise its authority for forty-two months**. It opened its mouth to blaspheme God, and to slander his name and his dwelling place and those who*

---

[76] Sulpicius Severus, *Sacred History* 2:28, 29 Translated by Alexander Roberts. From Nicene and Post-Nicene Fathers, Second Series, Vol. 11. E-Version, newadvent.org.

[77] The most detailed of these accounts is provided by Tacitus, *Annals*, 1544.

[78] Paulus Orosius, (early 5th century A.D.) *The Seven Books of History Against the Pagans*, (Washington DC, Catholic University Press: 1964), 7:7 E-Version, Questia.com.

> *live in heaven. It was given power to wage war against God's holy people and to conquer them* (Revelation 13:5-7a).

Following the great fire of A.D. 64, which consumed much of the capital city, rumors arose that Nero himself had set the fire. In an attempt to throw off suspicion, Nero fingered Christians as the culprits. Not long after the fire, which began on July 19, Nero began "damage control" and, until his death on June 9, A.D. 68, used Christians as scapegoats. More detail is provided by church historian Mosheim: "*The dreadful persecution which took place by order of this tyrant, commenced at Rome about the middle of November, in the year of our Lord 64. . . . This dreadful persecution ceased but with the death of Nero. The empire, it is well known, was not delivered from the tyranny of this monster until the year 68, when he put an end to his own life.*"[79] Almost to the day, this represents a period of three-and-a-half years, or forty-two months.

The Beast Is Associated With A Number

The number "6" in Roman numerals is made up of the letters, "VI". The ancient Greek number "6" was taken from the sixth letter of their alphabet, the letter "sigma" which looks like the English letter "s." Returning to the Babylonian empire and their sexagesimal system of numbers, the [computer] programmer considered that the possibility that their letter "A' equaled 6. Thus, from the three great world empires of history, he found that the composition of the number "666" spells the word VISA –

---

[79] Mosheim, *Historical Commentaries*, 1:138,139. As quoted in Kenneth L. Gentry Jr., *The Beast of Revelation*, Second Printing (Tyler, Texas: Institute for Christian Economics, 1994), p. 62.

the exact name of today's most accepted and popular credit card"[80]

It is widely accepted among historians that Nero never used cash, only plastic. As a part of his plan to establish a new world order, he insisted that Discover and MasterCard be abolished and...OK. I just couldn't resist. Attempts on the part of others to make something of John's reference to the number 666 are often humorous—hysterical even (as the actual above quotation illustrates). I'm not trying to put down an individual; I'm simply trying to make a point: ***it's easy to get a little crazy when we don't employ sound hermeneutics and careful exegesis.*** It is safe to say that John's reference to the number of the Beast had nothing to do with VISA (or the Pope, or Ronald Reagan or Mikal Gorbachev or Barak Obama). What does this cryptic message mean?

In the ancient world, there was no system for enumerating things. For this reason, the alphabets of most cultures served a dual purpose; phonetic symbols and numbers. We've all been frustrated trying to figure out when a movie was released or an older book printed because of the use of Roman numerals. At the very least, we know that I = 1, V = 5, X = 10, and so on. Both the Greek and Hebrew alphabets use a similar system. Each letter corresponds to a number.

---

[80] Jack Van Impe, 11:59 and Counting, pp. 106-107.

WINSOME WARRIORS

Greek Letter/Number Equivalents

1	α	alpha	10	ι	iota	100	ρ	rho
2	β	beta	20	κ	kappa	200	σ	sigma
3	γ	gamma	30	λ	lambda	300	τ	tau
4	δ	delta	40	μ	mu	400	υ	upsilon
5	ε	epsilon	50	ν	nu	500	φ	phi
6	ϛ	vau*	60	ξ	xi	600	χ	chi
7	ζ	zeta	70	ο	omicron	700	ψ	psi
8	η	eta	80	π	pi	800	ω	omega
9	θ	theta	90	ϟ	koppa*	900	ϡ	sampi

Hebrew Letter/Number Equivalents

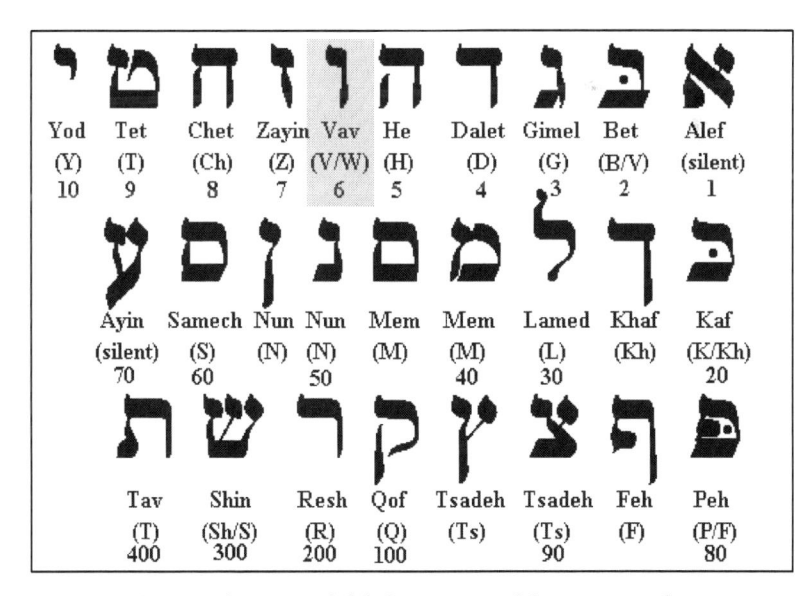

Yod	Tet	Chet	Zayin	Vav	He	Dalet	Gimel	Bet	Alef
(Y)	(T)	(Ch)	(Z)	(V/W)	(H)	(D)	(G)	(B/V)	(silent)
10	9	8	7	6	5	4	3	2	1

Ayin	Samech	Nun	Nun	Mem	Mem	Lamed	Khaf	Kaf
(silent)	(S)	(N)	(N)	(M)	(M)	(L)	(Kh)	(K/Kh)
70	60		50		40	30		20

Tav	Shin	Resh	Qof	Tsadeh	Tsadeh	Feh	Peh
(T)	(Sh/S)	(R)	(Q)	(Ts)	(Ts)	(F)	(P/F)
400	300	200	100		90		80

Given the two-fold function of letters in the ancient world, coded messages were often put in the form of numbers that represented letters. In Greek culture this is known as

251

isopsephia, and in Hebrew culture, it is called *gimatriya*. Coded messages were not foreign to the early church. Although not *isopsephia*, the now popular "fish" symbol (you know, the one you have on the back of your car) was actually a coded symbol known as an *acronym*. The Greek word for "fish" is "ixthus" or ἸΧΘΥΣ: taking the first letter of each of the words in the phrase "Jesus Christ, God's Son, Savior." (Ἰησοῦς Χριστός Θεοῦ Υἱός Σωτήρ) spells out the word for fish. Archeologists have discovered many instances where this symbol was strategically placed on buildings or caves to identify it as a safe place for Christians.

The practice of *isopsephia* and *gimatriya* was also common. A later Christian work known as the Sibylline Oracles (circa 150 A.D.) included this riddle:

When the virgin shall give birth to the Word of God the Most High, she shall give to the Word a Name, and from the east a star will shine in the midst of day gleaming down from heaven above proclaiming to mortal men a great sign. Yes, then shall the Son of the Great God come to men, clothed in flesh like mortals on earth. He has four vowels and in him, twofold the consonants ... and now I will declare to you the whole number ... eight monads, and to these as many decads, and eight hundreds his name will show.

To solve the riddle, the numeric value of all the letters in the name have to add up to 8 + 80 + 800. That same name must consist of 4 vowels and two consonants. The Greek spelling of "Jesus" is the answer:

Jesus = (In Greek) *Ιησous* = 10+8+200+70+400+200 or 888 (4 vowels; i,e,o,u and two consonants; s and s)

Among Jews, the practice of *gimatriya* was and still is popular. In Jewish culture, for example, the number seven figures prominently. It is a number associated with God, creation, and blessing. The Hebrew word *mazal* (מָזֹל) totals the number 77. Even today, you will hear Jews congratulate or toast one another with the words "*mazal tov*" or "good blessing." It is literally a blessing that calls for God's presence to abide with that person from that moment forward. In addition to being a blessing, its numeric value also carries with it an "extra" or hidden blessing, seven "two times over."

John's use of this practice should not surprise us. In order for the Beast to be Nero, his name must total the number six-hundred-sixty-six. John does not simply repeat the number "six" three times. Some have argued that John is using the number six, often associated with an anti-God value (one before seven) as a way of saying that the Beast is sinful and against God three times over. While this would be an appropriate way to describe the likes of Nero, there is no question that John wrote the full numeric value of six-hundred-sixty-six.

In the original text, John wrote that number in Greek. A quick tally of the numeric value of Nero's name with a Greek valuation totals 1005. But John was a Jew, writing to churches consisting of Jews. In fact, Revelation is regarded as one of the most "Jewish" books of the New Testament. A careful examination of the original Greek text of Revelation reveals that while John "writes in Greek, he thinks in

Hebrew."[81] We know from recent archeology that the Hebrew spelling of Nero's name was Nrwn Qsr (pronounced "Neron Kaiser) or "Nero Caesar."[82] This would make the Hebrew numeric valuation of Nero's name as follows:

נ = 50 ר = 200 ו = 6 נ = 50 ק = 100 ס = 60 ר = 200

thus:

נרון קסר = 666

The Solution To The Secret

Why wouldn't John just come out and say, "The Beast is Nero?" Why would John, writing in Greek, expect his readers to translate the number of the Beast into Hebrew? Why not just identify the Beast's number as 1005 so everyone could figure it out? Because John was no fool. Imagine you were living in say, North Korea at the time of this writing (2011). Kim Jong-il is the current dictator of that country. He wields power much like a Roman emperor would. Now imagine sitting at your computer in Pyongyang and posting on your blog that the President of Korea is the spawn of Satan and is soon to be destroyed for his beastly behavior and persecution of Christians. As fast as you can say "gulag" you would be arrested and never seen again. Is it not fair to assume that John took his Master's admonition to heart to be as "innocent as a dove" and as "shrewd as a snake?"

---

[81] R.H. Charles, *A Critical and Exegetical Commentary on the Revelation of Saint John*, 2 Volumes. (Edinburgh: T.& T. Clark, 1920). p. cxliii.

[82] D.R. hillers, "Revelation 13:18 and a Scroll from Murabba'at," *Bulletin of the American Schools of Oriental Research* 170 (April, 1963): 65.

We know that Paul, on more than one occasion, used his Roman citizenship to get out of a jam (Acts 21:27-26:32). This in no way impugns the integrity or faithfulness of Paul. Ultimately, his unwillingness to deny Christ, coupled with his high profile in the early Church, cost him his life at the hands of Nero. But Paul was unwilling to *unnecessarily* incur the wrath of Rome. John, already on Nero's "Most Wanted" list, would soon be exiled to the island of Patmos where he received the vision recorded in Revelation (Revelation 1:9). Rather than stir the pot and suffer immediate fallout, John referred to Nero in this cryptic way. While every educated person in John's day knew Greek, very few non-Jews knew Hebrew. This greatly reduced the likelihood that John would be "outed" as speaking ill of the emperor. John was eager to inform the saints without needlessly attracting the bad intentions of the Roman king. Even the great Saint Augustine recognized this dilemma. Commenting on Paul's remark in 2 Thessalonians 2:7 that "lawlessness" was already present, he wrote: *"What means the declaration, that the mystery of iniquity already works?... Some suppose this to be spoken of the Roman emperor, and therefore Paul did not speak in plain words, because he would not incur the charge of calumny for having spoken evil of the Roman emperor."*[83] John, like Paul, was not being cowardly but clever. As with every other detail regarding the "Beast" of Revelation, the Beast's number perfectly matches the emperor Nero.

---

[83] Saint Augustine, *The City of God*, Translated by Marcus Dods. *From Nicene and Post-Nicene Fathers, First Series, Vol. 2*. Edited by Philip Schaff. (Buffalo, NY: Christian Literature Publishing Co., 1887.) Revised and edited for New Advent by Kevin Knight XX, 19. E-Version newadvent.org

The Violent Death of the Beast

"Those who live by the sword, die by the sword." While most folks are familiar with that expression, few know its origins. Its roots can be traced to Jeremiah 15:2, where the prophet warned God's people that judgment was coming.

> *And if they ask you, 'Where shall we go?' tell them, 'This is what the LORD says:' 'Those destined for death, to death; those for the sword, to the sword; those for starvation, to starvation; those for captivity, to captivity'* (Jeremiah 15:2).

Christ used the same expression in Matthew 26:52 in his rebuke of the disciple who cut off the High Priest's servant's ear: *"Put your sword back in its place," Jesus said to him, "for all who draw the sword will die by the sword."* Drawing upon that same imagery, John, again speaking cryptically, explained how the Beast's reign would end.

> *All inhabitants of the earth will worship the Beast...He who has an ear, let him hear. If anyone is to go into captivity, into captivity he will go. If anyone kills with the sword, with the sword he will be killed* (Revelation 13:8-10a).

That Nero was fond of using the sword is beyond dispute. The Apostle Paul knew this all too well. He was beheaded in 67 or 68 A.D. by Nero. The Church Father Tertullian wrote to the Romans, *"Consult your histories; you will there find that Nero was the first who assailed with the imperial sword the Christian sect.*"[84] And, just as John predicted, Nero perished by the sword. The Imperial historian Suetonius recorded that when Nero knew he was about to be overthrown, *"he reproached himself for his cowardice in such words as these: "To live is a scandal and a shame — this does not become Nero, does not become him — one should be resolute at such times — come, rouse thyself!" And now the horsemen were at hand who had orders to take him off alive. When he heard them, he quavered: "Hark, now strikes on my ear the trampling of swift-footed coursers!" and drove a dagger into his throat, aided by Epaphroditus, his private secretary."*[85] With this last cowardly act, the reign of the Beast ended.

The Beast Dies And Rises Again?

In both chapters 13 and 17, John alluded to the fact that the Beast would die, and then rise again.

> *I saw one of his heads as if it had been slain, and his fatal wound was healed. And the whole earth was amazed and followed after the beast...The beast which was and is not, is himself also an eighth and is one of the seven, and he goes to destruction (Revelation 13:3; 17:11).*

---

[84] Tertullian, *The Exclusion of Heretics*. Translated by Peter Holmes. From *Ante-Nicene Fathers*, Vol. 3. Edited by Alexander Roberts, James Donaldson, and A. Cleveland Coxe. (Buffalo, NY: Christian Literature Publishing Co., 1885.) Revised and edited for New Advent by Kevin Knight. 21. E-Version, newadvent.org

[85] Seutonius, *The Lives of the Caesars*, The Life of Nero, p. 181.

WILL THE REAL ANTICHRIST PLEASE STAND UP

Where is there any record of Nero rising from the dead? There is none. But far from derailing the contention that Nero is the Beast, this detail actually confirms this view.

Remember, John shifted back and forth, sometimes in consecutive verses (Revelation 17:9-10) between a general identification of the Beast as a city/Kingdom (Rome) and a more specific identification (the man Nero). It is precisely the Beast in a general sense that John is referring to here. It is not the man, Nero, who will rise again, but the Kingdom or Roman Empire.

Notice that *"the whole earth was amazed and followed after the Beast"* (13:3b). What amazed everyone in the known world was that the Roman Empire could survive after the great "first family" had come to an end. The sword that brought an untimely end to Nero, was also believed to have signaled the death of the Beast considered generally, or the Roman Empire! As the last of the Julio-Claudian line of emperors there were no more blood-relatives waiting to seize power upon Nero's death. His death signaled unbelievable panic among those in Rome and the rest of the Empire. Almost immediately, civil wars broke out and there was a mad power-grab. Following Nero's death, in the space of just over a year, no less than four "emperors" seized power; Galba, Otho, Vetellius, and Vespasian. As Emory University professor Herbert Benario put it, *the aftermath of Nero's death was cataclysmic. Galba was the first of four emperors who revealed the new secret of empire 'that an emperor could be made elsewhere than in Rome.' Civil war ensued, which was only ended by the victory of the fourth* claimant, Vespasian, who established the brief dynasty of the Flavians. The dynasty of the Julio-Claudians was at an end.[86]

Tacitus, writing only a few years after Nero's death, gave this chilling account of what took place. It was *a period rich in disasters, frightful in its wars, torn by civil strife, and even in peace full of horrors. Four emperors perished by the sword. There were three civil wars; there were more with foreign enemies; there were often wars that had both characters at once. There was success in the East, and disaster in the West. There were disturbances in Illyricum; Gaul wavered in its allegiance; Britain was thoroughly subdued and immediately abandoned; the tribes of the Suevi and the Sarmatae rose in concert against us; the Dacians had the glory of inflicting as well as suffering defeat; the armies of Parthia were all but set in motion by the cheat of a counterfeit Nero. Now too Italy was prostrated by disasters either entirely novel, or that recurred only after a long succession of ages; cities in Campania's richest plains were swallowed up and overwhelmed; Rome was wasted by conflagrations, its oldest Temples consumed, and the Capitol itself fired by the hands of citizens. Sacred rites were profaned; there was profligacy in the highest ranks; the sea was crowded with exiles, and its rocks polluted with bloody deeds. In the capital there were yet worse horrors. Nobility, wealth, the refusal or the acceptance of office, were grounds for accusation, and virtue ensured destruction...Besides the manifold vicissitudes of human affairs, there were*

---

[86] Herbert W. Benario, *An Online Encyclopedia of Roman Rulers*, "Nero's Death and Its Aftermath." http://www.roman-emperors.org/nero.htm

prodigies in heaven and earth, the warning voices of the thunder, and other intimations of the future, auspicious or gloomy, doubtful or not to be mistaken. Never surely did more terrible calamities of the Roman People, or evidence more conclusive, prove that the Gods take no thought for our happiness, but only for our punishment... Such was the state of the Roman world, when Servius Galba, consul for the second time, with T. Vinius for his colleague, entered upon a year, which was to be the last of their lives, and which well nigh brought the commonwealth to an end. [87]

The words of Revelation 13:3 could not have been more true. One fatal wound to the sixth head (Nero) very nearly brought about the death of the seven-headed Beast (Roman Empire.) To the amazement of everyone, the beleaguered Empire which appeared to die with Nero, rose from the ashes of history to once again rule the world. To find the fulfillment of John's words regarding the revival of the Beast (Rome) we need look no further than 68-69 A.D. and the establishment of the new line of Roman Emperors.

But what of this "eighth" king? *"The beast which was and is not, is himself also an eighth and is one of the seven, and he goes to destruction"* (Revelation 17:11). Ken Gentry has written extensively on The Beast of Revelation. He shares the view that Nero was the Beast. In commenting on the objection that the Beast is identified as

---

[87] Tacitus, *The Histories*, Book 1: 2, 3,11; Translated by Alfred John Church and William Jackson Brodribb,

an eighth ruler, he writes, "*A consultation of the Greek text helps alleviate the apparent tension in this view. Exegetically, the chronological line of heads/kings is spoken of with careful exactness by use of the definite article, 'the.'* That is, if we translate John with exact literalness, he writes of the "kings" (emperors) in Revelation 17:10 as follows: "**the** *five fell,* **the** *one is,* **the** *other not yet come, and whenever he comes a little [while] him it behooves to remain." But the definite article is conspicuously absent in a literal translation of the reference to the eighth head/king in Revelation 17:11: "And the beast which was and is not, even he an eighth is." The definite article that clearly and repetitively defined the chronological series of head/kings ("the five," "the one," "the one to come") vanishes before the eighth is mentioned. Thus, this eighth king is "an eighth," i.e. it refers not to any one particular individual, but to the revival of the Empire itself under one who is outside of the originally specified seven kings*"[88] Once again, John had moved from speaking of specific kings to speaking of the empire generically. The eighth king is the Roman Empire as a whole.

Conclusion

As we align all the data regarding The Beast, it points without equivocation to Emperor Nero. Like The Antichrist, the Beast has come and gone, as has the Man of Lawlessness. Put away your calculators. Fold up the charts. John and Paul both understood the times in which they lived. They wrote to a first century Church that was in the throes of fierce

---

[88] Kenneth L. Gentry Jr., *The Beast of Revelation*, Second Printing (Tyler, Texas: Institute for Christian Economics, 1994) pp. 75-76

persecution at the hands of Judaism. In anticipation of an even greater assault, these remarkable students of Jesus' teaching warned their readers that the Old Covenant, rooted in the nation of Israel and centered in Jerusalem, was about to end. As Jesus had taught, they also pointed to clear signs that would precipitate Jesus' coming in judgment and the advent of a second wave of persecution at the hands of Rome. If the plethora of time indicators is correct, then John and Paul understood that the last days were mere decades away.

The implications for us are profound. If the already "obsolete" Old Covenant has been done away with, and if the rule of Christ is present now, then our calling could not be clearer. **The Church has been given the same mandate that Israel had, to bring the Gospel of the Kingdom to the nations. More than just striving to save souls (*the* foundational first step), we are heralds of New Order.** The transformative effects of the presence of the Kingdom are as far-reaching as the Kingdom itself. The Usurper will not take this laying down. The Dragon is "enraged" and has gone off to make war against God's people, *those who obey God's commandments and hold to the testimony of Jesus* (Revelation 12:17). It is pointless for us to look for or expect the coming of some great world-leader who will oppose Christ. The logical conclusion of such an expectation is withdrawal and fearful expectation. The last 150 years have shown the devastating effect of that kind of thinking.

Instead, we need to take the lessons of history and apply them to today. The Antichrist has long been forgotten. The man of lawlessness had his day in the sun, the Beast his fifteen minutes of fame. Each of them was "destroyed" at the flashpoint of God's glory, 70 A.D. Satan was defeated. His allies have been crushed by the coming of the Kingdom. The spoils of victory await all those who believe that we are "more than conquerors" in Christ Jesus. We can continue to scan the political horizon for The Antichrist or The Beast, or we can live with victory and courage and boldness now. "Will the real Antichrist, man of lawlessness, Beast, please stand up?" No. "Take a seat, chump. You've taken your cuts and you struck out. Game over."

Chapter Summary

Unfortunately, modern-day end time "experts" have conflated the Biblical teaching on The Antichrist, the Man of Lawlessness, and the Beast of Revelation. There is good reason to believe that those three monikers refer to three DIFFERENT individuals.

Despite the very limited teaching on The Antichrist, the current prophetic landscape is fascinated with this individual. What the writings of John tell us is that this individual was someone who was a contemporary of John himself. Most likely, he was a proto-Gnostic who espoused heretical teaching regarding Jesus Christ and salvation. Evidence from the first century suggests that this individual was one of three prominent first-century heretics; Cerinthus, Simon Magus, or the deacon Nicolas. The implications are clear: the Antichrist has come and gone. His arrival signaled the fast approaching day of judgment that culminated in the destruction of the Temple in 70 A.D. This is not to say that the same *spirit* of antichrist does not exist today. It does. It will continue to raise its unsightly skull until Christ appears a second time. But the notion that we should be looking for a *future* incarnation of this individual is in clear contradistinction to what the Bible teaches.

The Man of Lawlessness, of which Paul spoke only briefly, was a figure that was also closely tied to the Jewish Revolt and the destruction of Jerusalem. The most likely candidate was the Emperor Titus. Again and again, Titus matched the description that Paul gave of this man. History shows that, in every way, Titus met the criteria established by Scripture as to the identity of The Man of Lawlessness.

As for the Beast of Revelation, God's word is also explicit. As we collect the data that John provided in Revelation, a list of details emerged that pointed to a figure who was living at the time Revelation was written. All of the details of this shadowy figure, down to the very number of his name, push Nero into the exegetical light of day. For centuries, Biblical teachers and expositors have maintained that Nero was the Beast. There is no reason to think that our rich Christian heritage was wrong.

The implications for us are compelling. Put away your calculators, and throw away your charts. All of these individuals; The Antichrist, The Man of Lawlessness, and the Beast of Revelation, have gone the way of every one of Christ's opponents. Rising above history is the shadow of the risen Christ. Antichrists, Lawless men, and Beasts cannot hold a candle to the One who is Lord of Lords and

King of Kings. As it was in the first-century, so it will be today and forever. We have nothing to fear from any political or religious figure, any author or academic, who might oppose Christ and His Kingdom. Rather than bury our noses in elaborate timelines and colorful diagrams, we should bury our hearts in the Word of God. Our focus must shift away from nefarious figures and wicked world leaders who we suspect might be The Antichrist. Instead, we must herald from every street corner, every business and school, every movie theater and every church that Christ is Lord. Woe to anyone who opposes Him. Raise your opposition to The Kingdom at great risk to yourself. There is only one Kingdom that will last for eternity, and only one King who reigns forever, and His name is Jesus. Let your fascination linger over how Christ has called you and me to join Him in His great work of reclamation, reconciliation and redemption. Finding ways to more effectively do that is worth our greatest energies and resources.

CHAPTER 9

THE (NOT VERY SECRET) RAPTURE

"SATAN, WE SURRENDER!"

There ain't no grave can hold my body down.
There ain't no grave can hold my body down.
When I hear that trumpet sound I'm gonna rise right out of the ground. Ain't no grave can hold my body down
JOHNNY CASH "AIN'T NO GRAVE"

"Warning: In case of rapture, this car will be unmanned"
POPULAR BUMPER STICKER

According to the Lord's word, we tell you that we who are still alive, who are left until the coming of the Lord, will certainly not precede those who have fallen asleep. For the Lord himself will come down from heaven, with a loud command, with the voice of the archangel and with the trumpet call of God, and the dead in Christ will rise first. After that, we who are still alive and are left will be caught up together with them in the clouds to meet the Lord in the air. And so we will be with the Lord forever. Therefore encourage one another with these words.
1 THESSALONIANS 4:15-18

My fascination with the "end times" began in the most unlikely of places. I was cruising down South Dixie Highway in Miami, Florida with my dad. We had stopped at a light across from Dadeland Mall. The car in front of us had a bumper sticker that caught my eye. It read:

> **WARNING:**
> **In case of Rapture, this car will be unmanned**

I asked my dad, "What does that mean?" My father proceeded to explain to me that some people believed that at some point in the future, Jesus would come back "secretly." At that time he would "take" or "rapture" all those who were believers. Whatever those believers were doing, regardless of where they were, they would disappear, only to "return" seven years later—cars would run off the road, planes would crash, cups of coffee that had just been raised to mouths would fall harmlessly to the table or floor. This "coming" of Jesus was not His second coming, but only the first installment of His second coming. Seven years after this "secret" coming, after a time of great tribulation, Jesus would return again to establish an earthly Kingdom, reminiscent of the Kingdom of His ancestor King David. After one-thousand years, a great battle would rage, fought either with conventional or nuclear weapons. THEN, Jesus would come back the second time. All mankind would then be judged, and the eternal state would begin.

My mind began to race, envisioning all of the horrific consequences of a secret rapture. I nervously looked over my shoulder to see if any semis with fish symbols on their bumpers were bearing down on us. My dad could see the wheels turning in my 12-year-old brain. Before I could ask him "is that true," he assured me that the likelihood of that happening was pretty remote. Still, I remember being troubled for the rest of that day. Our home was near the flight path of planes that flew out of Miami International Airport. At one point I interrupted the pickup football game I was playing to watch a plane flying overhead, trying to determine if it looked "normal."

That weekend, after church, my dad came to my room with a book in his hand. It was a commentary on Revelation, titled *More Than Conquerors* by William Hendrickson. "Here's something that might help with what we talked about earlier in the week." A brief side note: my dad was converted later in life as an adult. He was (still is) overwhelmed by the grace of God. My earliest memories are of my dad, hunched over God's word, gobbling up every sentence. He acted as if he had some "catching up" to do, and he was determined to make up for all the lost years he had spent living in the Kingdom of Darkness. I think that was why he was always recommending books for me to read. He didn't want to see his son suffer the same fate. By the age of sixteen I had read *Calvin's Institutes*, *The Complete Works of Jonathan Edwards*, Berkhof's *Systematic Theology*, and a host of other "heavy" books that no teenage boy has any business reading. But my dad was and still is my hero. If he recommended it, it must be worth reading.

Much of what I read was just too deep. I couldn't wrap my young brain around a lot of it. But I can't help but think that the trajectory of my life was dramatically impacted by those years and those books. I remember turning the last page of *More Than Conquerors* and thinking to myself, "this is the most amazing stuff I have ever read." So began my lifelong pursuit of an understanding of the end that made sense for today. While my convictions have evolved, one thing has remained constant: the idea of a "secret rapture" seemed terribly inconsistent with what I read in the Bible. It does to this day.

What Is The "Secret Rapture?"

The "popular" teaching that has become a given in Evangelical circles is that we should expect a secret rapture someday. This teaching is part of the larger teaching concerning the perceived future role of the state of Israel and God's plan to rule the world from His political headquarters in Jerusalem. God's original plan was to establish a "centripetal" form of evangelism, where the nations would "stream" to Israel to learn the truth about the God of Israel. This is what many Old Testament prophets foretold.

> And I, because of their actions and their imaginations, am about to come and gather all nations and tongues, and they will come and see my glory. "I will set a sign among them, and I will send some of those who survive to the nations—to Tarshish, to the Libyans and Lydians (famous as archers), to Tubal and Greece, and to the distant islands that have not heard of my fame or seen my glory. They will proclaim my glory among the nations. And they will bring all your brothers, from all the nations, to my holy mountain in Jerusalem as an offering to the LORD—on horses, in chariots and wagons, and on mules and camels," says the LORD. "They will bring them, as the Israelites bring their

> *grain offerings, to the Temple of the LORD in ceremonially clean vessels* (Isaiah 66:18-20).

Christ's coming in the first-century was intended to inaugurate this great Kingdom. But the Jewish people rejected their Messiah.[89] Of course, God knew all of this in advance. In order to inspire "jealousy" in the hearts of His True People, God established a critical but *temporary* "people" who would do His bidding until Israel could be restored. This "new people" is the Church. Although God never intended the Church to be His primary instrument of redemption, He has given the task of sharing the Gospel to them for a season. At some point in the future, the Church will be taken out of the world, via a secret "rapture" that will signal the beginning of a seven-year period which includes the "great tribulation." During this time, God will once again use a remnant of the true chosen people, Jews, to evangelize the world. It is during this seven-year "church-raptured-Jews-evangelizing" period that the Antichrist will come to power. At the end of that seven years, Christ will come again to destroy His enemies and accomplish what He had intended from the beginning—a 1,000 year reign, from Jerusalem, to which the nations will come and give Christ His due.

This is an obvious oversimplification, and there is a great deal of dispute among those who hold to this worldview as to the particulars. As a whole, this group has come to be known as "premillenial dispensationalists," but

---

[89] In Scofield's notes on Matthew 4:17 he wrote "When Christ appeared to the Jewish people, the next thing, in the order of revelation as it then stood, **should have been** the setting up of the Davidic Kingdom."

as mentioned, there is not unanimity as to when the rapture will occur, what the role of the rebuilt Temple will be during the thousand-year reign of Christ, etc. As to the rapture itself, there is not much dispute—someday, the church will be taken out, making room for God to pursue His original intentions with the Chosen People of Israel. There are a plethora of websites and books and seminars and videos that will provide you with everything from a "rapture-ready" scorecard indicating how close we might be to the rapture, to lists of Scriptures that support this overall scheme, not to mention charts and diagrams that spell it all out in spine-tingling detail. Keep in mind that the issue before us is not simply, "will there be a secret rapture someday?" This teaching is part of a much larger body of teaching, which depends on this event as foundational to the rest. "Warning: In case there is **no** secret rapture, this dispensational house of cards comes tumbling down!" Our approach to this issue is the same as all the others—what does the Bible say?

What Does "Rapture" Mean?

The word "rapture" never actually appears in the Bible. It is a transliteration of a Latin word, *raptus*, which is taken from the Latin translation of the Bible written by Saint Jerome in the 382 A.D. That word is the translation given by Jerome for two words found in 1 Thessalonians 4. Can you find them?

> *Brothers and sisters, we do not want you to be uninformed about those who sleep in death, so that you do not grieve like the rest of mankind, who have no hope. For we believe that Jesus died and rose again, and so we believe that God will bring with Jesus those who have fallen asleep in him. According to the Lord's word, we*

THE (NOT VERY SECRET) RAPTURE

> *tell you that we who are still alive, who are left until the coming of the Lord, will certainly not precede those who have fallen asleep. For the Lord himself will come down from heaven, with a loud command, with the voice of the archangel and with the trumpet call of God, and the dead in Christ will rise first. After that, we who are still alive and are left will be caught up together with them in the clouds to meet the Lord in the air. And so we will be with the Lord forever. Therefore encourage one another with these words* (1 Thessalonians 4:13-18).

Jerome used the word *rapiemur* (from the Latin root *raptus*) to translate the Greek word *harpazo*-αρπαζω, which in English translations of 1 Thessalonians 4 is "caught up." The word *harpazo* has a number of different usages in the New Testament.[90] There are instances where the word *harpazo* can mean to "take" as in "movement in a direction." For example in 2 Corinthians 12:2-4, Paul uses *harpazo*.

> *I know a man in Christ who fourteen years ago was caught up to the third heaven. Whether it was in the body or out of the body I do not know—God knows. And I know that this man—whether in the body or apart from the body I do not know, but God knows— was **caught up** to paradise and heard inexpressible things, things that no one is permitted to tell* (2 Corinthians 12:2-4).

John, in Revelation 12:5 records, *She gave birth to a son, a male child, who "will rule all the nations with an iron*

---

[90] Here are all the New Testament occurrences of the word *harpazo*. Matt. 11:12; Matt. 12:29; Matt. 13:19; John 6:15; John 10:12; John 10:28; John 10:29; Acts 8:39; Acts 23:10; 2 Cor. 12:2; 2 Cor. 12:4; 1 Thess. 4:17; Jude 23

scepter." And her child was **snatched up** *to God and to his throne*

What is interesting about both of these last two examples is that the word "up" is supplied by translators without any real lexical or grammatical support. Although upward movement is implied (because in both cases heaven is thought of as being "up") there is nothing about the word itself that suggests specific direction, whether up, down or sideways.[91] In the vast majority of cases, *harpazo* is used to convey the idea of "snatching," "pulling" or "forcefully grabbing."

For example, Jesus consoled His disciples when He said *I give them eternal life, and they shall never perish; no one will* **snatch** *them out of my hand. My Father, who has given them to me, is greater than all; no one can* **snatch** *them out of my Father's hand.* (John 10:28-29). Jude encouraged the saints to have compassion on some, but for others who were at risk, *save (them) by* **snatching** *them from the fire...* (Jude 22-23). Luke, in recording the history of the early Church recounted how Paul was saved from the clutches of the Sanhedrin:

> *There was a great uproar, and some of the teachers of the law who were Pharisees stood up and argued vigorously. "We find nothing wrong with this man," they said. "What if a spirit or an angel has spoken to him?" The dispute became so violent that the commander was afraid Paul would be torn to pieces by them. He ordered the troops to go down and* **take**

---

[91] See especially Dr. Kelly Nelson Birks, "A Response to 'Silence Demands a Rapture,'" online at
http://www.preteristarchive.com/Modern/2002_birks_response-rapture.html

THE (NOT VERY SECRET) RAPTURE

him away from them by force and bring him into the barracks (Acts 23:9-10).

None of the uses of *harpazo* require a "secret rapture." The word itself says nothing one way or the other about cars and planes being unmanned at some point in the future. Nothing in Scripture, Greek lexicons or grammar texts demand that we understand *harpazo* to mean the movement of a physical body in an upward direction. Where, then, did this idea come from? Surely Biblical writers refer somewhere to this "catching up" as being akin to the modern idea of a secret rapture. Surely there is significant attestation among the early church fathers that this idea was the primary understanding of the teaching of the Apostles. To find the answer, we must begin with Jesus and then see what Jesus' disciples made of the teachings of their Master.

Jesus And The Rapture

In what has come to be known as "The High Priestly Prayer," Jesus poured His heart out for His disciples. He knew the road ahead would be difficult. The disciples were abuzz with questions about Jesus' departure and His return. They were sad. The thought of life apart from their Lord was almost more than they could bear. Cryptic at first, Jesus finally spoke plainly to His closest friends about what the future held—sadness would turn to joy. The Comforter would come. It would actually be "good" for the disciples that Jesus left. Then Jesus prayed, not only for them but for all disciples (17:20) He said:

> *I am coming to you now, but I say these things while I am still in the world, so that they may have the full measure of my joy within them. I have given them your word and the world has hated them, for they are not of the world any more than I am of the world. My prayer is not that you take them out of the world but that you protect them from the evil one. They are not of the world, even as I am not of it. Sanctify them by the truth; your word is truth. As you sent me into the world, I have sent them into the world. For them I sanctify myself, that they too may be truly sanctified* (John 17:13-19).

Although we are not "of" this world, we are "in" this world. And so we shall remain. At no time did Jesus even hint that they/we would be taken out of the world. Something as important as that would surely have been worth mentioning. If they were to escape the fiery trial ahead, why bother with things concerning the end? Like us, they were being sent into the world for a specific purpose—to share the Truth of the Gospel of the Kingdom—to preach that Gospel to the nations, all the while embracing the Kingdom ethic that Christ taught us to live by. Jesus gave no indication whatsoever that He expected His followers to be removed from the earth at some future date.

On another occasion, Jesus told His disciples what would happen at the "end of the age." He made no bones about the fact that He was revealing to His disciples the "secrets of the Kingdom" (Matthew 13:11). When Jesus came again, He would

THE (NOT VERY SECRET) RAPTURE

> *send out his angels, and they will weed out of his kingdom everything that causes sin and all who do evil. They will throw them into the blazing furnace, where there will be weeping and gnashing of teeth. Then the righteous will shine like the sun in the kingdom of their Father. Whoever has ears, let them hear* (Matthew 13:42-43).

Notice the clear progression: ***First***, those who are ***not*** aligned with The Kingdom are taken, then those who are. This is the exact OPPOSITE of the prevailing teaching regarding the secret rapture! Jesus immediately followed this parable with another.

In Matthew 13:47-51, Jesus stated,

> *Once again, the Kingdom of heaven is like a net that was let down into the lake and caught all kinds of fish. When it was full, the fishermen pulled it up on the shore. Then they sat down and collected the good fish in baskets, but threw the bad away. This is how it will be at the end of the age. The angels will come and separate the wicked from the righteous and throw them into the blazing furnace, where there will be weeping and gnashing of teeth. "Have you understood all these things?" Jesus asked. "Yes," they replied.*

Although the disciples often seem a few fries short of a happy-meal, on this occasion at least, they got it. Jesus will come again. He will gather everyone, but they will be separated out. ***First*** the wicked, then the righteous, and then the end will come. If they did indeed understand what Jesus meant, we should expect to see the same ideas reflected in the later writings of those same Apostles.

THE APOSTLES AND THE RAPTURE

It's not hard to imagine a single voice rising above the rest when Jesus asked the disciples if they understood. Peter had a way of standing out. When he wasn't sure what to say, he opened his mouth! Of course Peter matured. It's hard to believe that the same man who did his best Vincent Van Gogh impersonation in the Garden of Gethsemane is the same man who wrote:

> *Above all, you must understand that in the last days scoffers will come, scoffing and following their own evil desires. They will say, "Where is this 'coming' he promised? Ever since our ancestors died, everything goes on as it has since the beginning of creation." But they deliberately forget that long ago by God's word the heavens came into being and the earth was formed out of water and by water. By these waters also the world of that time was deluged and destroyed. By the same word the present heavens and earth are reserved for fire, being kept for the Day of Judgment and destruction of the ungodly. But do not forget this one thing, dear friends: With the Lord a day is like a thousand years, and a thousand years are like a day. The Lord is not slow in keeping his promise, as some understand slowness. Instead he is patient with you, not wanting anyone to perish, but everyone to come to repentance. But the day of the Lord will come like a thief. The heavens will disappear with a roar; the elements will be destroyed by fire, and the earth and everything done in it will be laid bare. Since everything will be destroyed in this way, what kind of people ought you to be? You ought to live holy and godly lives as you look forward to the day of God and speed its coming. That day will bring about the destruction of the heavens by fire, and the elements will melt in the heat. But in keeping with his*

THE (NOT VERY SECRET) RAPTURE

> *promise we are looking forward to a new heaven and a new earth, where righteousness dwells* (2 Peter 3:3-13).

The word "finality" comes to mind as we read Peter's words. God is patient. He is longsuffering. But His love will not suffer forever. A Day is coming when all bets are off--the jig is up. The timeline could not be plainer. There is a reservation for the earth and heavens—no table for two by the window, but a terrible day when the heavens and earth will be destroyed. It will come unexpectedly, like "a thief in the night." God will make good on the promise of Christ's triumphal return. It will not happen in stages, and when it does happen, it will leave no earth upon which "non-raptured" survivors can exist. Instead, "everything done in it (the earth) will be laid bare," i.e. the earth's inhabitants will be judged. Believers, who will be present through all of this, are urged to "live holy and godly lives" as they look forward not to a secret rapture but to the beginning of the new heaven and the new earth.

We need to keep in mind that Peter was addressing a specific problem with a specific solution. The problem? There were false teachers in the Church (2 Peter 2:1). Peter devoted an entire chapter (chapter 2) to describing these people. The solution? He was trying to keep the church from falling for false arguments which were predicated upon the assumption that Jesus was not coming back! "Rest assured," says Peter. "He is!"

Peter also gave us a glimpse into the timing of that day. I had always believed that Christ would come again on a day that was already marked on God's calendar—"On August

16, 2057..." Thus saith the Lord. But in reading 2 Peter 3 carefully, we see that "The Day" is not a static date in the future. That date moves. It is flexible. It is being adjusted. Slowly but unequivocally, that Day is being moved closer and closer to the present. Peter stated that we can "speed its (The Day) coming." How do we do that? By delivering the Gospel of the Kingdom to every creature on earth! By declaring boldly that Jesus reigns, that *"the Kingdom of the world has become the Kingdom of our Lord and of His Christ!"* (Revelation 11:15). Without regard to personal cost, we hasten that day by declaring the Lordship of Christ in every area of life, in every industry, every social structure, every family, every business, and every state capital.

God is waiting patiently for as many to come to repentance as possible. When that last life is transformed, when that last person is translated from the Kingdom of darkness into the Kingdom of His glorious light, the end will come. What will it be like? *It will be loud!* There will be a "roar." *It will be hot!* Everything will be destroyed by fire. *It will be messy!* Everything will melt. *It will be revealing!* Everything will be laid bare. Peter could not be clearer.

There will be no break in the action, no lag time, no disappearing acts. Granted, Peter, like all other Biblical writers, does not give a highly detailed account of the end. In almost every case, we find that Biblical writers zero in on only a few aspects of the second coming. We can assume that more will happen than what any Biblical writer records. Why? *Because by giving more detail, it would dilute the point that each writer was trying to make. It would be easy for readers to get caught up in details, parsing every word or phrase to find some hidden meaning or secret code or looking for fulfillments in every headline.* Sound familiar? This is why Peter made his description of the "end" abundantly simple and eminently clear. Despite the simplicity of his message, many have tried to fill in the gaps with ideas that simply don't appear in the text. Rather than imagining what Peter *might have said*, we need to take at face value what he *did say*. What will the end be like? As the great Italian theologian Guido Parousiachi said, "Bada bing, Bada boom!" Jesus will come again, and then, The End.

What Jesus' Best Student Wrote

Another of Christ's first century followers, the Apostle Paul was arguably Jesus' best student. While we don't know the particulars, Paul was given unique access to Christ in the days/years after his conversion (2 Corinthians 12:2-4; Galatians 1:11-20). He saw things that no other human had seen. Things were revealed to him that he dared not utter. It is with particular interest then that we look at what Paul wrote concerning The End. To the church in Corinth he wrote:

> *I declare to you, brothers and sisters, that flesh and blood cannot inherit the Kingdom of God, nor does the perishable inherit the imperishable. Listen, I tell you a mystery: We will not all sleep, but we will all be changed in a flash, in the twinkling of an eye, at the last trumpet. For the trumpet will sound, the dead will be raised imperishable, and we will be changed. For the perishable must clothe itself with the imperishable, and the mortal with immortality. When the perishable has been clothed with the imperishable, and the mortal with immortality, then the saying that is written will come true: "Death has been swallowed up in victory." "Where, O death, is*

> *your victory? Where, O death, is your sting?" The sting of death is sin, and the power of sin is the law. But thanks be to God! He gives us the victory through our Lord Jesus Christ* (1 Corinthians 15:50-57).

"Sleep" is a very Pauline way of saying "die." The mystery of that great Last Day was that not everyone would die. Those who were still alive when Jesus returned, along with those who had already died, would be "transfigured." Dead or alive, our bodies are not as they should be. Death only highlights the fact that we are dust. For those of us over 50, we know all too well that our "dustiness" is more evident every day! The change that we will experience will be signaled by a great blast from a trumpet. It will be no secret, and it will not last any longer than it takes to blink. From that moment on, God will put His final stamp of approval on the work of Christ as the last enemy, death, slides under the footstool of Jesus.

Earlier in the same chapter, Paul made reference to the finality of that great moment.

> *For as in Adam all die, so in Christ all will be made alive. But each in turn: Christ, the firstfruits; then, when he comes, those who belong to him. Then the end will come, when he hands over the Kingdom to God the Father after he has destroyed all dominion, authority and power. For he must reign until he has put all his enemies under his feet. The last enemy to be destroyed is death* (1 Corinthians 15:22-26).

Once death is dealt this final blow, the end will come.

There is no doubt that Paul had the same event in mind when he wrote 1 Thessalonians 4. It is this passage that has inspired the thinking of those who believe in a "secret rapture." Paul wrote:

> *Brothers and sisters, we do not want you to be uninformed about those who sleep in death, so that you do not grieve like the rest of mankind, who have no hope. For we believe that Jesus died and rose again, and so we believe that God will bring with Jesus those who have fallen asleep in him. According to the Lord's word, we tell you that we who are still alive, who are left until the coming of the Lord, will certainly not precede those who have fallen asleep. For the Lord himself will come down from heaven, with a loud command, with the voice of the archangel and with the trumpet call of God, and the dead in Christ will rise first. After that, we who are still alive and are left will be caught up together with them in the clouds to meet the Lord in the air. And so we will be with the Lord forever. Therefore encourage one another with these words* (1 Thessalonians 4:13-18).

The parallels between 1 Corinthians 15 and 1 Thessalonians 4 are unmistakable. In both cases, Paul referred to the "trumpet" of God. In both cases he made a distinction between those who had already died, and those who were still living when Jesus returns. In both cases, Paul told his readers that death will not have the last word. What has fueled the imagination of some is Paul's description of being "caught up" in the clouds. As we have already noted, the word "up" that most translations include is NOT part of the meaning of the word used there—it is implied, and inserting it makes the English text read more smoothly. Even if we concede that the word used here can mean that something is moved upward, there is nothing in Paul's words that *demands* a *secret* catching "up" into heaven, leaving behind bewildered residents and initiating a seven-year period of unparalleled suffering and the rise of the Antichrist!

Like Peter, what Paul said is simple and clear. He was addressing a specific problem—people were concerned with what happened to people when they died. Paul conceded that grief over the death of a loved one is natural. But we grieve *differently*. Paul built his argument on the resurrection of Jesus. Just as God raised Jesus from the dead, He would bring those who died in Christ with Him, i.e. they too would rise from the dead as the first to join Jesus at the second coming. As Jesus descended to earth, all those who had already died would join Him in His descent. Then, all graves, past and present, would be emptied. What a remarkable reunion! People who had recently lost a loved one or people who had never met their grandparent or great aunt would be able to see them again. Then those who were still living would also rise to meet Christ in the air. There are only two ways to meet Jesus: die or fly! That great resurrection would signal the end. This is what Paul meant when he said, "And so we will be with the Lord forever." The eternal state has begun. How will we know that this has happened? Jesus will shout, and the great *shofar* of heaven will sound. There can be no other meaning for the words "loud command" or "trumpet call." It will be noisy. Again, no secret, no great disappearing acts, only visible and loud indications that the end has come.

An Objection Considered

Matthew 24 has often been cited as a prime example of what those who believe in a secret rapture are talking about. Verses 36-42 read as follows:

THE (NOT VERY SECRET) RAPTURE

> *But about that day or hour no one knows, not even the angels in heaven, nor the Son, but only the Father. As it was in the days of Noah, so it will be at the coming of the Son of Man. For in the days before the flood, people were eating and drinking, marrying and giving in marriage, up to the day Noah entered the ark, and they knew nothing about what would happen until the flood came and took them all away. That is how it will be at the coming of the Son of Man. Two men will be in the field; one will be taken and the other left. Two women will be grinding with a hand mill; one will be taken and the other left. Therefore keep watch, because you do not know on what day your Lord will come* (Matthew 24: 36-42).

Is there anything in *this* passage that *DEMANDS* a secret rapture? As always, we need to understand Christ's words in their broader context. As we have already illustrated, this passage is NOT about the second coming, it is about the destruction of Jerusalem in 70 A.D. As the Roman legions under the command of Titus swept down upon Jerusalem, the outcome was devastating. The streets of the city literally ran red with the blood of those who were slaughtered. Following the notes of Flavius Josephus, historian Alfred Church gives this account of the final destruction of the Temple.

And while the Temple was burning, the soldiers ceased not to slay all whom they met; nor had they pity for youth, or reverence for old age, but put both old and young, people and priests, to the sword. And there went up a great and terrible clamour, the soldiers shouting aloud for joy, and the Jews crying out as they saw themselves surrounded with fire and sword, and the people bewailing the Temple, for even they who could scarce speak for the weakness of hunger, when they saw the burning of the Holy Place brake forth with loud lamentations. As for the Temple, and the hill whereon it stood, the ground could not be seen for dead bodies; and the soldiers trampled on heaps of corpses as they pursued them that fled.[92]

Despite the unparalleled carnage, not everyone was killed. Some were executed, while others were taken prisoner. Many were whisked away to other parts of the empire where they worked as slaves. Church once again gives us some idea of the scope and magnitude of the human tragedy surrounding the fall of Jerusalem.

Now the number of them that were taken captive was ninety-and-seven thousand in all; and the number of them that perished in the war was eleven-hundred-thousand. For a great multitude had assembled, according to custom, at the Feast of the Passover, and being overtaken suddenly by the war were not able to depart. And indeed, that so great a multitude could be gathered together in the City is manifest from the counting that was made in the days of Cestius. For when Nero made little account of the strength of the people, Cestius would have the priests take the number of the people. And they, when the Feast of the Passover was come, counted the number of the lambs that were slain for sacrifice; and the number was two-hundred-and-fifty-and-six thousand and five hundred; and for each lamb might be reckoned a company of ten men at the least.[93]

---

[92] Alfred Church, *The Story of the Last Days of Jerusalem from Josephus*, (London: Seeley and Company, Ltd., 1903) p. 102

[93] Ibid, p. 114

THE (NOT VERY SECRET) RAPTURE

Many were killed, but some were taken. Some died, others escaped. What Matthew described in these verses in chapter 24 is nothing more than that people who were working or walking side by side in those days would be set upon, and one would be taken captive, while the other would be left. So swift and terrible was the final assault on Jerusalem that the words of Matthew 24 are a perfect description of precisely what happened during the Jewish War.

What are we to make of Jesus' reference to the "days of Noah" in Matthew 24? While we need to be careful not to push analogies too far, it seems clear from the context that what Jesus was saying was that the fall of Jerusalem and subsequent end of the Jewish age would come *SUDDENLY* not secretly. When it came, those who embraced the old covenant would be caught unaware. Again, nothing in the text demands that this event be a secret. Almost every reference to Jesus' coming in judgment on the people of Israel and the old Temple-centric system was a call to watchfulness. Luke 12: 39-40; 1 Thessalonians 5:2, 4; Revelation 16:15; Matt 24:40-42; and Luke 21:34 all advocated being attentive to the signs and being prepared. *Why would Jesus encourage His followers to be watchful and to stay prepared if the very thing they were watching for would be a secret?* There is simply nothing in any of these texts that supports the idea of a secret rapture or a "coming-in-a-half" of Jesus.

So if the Biblical record is unable to produce any compelling evidence to support the idea of a secret rapture, then why is this idea so popular? If neither Jesus nor any of his first century followers suggested such an idea, where did it come from? It is precisely the origins of this teaching that is the "dirty little secret" of secret rapture proponents.

The Origins Of A Secret

The most common response I get to the teachings offered in this book is, "Why have I never heard this before?" That's ironic. Prior to the early to mid-19th century, it was the idea of a secret rapture that no one had ever heard of before. *In fact, NOTHING like today's secret rapture can be found in any of the teachings of the Church for the first eighteen-hundred years of its existence.* Before the fruit of this new teaching could ripen, the prophetic soil of the day needed to change. The prevailing **historic** view of Biblical prophecy could not support this radical new idea. A change from an historic to a **futuristic** view of Biblical prophecy was needed. The seeds of such a change were sown in the 16th century, during the Protestant Reformation.

One of the greatest contributions of the Reformation was a return to the authority of Scripture. By reestablishing *sola scriptura*, "Scripture only" as the basis for all sound doctrine, the reformers were responding to the error of the Roman Catholic Church which appealed to the traditions of the church as having equal authority to the Bible. Arising from the teaching that Scripture alone could provide us with God's Truth, the reformers looked at Biblical prophecy and correctly understood that the prophecies of Scripture were to find their fulfillment in history, i.e. a historical approach. Prior to the Reformation, the prevailing hermeneutic was that Biblical prophecy should be interpreted *allegorically* not historically. The allegorical method taught that Biblical writers intended something other than what was plainly expressed in a passage and should be interpreted differently than the plain meaning of words. This allegorical method argued that the "true" meaning of a passage could only be found in finding the *hidden* or *symbolic* meaning of prophetic passages. The Reformers moved away from that hermeneutic to one that looked for the meaning of prophecy in history. A more "literal" hermeneutic was adopted which tried to appreciate the actual "literature" being studied. Understanding prophetic symbols became less a matter of looking for hidden meanings and more a matter of looking for historical meanings.

Of all the reformers, Martin Luther and John Calvin stand out as thinkers who promoted this view. Prophecy was nothing if not historical. Unfortunately, their **application** of the meaning of prophecy was often driven by cultural realities. In applying prophecies to their own day both Luther and Calvin argued that the Antichrist was none other than the corrupt Papacy. Luther contended, *"Nevertheless, since few know this glory of baptism and the blessedness of Christian liberty, and cannot know them because of the tyranny of the pope, I for one will walk away from it all and redeem my conscience by bringing this charge against the pope and all his papists: Unless they will abolish their laws and traditions, and restore to Christ's churches their liberty and have it taught among them, they are guilty of all the souls that perish under this miserable captivity, and the papacy is truly the Kingdom of Babylon, yes, the Kingdom of the real Antichrist! For who is "the man of sin" and "the son of perdition" but he that with his doctrines and his laws increases sins and the perdition of souls in the Church, while he sits in the Church as if he were God? All* this the papal tyranny has fulfilled, and more than fulfilled, these many centuries. It has extinguished faith, obscured the sacraments and oppressed the Gospel."[94]

Calvin agreed. *"Some persons think us too severe and censorious when we call the Roman pontiff Antichrist. But those who are of this opinion do not consider that they bring the same charge of presumption against Paul himself, after whom we speak and whose language we adopt…I shall briefly show that (Paul's words in 2 Thessalonians 2) they are not capable of any other interpretation than that which applies them to the Papacy"*[95]

That virtually every other reformer agreed with their assessment is beyond dispute.[96] The Roman Church found itself with a major PR problem. An argument was needed that would deflect criticism away from the Papacy. In three different installments, the Church of Rome gathered its best and brightest thinkers to discuss how to respond to the criticisms spawned by the Reformation. From 1545-1563, the Council of Trent did just that, launching what has come to be known as "the Counter-Reformation." In particular, the

---

[94] Martin Luther, "A Prelude by Martin Luther on the Babylonian Captivity of the Church," Chapter 3, p. 536.

[95] John Calvin, *Institutes of the Christian Religion* (The Westminster Press: Philadelphia, 7th Printing, 1975) Book IV, Chapter VII, section 25, p. 1144.

[96] Wycliffe, Zwingli, Knox, Wesley, Tyndale, and Melanchthon, to name only a few, shared the conviction that the Antichrist was the Papacy. Lest we come down too hard on these thinkers, we need to remember that the Roman Church at this time was thoroughly corrupt. Political agendas had taken over the Church, and immoral behavior was rampant.

THE (NOT VERY SECRET) RAPTURE

Jesuit order was commissioned with finding an alternative to the Protestant application of Biblical prophecy.[97]

THE CHARGE OF THE JESUITS

Francisco Ribera (1537-1591), a doctor of theology took up the charge of the Council of Trent with great enthusiasm. In 1590, Ribera, himself a Jesuit, published a commentary on the Revelation of St. John. His commentary argued that the Antichrist/Beast was a wholly future individual who would persecute the Church. His approach came to be known as "futurism." Ribera argued that the bulk of The Revelation had to do with events far in the future, and that any application which tried to locate the meaning of John's prophecy in the sixteenth century or *any* history was misguided. He identified a seven year period as "the" great tribulation," and argued that most of Revelation pertained only to the three-and-a-half years prior to the second coming of Christ. While nothing like today's secret rapture teaching appears in the work of Ribera, he did introduce ideas that are common among those who hold to that idea, including: the rebuilding of the Temple in Jerusalem, the claims of the Antichrist to be God, and the establishment of a world government under the reign of the Antichrist. It is fair to say that Ribera's work opened the door for the idea of the secret rapture.

---

[97] It is critical for the reader to understand that I am NOT trying to assign some nefarious motivation to either the Council of Trent or the resulting work of Jesuit priests. I am convinced that the subsequent work of these Jesuit priests was motivated in large part by a desire to honor God and glorify Him. Some writers have suggested that the mere fact that "futurism" can be traced to Roman Catholic writers makes it immediately suspect. I do not agree. I believe that futurists are wrong in their application of prophetic texts, just as Calvin and Luther were wrong in applying references to the Antichrist to the Papacy.

Building on the work of Ribera, another Jesuit, Manuel LaCunza (1731-1801) wrote *The Coming of the Messiah in Glory and Majesty* ("La Venida del Mesías en Gloria y Majestad"). By his own admission, he wrote the book for several reasons: to make "the greatness and excellence" of Christ more well-known, to encourage other priests to "shake off the dust from their Bibles," to call sinners to repentance and faith in Jesus Christ, and, finally, to offer "some greater light" to the Jewish people.[98] Lacunza's work was met with more than a little controversy. Chief among his critics were his fellow Catholics, who reacted to Lacunza's identification of the Roman hierarchy as connected to the *second* beast of Revelation 13 and the whore of chapter 17.

Although his work was filled with novel ideas and controversial interpretations, perhaps the most interesting was his notion of two resurrections and two judgments. *Jesus Christ will return from Heaven to earth when His time comes, at the appropriate time and moment that the Father Himself has placed under His own power. He will come accompanied not only by the angels, but also by the saints previously resurrected—of those, I say, that will be judged worthy of that time and of the resurrection of the dead... He will not come in a hurry, but more deliberately than is usually thought. He will not only come to judge the dead but also and in the first place the living. Consequently, this judgment of the living and the dead cannot be only one judgment, but rather two very diverse judgments, not only in essence and in manner but also in*

---

[98] Manuel Lacunza, *The Coming of the Messiah in Glory and Majesty*, (L.B. Seeley and Son: London, 1827) pp.135-136

time. From this we conclude (and this is the main point that deserves attention) that there has to be considerable space of time between the awaited coming of the Lord, and the judgment of the dead or universal resurrection."[99] Lacunza also wrote at length about the special place of the Jews and the error of thinking that the Church had in some way become the "new" people of God.

Less noteworthy than the actual content of Lacunza's book was the influence that his "outside-the-box" thinking had on the man responsible for translating his work into English, Edward Irving. So enthralled was Irving with Lacunza's work that he taught himself Spanish in order to translate the *Coming of the Messiah,* the final edition of which included a 203 page introduction by Irving.

The Unnerving Edward Irving

Edward Irving (1792-1834) was born in Annan, Scotland. At the age of 17, Irving graduated from the University of Edinburgh with a Master's degree. Within six years, he had completed his doctoral studies and was licensed to preach. An engaging and fiery preacher, Irving soon found himself in the spotlight of the Scottish Presbyterian denomination that he served at Regent Square Church in London. His teachings regarding the gifts of the Spirit, and his contention that Christ possessed a "sinful human nature" caused more than a few raised eyebrows. According to Irving, it was only the operation of the Holy Spirit in the life of

---

[99] Manuel Lacunza, *The Coming of Messiah in Glory and Majesty* (London, England: JG Tillin, 2000), p. 96.

Christ that kept Him from sinning. Irving's popularity with the people continued to grow amidst miraculous healings and numerous signs and wonders at the Regent church, despite the growing suspicions by the London Presbytery that Irving was heterodox.

In May of 1832, Irving was removed from his position at the church, at which point he began his own church, the Newman Street Church. Amidst all the controversy and the meteoric rise of Irving to the status of spiritual "superstar," a little noticed event took place that would forever change the trajectory of Irving's life and teaching.

The Bonnie Lass Who Dropped a Bomb

While Irving translated Lacunza and locked horns with fellow Presbyterians, a sickly 15 year-old Scottish girl named Margaret MacDonald studied her Bible. A steady stream of individuals came and went from her Port Glasgow, Scotland home. They came regularly for prayer meetings and displays of the Spirit's power. Visions, healings, and prophetic utterances were regular occurrences. Somewhere between March and April of 1830, Margaret, a parishioner of Irving's Regent church, received a prophetic word from the Lord. After receiving numerous visions of the coming of the Lord, she recorded these visions and sent them in a letter to Irving. MacDonald wrote,

"Here I was, made to stop and cry out, 'O it is not known what the sign of the Son of Man is; the people of God think they are waiting, but they know not what it is. I felt this needed to be revealed...but suddenly what it was burst upon me with a glorious light. I saw it was just the Lord himself descending from Heaven with a shout...I saw the error to be

that men think that it will be something seen by the natural eye; but it is spiritual discernment that is needed..." [100] MacDonald contended that a "coming" of Christ was imminent, and that the second phase of His coming would be public, but the first would be secret and hidden. She continued,

"This was the oil the wise virgins took in their vessels - this is the light to be kept burning - the light of God - that we may discern that which cometh not with observation to the natural eye. Only those who have the light of God within them will see the sign of his appearance. No need to follow them who say, see here, or see there, for his day shall be as the lightning to those in whom the living Christ is. 'Tis Christ in us that will lift us up - he is the light - 'tis only those that are alive in him that will be caught up to meet him in the air. I saw that we must be in the Spirit, that we might see spiritual things..." [101] Included in MacDonald's prophetic words was the identification of the Antichrist as Robert Owen (1771-1858), a leading socialist of the early nineteenth century. Her written account of those visions ended with the words, *"This is what we are at present made to pray much for, that speedily we may all be made ready to meet our Lord in the air—and it will be. Jesus wants his bride. His desire is toward us. He that shall come, will come, and will not tarry. Amen and Amen. Even so come Lord Jesus."*

---

[100] http://www.Bibleprophesy.org/vision.htm

[101] Robert Norton, *Memoirs of James and George MacDonald* (Port-Glasgow, Scotland: 1870), pp. 171-176.

The effect of MacDonald's vision upon Irving was immediate and profound: *"The substance of...Margaret Macdonald's visions or revelations, given in their papers, carry to me a spiritual conviction and a spiritual reproof which I cannot express."* For Irving, MacDonald's visions provided the final confirmation for his burgeoning ideas. From 1830 until his death, Irving devoted his considerable energies to writing and speaking, promoting his convictions that: the pre-tribulation rapture of the Church was imminent, this rapture would be a secret, there was a radical distinction between the Gentile Church and the Jews, the latter were destined to rule with Christ in an earthly millennial Kingdom seated in Jerusalem, and that the "latter rain" of God's Spirit would precipitate the imminent return of Christ.[102] IT IS IN THE WRITINGS OF MACDONALD AND IRVING THAT WE FIND THE **VERY FIRST** ORGANIZED TEACHING OF WHAT SURVIVES TODAY AS THE DOCTRINE OF THE SECRET RAPTURE. By Irving's own reckoning, his ideas were so new and so unprecedented that *"I did not know of one brother in the ministry who held with me in these matters...So novel and strange a doctrine...did not fail to call down upon my head all possible forms and degrees of angry and intemperate abuse."*[103] What could account for the incredible popularity of this relatively young and heretofore unheard of teaching? How, over the course of

---

[102] Ibid. Lacunza. Irving's "Preliminary Discourse," pp. 4-5. The first 127 pages of the English translation of the book are Irving's teachings regarding the end-times. It provides a wealth of information regarding Irving's beliefs as well as illustrating his indebtedness to Lacunza.

[103] Edward Irving, *The Reverend Edward Irving's Preliminary Discouse to the Work of Ben Ezra (Lacunza)* entitled *the Coming of the Messiah in Glory and Majesty*, 1859 reprint, pp. 7-8.

less than 100 years, did this teaching become the majority report among evangelical Christians?

The Rapture: A Secret No More

An Irish preacher/attorney, John Nelson Darby (1800-1882) helped begin the Plymouth Brethren. Feeling that the established Church of England was corrupt, the Brethren sought to create a holy and pure fellowship of believers that eschewed the then popular distinction between clergy and laity.

In 1830, Darby visited Scotland and personally investigated Margaret MacDonald's prophecies. It was here that Darby was introduced to the teachings of MacDonald/Irving, and, via Irving, to the writings of Lacunza. A prolific writer and tireless teacher, Darby began to expand on the ideas being forwarded by Irving and others. From 1831-1833 Darby participated in the Powerscourt Conference, a gathering of Bible students organized by his friend, the wealthy Lady Powerscourt. It was at this conference that Darby began to espouse his unique blend of Lacunzian-Irvingite theology.

It is important to note that, along with his elaborations on the new "rapture-theology," Darby also taught what can only be considered the logical conclusion of such a teaching. If the Olivet Discourse is wholly future, then the second "coming" of Christ must be preceded by all the horrible events described there. For Darby, it was essential to understand that things would only get worse as we approached the "great tribulation" and the rapture. In fact, we should *welcome* bad news as a sign that the rapture was imminent and that the millennial reign of Christ could not be far behind. Speaking in 1840, Darby remarked, *"What we are about to consider will tend to show that, instead of permitting ourselves to hope for continued progress of good, we must expect a progress of evil; and that the hope of the earth being filled with the knowledge of the Lord before the exercise of His judgment, and the consummation of this judgment on the earth, is delusive... Truly Christendom has become completely corrupted, the dispensation of the Gentiles has been found unfaithful: can it be restored? No! Impossible."*[104] It's not hard to see how small a jump it is from this kind of thinking to the "Circle- the wagons!" mentality that pervades much of the Church today.

In the 1830's and 1840's, Darby traveled extensively in Britain and Europe, during which he established himself as a leading interpreter of Biblical prophecy. From 1862 to 1877, Darby expanded his travels to include North America. As Darby continued to expand on the secret rapture and the radical distinction between the Jews and the Church, some of his published works fell into the hands of Cyrus Ingerson Scofield (1843-1921), fellow attorney and sometime public official.

The Rapture Goes Public

Scofield was a man of enormous energy for both good and bad. He most certainly would have embraced Luther's suggestion, "Be a sinner, and sin boldly" (although we dare not forget to finish the sentence: "but believe more boldly

---

[104] Speech in Geneva, 1840, in William Kelly, ed., *The Collected Writings of J.N. Darby*, Prophetic no. 1, vol. 1 (Kingston-on-Thames: Stow Hill Bible and Tract Depot, undated), 471, 486

still!) After his "conversion,"[105] Scofield continued to engage in behavior that can only be described as scandalous. Even as great a hero of the faith as King David, a "man after God's own heart" was guilty of egregious behavior. But a person's true character is revealed in how they respond to their failures and disobedience. There is no indication that Scofield ever repented of abandoning his first wife and two children, having an affair with his soon-to-be second wife, defrauding supporters of thousands, stealing money from his mother-in-law, losing his post as assistant District Attorney for blackmail, being arrested for forgery, or being convicted of fraud, spending six months in jail for that crime.[106]

Undaunted, C.I. Scofield, after a number of ill-fated moves and career changes, settled in Dallas, Texas. It was there, in October of 1882, that he took the position of pastor at a small Congregational Church. By this time, Scofield had already been introduced to the teachings of Darby through his friend and personal mentor, Rev. James H. Brooks (1830-1897). By 1888, Scofield's church had grown to the point where it could afford to pay him a full-time salary and subsidize the study leaves that would ultimately produce the reference Bible that bears his name. In that same year, Scofield published *Rightly Dividing the Word of Truth* as a

---

[105] The details of Scofield's conversion are dubious at best. Recent research has shown that his own account of that event included fabrications regarding the time, place, and other particulars. Cf. Joseph Canfield, *The Incredible Scofield and His Book*, (Ross House Books: Vallecito, California, 1988), p. 65-68.

[106] As far as I know, the only carefully researched and critical study of the life of C.I. Scofield is the above footnoted book by Canfield. As might be expected, this book has met with violent opposition from those who look to Scofield as the man who brought the ideas of Darby and others to popularity. Canfield chronicles some of this reaction in the Foreword. To date, no serious refutation of Canfield's findings has been produced.

tool to assist in the teaching of the re-warmed ideas of Darby and Brooks. The title, taken from 2 Timothy 2:15, expanded on Paul's encouragement to "rightly divide" the Word of Truth by suggesting that the Bible could be *divided* into seven arbitrary periods, or "dispensations." The sixth dispensation was the "grace age," our current age, which Scofield suggested was God's "plan B" in light of Israel's rejection of their Messiah. Scofield argued that, at some time in the future, God would initiate a second attempt to establish a Jewish run world empire, under the head of Christ Himself, who would sit on a throne in Jerusalem for a thousand years. With the encouragement of Rev. Brooks and other friends, Scofield determined to elaborate on his ideas and publish his "notes" alongside related Scriptures in a "study" Bible.

Along with his duties as pastor/author/speaker, Scofield also served as the head of the Southwestern School of the Bible, which would become Dallas Theological Seminary. Largely through the efforts of Rev. Brooks, Scofield was also introduced to soon-to-be lifelong friend, Dwight L. Moody (1837-1899), who founded the famous Bible institute that bears his name. In 1890, Scofield began a Bible correspondence course in which he continued to promote the ideas of Darby, coupled with his own unique elaborations. The course continued until his death in 1914, at which point it was taken over by Moody Bible Institute.

After serving the Dallas church for fourteen years, Scofield accepted a call to Moody's home church in Northfield, Massachusetts, a post he assumed in 1895. Moody had already launched the Northfield Summer Conferences for Scripture as a way to give attendees an opportunity to "search the Scriptures." It was at one such conference that Scofield was introduced to Robert Scott of Morgan and Scott Publishing, a group closely linked to the Plymouth Brethren. Neither Scofield nor Scott could foresee the significance of their meeting.

By early 1903, failing health and increased devotion to completing his Bible compelled Scofield to resign his pastorate at the Northfield church. In early 1904, Scofield traveled to Europe for research, where he was taken in by Robert Scott at his home near Dorking, England, the same Robert Scott he first met at a Northfield Summer Conference. It was during this visit that Scott introduced Scofield to McHenry Fowde, head of the Oxford Bible Publishing House of Great Britain. Although his Bible was not yet completed, *it was agreed that the greatest publisher in the English speaking world, Oxford House, would publish Scofield's Bible upon completion.* On January 15, 1909, the first edition of the Scofield Reference Bible was published. In 1917, a revised edition was published, and it has been the standard ever since.

Featured in his Bible notes were teachings taken directly from the work of Darby and Brooks, a fact that was apparently not worth mentioning by Scofield. Chief among those ideas were: a radical distinction between the Church and Israel (Irving and Darby were critical in the development of the Christian-Zionist movement), the unconditional nature of the Abrahamic covenant, the "gap" between Daniel's 69th and 70th "week," the failed attempt of Christ to re-establish the Davidic Kingdom with his first coming, the secret rapture, the literal reign of Christ for a thousand years from a throne in Jerusalem after his second coming (Part A), the rebuilding of the Temple, the resurrection of ancient Temple practices including sacrifices, the ultimate failure of the Church, the idea that Israel would someday be attacked by a Russian led coalition, the great final Battle of Armageddon, and the eventual return of Christ (Part B).

The place of the secret rapture in Scofield's teaching was central. God had two people—Israel and the Church. He also had two different plans for these two groups. For Israel, God had an earthly Kingdom planned, with the seat of government in Israel, with Christ seated on a throne there, where He would rule in power for 1000 years. According to Scofield, Christ originally planned to set this earthly Kingdom up at His first coming, but Israel rejected Him. Although Christ did succeed in setting up His Kingdom in a very limited way, the promised earthly Kingdom would not come until after His second coming. For a dispensation (Grace), God had chosen to call to Himself another people known as "The Church." At some point in the future, God would "rapture" the Church in a secret event, at which time He would proceed with His original plan to establish an earthly Kingdom for the nation of Israel. Christ would first come *for* His Church (The Rapture) and then He would come *with* His Church (The Revelation). If these ideas sound familiar, it is because Scofield's ideas represent THE majority report among evangelicals today.

Is it any wonder? With all the relationships and connections that Scofield had, his study Bible became the foundation for every pastor, Bible teacher and theologian who held to a "dispensational" view of Scripture and Biblical prophecy. It is fair to say that EVERY modern study Bible is patterned after Scofield's amazing publication. Complete with notes alongside Scripture, cross-references, chapter and paragraph headings, and intriguing charts/diagrams, Scofield managed to carve out a place in history relative to Bible study that is unmatched by anyone before or since. To this day, Moody Bible Institute and Dallas Theological Seminary continue to churn out graduates who are steeped in the dispensational teachings of Scofield. Unfortunately, Scofield's views were largely those of his Brethren "brethren" and the disciples of Irving and Darby. Unheard of prior to the mid to late 19th century, Scofield managed to turn more than 1800 years of Biblical study and exegesis completely on its head. Just like the "secret rapture" teaching that appears NOWHERE in Scripture (except in the notes of editions of the Scofield Reference Bible), so most of the teachings included in Scofield's Bible are nothing more than the unbiblical, reworked ideas of his contemporaries. Why does it matter? What difference does it make that these novel ideas became the "gospel" of prophetic interpretation and end-times understanding? *Because they have fostered a latent pessimism and a commitment to disengage from the world around us that has fostered the wholesale handing over of whole areas of life to the rule of Satan.* Not only do we subtly celebrate "bad" news, but we also function as survivalists rather than subversives. I challenge every reader to consider the waning influence of the church in our society over the past 150 years. A major contribution to that trend is the very teaching we have just briefly reviewed. And it gets worse.

In Heaven For Seven?

It is hard to imagine a more depressing or bleak picture than the one painted by Scofield and his contemporaries. In that system, believers are "raptured," and for seven years enjoy the glorious and perfect presence of God Himself. Then, THEY ARE REINTRODUCED TO A FALLEN AND SINFUL WORLD DURING THE MILLENNIUM, WHERE THEY LIVE, NOT FOR SEVENTY OR EIGHTY OR EVEN A HUNDRED YEARS, BUT FOR A FULL THOUSAND YEARS! This is not a teaching of hope, but of failure. This is not a teaching of joy, but of a purgatorial-like state that those who are alive when Christ raptures His saints must endure. At the core of the secret-rapture myth is a worldview that is defeatist. With blatant disregard for the abundant and clear time-frame references in Scripture, this view is part of a system that not only expects but welcomes the waning influence of Christ-followers in the world. Because of the influence of this view over the last 150 years, the Church has lost sight of its mandate and has given up any significant influence in our culture.

The issue is not simply to make our world more "moral." Rather, as winsome warriors, we must proclaim what *is* as part of what *will be*. The present "realities" are not as "real" as they seem. Our first priority must be to fight to bring the Gospel of the Kingdom to all the peoples of the earth. Even that is not ultimate. Ultimately, it is the fame and glory of God that we proclaim to the nations. As more and more peoples embrace that truth, genuine "virtue" is the necessary fruit of that. It is *not* correct to assume that if more and more people get "saved" that a more virtuous society *necessarily* results. It *is* correct to say that as more and more people are saved, and taught to observe "all things" that Christ taught us, what develops is a robust Christian worldview that has the glory and fame of God at its core. With that as the beginning and the end of all our endeavors,

THE (NOT VERY SECRET) RAPTURE

virtue becomes possible and the Kingdom begins to flourish in every arena of life! The defeatist "the world-is-getting-worse-and-worse-and-isn't-that-great" worldview that the secret rapture teaching is built upon makes that kind of personal and cultural transformation impossible.

As we have seen, the millennial reign of Christ is NOW. God's affections are not rooted in a people, but in Himself. Our hope is not in escaping this world, but in transforming this world as heralds of a new Kingdom and a new King.

Artist's rendering of the "secret rapture." Although there are many websites that feature this dubious doctrine, there are also a number that try to set the record straight with sound biblical teaching. One such site, www.noscretapture.com, provides a number of compelling and well-thought out arguments regarding the so-called secret rapture. Author, speaker and radio host Steve Wohlberg authored this site, and has written an easy to read, scholarly book, titled *The Rapture Delusions*, which thoroughly dismantles the secret rapture theory.

WINSOME WARRIORS

The (Short) History of the Secret Rapture

The chart below will help the reader see the *recent* nature of the secret rapture teaching, as well as the historical connections that account for it. The darker the figure, the more prominent their role in popularizing this theory.

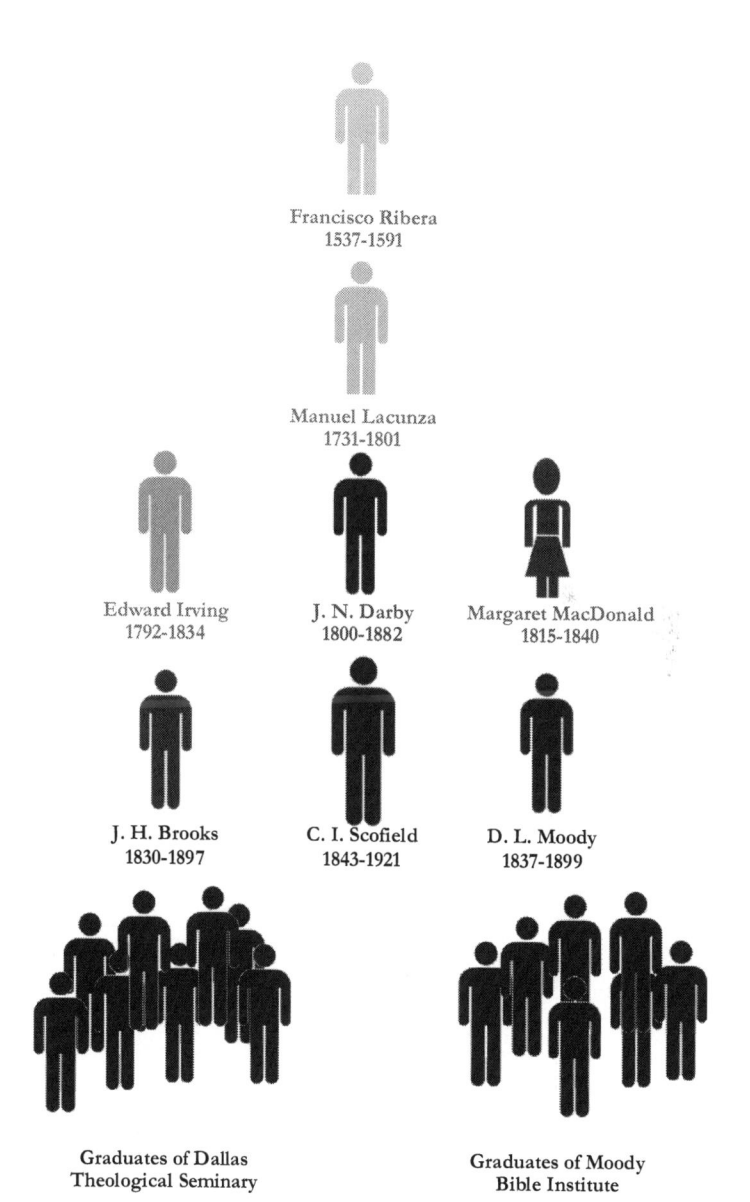

Francisco Ribera
1537-1591

Manuel Lacunza
1731-1801

Edward Irving
1792-1834

J. N. Darby
1800-1882

Margaret MacDonald
1815-1840

J. H. Brooks
1830-1897

C. I. Scofield
1843-1921

D. L. Moody
1837-1899

Graduates of Dallas
Theological Seminary

Graduates of Moody
Bible Institute

So What Will Happen?

There will be no installments of Christ's return. There will be no delay between a "first-and-a-half" and second appearing. There will be no departure of believers for seven years. The greatest hope of all believers (1 Cor. 15:19) is that someday, the Lord Christ Himself will crack open the sky and come again. It will happen "like a thief," at a time when the lost will not expect it (1 Thessalonians 5:2). Like a powerful magnet surrounded by metal particles, Jesus will draw all men to Himself (1 Thessalonians 4:15-17). In rapid-fire succession, first those who have died (1 Thessalonians 4:16), then those who are still alive (1 Thessalonians 4:17) will be caught up to meet Him (1 Thessalonians 4:17). As Christ descends through the clouds (Acts 1:9-11), He will shout the final "Amen!" as the trumpet of heaven deafens humanity (1 Thessalonians 4:16). Both the living and the dead will watch in amazement as the earth melts in the face of the white-hot justice of God (2 Peter 3:10). All mankind will be judged, and eternity will begin (Revelation 20:11-15). Period (1 Thessalonians 4:17b).

Chapter Summary

The Scriptures are devoid of any teaching that approximates the current so-called "secret rapture" idea. If anything, Jesus taught precisely the opposite. His desire was NOT that we be taken from this world, but that we be protected from the Evil One. Nor did Jesus' disciples teach such a doctrine. In one place, the apostle Paul refers to the final moment in history when we will all be taken up to meet Christ at His final appearing. The idea that all believers will be whisked away, leaving a cadre of Jewish evangelists to spread the Gospel of the Kingdom during a thousand-year reign of Christ is ludicrous. By weaving together a variety of unrelated Scriptures, proponents of this teaching have created an unsightly doctrinal tapestry that looks bad from both the front and the back.

The amazing popularity of this doctrine belies the embarrassing history that produced it. With absolutely no church tradition or pedigree to support it, this idea was invented in the early to mid-19th century by well intentioned but misguided teachers and pastors. The single greatest contributor to the spread of this doctrine was Cyrus Scofield, who published this teaching as a part of his first-of-its-kind study Bible. For the same reasons that study Bibles are standard issue today, Scofield's Bible enjoyed unprecedented popularity. Due in large part to Scofield's personal connections, the two most popular seminaries/Bible institutes of that time both embraced this teaching, churning out generations of pastors and Bible teachers who embraced the idea of a secret-rapture.

Despite the entertaining and popular teaching that is the secret rapture, the Word of God knows no such thing. There will be no secret rapture. There will be no "completion" of God's original purposes with the state of Israel. There will be no Jewish Missionary Society that evangelizes a now "believer-deficient" world. There is no "special" means of salvation for Jews apart from the same need to be born again that applies to all who are lost. There will be no utopian world that will exist with Christ, seated on a literal throne in Jerusalem, complete with the resurrection of old Temple practices, complemented by a steady stream of people who come to Jerusalem to be saved. While not as doctrinally "sexy" as the so-called secret rapture, the truth is that Jesus will appear again someday. He will gather all of humanity to Himself, first the dead in Christ, then the rest of mankind, at which time we will all be judged and assigned our eternal home.

The implications for us are numerous. New is not always better. Despite repeated attempts on the part of dispensationalists to find some historical precedent, nothing approximating the current teaching existed prior to the 19th century. We should also take to heart the need to thoroughly vet any teaching or doctrine that has a dubious pedigree. Finally our hope in the glory of God should not rest on some future, idyllic existence that violates the very heart of the Great Commission. It is not to one nation that God's purposes are focused, but to all the nations of the earth. And our hope for the future cannot be focused on whether or not we will experience a "great tribulation" or be taken to Heaven and placed in a seven year holding pattern. It is not for some future earth that we are commanded to pray, "your Kingdom come, your will be done, on earth as it is in Heaven." That prayer concerns this earth—our world, to which Christ commanded us to go and make disciples. "Warning: In Case of the actual Biblical teaching on the Rapture, This Car Will Become Completely Irrelevant."

CHAPTER 10

THE WAIT OF THE WORLD

PASSING THE PROPHETIC BATON

In my vision at night I looked, and there before me was one like a son of man, coming with the clouds of heaven. He approached the Ancient of Days and was led into his presence. He was given authority, glory and sovereign power; all peoples, nations and men of every language worshiped him. His dominion is an everlasting dominion that will not pass away, and his Kingdom is one that will never be destroyed.
DANIEL 9:13-14

Your land will be laid waste, and your cities will lie in ruins. Then the land will enjoy its sabbath years all the time that it lies desolate and you are in the country of your enemies; then the land will rest and enjoy its sabbaths. All the time that it lies desolate, the land will have the rest it did not have during the sabbaths you lived in it...For the land will be deserted by them and will enjoy its sabbaths while it lies desolate without them. They will pay for their sins because they rejected my laws and abhorred my decrees.
LEVITICUS 26: 35, 43

Daniel and Revelation: Passing the Baton

Ask any track and field athlete who runs in relays what the most important part of the race is, and they will always tell you: "Passing the baton." The most significant Old Testament book having to do with the "end-times" is the book of Daniel. It is intimately connected to Revelation. As a result, the visions and dreams that Daniel interpreted and saw are essential to understanding Revelation. They provide the historical foundation upon which Revelation is built. It is as if Daniel reached across time and passed the baton of prophecy to the apostle John. Where Daniel left off, John picked up. The events that Daniel described were fulfilled before and during the life of Christ. Revelation chronicles events that occurred not long after the life of Christ.

The most significant chapter in all of Scripture relative to our philosophy of history is Daniel 2. The vision that Daniel interpreted carried his readers from a great image in Babylon to a manger in Bethlehem. Coupled with chapter 7, these visions do more to inform a Christian understanding of history than any others. The timeline that Daniel offered up began in 603 B.C., the second year of the reign of the greatest monarch to date, King Nebuchadnezzar.

The king was greatly troubled by the dream he had, and it caused him to lose sleep (Daniel 2:1). The greatest soothsayers and sorcerers of the Kingdom were summoned to tell the king the meaning of his dream. He shrewdly denied requests to share the content of the dream, knowing full well that anyone can "make up" an interpretation of something they have been told, whereas only a true diviner of truth could know the content AND the interpretation without being given any clues. Daniel 2:10 provided the perfect introduction to Daniel and his friends: *"There is not a man on earth who can meet the king's demand..."* Precisely. Any hope for understanding could not rest with a man, but with God Himself. As the Protagonist of the entire chapter, God Himself, was "set up" in verse 11: *"No one can show it to the king except the gods, whose dwelling is not with flesh."* The faux wise men of Babylon had unwittingly hit the nail on the proverbial head. No "man" can do what you ask, but "God" can.

In a rash display of arrogance and anger, the king responded by decreeing that every wise man in the Kingdom would suffer the same fate as those who were granted an audience—death. In marked contrast, Daniel responded to his imminent demise with *"prudence and discretion"* (2:14). In an amazing display of faith, Daniel requested an audience with the king so that *"he might show the interpretation to the king"* (2:16). Before conferring with his friends or inquiring of the Lord, Daniel was confident that the God of Israel was in this, and that He would deliver both Daniel and his friends. Never a Lone Ranger, Daniel proceeded to confer with Shadrach, Meshach and Abednego, aka Hananiah, Mishael, and Azariah. They all prayed for *"mercy from the God of heaven,"* and Daniel received the interpretation of the dream in the form of a vision. Before the chapter shares the meaning of the dream with the reader, **the real point of the dream is revealed—that God is sovereign over history, and it is He who sets up and deposes the rulers of the earth.** *"He changes times and seasons; he removes kings and sets up kings...He reveals deep and hidden things; He knows what is in the darkness, and the light dwells with Him"* (2:21-22). For the sake of His own glory, and to the praise of His glorious grace, the God of heaven would set up one Kingdom as He brought down four others.

Daniel was quickly brought before King Nebuchadnezzar. When asked if he knew the content of the dream and its meaning, Daniel's answer must have shocked the monarch: *"No wise men, enchanters, magicians, or astrologers can show to the king the mystery that the king has asked"* (2:27). Before the king could say "off with their heads," Daniel again pointed the king and the reader to the main character of this unfolding drama: *"...but there is a God in heaven who reveals mysteries, and He has made known to King Nebuchadnezzar what will be in the latter days"* (2:28). Daniel's reference to "the latter days" is a clear indication that the things he would speak of had to do with events in the distant future. A better translation might be "at the end of the era," meaning a long (but not interminable) time from now that will usher out one thing and introduce another. This phrase carried with it the idea of fulfillment; as if God's long-planned retaking of lost ground would begin in earnest in the days under consideration.[107]

Before we look at the specifics of the interpretation, we need to remember that we are dealing with visions and dreams. As with all apocalyptic literature, the meaning of symbols and metaphors cannot be pushed too far. The dream that Daniel interpreted had to do with the grand sweep of history and the definitive triumph of God's plans over man's plans. Trying to match every minute detail of the dream with a moment in history demands too much of the text.

---

[107] John Goldingay, *Daniel* (Word Biblical Commentary: Dallas, Texas) 1989, pp. 48-49.

Daniel proceeded to tell the king that he saw an immense statue that radiated light and was "frightening" in appearance. The image was composed of five ingredients: gold, silver, bronze, iron, and clay. As the king watched, a supernatural stone *"cut out by no human hand"* (2:34) rolled toward the statue, struck it, and broke the statue into pieces. After being broken apart, the pieces of the statue proceeded to disintegrate and become like *"the chaff of the summer threshing floor"* (2:35). The wind then carried the pulverized remnants of the statue away, so that *"not a trace of them could be found"* (2:35). The same stone that struck the statue then began to grow until it became the size of a *"great mountain"* that covered the entire earth (2:35). As we are soon to discover, Nebuchadnezzar had good reason to lose sleep over this dream.

The statue, we are told, represented four successive Kingdoms. The first, the head of gold, represented the Babylonian Kingdom over which Nebuchadnezzar ruled. The latter's rule was far-reaching, but only because the God of heaven had permitted him to assume that role (2:37-38). The silver in the statue represented another Kingdom, "inferior" to Babylon, which would come to power "after" Babylon fell, referring to the Medo-Persian Empire which ultimately conquered Babylon and became the next great world power. A third Kingdom followed, which would "rule over all the earth," referring to the Greek empire established by Alexander the Great. A fourth Kingdom, which received special treatment in the dream, would take the place of Greece. Several features of this Kingdom were: it would be as "strong as iron" (2:40). It would also "break and crush all these" other Kingdoms (2:40). This Kingdom would be a "divided Kingdom," being "partly strong and partly brittle"

(2:42). It would also be characterized by an attempt to mix races through marriage in an attempt to create a sort of "melting pot," but these unions would ultimately fail to produce the desired political effect (2:43). Finally, in the *"days of those kings,"* (i.e. the kings of the fourth empire), *"the God of heaven will set up a Kingdom that shall never be destroyed, nor shall the Kingdom be left to another people"* (2:44). Unlike the other Kingdoms, this Kingdom would "stand forever" and it would account for the complete destruction of the other four (2:44).

The only Kingdom that can possibly be the fourth Kingdom, chronologically, culturally and historically is the Roman Empire. Daniel concluded his explanation with a "take it to the bank" dénouement: *"the dream is certain and its interpretation sure"* (Daniel 2:45). Uncharacteristically, Nebuchadnezzar responded as every opponent to the Kingdom of God should: he *"fell upon his face"* and declared *"Truly, your God is God of gods and Lord of kings, and a revealer of mysteries"* (2:47).

Prophesied Empires
- Babylon
- Medo-Persia
- Greece
- Rome
- Europe
- 2nd Coming of Christ — Daniel 2:44

Although most students of the Bible acknowledge that the empires represented by the statue in Daniel's vision are Babylon-Rome, many (as the chart to the left illustrates) argue that there is a "dual-fulfillment" to this prophecy. A RESURRECTED Roman Empire (European Union?) will, at some point in the future, rise again to dominate the world and wage war against God's people. Nothing in God's Word supports this teaching.

WINSOME WARRIORS
THE KINGDOMS OF DANIEL 2 & 7

Neb. Dream Daniel 2	Daniel's Vision Daniel 7	Kingdoms	Dates
Gold	Lion	Babylonia	605-539 B.C.
Silver	Bear	Medo-Persia	539-336 B.C.
Bronze	Leopard	Greece	336-133 B.C.
Iron	Beast	Rome	133 B.C.-476 A.D.

The same movement of world history that we find described in Daniel 2 is taken up again in chapter 7. While both chapter 2 and 7 deal with the same world powers, the latter does so with greater detail and greater specificity. In both cases, the overriding concern of the author was to assure his readers that **despite the attempts of world powers to threaten God's People and His Kingdom, God Himself will not only vindicate His people, but He will give them another Kingdom** that will vanquish all the others and that will never fade and never be destroyed.

Like Nebuchadnezzar in chapter 2, the dream of chapter 7 "disturbed" Daniel (7:15). It occurred in 555 B.C. at the onset of the reign of Belshazzar. While there is no detailed **interpretation** of this dream as in chapter 2, it was undoubtedly a second iteration of what was described there. Instead of four segments of a statue, Daniel saw four impressive and frightening beasts rising from the sea, each symbolizing successive Kingdoms, a fact made explicit in verse 7:17. Their characterization as beasts was indicative of their opposition to God. Scripture often portrays those who are Godless as beasts (cf. for example Psalm 49:20 and Psalm 73:22). The Kingdoms represented are Babylon, Medo-Persia, Greece and Rome. As in chapter 2, the first beast lost its power, indicated by the removal of its wings. The second beast, the Medo-Persian Empire, "devoured" the Babylonian empire. The three "ribs" in its mouth are most probably referring to the three great Babylonian kings, Nebuchadnezzar, Evil-Merodach and Belshazzar. The third beast had four wings and four heads, symbolic of the four "rulers" who divided up the vast empire of Alexander the Great: Cassander, Lysimachus, Seleucus I, and Ptolemy I.

Paralleling chapter two, the fourth empire/beast was given special attention. No doubt this is due to the special impact that this empire would have in the life of Christ and the early church. The description of the fourth beast conjures up ominous images, with evocative adjectives used to describe it: terrifying and dreadful and exceedingly strong (Daniel 7:7). Like the iron of the great statue, this beast sported "great iron teeth," ideal for devouring (7:7). The fourth beast was more powerful than all the others (7:23), a description of the world domination of the Roman Empire which would "devour the whole earth and trample it down..." (7:23). Like the beast of Revelation 17, this beast had "ten horns," possibly symbolizing ten provincial governors or, more likely, the ten Roman emperors who reigned until the beginning of the Jewish War in 67 A.D.

The "little horn" that is introduced in 7:8 is identified as one who "came up among them." Later in chapter seven we are told that this little horn came "after" the other ten (7:24). Prior to this eleventh king, three others were displaced, or "plucked up," language that suggests the work of God Himself.[108] Although the identity of the little horn has been hotly debated, Daniel gives a number of clues as to his identity. There is no question but that the little horn, like the other ten horns, represents a "king."

Left: Statue of the Roman Emperor, Titus Flavius Caesar Vespasianus Augustus, or, Titus.
Below: Close-up of the inscription at the top of the Arch of Titus. It reads: *The Roman Senate and People to Deified Titus, Vespasian Augustus, son of Deified Vespasian.*

Arch of Titus Detail: Inscription

---

[108] The verb here for "plucked" is passive in voice, suggesting that they had this done to them by someone/something else.

Biblical "clues" to the identity of the "little horn:"

Biblical Text	Clue
(7:8; 24)	• The little horn appears as one of the ten horns, but reigns "after" them, making him an eleventh.
(7:8)	• He follows three other kings whose reigns end precipitously or prematurely.
(7:24)	• The little horn plays some role in the displacement of the other three kings.
(7:8, 20, 25)	• The little horn appears boastful and arrogant.
(7:20)	• The little horn seems greater than his predecessors.
(7:25)	• The little horn wages "war" with God's people for three-and-a-half years.
(7:26-27)	• It is during the reign of the little horn that the Kingdom of God will come and the saints will begin to reign with Christ.
(7:20, 24)	• The little horn is somehow distinct from his predecessors.
(7:25)	• The little horn will try to change the "set times and laws" of his kingdom.

The most likely candidate for the little horn is the Roman emperor Titus (79-81 A.D.)[109] The greatest detail on

---

[109] The Jewish Rabbi who is credited with providing the foundation for all Jewish commentaries that followed was **Rabbi Shlomo Itzhaki**, or Rashi(1040-1105 A.D.). In his commentary on Daniel, written in the late 11th century A.D. he identified the

the reign of Titus came from the Roman historian Suetonius. He identified Titus as the eleventh Roman emperor.[110] Most intriguing was the fact that Titus' father, Vespasian, the tenth emperor, ruled in almost perfect concert with his son. Suetonius noted: *From that time on* (the time of Vespasian's ascension to the throne) *he (Titus) never ceased to act as the emperor's partner and even as his protector. He took part in his father's triumph and was censor with him. He was also his colleague in the tribunicial power and in seven consulships. He took upon himself the discharge of almost all duties, personally dictated letters and wrote edicts in his father's name, and even read his speeches in the senate in lieu of a quaestor.[111]* As early as 70 A.D., Titus was declared emperor by his troops.[112] *For all intents and purposes, what can be said of Vespasian can also be said of Titus.*

Prior to the reign of Vespasian, three other emperors occupied the throne for very short periods. All three met with violent ends. Galba reigned for seven months, from 68-69 A.D., Otho for three months, from January 69 A.D. to April, and Vitellius for another eight months, from April to December of 69 A.D. Although Vespasian was the next emperor, it was Titus who was personally responsible for the execution of Vitellius.

"little horn" as Titus. Most Jewish commentators since have concurred. Cf. www.chabad.org for Rashi's commentary.

[110] C. Suetonius Tranquillas, *The Lives of the Twelve Caesars*, Life of Titus, Loeb Classical Library, 1914, Book 9

[111] C. Suetonius Tranquillas, *The Lives of the Twelve Caesars*, Life of Titus, Loeb Classical Library, 1914, Section 6, p. 329.

[112] Titus did not officially reign as Emperor until 79 A.D

Although Titus grew into the position of emperor, emerging as one of Rome's finest, he was not immune to the vices and excesses of most emperors. The little horn is identified in Daniel 7 as being "arrogant," and Titus certainly matched that description. Again, Suetonius observed: *He also assumed the command of the Praetorian Guard, which before that time had never been held except by a Roman knight, and in this office conducted himself in a somewhat arrogant and tyrannical fashion.*[113] Titus was also given the status of "god" due to his handling of the Jewish Revolt and the complete destruction of the Temple in 70 A.D. The still surviving Arch of Titus is inscribed with the words, *"The Roman Senate and People to Deified Titus, Vespasian Augustus, son of Deified Vespasian."*

Vespasian and Titus zealously appealed to numerous "omens" that supposedly foretold their rise to power, making their ascent to the throne an unmistakable act of the gods. Like his father before him, Titus declared himself emperor *before* receiving Senatorial approval. In the name of restoring stability, he also had conferred upon himself a number of privileges and prerogatives that none of the Julio-Claudians enjoyed.[114]

History distinguished Titus as the second emperor of the critically important Flavian dynasty. With the death of Nero (the last of the Julio-Claudian line) and the twenty months of chaos/civil war brought on by Galba, Otho, and

---

[113] Ibid, p. 329

[114] A surviving fragment of a law known as the *lex de imperio Vespasiani* suggests that Vespasian/Titus were the most autocratic rulers up to that time.

Vitellius, Titus' father provided the empire with desperately needed stability. He acted quickly to make sure his reign lasted beyond himself. Vespasian was the first emperor to actually appoint a successor, his son Titus (also a first) and to officially give him the name "Caesar." All of these details help move Titus to the front of the line in meeting the criteria that Daniel gave us in chapter 7.

Another distinction of the little horn was that he *"will try to change the set times and the laws"* (Daniel 7:25). Under the reign of Titus, two significant pieces of legislation were passed. First, he ended the longstanding practice of trying individuals suspected of treason. Every previous emperor had used the *lex maiestas* to silence political opponents. For the first time in the history of the empire, that practice was abolished. In another piece of landmark legislation, Titus also introduced what survives today as the prohibition of "double jeopardy," or the law that prohibits someone from being tried for the same crime twice. Although both pieces of legislation were later overturned, they stand out as significant for their time.

The most culturally and spiritually significant event in the life of Titus was The First Jewish-Roman War (67-73 A.D.) or The Great Revolt. Nero (then emperor) first appointed Vespasian as the commander of the army assigned the task of putting down the revolt. That distinction quickly passed to Titus, and for close to three-and-a-half years, Titus successfully fought Jewish forces, culminating in the razing of the Temple in 70 A.D. Titus was ultimately responsible for putting down the Jewish rebellion. Jews, and to a lesser degree, Christ-followers, fell by the sword or were captured and crucified.[115] The human toll in Jerusalem alone included virtually all of the more than six-hundred thousand who defended the city against the Romans.[116] In a very real sense, Titus was personally responsible for making war against God's people (Daniel 7:21).

As we have already noted, the significance of 70 A.D. cannot be overstated. *Tisha B'Av*, or July 30, 70 A.D., is appropriately called the "saddest day in Jewish history."[117] It is on this date that The Kingdom came in a way that forever changed history. Although the crucifixion, resurrection and ascension of Christ stand alone as the focal points of history, the timeline of the Kingdom was once-for-all changed as the old covenant ended with the razing of the Temple on that day in July. God used Titus to usher in the Kingdom of God. Again, Titus fits nicely as the little horn, under whose authority the Kingdom came as never before.

It is not surprising that this dramatic change came at the hands of a pagan empire. The story of God's dealings with his people is filled with examples of God using pagan

---

[115] Max Dimont *Jews, God, and History* (2nd ed.).(New York, New York: Signet Classic, 1962), p. 101 "To make sure that no food or water supply would reach the city from the outside, Titus completely sealed off Jerusalem from the rest of the world with a wall of earth as high as the stone wall around Jerusalem itself. Anyone not a Roman soldier caught anywhere in this vast dry moat was crucified on the top of the earthen wall in sight of the Jews of the city. It was not uncommon for as many as five hundred people a day to be so executed. The air was redolent with the stench of rotting flesh and rent by the cries and agony of the crucified. But the Jews held out for still another year, the fourth year of the war, to the discomfiture of Titus."

[116] , Cornelius Tacitus "Book 5". *The works of Cornelius Tacitus: with an essay on his life and genius, notes, supplements*. (Philadelphia, PA: Thomas Wardle, 1844) p. 504.

[117] Joseph Telushkin, *Jewish Literacy: Most Important Things to Know About the Jewish Religion, Its People and Its History*. (New York, NY: William Morrow & Co, 1991) p. 656

and Godless people to judge His Own.[118] But the "judges" do not escape their own judgment. Although they were merely instruments in the hands of the Grand Puppet Master, they were still held responsible for their violence against God's people. The same can be said for Titus. Daniel's vision included the ultimate fate of the little horn (7:26-27). That fate came at the hands of the main characters of chapter seven; the "Ancient of Days" and "one like a son of man."

In Daniel 7:9, The Ancient of Days set up His throne and opened the books (7:10). He was seated on a throne of fire, while a river of fire emanated from Him, symbolizing the purifying effect of His judgment upon all the beasts and the little horn in particular (7:9-11). Using language that anticipated Matthew 24, *"one like a son of man"* (The Christ) comes *"with the clouds of heaven"* (Matthew 24:30) and received the dominion and glory of the Kingdom (7:13-14). With the destruction of Jerusalem, the prophecy of Daniel 7:14, originally given in Genesis 12:3, became a reality. The ethnocentric and exclusive religion of Israel gave way to the Gospel of the Kingdom and became available to *"all peoples, nations, and languages"* (7:14). The dire predictions for his own people were not lost on Daniel. At the very least, he intuited the significance of what he saw: *"my spirit within me was anxious, and the visions of my head alarmed me"* (7:15). As the blood drained from his face (7:28), Daniel pondered the implications of what he had seen.

---

[118] Many of the Minor Prophets struggle with this fact—note especially Habakkuk, who cannot conceive of the fact that God would use the pagan Babylonian empire to judge His own People. (Habakkuk 1:5-6)

The bad news for Daniel is contrasted with the almost inconceivably good news for the now expanded and multi-national People of God. Christ does not rule alone.

> *And the Kingdom and the dominion and the greatness of the Kingdoms under the whole heaven shall be given to the people of the saints of the Most High; their Kingdom shall be an everlasting Kingdom, and all dominions shall serve and obey them* (Daniel 7:27).

Daniel saw a day when not only Christ would reign, but the saints would reign with Him.

As we have seen, Daniel had much to say about the events that occurred during and around the lifetime of Jesus' "beloved" disciple John. Recalling our metaphor of the relay runner, Daniel received the "baton" of prophecy. He recorded events that would take us up to the time of Christ and His disciples. Many of the prophecies that Daniel foretold would come to pass in the lifetime of John. The imagery of "sealing up" the prophecy suggested Daniel would have to wait for the things he saw to be fulfilled. In so doing, he reached across time and handed the baton of prophecy to John, who then received his own vision which the latter recorded in Revelation. It was an almost seamless transition. But before Daniel could finish his leg of the race, there was one more prophecy that he had to record. In one of the most stirring and stunning prophecies of the Old Testament, Daniel introduced us to the prophetically critical "seventy-weeks" in Daniel 9.

THE NOTORIOUS 70-WEEKS

The implications of what Daniel had seen thus far were beginning to sink in. The future for his people was grim. As he pondered that prospect, Daniel, as part of his daily "quiet time," read Jeremiah 25:1-15 and Jeremiah 29:1-23. Daniel read that the exile that he was a part of would not last forever.

> *"But when **the seventy years are fulfilled**, I will punish the king of Babylon and his nation, the land of the Babylonians, for their guilt," declares the LORD, "and will make it desolate forever. I will bring upon that land all the things I have spoken against it, all that are written in this book and prophesied by Jeremiah against all the nations. They themselves will be enslaved by many nations and great kings; I will repay them according to their deeds and the work of their hands...This is what the LORD says:* ***"When seventy years are completed for Babylon****, I will come to you and fulfill my gracious promise to bring you back to this place"* (Jeremiah 25:12-14; 29:10 emphasis added).

Daniel realized that the seventy year exile of God's people was nearly done. Beginning with the death of king Josiah in 608 B.C., Daniel correctly surmised that it could not be much longer to wait. The fall of Babylon to Cyrus the Great occurred in 539 B.C., making the timing of Daniel's prayer in chapter 9 very close to that year. Daniel was hoping and literally praying that the end of Israel's exile had come. But, as Daniel was about to discover, he was far too short-sighted. **God's plan for restoring His people extended far beyond a physical return to their homeland. The deeper and much more significant restoration of God's people would take much** longer. This is at the heart of the message that the angel Gabriel brought to Daniel in chapter 9.

Unlike the previous chapters, this prophecy was rooted in Scripture, not a vision or dream. As Daniel read the prophecies of Jeremiah, he was overcome with the sin and rebellion of the Jewish people. No less than twenty-two times in Daniel 9:4-16, Daniel referred to the "sin," "shame," "rebellion," "disobedience," and failure to listen on the part of his people. Daniel's spirit was flooded with shame, and he poured his heart out in confession and repentance. Daniel acknowledged that God kept His part of the covenant and that He loved to bless (9:4) despite the reckless disregard of Israel for their God.

The focus of Daniel's confession then turns to the "desolation" of Jerusalem and the Temple (9:2, 12, 16-18). Once again, Daniel failed to see the much more significant desolation of the hearts of God's people. A return to Jerusalem would only address their physical return from exile. As always, God's concern is that His people fulfill their covenant responsibility to bring the truth about the God of Israel to ALL the nations. As Daniel was about to learn, rebellion, judgment and restoration are not merely a matter of where one's body is, but where one's heart is.

Appropriately, Daniel acknowledged that what was at stake was the reputation of God Himself, and that it was for His own name's sake that He should act (9:16-19). Daniel's thinking was on the right track, but he failed to see that God's agenda was about much more than just *one* people and *one* city. From Daniel's perspective, as long as Jerusalem lay in ruin, and as long as the Temple remained unrestored, God's glory suffered. Daniel could not possibly have been prepared for the answer to his prayer, or for what God had in store for both His holy city and His dwelling place, the Temple. That answer began in Daniel 9:20.

The interpretive key to Daniel 9 is the number seven and multiples of seven. At the heart of God's great creative and "re-creative" work is the number seven. On the seventh day, God rested—not because He was tired or bored, but because His desire was to weave a key thread into the fabric of life—the principle of "Sabbath." From the beginning, God's people had been commanded to enjoy a Sabbath. The Sabbath was to be the axle upon which all of life turned. In addition to the weekly observance of Sabbath, every seventh year, the Israelites were to exercise this same principle by giving the land a "Sabbath of rest" by not sowing or reaping.

> *"Speak to the Israelites and say to them: 'When you enter the land I am going to give you, the land itself must observe a Sabbath to the LORD.* **For six years sow your fields, and for six years prune your vineyards and gather their crops. But in the seventh year the land is to have a year of Sabbath rest, a Sabbath to the LORD**. *Do not sow your fields or prune your vineyards. Do not reap what grows of itself or harvest the grapes of your untended vines. The land is to have a year of rest. Whatever the land yields during the Sabbath year will be food for you—for yourself, your male and female servants, and the hired worker and temporary resident who live among you, as well as for your livestock and the wild animals in your land. Whatever the land produces may be eaten"* (Leviticus 25:2-7 emphasis added).

THE WAIT OF THE WORLD

In addition to giving the land a Sabbath, that same Sabbath of rest was to extend to debts and ownership of both property and people. Called the year of *"shemitah"* or release, Sabbatical years reminded God's people that we are only stewards of what God has given us, not owners, and that the plight of the poor must always be considered.

> *At the end of every seven years **you must cancel debts.** This is how it is to be done: Every creditor shall cancel any loan they have made to a fellow Israelite. They shall not require payment from anyone among their own people, because the LORD's time for canceling debts has been proclaimed...Be careful not to harbor this wicked thought: "The seventh year, the year for canceling debts, is near," so that you do not show ill will toward the needy among your fellow Israelites and give them nothing. They may then appeal to the LORD against you, and you will be found guilty of sin* (Deuteronomy 15:1-2, 9).

Again in Deuteronomy 31, God made His will clear.

> *Then Moses commanded them: "At the end of every seven years, in the year for canceling debts, during the Festival of Tabernacles, when all Israel comes to appear before the LORD your God at the place he will choose, you shall read this law before them in their hearing. Assemble the people—men, women and children, and the foreigners residing in your towns—so they can listen and learn to fear the LORD your God and follow carefully all the words of this law. Their children, who do not know this law, must hear it and learn to fear the LORD your God as long as you live in the land you are crossing the Jordan to possess* (Deuteronomy 31:10-13).

Sabbatical years were to begin during the month of *Tishri* which corresponds roughly to our October (Leviticus 25:9). After seven cycles of Sabbatical years (49 years or 7 X 7), the Israelites were commanded to celebrate the "year of Jubilee," during which all property reverted back to its original owner.

> *Count off seven Sabbath years—seven times seven years—so that the seven Sabbath years amount to a period of forty-nine years. Then have the trumpet sounded everywhere on the tenth day of the seventh month; on the Day of Atonement sound the trumpet throughout your land.* **Consecrate the fiftieth year** *and proclaim liberty throughout the land to all its inhabitants. It shall be a jubilee for you; each of you is to return to your family property and to your own clan. The fiftieth year shall be a jubilee for you; do not sow and do not reap what grows of itself or harvest the untended vines. For it is a jubilee and is to be holy for you; eat only what is taken directly from the fields.* **In this Year of Jubilee everyone is to return to their own property** (Leviticus 25:8-13 emphasis added).

To Israel's great shame, there is no record of either the Sabbatical years or the Year of Jubilee **ever** having been observed. In addition to Israel's disregard for the ethical demands God has placed on her, they ignored perhaps their greatest distinctive—Sabbatical and Jubilee. God was very specific as to the repercussions of such disobedience.

> *If in spite of this you still do not listen to me but continue to be hostile toward me, then in my anger I will be hostile toward you, and I myself will punish you for your sins* **seven times over** *...I will scatter you among the nations and will draw out my sword and pursue you. Your land will be laid waste, and your cities will lie in*

> ruins. **Then the land will enjoy its sabbath years** *all the time that it lies desolate and you are in the country of your enemies; then the land will rest and enjoy its sabbaths.* **All the time that it lies desolate, the land will have the rest it did not have during the sabbaths you lived in it...** *For the land will be deserted by them and will enjoy its sabbaths while it lies desolate without them. They will pay for their sins because they rejected my laws and abhorred my decrees* (Leviticus 26:27-28, 33-35, 43 emphasis added).

God made clear that the consequences of failing to keep the Sabbatical years would result in one year of captivity for each Sabbatical year that went unobserved (2 Chronicles 36:20-21; Jeremiah 34:8-17). This principle, one year for each day, is not without precedent. The Israelites were punished with forty years of wandering in the wilderness before entering the Promised Land because they had squandered forty days of reconnaissance. *For forty years—one year for each of the forty days you explored the land—you will suffer for your sins and know what it is like to have me against you* (Numbers 14:34). In Daniel's case, Israel was punished with one year of captivity for each of the Sabbatical years they failed to observe. Over the past 490 years (70 Sabbatical cycles), the land should have enjoyed seventy Sabbatical years. Those years were lost due to Israel's unwillingness to observe them. God restored those seventy "lost" years by giving them back to the land.

For close to seventy years, Israel had been held in captivity by the Babylonians/Medo-Persians, giving the land the seventy years of rest that it had never experienced (Leviticus 26 & 2 Chronicles 36). Daniel pled,

> *Now, our God, hear the prayers and petitions of your servant. For your sake, Lord, look with favor on your desolate sanctuary. Give ear, our God, and hear; open your eyes and see the desolation of the city that bears your Name. We do not make requests of you because we are righteous, but because of your great mercy. Lord, listen! Lord, forgive! Lord, hear and act! For your sake, my God, do not delay, because your city and your people bear your Name* (Daniel 9:17-19).

The remarkable answer that Daniel received addressed both the shorter story of God's dealings with His people, and the longer story of His dealings with the nations. The shorter story of rescue for Israel would move their bodies from one land to another. The longer story of redemption would move their hearts from one Kingdom to another. That this was God's plan all along is evident from words like these:

> *When all these blessings and curses I have set before you come on you and you take them to heart wherever the LORD your God disperses you among the nations, and when you and your children return to the LORD your God and obey him with all your heart and with all your soul according to everything I command you today, then the LORD your God will restore your fortunes and have compassion on you and gather you again from all the nations where he scattered you. Even if you have been banished to the most distant land under the heavens, from there the LORD your God will gather you and bring you back. He will bring you to the land that belonged to your ancestors, and you will take possession of it. He will make you more prosperous and numerous than your ancestors. The LORD your God will circumcise your hearts and the hearts of your descendants, so that you may love him with all your heart and with all your soul, and live. The LORD your*

> *God will put all these curses on your enemies who hate and persecute you. You will again obey the LORD and follow all his commands I am giving you today. Then the LORD your God will make you most prosperous in all the work of your hands and in the fruit of your womb, the young of your livestock and the crops of your land. The LORD will again delight in you and make you prosperous, just as he delighted in your ancestors, if you obey the LORD your God and keep his commands and decrees that are written in this Book of the Law and turn to the LORD your God with all your heart and with all your soul* (Deuteronomy 30:1-10).

Notice that God is concerned with more than just where His people's bodies are (bringing them back to the Land). He is far more concerned with where their hearts are (*so that you may love me with all your heart and with all your soul...*). The resolution of the first concern (their bodies) would be accomplished very soon. God's people would be brought back to the Land and His sanctuary would be restored. But the bigger concern (their hearts) would take longer—490 years to be exact. Israel had broken covenant with God and had been punished as a result. But the amount of time it would take *to finish transgression, to put an end to sin, to atone for wickedness, to bring in everlasting righteousness, to seal up vision and prophecy and to anoint the Most Holy Place...* would take much longer (Daniel 9:24). Why "seventy sevens" or four-hundred-ninety years? With beautiful divine symmetry, Gabriel informed Daniel that true restoration would take 490 years. Using the Sabbatical year formula that this passage assumes, we can calculate that from the establishment of the Kingdom of Israel until the Babylonian captivity was roughly 490 years. Then commenced the seventy years of exile before Jerusalem and the Temple were rebuilt, followed by another 490 years to restore the hearts of God's people and bring the Gospel to the nations.[119] Daniel was primarily concerned with the return from exile. God was primarily concerned with renewing His covenant with the True Israel so that they could be the blessing to the nations that He intended from the beginning.

To summarize, it took God's people 490 years to get into this mess, and it would take another 490 years to get them out![120] With this as our foundation, let's look specifically at what Gabriel's words to Daniel in 9:20-27 actually meant.

Seventy Sabbatical Years or 490 Years	Seventy Years In Exile	Seventy Sabbatical Years or 490 Years
Time Required to Store Up God's Wrath	1 Year for Every "Sabbath" The Land Did Not Receive	Time Required to Establish a New Covenant

In verses 20 and 21, Daniel was reintroduced to the angel Gabriel. His purpose in coming to Daniel was clear—to give Daniel *"insight and understanding"* (v. 22). The moment

---

[119] Bob Pickle has provided a landmark analysis of when the Sabbatical years fell on the Jewish calendar. Comparing the two best attempts at identifying those years, the 1856 Zuckermann table and the 1973 Wacholder table, Pickle concludes that the Zuckermann table is correct. For a copy of that analysis, go to *"When Were the Sabbatical Years"* at http://www.pickle-publishing.com/papers/sabbatical-years.htm.

[120] I am thoroughly indebted to Peter J. Gentry for his amazingly well written and documented article *Daniel's Seventy Weeks and the New Exodus*, *SBJT* 14.1 (2010): 26-44. In that article, Gentry argues that just as God brought His people out of Egypt and established a covenant with them, so Daniel's Seventy Weeks speaks of another great "exodus" and the restoration of God's covenant with His people.

Daniel began to confess the sins of his people, a "word" went out from the Lord. In the original language, "word" suggests a decree or a covenant. God had ordained that it would take "seventy sevens" to regain the hearts of His people and truly end their exile. There is an ever shrinking debate over the meaning of the word "weeks" or "sevens" here. In Hebrew, the word *savua* is translated "week," a period of seven days. But Daniel's quotation of Gabriel meant something different in 9:24. This seems clear when compared to Daniel's use of the same word in 10:2-3. There he made his meaning explicit by using the expression "week of days." This is the only instance in the entire Old Testament where the expression "week of days" is used. This makes sense given the close proximity to a different and figurative use of the word *savua*, "week" in 9:24. It is as if Daniel is telling the reader, "I know I used the word "week" in a different sense in chapter 9, but in chapter 10 I mean the reader to understand the word normally. To make sure you get that, I am going to spell it out for you in chapter 10—a "week" means seven days there, precisely because it doesn't mean that in chapter 9." The most natural understanding of *savua* in chapter 9 is to take the word "week" to mean a seven YEAR period, not a seven DAY period.

Accordingly, there would be seventy of these seven-year periods as it related specifically to the restoration of the True Israel and the rebuilding of the earthly Jerusalem, and the revelation of the Heavenly Jerusalem (Daniel 9:24). This period would commence after the 70 year exile had been completed. We are told that this 490 year period would be required to accomplish six things: 1. To finish transgression, 2. To put an end to sin, 3. To atone for wickedness, 4. To bring in everlasting righteousness, 5. To seal up vision and prophecy, and 6. To anoint the Most Holy Place" [121](9:24). Seen in the broader context of restoring the covenant with His People, the first three objectives to be accomplished during the "seventy sevens" had to do with ethnic Israel; Ethnic Israel needed to "finish" or "complete" their rebellion against God, atonement had to be made for that rebellion, and they needed to be forgiven. The last three objectives had a much broader application. Once ethnic Israel had been dealt with, God's original intention for the *True Israel* could be accomplished. Although natural Israelites were included in the last three objectives, God's plan had always been for Israel to be part of a much greater and diverse People, the True Israel composed of all those who put their trust in The Messiah. Once the 490 years was up, the world (not just Israel) would experience unprecedented access to the God of Israel, introducing "everlasting righteousness," the fulfillment of all prophecy up to that point, and the consecration of the "most Holy Place." Even a quick glance at the New Testament illustrates how these six prophesies were fulfilled in and around the lifetime of Christ.

1. *"To finish transgression..."*
This was fulfilled as the sins of God's people finally reached their tipping point, and the wrath that God had stored up toward ethnic Israel was finally unleashed in the

---

[121] The reference to the "anointing of the Most Holy Place" should not be confused with a reference to the physical Temple. All 6 of these things point directly to Christ. While it is easier to assign the first five things with the work of Christ, the reference to the Most Holy Place has confused some. Like the other five, the sixth thing is a reference to the "True Temple," or Jesus Christ. In John 2:13-22 Christ himself made this connection when debating with the religious leaders of His day. John makes the same connection in Revelation 21:22 where we are told that there is no Temple in the New Jerusalem because the "Lamb" is the true Temple.

destruction of Jerusalem (Matthew 3:7; 21:33-45; 23:32,35,36,38; Luke 11:47-51; 1 Thessalonians 2:14-16).

2. *"To put an end to sin..."*
This was fulfilled as the obsolete old covenant way of dealing with sin was forever ended with the death of Christ (John 1:29; Matt 1:21; Acts 10:43; Hebrews 9:12-14, 26; 10:9-14).

3. *"To atone for wickedness..."*
This was fulfilled in the propitiation for our sins offered by Christ on the cross (Romans 5:8-11; 2 Cor. 5:17-21; Hebrews 2:17; Col 1:12-21).

4. *"To bring in everlasting righteousness..."*
This was fulfilled as Christ's death/resurrection introduced us *to "a righteousness from God apart from the law..."* (Romans 3:21-26; 4:13; 5:17, 18; 9:30, 31; 14:17; Hebrews 9:12; 2 Thessalonians 2:16; 1 Corinthians1:30; 2 Corinthians 9:9).

5. *"To seal up vision and prophecy..."*
This was accomplished as Christ fulfilled all prophecy regarding the Messiah and revealed that the Old Testament Scriptures had always been speaking of Him (Matthew 13:14,15; 17:5; John 1:1; 12:39-41; Acts 7:37; 28:25-27; Romans 1:1-2, 3:21, 16:25-26; Ephesians 2:11-17; 3:3-6; Colossians 1:26; Hebrews 1:1-2; 1 Peter 1:9-11; 2 Peter 1:19-21).

6. *"To anoint the most holy ..."*
This was fulfilled as Christ received the anointing of the

Holy Spirit, enabling Him to function as a perfectly surrendered Human Being (Matthew 3:15-17; Luke 4:18; John 1:32; Acts 2:32,33,38,39; 4:26,27; 10:37,38,44,45; Hebrews 9:22-24).

Gabriel proceeded to tell Daniel **when** these things would be accomplished. *"From the time the word goes out to restore and rebuild Jerusalem until the Anointed One, the ruler, comes, there will be seven 'sevens' and sixty-two 'sevens'"*(9:25). In other words, from the time the decree to rebuild Jerusalem went out, until the coming of the Anointed One, 483 years would go by (7 + 62 X 7). Before we explain when this prophetic clock started ticking, we need to identify the "Anointed One" or "ruler" that Gabriel spoke of.

The rules of grammar and the absence of any clear indications to the contrary demand that the two terms—"Anointed One" and "ruler" in verse 25—must refer to the same individual. The same rules demand that the "Anointed One" in verse 26 also refers to the same individual. There is a standard term in Hebrew for "ruler," the word *melek-*מֶלֶךְ It is used to describe a king/ruler who sees his role as absolute monarch and who uses his position to prosper himself at least as much as his subjects. That word is NOT used here. Instead, the word *nagid-*נָגִיד is used. Although *nagid*, used in isolation, can refer to any king or monarch who assumes the throne, it is rarely used in conjunction with the word for "anointed one," or *masiah-*מָשִׁיחַ Whenever the words *nagid* (ruler) and *masiah* (anointed one) are used together, they refer ONLY to an anointed king/ruler who sees himself as divinely appointed for the purpose of benefiting God's People (1 Samuel 9:16; 10:1; 1 Chronicles 29:22). If a likely candidate for the "Anointed One" and "ruler" of Daniel 9 is beginning to emerge, it is for good reason. As theologian John Oswalt notes, "the reference in Daniel 9 is the only unambiguous reference to *masiah* (The Messiah) as the eschatological Anointed One, in the entire Old Testament."[122] The "Anointed One" and "ruler" of Daniel 9:25 & 26 is none other than Jesus Christ.

To review: from the time of the decree to rebuild Jerusalem goes out, until the coming of the Messiah (*nagid/ masiah*), 483 years would transpire. Using the Sabbatical Year formula as our template, the decree that began the 70 week timeline was issued in 457 B.C. by King Artaxerxes to the prophet Ezra (Ezra 7:11-26). The original decree to rebuild Jerusalem/the Temple was issued in 537 B.C. by Cyrus. That work stopped due to hostility from opponents of the plan. This matched perfectly with the words of Gabriel who acknowledged that the work to rebuild the city/Temple would be done "in times of trouble" (Daniel 9:25). A second decree was then issued by Darius to complete the work (Ezra 6). In Ezra 7, we read how the supporting infrastructure for the city/Temple needed to be completed, a task sanctioned by Artaxerxes in 457 B.C. What is amazing about all these orders is that Scripture views them all as one decree!

> *So the elders of the Jews continued to build and prosper under the preaching of Haggai the prophet and Zechariah, a descendant of Iddo. They finished building the Temple according to the command of the God of*

---

[122] J. Oswalt, "מָשִׁיחַ," *New International Dictionary of Old Testament Theology and Exegesis* (ed. William A. VanGemeren; 5 vols; Grand Rapids:Zondervan, 1997), 2.1126. as quoted by Peter J. Gentry, *Daniel's Seventy Weeks and the New Exodus*, SBJT 14.1 (2010): 33.

> *Israel and the decrees of Cyrus, Darius and Artaxerxes, kings of Persia* (Ezra 6:14).

Each successive decree was viewed as an extension of the previous one.[123] Most striking about Artaxerxes' order in 457 B.C. is that it coincided perfectly with the beginning of a Sabbatical year.[124] Counting from 457 B.C. the 69 weeks that we are told should bring us to the "Anointed One" take us to the year 27 A.D. With laser like precision, the prophecy of Daniel 9 introduced us to the life and public ministry of Jesus Christ, which began at precisely that time!

As we move further into the text, we find ourselves faced with a stream of references that seem to jump from one to another with no apparent connection. Much of the confusion surrounding Daniel 9:25-27 has to do with the classic Hebrew prose in which Gabriel's message was delivered. "The approach in ancient Hebrew literature is to

---

[123] "The decrees of Cyrus, Darius and Artaxerxes 7th year are referred to in Ezra 6:14 as if they are but one decree. It is as if Cyrus began the decree and Artaxerxes finished it, which explains why Daniel 9:25 speaks of one "commandment to restore and rebuilt." Once this commandment process was complete, the 70 weeks could begin." An Examination of of Anderson's Chronological Errors Regarding Daniel 9's First 69 Weeks" at http://www.picklepublishing.com/papers/sir-robert-anderson.htm. P. 13 under "Conclusions" #6.

[124] Robert Pickle has provided excellent research into the dates for Sabbatical years. In particular, Pickle compares the two academic "standards" for calculating when the Sabbatical years were, those provided by Benedict Zuckerman in 1856 and the more recent research of Ben Zion Wacholder. Using computer generated models and careful examination of data from a variety of Biblical and extraBiblical sources, Pickle concludes that Zuckerman's calculations are indeed correct. He writes: "of the various interpretations of Daniel 9 that have been proposed over the centuries, there is one that fits Zuckerman's sabbatical dates. That is the interpretation that commences the 70 weeks with the decree of Ezra 7 in 457 B.C. and ends it in 34 AD. Christ's death, under this scenario, occurs in the precise middle of the 70th week, in the spring of 31 AD." Online "When Were the Sabbatical Years?" http://www.picklepublishing.com/papers/sabbatical-years.htm, p. 10 under "Conclusion and Application."

take up a topic and develop it from a particular perspective and then to stop and start anew, taking up the same theme again from another point of view."[125] Imagine listening to Queen's rock classic "Bohemian Rhapsody." At one point the chorus sings *"(Let him go!) Bismillah! We will not let you go (Let him go!) Bismillah! We will not let you go! (Let me go!) Will not let you go! (Let me go!) Will not let you go! (Let me go!) Ah no, no, no, no, no, no, no."*

If you listen to the song with stereo equipment, you will notice that the chorus is sung sequentially, with music coming from the right speaker, then the left, and so on. It is up to the listener to put the words together in order to make sense. The chorus is actually a conversation, the left and right speakers representing the two people (groups) in the conversation. Such is the case with Daniel 9:25-27. The reader is introduced to the same event from different perspectives. It is up to the reader to "listen" to the right, then the left "speaker" and make sense of what they are hearing/reading. Gabriel's message took up one event, moved on to another at a different time, then moved **back** to the original event, and then **back** again to the later event. Our tendency as Westerners is to read this passage in a linear fashion. This is what most often keeps us from understanding it correctly. The last or 70th week was described in both verses 26 and 27 with additional references to events that fell outside of the 70th week included in the same verses. If we try and read these verses in "order" we will be hopelessly confused. As we

---

[125] Peter J. Gentry, *Daniel's 70 Weeks and The New Exodus*, p. 36.

will see, this literary structure helps make much more sense of what follows.

Verse 26 takes us to a time "after the sixty-two-sevens." Sometime after the 69th week (7 + 62) the "Anointed One" would be put to death and "will have nothing." The words translated "will have nothing" are awkward, and could just as easily be translated, "but not for himself."[126] This translation fits more precisely with what we know about the death of Christ as an "atoning sacrifice" for our sins. We are then introduced in verse 26b to another event that occurred sometime after the 69th week. We are not told how long after the 69th week this event occurred, or even if it occurred within the 70th week. There is nothing in the text that DEMANDS that the events described in 26b and 27b occurred **during** the seventieth week, only sometime **after** the 69th.

We know from our examination of Matthew 24, that Christ Himself foretold that it was **He** who would ultimately destroy the Temple and the city of Jerusalem. We also know from the most reliable extra Biblical source on the destruction of Jerusalem, Josephus's *The Wars of the Jews*, that it was the Jewish Zealots who were ultimately responsible for the destruction of the Temple and the city of Jerusalem.[127] As we lay the words of Gabriel in Daniel 9 over history, we see a perfect match. *"The people (the Jews) of the ruler who will come (Christ) will destroy the city and the sanctuary."* In one of the greatest ironies of history, the very Messiah who

---

[126] Peter J. Gentry, *Daniel's 70 Weeks and The New Exodus*, p. 37.

[127] Josephus: *The Wars of the Jews*, 6.2.1-5, pp.877-880.

vicariously gave His life for His people would also bring in the final judgment upon those same people.

The final or "seventieth week" ran from 27-34 AD. Midway through this week, or roughly 31 AD, the Anointed One was "cut-off," referring to the crucifixion, which we know occurred sometime around 31 AD. This same death would "confirm a covenant" with many, a clear reference to the "many" of which Isaiah prophesied.

> *Yet it was the LORD's will to crush him and cause him to suffer, and though the LORD makes his life an offering for sin, he will see his offspring and prolong his days, and the will of the LORD will prosper in his hand. After he has suffered, he will see the light of life and be satisfied;* **by his knowledge my righteous servant will justify many,** *and he will bear their iniquities. Therefore I will give him a portion among the great, and he will divide the spoils with the strong, because he poured out his life unto death, and was numbered with the transgressors.* **For he bore the sin of many***, and made intercession for the transgressors* (Isaiah 53:10-12).

Christ's death brought an end to the old Jewish system of sacrifice (Daniel 9:27) and once and for all atoned for sin (Hebrews 10:5-18). Gabriel's message continued to switch back and forth from the left speaker to the right speaker as he pronounced the final judgment that would ultimately befall the Temple and the city of Jerusalem. Referring to the pagan Roman armies under the command of Titus, Gabriel explained that the final indignation would occur at the hands of this "ruler" (Titus) who would set up his pagan ensigns in and around the holy city/Temple. Of course, he would not escape his own judgment (the "little horn"), which was foretold in detail in Daniel 7.

Pulling all these insights together, a proper reading of Daniel 9:25-27 would look something like this (with explanations added parenthetically).

> *"Know and understand this: From the time the word goes out to restore and rebuild Jerusalem* (in 457 B.C., at the command of Artaxerxes) *until the Anointed One* (The Messiah), *the ruler* (Jesus Christ), *comes, there will be seven 'sevens,'* (49 years) *and sixty-two 'sevens'* (434 years; a total of 483 years). *It* (Jerusalem) *will be rebuilt with streets and a trench,* (complete with infrastructure and political authority in place) *but in times of trouble* (the work will move forward haltingly, with periods of resistance stopping the rebuilding effort). *After the sixty-two 'sevens,'* (after the 483 years, sometime during the 70th week) *the Anointed One* (Jesus Christ) *will be put to death* (crucified) *and will have nothing.* (Or "but not for Himself," i.e. for the sake of atonement for others). *The people (The Jewish people) of the ruler* (Jesus Christ) *who will come will destroy the city and the sanctuary* (i.e. be ultimately responsible for the destruction of Jerusalem/The Temple). *The end will come like a flood: War will continue until the end* (until the total destruction of Jerusalem—it will begin sometime after the 70th week), *and desolations have been decreed* (the fruit of the infighting of the Jewish rebels and zealots who profaned the Temple). *He* (Jesus Christ) *will confirm a covenant* (a new

covenant which includes, but is not exclusive to, Israel) *with many for one 'seven'* (the "many" of which Isaiah spoke in Isaiah 53:10-12). *In the middle of the 'seven'* (Sometime around 31 AD) *he* (Jesus Christ) *will put an end to sacrifice and offering* (through His "once for all" sacrifice on the cross). *And at the Temple* (sometime after the 70th week) *he* (soon-to-be emperor Titus) *will set up an abomination that causes desolation* (by surrounding the holy city with foreign armies and then sacrificing to their gods on the Temple mount), *until the end that is decreed* (the judgment of the "little horn") *is poured out on him* (Titus)."

This is the most consistent and straightforward reading of the text. The significance of all this is that Daniel recorded events, most of which would occur centuries after he wrote them (hence the command to "seal up" the prophecy--Daniel 12:9). Daniel's prophecies in chapters 2, 7, and 9 provide the foundation upon which the vision of Revelation is built. In predicting the rise of the Roman Empire, the death of the Messiah, and the establishment of the Kingdom in a new and fresh way, Daniel paved the way for the words recorded in Revelation. Daniel plotted out the high points of history until the first century AD, and John then filled in the details of what would happen from the first century onward. IN BOTH CASES, THE QUESTION THAT WAS BEING ANSWERED IS, WHAT WILL BE THE FATE OF GOD'S PEOPLE, AND WHEN WILL THE PROMISED KINGDOM COME INTO ITS OWN? Daniel, like John, faced the dilemma that living by sight always presents: What are we to make of what we see, as opposed to what we know by faith? Daniel, having answered that question regarding events BEFORE the coming of the Messiah now passed the baton to John who turned to events that would transpire AFTER the coming of the Messiah. That is the subject of Revelation.

Chapter Summary

The books of Daniel and Revelation are closely connected, the prior explaining one phase of the history of the Kingdom of God, the latter picking up where Daniel left off. Daniel is primarily concerned with the disposition of God's people and the historical development of the Kingdom.

Daniel 2 and 7 provide us with a "40,000 foot view" of the growth of the Kingdom Using the metaphors of both a great statue and fierce beasts, respectively, Daniel foretold that 4 great earthly kingdoms would arise and confront the Kingdom of God, and that all of them would suffer the same fate—destruction. Conversely, the Kingdom of God would not only be established during the time of the fourth kingdom, the Roman Empire, but it would actually grow to include people from all nations, tribes, and tongues.

In chapter 9, Daniel proceeded to explain what would happen in the years from the return from exile to the death of the Messiah (457 B.C. - 33 A.D.). It would take 490 years to "rebuild" the hearts of His People, not people in name only, but People who represented the True Israel. That 490 year period would see: the completion of the rebuilding of Jerusalem/The Temple, the continued rebellion of the Jewish people, the coming of the Messiah, the subsequent judgment of the Jewish people, culminating in the destruction of the Temple, and the establishment of the Kingdom in a new and fresh way that confirmed how obsolete the Old Covenant was. There is no indication anywhere in Scripture that suggests we should understand these three critical chapters, Daniel 2, 7, and 9, in any other way than what appears to be the plain, natural meaning. To suggest that these chapters are actually speaking of future kingdoms, or that these prophecies actually had a "double-fulfillment" flies in the face of the clear instructions that Daniel was given regarding what he was shown. He was told to "seal up" the words of his prophecy because their content had to do with things that would happen at or around the coming of the Messiah.

Using the Sabbatical Year formula that Daniel assumes, we see that Daniel, in the 9th chapter, predicted with mind-blowing accuracy the events surrounding the life of Christ and the destruction of the Temple in 70 A.D. Picking up on the very same themes, the book of Revelation declared with unmistakable clarity that God is still pursing Shalom/Rest for His People and His world. That Shalom, that Rest, is best captured in the number 7, the day upon which God rested and the day around which all of life was to revolve for God's People. The same number 7, which figures so prominently in Daniel is used with the same kind of intentionality in Revelation. Like two runners in a cosmic relay, Daniel and John enjoyed the perfect passing of the baton.

There are several implications that Daniel offers us. First, it is pointless to oppose God's Kingdom initiatives. No matter how strong or opulent the building materials, no matter how fierce the opposition, the "Rock" of the Kingdom will crush them all, and grow to fill the earth. We are in that phase of redemptive history now. The Rock is growing. The "Son of Man" is reigning. The only thing that keeps us from seeing that is the eyes of sight.

Second, God's people are actually reigning with Him now! It is too small a thing for God to have a People composed of one ethnicity or one language. His intentions have always been to create a People from every nation. More dramatic still, His intentions have always been to have that same People reign with Him as His Kingdom expands. Like secret agents, God's people are systematically infiltrating every square inch of enemy territory. Using methods that are totally foreign to the ways of the World, winsome warriors are being recruited and called to wage war against all the other kingdoms that continue to pop up, both personal and political.

Finally, Daniel provides great insight into how history works. Things are never as they appear. Evil never ULTIMATELY triumphs. Every ruler, politician, king or prime minister is nothing more than a pawn in the hands of Christ. At the very least, a thorough understanding of Daniel should forever change the way we watch the evening news or read the daily paper. The "template" that God has placed over history is revealed to us in the book of Daniel. There is no reason to think that that template has changed.

In the closing frames of the most recent film adaptation of C.S. Lewis' *The Lion, the Witch, and the Wardrobe*, the Lion Aslan, the Christ-figure, can be seen from a distance walking along the beach. The camera briefly switches back to the main characters, then once again pans back to the beach—the Lion is gone. But the unmistakable paw prints that He left can still be seen. It is an apt word-picture. The paw prints of the great Lion of Judah are all over history. While we may not be able to see with perfect clarity, the fact remains that Aslan is on the move. Daniel believed it. Do we?

CHAPTER 11

A Scroll Down Memory Lane (Part 1)

THE "TRUE ISRAEL" REVEALED

The revelation of Jesus Christ, which God gave him to show his servants what must soon take place. He made it known by sending his angel to his servant John.
REVELATION 1:1

The study of Revelation either finds a man mad, or leaves him that way.
JOHN CALVIN

Please don't be deceived by those people who come along and say, "The book of Revelation is apocalyptic; therefore, you can't understand it." That's a bunch of nonsense — just nonsense. I heard that for years. "It's apocalyptic! It's apocalyptic!" The word scared me to death. It sounded like a disease.
DR. DAVID R. REAGAN

SCROLL DOWN MEMORY LANE (1)

Arguably the greatest thinker of the Protestant Reformation, John Calvin (1509-1564) remarked that *"The study of Revelation either finds a man mad, or leaves him that way."* It is not surprising then that although he wrote commentaries on almost every book of the New Testament, he declined to do so for Revelation.[128] It's tough to argue with Calvin. But as erudite as he was, he was wrong about Revelation. A simple, plain reading of the text is possible, and the **meaning** of John's words can be understood. Yes, there are many symbols and images that at first blush appear confounding. And yes, the **applications** of John's record of Christ's revelation are endless. That is precisely where most readers make their mistake. Before we can **apply** the message of Revelation, we must first understand the **meaning** of Revelation, a task that is eminently achievable. If you doubt that goal can be reached, you need look no further than the very first word of Revelation.

Revelation begins with the word *apokalupsis*-αποκαλυπσις, from which we get our English word "apocalypse." The word means "a revelation" or an "unveiling." Other New Testament uses of this same word only confirm that clarity and insight are the takeaways from reading Revelation, not "maddening" confusion.

For example, in Matthew 11:25 we read, *At that time Jesus said, "I praise you, Father, Lord of heaven and earth, because you have hidden these things from the wise and learned, and **revealed** them to little children."* Luke

---

[128] Calvin also failed to complete commentaries on 2 and 3 John before his death in 1564.

2:32 comments that the coming of The Christ was to be *a light for (αποκαλυπσις)* **revelation** *to the Gentiles, and the glory of your people Israel.* In commenting on his understanding of the Gospel, Paul says *I did not receive it from any man, nor was I taught it; rather, I received it by* **revelation** *from Jesus Christ* (Galatians 1:12). Paul reminded the Thessalonians that they would recognize the "man of lawlessness" because he would be "revealed." There was no need to worry that they would miss the "day of the Lord" because this man's coming would be an *αποκαλυπσις* (2 Thessalonians 2:3).

Far from intending to obscure facts or confuse readers, Revelation was written to pull back the curtain of time and give us a rare glimpse of the flow of history from Heaven's perspective. Unlike the would-be-wizard of the Emerald City, we must pay very close attention to the Man behind the curtain—He is pulling levers and moving knobs that have everything to do with our past and our future—no parlor tricks and special effects, but the destiny of every person and everything. This is what the *αποκαλυπσις* of Jesus Christ was intended to show its readers. In short, what John saw and then recorded was an "unveiling," a "revelation" that was intended to motivate and reassure his readers precisely because they **would** be able to understand what he was writing about. The same can be true for us. That understanding begins by reviewing the authorship and the intended recipients of this *αποκαλυπσις*.

Who And When Tells Us What

There is almost no debate as to who wrote Revelation or to whom it was written. *"John, to the seven churches in the province of Asia"* (Revelation 1:4). It is easy to pass over such a straightforward introduction. But the entire drift of Revelation is toward these churches, and, by application, to the Church at large. Something prompted John to write when he did, and to whom he did. If we lose sight of that fact, we are destined to become lost in a maze of beasts and bowls and seals and saints. Revelation is a specific book written to a specific group at a specific time in order to address a specific problem. There is a "key" that will help us unlock that problem.

The Conundrum Of The Church

I recently moved to a new office. The key to my office was made from the same blank as several other keys on my key-ring. For weeks, I would fumble with each key before finding the one that unlocked my office door. My wife suggested I paint some finger-nail polish on the one that opened my office, making it easier to find. As the Guinness commercial opines, "Brilliant!"

The Revelation of Jesus Christ is no different. The "key" to understanding this book is found in Revelation 1:9; and 2:9; and 2:13; and 6:9-11; and 7:13-17; and 12:11; and 13:7; and 14:12, 13; and 16:5-6; and 17:4-6; and 18:20, 24; and 19:2-3; and 20:4. No nail polish required, just a *big* key-ring. Each of those passages addressed the suffering of God's saints and the plight of those who had already given their lives for the sake of the Gospel. The regular reference to martyrs in Revelation makes it abundantly clear that this was the "problem" the first century Church faced. How could God sit idly by while His sons and daughters continued to feel the wrath of both Judaism and the Roman Empire? Revelation's answer is that He could not, and He will not. Their cry had reached the throne room of heaven, and the promise of vindication was just around the historical corner. At the heart of the entire book of Revelation is the answer to the question, "Will God avenge the deaths of His saints who have lost their lives for Christ?"

Those saints lost their lives first at the hands of Judaism and then the Roman Empire. They were enduring great suffering, and many had already been martyred. John quickly established his affinity with the recipients of Revelation by identifying himself as a "companion in the suffering" they were experiencing (1:9). In the face of this withering persecution, the first-century church was having serious doubts as to the goodness and greatness of God. Faithfulness and obedience seemed to result in things getting worse, not better, and the enticements of the World seemed an attractive alternative. It was not a great logical leap to argue, "If God seemed inattentive to the cries of His saints, how attentive would He be to minor indiscretions and peccadilloes on my part?" Little has changed in the intervening 2,000 years. We have all found ourselves wondering in the midst of hard times, "Where is God?"

The fact that we have all been there does not mitigate the fact that the very thing that gives us the victory in those times—our faith—is the very thing we struggle with the most (1 John 5:4). Like the first-century Church, we are all tempted to live by the eyes of sight. But our calling is higher. *"We live by faith, not by sight"* (2 Corinthians 5:7). Our faith calls us to see things that no one else can see, *not because they are not there, but because they can only be seen with the eyes of faith.* This is precisely what John was exposed to in the Revelation of Jesus Christ. He saw things that only faith could give him access to. The message that Christ gave John was both chilling and exhilarating. **The vision was intended to encourage believers** who were experiencing great persecution, by assuring them that the two great persecutors of the Church, Judaism and Rome, would suffer God's judgment in the near future. The death of God's saints had NOT gone unnoticed. Christ himself was serving notice that nobody messes with God's children without paying the price—Nobody. Appearances to the contrary, the Day was coming, and quickly at that, when those who were persecuted and martyred would be avenged. This is the glorious hope of Revelation. While the *application* of this hope is equally glorious for the Church today, the *meaning* of Christ's revelation to John was immediately applicable for those saints living in the first century.

How were the believers of John's day to respond in the face of God's apparent inaction? Give in? Give up? Embrace the ways of the World because the path of righteousness was too hard, not to mention the fact that it could get you killed!? Christ's message to the Church in Asia Minor was not simply to "hang on!" Instead, they were to "overcome." The irony of that suggestion must have been palpable for John's first-century audience. "Overcome?" "John, are you living in a parallel universe?" "We are dying here!" "We are on the run!" "We are incapable of withstanding the ferocious assault of both Judaism and Rome." The appropriate response? OVERCOME!? That is precisely the point throughout The Revelation. The early Church, like the Church today, was called to "overcome" everything that set itself up against the authority of the risen Christ. To each of the seven churches to which John wrote, he gave the same call to battle:

> *"To him who overcomes, I will give the right to eat from the Tree of Life"* (Ephesus; 2:7). *"He who overcomes will not be hurt at all by the second death"* (Smyrna; 2:11). *"To him*

> who overcomes, I will give some of the hidden manna" (Pergamum; 2:17). "To him who overcomes and does my will to the end, I will give authority over the nations..." (Thyatira; 2:26). "He who overcomes will, like them (the righteous in Sardis), be dressed in white..." (Sardis; 3:5). "Him who overcomes I will make a pillar in the Temple of my God" (Philadelphia; 3:12). "To him who overcomes, I will give the right to sit with me on my throne, just as I overcame and sat down with my Father on His throne" (Laodicea; 3:21).

Like the Church then, the Church now is called to do more than simply circle the wagons and hang on for the "rapture." *"No, in all these things we are more than conquerors through Him who loved us."* (Romans 8:37). "More" than conquerors? Yes! We do *more* than simply defeat the enemy. We plunder the enemy. We take the very things that the World and Satan have devised against us and we redeem them. The same power that raised Christ from the dead is now used to take things that were intended for evil and use them for good (Genesis 50:20).

> *"For though we live in the world, we do not wage war as the world does. The weapons we fight with are not the weapons of the world. On the contrary, they have divine power to demolish strongholds. We demolish arguments and every pretension that sets itself up against the knowledge of God, and we take captive every thought to make it obedient to Christ"* (2 Corinthians 10:3-5).

That war was to be fought by the first-century Church, with victory assured, JUST AS IT IS TODAY. *This is the message of The Revelation.* For first-century followers of Christ, their calling was clear: remain faithful and obedient—do not give in or give out—do not live timid or frightened lives—live boldly and confidently--your destiny is to reign with Christ in the Kingdom He came to establish, BOTH THEN, AND NOW. *This is the message of The Revelation.* Inch by inch, decade by decade, institution by institution, life by life, the Kingdom is rolling on, crushing everything that stands in its way. If you doubt it, wait and see—see what God will do as he fiercely protects His Own and destroys all those who threaten His bride, BOTH THEN, AND NOW. *This is the message of The Revelation.*

Why The "When" Is Critical To The "What"

If Revelation's central theme is that the saints must overcome in the face of current persecution, then the timing of the book must be there to support such an interpretation. If the book was written at a time of relative "peace" for the church, then Revelation is robbed of much of its power. The question of "when" Revelation was written raises two separate questions: first, when did the events described in Revelation come to pass; and second, when did John actually record the vision he saw? Both questions can be answered definitively. As to the first question, *the book of Revelation records things that have already come to pass. With the exception of the last two and a half chapters, everything John wrote about has already been fulfilled.* While there is no need to go into great detail in rehashing the question of imminence in the book of Revelation, a quick review will be helpful.

Words, Words, Words

There are three word groups that John used in reporting what he was told. The first was the word ἐν τάχει-*en tachei*, commonly translated as "soon." It is used in the following:

> Revelation 1:1: *The revelation from Jesus Christ, which God gave him to show his servants what must **soon** take place. He made it known by sending his angel to his servant John*...Revelation 2:16: *Repent therefore! Otherwise, I will **soon** come to you and will fight against them with the sword of my mouth*...Revelation 3:11: *I am coming **soon**. Hold on to what you have, so that no one will take your crown.* Revelation 22:6: *The angel said to me, "These words are trustworthy and true. The Lord, the God who inspires the prophets, sent his angel to show his servants the things that must **soon** take place.* Revelation 22:7: *Look, I am coming **soon**! Blessed is the one who keeps the words of the prophecy written in this scroll*...Revelation 22:12: *Look, I am coming **soon**! My reward is with me, and I will give to each person according to what they have done.* Revelation 22:20: *He who testifies to these things says, "Yes, I am coming **soon**." Amen. Come, Lord Jesus.*

The second is the word μελλο-*mello*, which we normally translate as "later" or "about to," or "going to come." It is used in:

> Revelation 1:19: *Write, therefore, what you have seen, what is now and what will take place **later**.* Revelation 3:10: *Since you have kept my command to endure patiently, I will also keep you from the hour of trial that is **going to come** on the whole world to test the inhabitants of the earth.*

The final word group surrounds the word ενγυs-*engus*, translated "near," or "at hand." It is used in

> Revelation 1:3: *Blessed is the one who reads aloud the words of this prophecy, and blessed are those who*

> *hear it and take to heart what is written in it, because the time is near.* Revelation 22:10: *Then he told me, "Do not seal up the words of the prophecy of this scroll, because the time is near."*

As we have already noted, this last passage stands in direct contrast to the instructions given to Daniel regarding the vision he saw. In Daniel 12:4, he was given precisely the **opposite** command that John received, being told TO seal up the words of that prophecy. The contrast is obvious. If Daniel was told to seal up the words of his prophecy because the events he foretold were historically far off, then it makes sense to assume that John's words were not to be sealed because the events he foretold were historically "near," not thousands of years in the future. The fulfillment of much of Daniel's prophecy began less than five-hundred years after his vision. The *plain* understanding of what John was told must mean that the fulfillment of John's prophecy would begin much sooner than Daniel's.

My appeal to what is plain and obvious is just that. Scholars continue to debate the fine-points of Greek grammar and lexical range of meanings[129] regarding these words ($\epsilon\nu$ $\tau\alpha\chi\epsilon\iota$, $\mu\epsilon\lambda\lambda o$ and $\epsilon\nu\gamma\upsilon s$). But there is nothing metaphoric about these time frame references. There is no apocalyptic imagery surrounding those words or any appeal to Old Testament language. There is nothing to suggest that John might be using words that could possibly be interpreted as anything other than what their plain and simple meaning would suggest. "Soon" means soon, "at hand" means imminent, and "about to" means

---

[129] For example, Kenneth Gentry in *Before Jerusalem Fell* argues for imminence, while Norman Geisler in *A Friendly Response to Hank Hanegraaff's book, The Last Disciple* at www.normangeisler.net argues from a futurist perspective.

just around the corner. John intended his words to be immediately applicable to his first-century readers, and he was told that what he saw would begin unfolding in the very near future. That is what these words MEAN. The fact that there are nearly a dozen such references in Revelation leaves little doubt that what John saw was going to happen to the very people to whom John first wrote.

So what are *we* to do with the message that Christ brought to His first-century followers? Ah, now we are talking APPLICATION. We will deal with that briefly in later chapters and at length in the next book in this series. Suffice it to say that there is application-a-plenty for us today, and for the Church of all ages. But that does not change the clear, incontrovertible fact that the prophecies given in the book of Revelation are, for the most part, fulfilled, just as the plethora of imminent time-frame references in the book itself would suggest.

Revelation: A Blind Date?

Scintillating: (adjective) "possessing or displaying a dazzlingly impressive liveliness..." Trying to determine "when" the book of Revelation was written (our second "when" question) is not scintillating reading. In fact, it is dryer than a mummy's pocket. Despite this question's lack of excitement, it is important. If, as we are suggesting, the book of Revelation described the coming judgment of disobedient Israel, culminating in the destruction of the Temple in 70 A.D. and the beginning of the judgment of the Roman empire beginning with Nero, then John must have received and published his account of the vision prior to the fall of Jerusalem and the end of Nero's reign. **Describing something that has already happened does not meet the criteria of prophecy.** No vision of things that had already occurred would have been required when looking through the archives of the *Jerusalem Daily* would do. When was Revelation written?

There are two popular answers to that question, the early date (prior to 70 A.D., sometime during or around the reign of Nero, 54-68 A.D.) and the late date (after 81 A.D., sometime during or around the reign of Domitian, 81-96 A.D.). Both camps have something of an ideological axe to grind. Many who favor a late date argue that most of the New Testament was written late into the first-century. Why? This supports their conviction that much of the New Testament is inaccurate. They argue that most of what survives today as "God's Word" is the result of wishful thinking on the part of Jesus' disciples. Historically far removed from the actual events, Jesus' disciples relied on vague memories or outright fabrications that were more a reflection of their own agendas than of what actually happened. Arguing for a later date helps bolster that argument. How?

On The Outside Looking In

We have all played the game "telephone," where one individual seated in a circle of people whispers a sentence to the person next to them, who then whispers the same sentence to the next person, and so on. By the time it reaches the final person, the original sentence is a far cry from what the original person in the circle actually said. The farther removed you are to the original, the harder it becomes to accurately relay what was said. By pushing back the dates of New Testament books, especially the Gospels, liberal scholars are more apt to dismiss much of what we read as "unreliable." Those who favor an earlier date are more apt to view the New Testament as reliable and authoritative.

There are two sources of evidence for determining the date of Revelation. One is external evidence, the other internal. The external evidence pertains to the writings of early Church fathers and extra-Biblical history. This is beyond the scope of this study. What we *can* say is that there is an increasing corpus of evidence that recommends an earlier date.[130] For our purposes, it is important to look at Revelation itself to determine what evidence there is to support an early date.

REVELATION'S REVELATION OF AN EARLY DATE

As dubious as the external arguments for a late date may be, the book of Revelation itself provides tantalizing clues as to the date of its composition. The most compelling evidence for an early date for Revelation is found in Revelation 17:9-10:

> *This calls for a mind with wisdom. The seven heads are seven hills on which the woman sits. They are also seven kings. Five have fallen, one is, the other has not yet come; but when he does come, he must remain for only a little while.*

As we have already discussed, this statement is a reference to the "kings" or emperors of Rome.[131] There is no doubt that ancient extra-Biblical sources often referred to emperors as "kings."[132] Scripture itself bears this out. In John 19:15, the

---

[130] For an excellent study of the external evidence, Cf. K.L. Gentry, *Before Jerusalem Fell: Dating the Book of Revelation* (Tyler, TX: 1989).

[131] Chapter 7, "The Beast Is a Political Figure."

[132] The writings of Nero's own court official, Seneca, include references to Nero as "king." Seneca, *On Clemency* 2:12.

priests reject Jesus as their king in the presence of Pilate by shouting, *"We have no king but Caesar!"* In Acts 17:7, *some "bad characters from the marketplace"* try to incite a riot at the home of Jason by arguing that he has befriended Paul and Silas, *who "act contrary to the decrees of Caesar, saying that there is another king, Jesus."* The "seven hills" that the beast represents is the city of Rome, and the seven heads of the beast also represent that same city's "kings."

John left little doubt that one of those kings, the sixth, was alive and reigning as he was writing. The first five had "fallen," a word used in the past tense to suggest that they were no longer reigning or living. The seventh king was yet to come, and he would reign for only a short period. As we have seen, counting from the first Roman emperor, Julius Caesar, we land squarely on Nero as the sixth king, followed by Galba who, by any reckoning, reigned only a short time—seven months. Nero reigned from A.D. 54-68, placing the writing of Revelation at some time during that span.

The Twin Towers Of Judaism

Another strong argument for an early date has to do with the Jewish Temple. Ask anyone who is old enough to remember September 11, 2001, "What is the first thing you look for when you see a picture or representation of Lower Manhattan?" The answer is almost always the same: "I scan the skyline for the Twin Towers of the World Trade Center." If they appear in a movie or a photograph, you immediately know something about WHEN that movie was made or that picture taken—it was before 9-11-01. That event is so indelibly impressed upon our consciousness that none of us will ever be able to look at that skyline the same again. For

Jews living in the first century, Herod's Temple was similar. The analogy breaks down in that the Temple was *far more* significant to Judaism than the Twin Towers could ever be to our national psyche. When the Temple was razed in A.D. 70, it truly was "the end of the age" for Judaism.

As we scan the apocalyptic skyline of Revelation, one building stands out: The Temple.

> *I was given a reed like a measuring rod and was told, "Go and measure the Temple of God and the altar, with its worshipers. But exclude the outer court; do not measure it, because it has been given to the Gentiles. They will trample on the holy city for 42 months"* (Revelation 11:1-2).

Should we take this passage literally as describing the actual Temple? There are a number of clues that suggest an unequivocal "yes."

Notice that the future tense is used in describing what "will" happen to this Temple—"they WILL trample on the holy city for 42 months." The reference to 42 months coincides EXACTLY with the length of the Jewish War, which began with the siege of Jerusalem in the Spring of A.D. 67 and culminated in the destruction of the Temple in August of A.D. 70. John was told to "exclude" the outer court in his measurements because it "has" (present tense) been given over to the Gentiles. It is a matter of historical record that early on in the Jewish War, Vespasian was able to secure the outer court of the Temple in A.D. 68. It was not until A.D. 70 that the entire Temple was captured. All of these references are simply too consistent with the historical facts of the siege and destruction of the Temple to be read as symbolic. John is literally describing some things that had happened, and some things that were yet to happen to the very real and very literal Herodian Temple.

Just a few verses after John was told to measure the Temple and its worshippers, he wrote that this Temple was located in a "great city." If John was referring to a literal Temple, we would expect him to refer to that city as Jerusalem—and he does! In verse 8, he wrote *"Their bodies (the two witnesses) will lie in the public square of the great city--which is figuratively called Sodom and Egypt—where also their Lord was crucified."* The fact that John made an overt distinction between a figurative designation for this city (*Sodom*: Isaiah 1:9-10; Ezekiel 16:46-49) and a literal designation (*where also their Lord was crucified*) is further proof that he meant us to understand the city as Jerusalem and the Temple to be the very one that stood in that city. There is no doubt that our Lord was in fact crucified in Jerusalem (Matthew 16:21; Mark 10:32-34; and Luke 9:51; 19:28).

One final reason for believing that John referred to a literal Temple in Jerusalem is the fact that Jesus made the very same reference to the Temple. The story in Luke 21, with its Synoptic parallels in Matthew 25 and Mark 13, unfolded as follows:

> *Some of his disciples were remarking about how the Temple was adorned with beautiful stones and with gifts dedicated to God. But Jesus said, "As for what you see here, the time will come when not one stone will be left on another; every one of them will be thrown down." "Teacher," they asked, "when will these things happen? And what will be the sign that*

> *they are about to take place..."When you see Jerusalem being surrounded by armies, you will know that its desolation is near. Then let those who are in Judea flee to the mountains, let those in the city get out, and let those in the country not enter the city. For this is the time of punishment in fulfillment of all that has been written. How dreadful it will be in those days for pregnant women and nursing mothers! There will be great distress in the land and wrath against this people. They will fall by the sword and will be taken as prisoners to all the nations.* **Jerusalem will be trampled on by the Gentiles until the times of the Gentiles are fulfilled"** (Luke 21:5-24 emphasis added).

The similarities between Jesus' words and the instructions given to John in Revelation are too close to be coincidental. All commentators agree that Jesus' words in Luke 21 should be understood as literal. If Jesus and John were describing identical events, then BOTH should be understood literally.

So, what does all this have to do with an early date for the writing of Revelation? There is no hint in Revelation that the Temple had already been destroyed when it was written. On the contrary, there is compelling evidence that the Temple was still standing as John wrote. There is no reason to believe that John was describing a "spiritual" Temple or that he was using figurative language. When he wrote Revelation, Herod's Temple was standing, which means that Revelation must have been written prior to A.D. 70.

Conclusion: Inside Out

From within and without, the testimony of Revelation and the early Church is compelling—Revelation was written prior to 70 A.D. This supports the argument that the prophecies of Revelation had to do with events that began unfolding prior to 70 A.D.

Chapter Summary

The Revelation of Christ that was given to John was unambiguously intended for first-century Christians. Rather than pointing to events that would occur thousands of years in the future, John was told repeatedly that the vision he saw would begin to unfold within his own lifetime, or "soon." Attempts to argue otherwise are either strained or simply irrational.

In support of this argument is the fact that the book of Revelation was written much earlier than some have suggested. Probably written in the late 60's of the first century, the internal evidence from Revelation itself supports this fact. John referred specifically to seven "kings" from the empire represented as a beast. Most probably the Roman Empire, John made clear that five emperors had already come and gone, one was currently reigning, and the seventh would reign for only a short time. This would make the sixth emperor Nero and the seventh Galba, who reigned for only a few months. John would had to have written Revelation sometime between 54 and 68 A.D., the span of Nero's reign.

The most compelling internal evidence from Revelation is the fact that John wrote without any mention of the destruction of the Temple in 70 A.D. In fact, there are numerous references to the Temple that suggest it was still standing when John wrote. To think that John would have failed to note that the Temple had been destroyed, fails to take into account how important that building was to every Jew, John included. When John wrote Revelation, a literal Temple was still standing in Jerusalem, demanding that Revelation was written sometime before 70 A.D.

CHAPTER 12

A Scroll Down Memory Lane (2)

THE FURY OF THE WARRIOR KING

I saw heaven standing open and there before me was a white horse, whose rider is called Faithful and True. With justice he judges and makes war. His eyes are like blazing fire, and on his head are many crowns...He is dressed in a robe dipped in blood, and his name is the Word of God. The armies of heaven were following him, riding on white horses and dressed in fine linen, white and clean. Out of his mouth comes a sharp sword with which to strike down the nations. "He will rule them with an iron scepter." He treads the winepress of the fury of the wrath of God Almighty. On his robe and on his thigh he has this name written: KING OF KINGS AND LORD OF LORDS.
Revelation 19:11-16

St. John's primary concern in writing the Book of Revelation was just this very thing: to strengthen the Christian community in the faith of Jesus Christ's Lordship, to make them aware that the persecutions they suffered were integrally involved in the great war of history.
DAVID CHILTON, DAYS OF VENGEANCE

Don't mess with God's children. And don't mess with God's plan to reclaim the nations as His own and establish His Kingdom like never before. That is the unequivocal message of Revelation. In two great sweeping movements of God's judgment, the enemies of the Church were destroyed. As Satan launched his furious counterattack to reclaim the nations and destroy the infant Church, God's Anointed ultimately triumphed. John saw what Daniel could only hope for:

> *As I watched, this horn was waging war against the holy people and defeating them, until the Ancient of Days came and pronounced judgment in favor of the holy people of the Most High,* **and the time came when they possessed the Kingdom** (Daniel 7:21-22).

Organizing Principles

As we saw with the first word of chapter 1 ($\alpha\pi o\kappa\alpha\lambda\upsilon\pi\sigma\iota\sigma$), Revelation is not the great mystery that so many have made it. By using the following organizing principles, Revelation becomes eminently understandable.[133]

Time Frames: We MUST keep the clear time frame references of Revelation front and center. Most of the vision that John saw described events that fell sometime in or near the first century. By taking the time-frame references at face value, it is possible to make sense of most of Revelation.

---

[133] Israel Warren's excellent commentary on Revelation identifies similar principles. "Are there any reliable guides to our path as we attempt to enter the obscure mazes before us...we may name three...The first is, the express declaration of the first verse of the book that it was to relate to "things which must shortly come to pass." The second is, the analogy of other Scriptures of a similar character...The third is the actual history of the times covered by these predictions." Israel P. Warren, *The Book of Revelation: An Exposition*. (New York: Funk & Wagnalls, 1886), pp. 94-95.

Symbolism: As is common with most prophetic literature, Revelation is crammed with symbols. *"In order to read Revelation in the natural sense intended by its author it will be impossible to interpret it "literally" (or by the explicit sense) or even by the rule of "literal where possible..."* "One simply cannot suppress the fact that this book is not a simple narrative to be read in a matter-of-fact fashion, but is rather an ornate series of symbols and similitudes which must be understood as referring to historical events and spiritual principles which lie beyond the things explicitly mentioned in the text."[134] As a rule, "when in doubt, figure the symbol out!" Unless the text gives clear reasons for NOT interpreting what we read symbolically, it is a gross violation of sound hermeneutics to understand things otherwise. In many cases, the text itself will explain the symbolism. If not, it is up to us to look for the meaning of the symbols that fill Revelation by comparing those symbols with their use in other parts of Revelation or other Scriptures.

Shalom: מלס. Picking up precisely where Daniel's prophecy left off, Revelation communicates God's intention to restore מלס (shalom) to the whole earth. Most commentators recognize the prevalence of the number "seven" in Revelation (it is used 55 times). Beyond references to the "complete" or "perfect" nature of that numeral, few point to the significance of the "rest" that God had always intended for His people and His planet. It is more than incidental that almost everything in Revelation revolves

---

[134] Greg Bahnsen, *Hermeneutics in the Book of Revelation*. (Nacogdoches, TX: Covenant Media Foundation, 1984), p. 10. Bahnsen does an excellent job of explaining the historic-Reformed understanding of "literal interpretation." This is the correct view.

around the number "seven" or its antithesis, the numeral "six."

The Old Testament: We cannot understand Revelation without understanding John's incredible indebtedness to the Old Testament. *So many of the symbols that we find in Revelation find their meaning in the Old Testament.* Consider the following:

Fact #1: In the 404 verses that make up Revelation, there are 278[135] references to Old Testament Scriptures.

Fact #2: There is not a single Old Testament book that is not quoted or referred to in Revelation.

Fact #3: The three most referred to Old Testament books in Revelation are Ezekiel, Daniel, and Isaiah.

Fact #4: The first book of the Bible begins in a Garden which features a great River and the Tree of Life, and Revelation concludes in a city with a great River and the Tree of Life

Fact #5: John obviously saw his vision as the culmination of many Old Testament prophecies and teachings. Some key comparisons are:

Deut 4:2; 12:32	Rev. 22:18-19
Isaiah 13-14	Rev. 18

---

[135] This is a conservative estimate. The number of Old Testament passages used or referred to range in number from 250 (Tenney), 400 (Westcott & Hort), 500 (Ezell and Scroggie i.e. some verses contain more than one OT reference), and 518 (VanHoye). Regardless of which number we use, the point is inescapable--John's indebtedness to the Old Testament cannot be overstated.

SCROLL DOWN MEMORY LANE (2)

Isaiah 63:3	Rev. 19:13
Isaiah 65	Rev. 21-22
Dan. 2:28-29	Rev. 1:1; 19; 4:1
Dan. 12:4,9	Rev. 22:10
Dan. 7:13-14	Rev. 1:12-16
Ezek. 2-3	Rev. 5
Ezek. 9	Rev. 7
Ezek. 16	Rev. 11:8
Ezek. 39	Rev. 19
Ezek. 38-39	Rev. 20:7-9
Ezek. 47	Rev. 22
Zech. 4	Rev. 11

To say that Revelation relies heavily upon the Old Testament is to state the obvious. The interpretive key to much of Revelation is an understanding of the Old Testament. Revelation is an exposition of all that the Old Testament spoke to regarding the Kingdom. Revelation integrates the teaching of both the eighth century B.C. prophets and the sixth century B.C. prophets into a breathtaking conclusion to all that was foretold. Even the hoped for "remnant" that was so much a part of Isaiah and Ezekiel find their fulfillment in the pages of Revelation. In the next few pages, we will take a "40,000" foot view of this amazing Vision. *It is essential that any serious student of Revelation look carefully at those instances where John appeals to or quotes the Old Testament. The context and meaning of Old Testament passages has everything to do with understanding the message of Revelation.* That puts many of us behind the eight-ball.

Our knowledge of Scripture is woefully inadequate, especially the Old Testament. Revelation will force us to dive into the Old Testament with fresh enthusiasm. Far from being a dry, pedantic exercise, this will prove to be a great boost to our faith. If that is so, then we can be certain that we will walk away from Revelation with a more profound and stirring picture of what the Old Testament People of God longed for: **Messiah!** The Old Testament, like Revelation, points with laser-like focus to the One True King, The Messiah and His Kingdom. Jesus made this clear when He spoke to the disciples on the road to Emmaus after His resurrection.

> He said to them, "How foolish you are, and how slow to believe all that the prophets have spoken! Did not the Messiah have to suffer these things and then enter His glory?" ***And beginning with Moses and all the Prophets, He explained to them what was said in all the Scriptures concerning Himself"*** (Luke 24:25-27, emphasis added).

EVERYTHING in the Bible is, in some way, about Jesus Christ! It stands to reason that if the Old Testament is primarily about Jesus Christ, then the one book of the Bible that has the most to do with His exaltation and glory should as well. I urge every student of Revelation to use/purchase a good study Bible and cross reference the many images and metaphors used in Revelation. At the very least, use a concordance to look up the images found in Revelation that are drawn from the Old Testament. Your understanding of this book will be greatly enhanced.

The Reign of Christ: Following on the heels of the previous principle, Revelation is about nothing if not the present and future reign of Christ. Despite appearances to the contrary, Christ, **along with the saints**, rules over the earth. The very thing that prompted the vision of Revelation was the apparent failure of Christ to protect His Church. In scene after scene, Christ's enemies are vanquished and martyrs are vindicated. Revelation leaves no doubt as to Who rules the nations and who rules along with Him.

Using these principles to guide our interpretation, the content of Revelation can be broken down as follows:[136]

1:1-8: Introduction

In the first eight verses John announced the major themes of the book. Here we are introduced to the author, the recipients, the type of literature, and, as we have seen, the time frame for the fulfillment of the vision.

1:9-3:22: The Church in the World

Christ issued a challenge to seven churches, the first century recipients of this revelation. He urged them to remain faithful and obedient despite the apparent failure of God to protect them. Each church was called to "overcome." The connection between "overcoming" and martyrdom is made explicit in 12:11: *And they overcame him because of the blood of the Lamb and because of the word of their testimony, and they did not love their life even when faced with death.*

4:1-11:19: The First Enemy Defeated—Judaism

Many people fail to consider that the first great persecutor of the Church was organized religion—in this case, Judaism. We normally associate the early persecution of the Church with images of the Coliseum, replete with lions tearing

---

[136] As stated in the preface, this summary of the content of Revelation is not unique to me. Countless scholars and commentators share the same view, among them: Israel P. Warren, Jay Adams, Greg Bahnsen, G.I. Williamson, Henry Cowles, G.B. Caird, and Robert H. Mounce to name only a few.

Christians apart. But the first group to try and stop the advance of Christ's Kingdom was His own race, the Jewish people. In chapters 4-11, God promised His Church that He would vindicate them and defeat their great enemy, organized Jewish religion.[137] It is critical to remember that by "organized Jewish religion" we DO NOT mean the religious observance of those who held true to the Old Testament and the historic faith of Israel. This was the faithful Remnant that the prophets often spoke of and with which Revelation is intimately concerned. The organized religion of Jesus' day represented a **rejection** of true faith. Promoted by the Scribes and Pharisees and perpetuated in the Talmud, this religion sought to maintain an exclusively Jewish faith and the hope of a literal, future restoration of the political fortunes of Israel. The organized religion of Jesus day looked forward to a literal, earthly Kingdom with Jerusalem as its capital city and a Messiah in the mold of the warlike King David. Jesus' teaching on the Kingdom represented a faithful reading of the Old Testament and the fulfillment of the promise of a Kingdom composed of people from every nation. It is precisely these conflicting views that resulted in Jesus' crucifixion and the subsequent persecution of those who followed Him.

Chapter 12: Transitional Chapter

In this chapter we move from the defeat of one enemy to the introduction of another. Just over 1,400 miles from Jerusalem, Rome is a world apart, culturally and religiously. The vision uses this chapter to facilitate that transition.

---

[137] Israel P. Warren provides great insight into the relationship between Jesus prophecy in Matthew 24 and Revelation 4-11. Cf. Israel P. Warren, *Revelation*. Pp.166-173.

13:1-19:21: The Second Enemy Defeated—Rome

In this section, we are introduced to the second great enemy of the Church—the Roman Empire. With greater resources and greater reach, this second wave of persecution was more intense than the first. As with the first enemy, this one, too, would undergo the fierce judgment of God and experience the glorious victory of the Church. These chapters introduce us to the *beginning* of God's judgment of the Roman Empire. The clash of two great world empires is portrayed. In these chapters, the great "rock" of Daniel's dream becomes a mountain, as the legs and feet of the "iron" enemy are ultimately destroyed and "blown away."

Chapter 20: Transitional Chapter

Another transitional chapter is inserted to help move us from the time shortly after the vision was recorded, to a time in the future. This chapter describes the current state of Satan, and the coming impact of his brief but furious last ditch effort to reclaim the nations.

22:1-22:21: The New Eden

In these chapters, we see the consummation of every Christian's hope. In breathtaking detail, John is shown the "New Jerusalem" and the perfect and complete reign of Christ. The great story of God's self-revelation ends precisely where it began, in the Garden of Eden. Just as the original residents of Eden were created to perfectly enjoy God's presence, so, one day, we too will enjoy His presence perfectly. Perhaps the most amazing feature of these chapters is that Heaven literally comes to earth.

The "new heaven and earth" are not only a future reality, but also a present reality.

With these organizing principles tucked firmly under our brains and this summary of the content of the Revelation in view, we are now ready to review the actual content of the book.

Chapter 1: The Main Thing

Every good story includes three elements; the protagonist (who the story is about), the problem ("and then what happened?") and the product (result). In Revelation 1:1, John introduced his readers to the Protagonist: *The revelation of Jesus Christ.* John then proceeded to give the greatest reassurance possible to both his first-century readers and to us. *"Jesus Christ (is)...the ruler of the kings of the earth."* (1:5). There is not a king or ruler or president or prime minister or politician or dictator who can move one inch beyond what Christ has commanded. Just as Daniel had declared, *"God changes times and seasons; He removes kings and sets up kings"* (Daniel 2:21).

This same God approached John just as He had Daniel, by literally laying hold of him and introducing Himself as a "son of man" (Daniel 8:18/Revelation 1:17; Daniel 7:13/Revelation 1:13). Just as He had promised (Matthew 24, Mark 13, Luke 21), Jesus announced an imminent return. *"He is coming with the clouds"* (1:7); the same judgment language He used in Matthew 24.[138] This

---

[138] Cf. Gen. 15:17; Exod. 13:21-22; 19:9, 16-19; Ps. 18:8-14; Isa. 19:1; Ezek. 32:7-8; Nahum 1:2-8; Matt. 24:30; Mark 14:62; Acts 2:19 for more examples of how God "rides" the clouds and uses them to make His presence known, especially in His role as Judge.

coming would be seen by those who *"pierced Him"* (1:7); the very thing He had warned the High Priest of in Matthew 26:64. As a number of commentators have noted, a better translation of verse 7b would be *"and all the tribes (of Israel) of the land (of Israel) will mourn because of Him."*[139] The great and terrible day that would mark the end of the Old Covenant was about to commence, and the Kingdom was about to be handed over from one people—ethnic Israel—to another People--true Israel/the Church. (Matthew 21:43)

That the Church was the target of this Revelation is without question. John was told to write down what he saw at the booming ("like a trumpet") request of a dazzling figure, "a son of man." In His hands He held seven stars, and He stood in the midst of seven lampstands. The stars, we are told (Revelation 1:20), were angels assigned to each of the seven churches which were represented by the lampstands. The fact that John was asked to write down what he saw should give us pause. John was not transcribing a memo, or copying a manuscript. Nor was he reporting the highlights of a political rally or describing the outcome of a football game. John was being asked to put into words things that were indescribable—things he had never seen before—animals and creatures and activities and people that would be difficult to describe under any circumstances! Is it any wonder that we might find it hard to interpret the meaning of things that John had trouble even describing! While the particulars of

---

[139] See David Chilton, *The Days of Vengeance: An Exposition of the Book of Revelation*, (Dominion Press: Ft. Worth, Texas) 1986. P. 39

some of the things that John recorded are impossible to know with absolute certainty, we can be sure of the overarching themes of the book and the time-frame in which those things were to occur. At the heart of everything that John recorded was an invitation to drink in a vision of Christ that was powerful and compelling, and a conviction that this same Christ was fighting for His Bride.

Chapters 2-3: The Truth About the Church

While a detailed exposition of the letters to the seven churches is beyond the scope of our study, we can make several general observations. Two of the churches receive only praise—Smyrna and Philadelphia. But five of the seven churches were in need of some sort of reworking, and one, Laodicea received only criticism. The ironic thing is that none of these churches was more than 50 years old. It seems that no institution is like the church when it comes to giving in to forces that make it tame, predictable and boring—unnecessary and uninteresting—committed to walking by sight, quick to embrace the world's values, and slow to live like citizens of The Kingdom. The "natural" drift always seems to be away from God's loving embrace and into the waiting arms of the world.

ALL of the major themes of Revelation are sounded in the letters to the churches:

Persecution:

> *Do not be afraid of what you are about to suffer. I tell you, the devil will put some of you in prison to test you, and you will suffer persecution for ten days. Be faithful, even to the point of death, and I will give you life as your*

victor's crown (Revelation 2:10; The church at Smyrna).

Resistance to Compromise:

I know where you live—where Satan has his throne. Yet you remain true to my name. You did not renounce your faith in me, not even in the days of Antipas, my faithful witness, who was put to death in your city—where Satan lives (Revelation 2:13; The church at Pergamum).

Nevertheless, I have this against you: You tolerate that woman Jezebel, who calls herself a prophet. By her teaching she misleads my servants into sexual immorality and the eating of food sacrificed to idols... Now I say to the rest of you in Thyatira, to you who do not hold to her teaching and have not learned Satan's so-called deep secrets, 'I will not impose any other burden on you, except to hold on to what you have until I come' (Revelation 2:20, 24-25; The church at Thyatira).

I know your deeds. See, I have placed before you an open door that no one can shut. I know that you have little strength, yet you have kept my word and have not denied my name (Revelation 3:8; The church at Philadelphia).

Endurance:

Since you have kept my command to endure patiently, I will also keep you from the hour of trial that is going to

> *come on the whole world to test the inhabitants of the earth* (Revelation 3:10; The church at Philadelphia).

Victory!:

"To the one who is victorious, I will give the right to sit with Me on My throne, just as I was victorious and sat down with My Father on His throne" (3:21). In each of the seven letters, Christ urged the Saints to be "victorious" (to "overcome") (2:7, 11, 17, 26, 3:5, 12, 21). These themes are captured in this challenge: "Prepare for the coming persecution..." The point is this—life is hard and it promises to become harder. There are times when you will wonder if God cares, if faith matters, if Jesus is really with you, and if He is really reigning over the World. What you see will often compel you to answer a resounding "no" to those questions. Don't give in. Press on—keep trusting, ask for more faith. Eternal life awaits you! Your destiny is glory! Your inheritance is within reach! Victory awaits those who trust in the conquering Rider (6:2), the conquering Lion (5:5) and the conquering Horseman! (19:11-16).

Vindication:

> *Do not be afraid of what you are about to suffer. I tell you, the devil will put some of you in prison to test you, and you will suffer persecution for ten days. Be faithful, even to the point of death, and I will give you life as your victor's crown.* (Revelation 2:10; The church at Smyrna).
>
> *To the one who is victorious and does my will to the end, I will give authority over the nations—that one 'will rule them with an iron scepter and will dash them to pieces like pottery' just as I have received authority from my*

> *Father. I will also give that one the morning star* (Revelation 2:26-28; The church at Thyatira).

In addition, each of the churches was encouraged to "open its ears!" "He who has an ear, let him hear" is repeated to every church. In other words, "listen up—this stuff is important!" Notice they are not challenged to open their eyes. In fact, that was their biggest problem. They were living by sight and in danger of giving in to the World. But they would be vindicated! The high-notes of the letters to the seven churches are just as relevant today. *The very inheritance that the first-century Church pined for is ours now.*

Chapters 4-6: The First Great Enemy

As we turn the page from Revelation 3 to chapter 4, there is little doubt that "we are not in Asia Minor anymore, Toto!" A great "door" was opened, and John was ushered into Heaven itself. The scene that unfolded mirrored Daniel's observations of Heaven's throne room in Daniel 7:9-14. It is critical to remember that all that follows is seen from Heaven's perspective. So many commentators try to interpret Revelation from an earthly perspective. This is backward! What John sees can only be understood through the lens of heaven. The clear focus of Revelation was what was happening in Heaven. Although the earth felt the effects of decisions and actions that emanated from there, the heart of the vision was the glory of God and His divine prerogatives as they flowed from His throne.

As soon as John entered the door to Heaven, he was "at once in the spirit" (Revelation 4:2), and he joined a worship service already in progress. As David Chilton rightly observes, *"Revelation is not, of course, a manual about how to 'do' a worship service; rather, it **is** a worship service, a liturgy conducted in heaven as a model for those on earth (and incidentally instructing us that the Throne-room of God is the only proper vantage point for viewing the earthly conflict between the Seed of the Woman and the seed of the Serpent)."*[140]

It is significant that John sees

> *a throne in heaven with someone sitting on it. And the one **who sat there** had the appearance of jasper and ruby. A rainbow that shone like an emerald encircled the throne* (4:2-3 emphasis added).

In all of the furniture and trappings of both the Tabernacle and the Temple, we are never told that there were chairs. No one sat when serving God in either place. The writer of Hebrews reminded his readers that in addition to following the carefully prescribed regulations under the "first covenant" for the construction of the tabernacle that *"when everything had been arranged like this, the priests entered regularly into the outer room to carry on their ministry"* (Hebrews 9:6). The same writer observed *"Unlike the other high priests, He (Jesus) does not need to offer sacrifices day after day, first for His own sins, and then for the sins of the people"* (Hebrews 7:27).

It was this "regular" entry and "day after day" routine that made chairs superfluous. Now, John saw that very thing, a chair on which is a figure in repose. The significance is not that there was a throne in Heaven, but that John saw this magnificent figure **seated** on that throne. In stark

---

[140] David Chilton, *The Days of Vengeance,*), p. 23.

SCROLL DOWN MEMORY LANE (2)

contrast to the constant need of forgiveness and sacrifice that the Old Covenant system represented, the work of Christ was symbolized as being complete. Our great Warrior-King has won the victory. "Now that the work is done, have a seat!"[141]

As John was ushered into the throne room of Heaven, he was introduced to two groups: the 24 Elders and the four creatures (Revelation 4:4; 4:6-8). Like the "chorus" in the plays of Euripides or Sophocles, the twenty-four Elders comment with a collective voice on the dramatic action throughout the vision. They represent the Church in general and martyrs in particular. The fact that they were "dressed in white" (4:4) is consistent with the way that martyrs are always described in Revelation (6:11; 7:9, 13:14). The number 24 is also symbolic of the priestly role they filled—in the tradition of the Aaronic priesthood, which was told to create 24 divisions (1 Chronicles 24:6-19).

John was then introduced to four creatures that would have been familiar to him. His mind would have been drawn immediately to Ezekiel 1. The four creatures are nearly identical to those Ezekiel described (Ezekiel 1:5-14). Of course, reading about them and actually standing in their presence are two very different things! Unlike the portly harp strumming infants of greeting card fame, these creatures were terrifying. More importantly their presence did not bode well for Israel. John would have known that these creatures portend judgment for His people (Ezekiel 2ff.). John observed these creatures engaged in a great antiphonal

---

[141] Christ is regularly described as being "seated" at the right hand of God: Ephesians 1:20; Ephesians 2:6; Colossians 3:1; Acts 2:34; Hebrews 1:3, 13; Hebrews 8:1; Hebrews 10:12; Hebrews 12:2.

chorus singing *"Holy, holy, holy is the Lord God Almighty, who was, and is, and is to come* (Revelation 4:8). Their chorus prompted the 24 elders to fall on their faces and worship: *"You are worthy, our Lord and God, to receive glory and honor and power, for you created all things, and by your will they were created and have their being"* (4:11). John confirmed what Isaiah saw hundreds of years earlier (Isaiah 6:2-3). This type of worship goes on "day and night."

In chapter 5, John was introduced to the "sentencing phase" of a great trial. The sentence was represented by a *"scroll with writing on both sides and sealed with seven seals"* (Revelation 5:1). Once again, John was exposed to the number seven. God was pursuing "Shalom," for Himself and for His Creation. But who was worthy to initiate the great final phase of God's redemptive and restorative purposes?

Although the scroll had yet to be opened, John could imagine the nature of its contents. Its description as a "scroll" with "writing on both sides" must have conjured up images of Ezekiel 2:

> *He said to me, "Son of man, stand up on your feet and I will speak to you..." He said: "Son of man, I am sending you to the Israelites, to a rebellious nation that has rebelled against me; they and their ancestors have been in revolt against me to this very day. The people to whom I am sending you are obstinate and stubborn... You must speak my words to them, whether they listen or fail to listen, for they are rebellious. But you, son of man, listen to what I say to you. Do not rebel like that rebellious people..." Then I looked, and I saw a hand stretched out to me. In it was a scroll, which he unrolled before me. On both*

> *sides of it were written words of lament and mourning and woe* (Ezekiel 2:1, 3-4, 7, 9-10).

John responded to what he saw with tears. Despite the lamentable future for his own people that a scroll like this would suggest, what prompted John's tears was the fact that God's plan could not move forward (Revelation 5:3-4). There was no one to open the scroll. Then John was informed that the "lamb" he saw in verse 6 (the first of 30 references to the Lamb in Revelation) was none other than "the Lion of the tribe of Judah, the Root of David" (5:5), and that He was worthy to open the scroll. The words of the elder in verse 5 echoed the words that Jacob spoke to his fourth son:

> *You are a lion's cub, Judah; you return from the prey, my son. Like a lion he crouches and lies down, like a lioness—who dares to rouse him? The scepter will not depart from Judah, nor the ruler's staff from between his feet, until he to whom it belongs shall come and the obedience of the nations shall be his* (Genesis 49:9-10).

The potential crisis had been averted. The scroll **could** be opened.

The "lion/lamb" is described as having "seven horns and seven eyes" (Revelation 5:6). John could not miss that the lamb looked *"as if it had been slain"* (5:6), an obvious reference to the crucifixion and a metaphor that John himself had used (John 1:29). Peter (1 Peter 1:19) and Paul (1 Corinthians 5:7) both used the same word picture to describe Christ. John was told that the horns and the eyes of the lamb *"are the seven spirits of God sent out into all the earth"* (Revelation 5:6). God's perfect Shalom was destined to cover the globe. What qualified the lamb as worthy to open the scroll? Verse 5 used the past tense to describe the work of the Lion of the tribe of Judah--He "**has** triumphed." It was precisely because He had **already** defeated Satan that the Lamb was worthy to open the scroll and mete out the judgment that He warned of so often during His earthly ministry. Once again the twenty-four Elders and four Creatures move the action along by leading a chorus that proclaimed the Lamb's worthiness to open the scroll (5:9-10).

Chapter 5 concludes with a familiar scene. The four creatures affirm God's will with a rafter-shaking "Amen," and the 24 elders once again fell down and worship The Lamb.

Chapter six introduces another common theme in Revelation: VINDICATION! One of the four creatures invited John to come and see a new figure, a bow-wielding (Habakkuk 3:9-11; Psalm 45:3-5), crown-wearing rider whose intentions were clear: "Conquest" (Revelation 6:2). There is little doubt as to the identity of this Rider—He is Christ. The Rider mirrors the figure in chapter 19 who is undeniably Christ. In both cases He rides a "white horse." The fact that He was "given a crown" foreshadows Revelation 14:14, where He will be identified as "one like a Son of Man," another common reference to Christ. Like a shotgun mounted over a fireplace, the Rider has taken the "bow" that hung over the throne (4:3) and He now wields it with violent intent.[142]

As the scroll is unfurled more seals are broken. The calamities that the corresponding horsemen bring match exactly the warning given by Ezekiel:

> *This is what the Sovereign Lord says: "How much worse will it be when I send against Jerusalem my four dreadful judgments--sword and famine and wild beasts and plague--to kill its men and their animals!"* (Ezekiel 14:21).

Centuries before Ezekiel, Moses had warned of the very same things in Leviticus 26 and Deuteronomy 28. The price for disobedience would include "the sword," "famine and plague," and attacks from "wild beasts." Even the particulars of God's judgment were foretold by Moses.

> *"If in spite of this you still do not listen to me but continue to be hostile toward me, then in my anger I will be hostile toward you, and I myself will punish you for your sins seven times over. You will eat the flesh of your sons and the flesh of your daughters"* (Leviticus 26:27-29).

Josephus recorded the grisly details of this very kind of cannibalism that occurred during the siege of Jerusalem.[143]

---

[142] When God established His covenant with Noah, he confirmed His peaceful intentions by setting a "bow" in the sky (Genesis 8:20-21). The very same "bow" which Ezekiel saw in Ezekiel 1:26-28 is apparently still there in Revelation 4. Chilton gives a complete and compelling argument for this: Chilton, pp. 83-84.

[143] Josephus, *Wars of the Jews*, Book 5, chapter 10, section 2.

What John saw and heard in the breaking of the first four seals was the culmination of all these prophecies. Although God's love suffers long, it does not suffer indefinitely. In Matthew 24, Jesus had warned of "wars and rumors of wars" (24:6-7a). The second horse of Revelation 6 took peace from the earth and made people "kill each other." As the fourth seal was broken, we see the words of Jesus fulfilled as "famine and plague" swept across the land (Matthew 24:8).

In the midst of these pronouncements of doom, we are told what was driving all this action along.

> *I saw under the altar the souls of those who had been slain because of the word of God and the testimony they had maintained. They called out in a loud voice, "How long, Sovereign Lord, holy and true, until you judge the inhabitants of the earth and avenge our blood?" Then each of them was given a white robe, and they were told to wait a little longer, until the full number of their fellow servants, their brothers and sisters, were killed just as they had been* (Revelation 6:9-11).

The cry "how long" is a common plea for justice (Psalm 35:17; 80:4; 89:46; Habakkuk 1:2). How long indeed!? The time had come for the vindication of the True Israel. Despite appearances, no one had gotten away with murder. On the basis of His atoning work on the cross, the Lamb of God would avenge the fallen saints. That vindication would have to wait only a short time, until Jesus' warning in Matthew 24:9 had been fulfilled, just as Revelation 6:11 suggests.

Although the object of this impending doom has not yet been revealed, it is not difficult to see where all this is headed. Compare the words of Jesus in Luke 21:9ff and Mark 13:1-37 to the judgments described in chapter 6. Then compare Revelation 6:12-17 with Luke 23:27-30. Jesus was clearly describing the same thing that John saw. Both are sounding the death knell for a city. Jerusalem: the center of the Old Covenant system—Jerusalem: propagator of a religion selfishly rooted in a single ethnic identity—Jerusalem: still pressing for an earthly Kingdom—Jerusalem: the epicenter of the persecution of the Saints—Jerusalem: home to false religion and idolatry. Jerusalem is being marked for destruction.

As the sixth seal was opened, the scene recalled the words of Isaiah:

> *All the stars in the sky will be dissolved and the heavens rolled up like a scroll; all the starry host will fall like withered leaves from the vine, like shriveled figs from the fig tree* (Isaiah 34:4).

The identical "shaking" imagery that Christ used in Matthew 24:29 is used here. While debating the imminent nature of Revelation, some commentators have rejoined "when did the moon turn to blood, when did the stars fall from the sky, when did the sun stop shining?" Such an interpretation fails to account for the highly symbolic nature of words like these. Revelation, like Isaiah, was attempting to convey the intense nature of the judgment that was coming. It is this very intensity that prompted the recipients of this judgment to cry out to the mountains, "fall on us and hide us" (Revelation 6:16). Drawing upon the imagery of Hosea 10:6-8 and Isaiah 2:10, 19, Christ had earlier spoken of this very thing:

> *A large number of people followed him, including women who mourned and wailed for him. Jesus turned and said to them, "Daughters of Jerusalem, do not weep for me; weep for yourselves and for your children. For the time will come when you will say, 'Blessed are the childless women, the wombs that never bore and the breasts that never nursed!' Then "'they will say to the mountains, "Fall on us!" and to the hills, "Cover us!"'* (Luke 23:27-30).

Chapter 7: The True "Palm Sunday"

The impending judgment upon Jerusalem now hits the "pause" button. After the opening of the sixth seal, but before the seventh, John was introduced to four angels who were responsible for the delay in judgment (Revelation 7:1-3a). They were "holding back the *four winds* of the earth" (7:1), a common metaphor for God's impending judgment (Psalm 104:3-4; Hosea 13:15-16; Genesis 41:27).

In the midst of God's fierce wrath, we are reminded of His great mercy. This brief respite may well be describing the cessation of the Jewish War in 68 A.D. that permitted so many believers to escape. It is significant that the four angels kept the "judgment-wind" of God from "blowing...on any tree" (Revelation 7:1). "Trees" are a common way of speaking of the righteous (Exodus 15:17; Psalm 92:12-14; Jeremiah 17:5-8). They were to be spared, at least to some degree, from the coming judgment. Just as the land of Goshen was spared many of the plagues that befell Egypt, God placed His seal of redemption upon a large number of "the tribes of Israel" (Revelation 7:4), promising to deliver them from the fury to come. With unmistakable symbolism, a perfect number of Jews are marked for mercy, 12,000 from each of the 12 tribes of Israel (7:5-8).[144] It is important to remember that the first believers were Jewish.

This group, the 144,000, was the "true Israel," the "remnant" that God had always promised would be maintained (Isaiah 6:13; Romans 9:27-28). Their "marking" is lifted directly from the prophecy of Ezekiel:

> *Now the glory of the God of Israel went up from above the cherubim, where it had been, and moved to the threshold of the Temple. Then the LORD called to the man clothed in linen who had the writing kit at his side and said to him, "Go throughout the city of Jerusalem and put a mark on the foreheads of those who grieve and lament over all the detestable things that are done in it." As I listened, he said to the others, "Follow him through the city and kill, without showing pity or compassion. Slaughter the old men, the young men and women, the mothers and children, but do not touch anyone who has the mark. Begin at my sanctuary." So they began with the old men who were in front of the Temple"* (Ezekiel 9:3-6).

Ezekiel's glimpse into the future was now fulfilled.

---

[144] A careful look at the list of tribes reveals the absence of Dan and Ephraim, and the inclusion of Joseph. Dan and Ephraim had been "cut off" from Israel due to their idolatrous behavior (Gen. 49:17; Amos 8:14; Isa. 7:8). There is no room in the New Jerusalem for "idolaters" (Rev. 21:7-8).

It is also important to note the difference between what John *heard* and what John *saw*. While he *heard* that the number of those sealed is 144,000, he *saw* a "multitude that no one could number" (Revelation 7:9). This multitude was composed of people from every "nation, tribe, people and language" (7:9). John intended us to understand these two groups progressively. The one, the remnant, the True Israel, was enfolded by the "great multitude." What began as a primarily Jewish movement expanded to include people from every nation. This way of thinking was not new. Isaiah foretold the same progression:

> *And now the LORD says— "he who formed me in the womb to be his servant to bring Jacob back to him and gather Israel to himself, for I am honored in the eyes of the LORD and my God has been my strength—he says: "It is too small a thing for you to be my servant to restore the tribes of Jacob and bring back those of Israel I have kept. I will also make you a light for the Gentiles that my salvation may reach to the ends of the earth"* (Isaiah 49:5-6).

Paul made clear that the Church was the "Israel of God" (Galatians 6:16) and "Abraham's seed" (Galatians 3:29). The historical progression of the "chosen People," from ethnic Israel to the multi-ethnic Church is undeniable. As we saw in our study of Romans 9-11, God's intentions were always to have a chosen people comprised of individuals from all the nations.

That this innumerable group also represented martyrs is made clear by their apparel. They were all wearing the same "white robes" that the martyred saints of

6:11 were given (7:9b). What is implicit in verse 9 is made explicit in verse 14.

> Then one of the elders asked me, "These in white robes—who are they, and where did they come from?" I answered, "Sir, you know." And he said, "These are they who have come out of the great tribulation; they have washed their robes and made them white in the blood of the Lamb (Revelation 7:14).

These saints, Jew and Gentile alike, had endured the "great tribulation" that was the Jewish War (66-73 AD) and the "great distress, unequaled from the beginning of the world until now," that Jesus spoke of in Matthew 24:21.

Revelation 7:9 described this great throng of people as holding "palm branches." The reader is immediately drawn to the scene from Christ's entry into Jerusalem. There, Jesus was welcomed into the city with the waving of palm branches (John 12:13). *It is significant that there are only two places in all of Scripture that use this term,* םירמת *or "palm."* Clearly John was making a contrast/comparison between the two events. A brief look at the use of "palms" in the cultic life of first-century Judaism will give us insight into what John intended.

Because of our lack of understanding of Jewish Feasts and celebrations, it is easy to miss the significance of "palms" on what we traditionally call "Palm Sunday." We know that Jesus entered Jerusalem just before the Passover (sometime in mid-Spring; John 12:1). *There is no part of Passover that includes palm branches.* The use of palms is reserved for *Sukkot* (The Feast of Booths), celebrated in the Fall. Why are the people of Jerusalem engaging in a ritual reserved for Sukkot in the days just before the celebration of Passover? Many commentators have noticed the inconsistency, the more liberal of which conclude that the Gospels are simply in error. This fails to consider what the people of Jerusalem intended by their use of palm branches as Jesus rode into Jerusalem.

Beginning in the second-century B.C., palms became increasingly associated with Jewish nationalism. Particularly during and after the Maccabean Revolt (164-63 B.C.), during which Israel threw off foreign occupiers, the palm branch was identified as *the* symbol of Jewish independence. The events surrounding The Revolt are highlighted in the extra-Biblical books of 1 and 2 Maccabees. There we find references like these: *On the twenty-third day of the second month, in the one hundred seventy-first year,* **the Jews entered it with praise and palm branches**, *and with harps and cymbals and stringed instruments, and with hymns and songs, because a great enemy had been crushed and removed from Israel. Simon decreed that every year they should celebrate this day with rejoicing. He strengthened the fortifications of the Temple hill alongside the citadel, and he and his men lived there* (1Ma 13:49-52 NRS).

And later, when they rededicated the Temple,

Now Maccabeus and his followers, the Lord leading them on, recovered the Temple and the city; they tore down the altars that had been built in the public square by the foreigners, and also destroyed the sacred precincts. They purified the sanctuary, and made another altar of sacrifice; then, striking fire out of flint, they offered sacrifices, after a lapse of two years, and they offered incense and lighted lamps and set out the bread of the Presence. When they had done this, they fell prostrate and implored the Lord that they might never again fall into such misfortunes, but that, if they should ever sin, they might be disciplined by him with forbearance and not be handed over to blasphemous and barbarous nations. It happened that on the same day on which the sanctuary had been profaned by the foreigners, the purification of the sanctuary took place, that is, on the twenty-fifth day of the same month, which was Chislev. They celebrated it for eight days with rejoicing, in the manner of the festival of booths, remembering how not long before, during the festival of booths, they had been wandering in the mountains and caves like wild animals. Therefore, carrying ivy-wreathed wands and **beautiful branches and also fronds of palm**, *they offered hymns of thanksgiving to him who had given success to the purifying of his own holy place. They decreed by public edict, ratified by vote that the whole nation of the Jews should observe these days every year* (2Ma 10:1-8 NRS).

The events of the first "Palm Sunday" are as clear a statement as any that the Jews of Jesus' day were looking to Him to restore the *political* fortunes of Israel. The presence of palm branches was akin to waving flags with Stars of David emblazoned on them. Like Judas Maccabeus, and like King David before him, the people of Jerusalem were calling out for Jesus to use his apparent "powers" to lead another revolt and re-establish the

Kingdom of David. Again, they were looking for a literal Kingdom, with literal borders, ruled by literal kings sitting on literal thrones, directing literal armies. From a military standpoint, imagine the appeal of Jesus. Military losses? He can raise the dead! Casualties of war? He can heal the wounded! Supply problems? He can create food from the most meager supplies! There is no need to speculate as to Jesus' response to the palm-branch wielding crowd that met Him that first "Palm Sunday." In as clear a reference to 70 A.D. as exists in the New Testament, we read:

> *As he approached Jerusalem and saw the city, he wept over it and said, "If you, even you, had only known on this day what would bring you peace—but now it is hidden from your eyes.* ***The days will come upon you when your enemies will build an embankment against you and encircle you and hem you in on every side. They will dash you to the ground, you and the children within your walls. They will not leave one stone on another, because you did not recognize the time of God's coming to you*** *"* (Luke 19:41-44, emphasis added).

Only days later the same crowd would be crying out, "Crucify Him!" The same crowd that urged Pilate, *"Let His blood be on us and on our children,"* could never have imagined that within a generation, their own curse and the words of Jesus would come crashing down upon them.

In stark contrast to Jesus' entry into Jerusalem, another throng "that no one could count" is now waving palm branches before the Lamb who sits on the throne. THIS TIME, the palm branches are appropriate. THIS TIME, the throng of celebrants recognize their Messiah for who He truly is. THIS TIME, the multitude sees the coming Kingdom in its proper context. THIS is the Kingdom that Jesus died and rose to establish. "Amen! *Praise and glory and wisdom and thanks and honor and power and strength be to our God forever and ever. Amen!* (Revelation 7:12).

The vivid contrast is made complete as this crowd is vindicated (7:15-17) rather than condemned. Imagine the joy and relief these martyred saints must have experienced! Their cry of "how long" (6:10) had been answered. They were translated from a life of deprivation and loss to the very presence of God. One can only imagine the elation of the Elder who declared to John on their behalf, "NEVER AGAIN!"

> *They are before the throne of God and serve him day and night in his Temple; and he who sits on the throne will shelter them with his presence. 'Never again will they hunger; never again will they thirst. The sun will not beat down on them,' nor any scorching heat. For the Lamb at the center of the throne will be their shepherd; 'he will lead them to springs of living water.' 'And God will wipe away every tear from their eyes'* (Revelation 7:15-17).

CHAPTER 8-11: "IT'S QUIET: TOO QUIET."

It is not hard to imagine John leaning in toward the Elder who had just given him this explanation and remarking, "It's quiet...too quiet." Like a premier film maker, God orchestrated a moment of great narrative tension in chapter 8. "This is the silence of solemn, portentous, expectation!"[145] Thus far, all the woes that were to befall the land have been deferred. Like the quiet before the storm, suddenly all Heaven breaks loose!

The catalyst for the action that follows is, of all things, prayer! Before the trumpets can sound, God's people must pray. As G.B. Caird confirmed, "God will not win His victories through the devotion of the martyrs alone, but only if that devotion is supported by the prayers of the whole church."[146] While He was still on earth, Jesus told His disciples a parable in anticipation of this very moment, a parable intended to encourage them to *"always pray and never give up"* (Luke 18:1). A widow, who would have had virtually no rights in this culture (not unlike first-century followers of The Way), implored a judge *"who neither feared God nor cared what people thought"* to "grant me justice against my adversary" (18:2-3). It is significant that the focus of her plea was "justice" which figured prominently in the parable; the judge determined that *"she will get **justice**"* (18:5), and Christ asked His disciples rhetorically, *"Will not God bring about **justice** for His chosen one?"* (18:7). He concluded, *"He will see that they get **justice**, and quickly!"* (18:8).

Revelation 8 is the proof that Jesus' words were true. Justice is finally served! *"The smoke of the incense, together with the prayers of God's people, went up before God from the angel's hand"* (Revelation 8:4). As the fragrance of the prayers of God's People wafted through Heaven, judgment was released—*"Then the angel took the censer, filled it with fire*

---

[145] Henry Cowles, *The Revelation of John*, (New York: 1871), p.82

[146] Caird, p. 107.

from the altar, and hurled it on the earth; and there came peals of thunder, rumblings, flashes of lightning and an earthquake" (8:5). The Jewish historian Josephus described just such a day as the armies of Rome surrounded the Temple: *"for there broke out a prodigious storm in the night, with the utmost violence, and very strong winds, with the largest showers of rain, with continual lightnings, terrible thunderings, and amazing concussions and bellowings of the earth, that was in an earthquake...anyone would guess that these wonders foreshadowed some grand calamities that were coming."*[147] The parallels between what Josephus described and what Revelation recorded are striking.

The use of fire from the "altar" to burn the "earth" could mean only one thing. We can be sure that the significance was not lost on John. As Old Testament Israel entered the land of promise, they we given careful instructions for "handling" the pagan cities they encountered. These cities were to be offered as burnt offerings to the Lord. In this way, they would be "purified" for having profaned the land. The fire that was used to burn the targeted city and its contents was fire that was set using coals from the altar. Charged with carrying coals from the altar with them wherever they went, the priests of Israel were responsible for starting the fire—it was "God's fire."[148] There could be no mistake as to Who was ultimately responsible for the destruction of each city.

---

[147] Josephus, *The Wars of the Jews,* Book 4, Chapter 4, Paragraph 5, p. 812

[148] The story of Nadab and Abihu drives home the point of using "unauthorized" fire, i.e. fire that did not come from the altar. The penalty? Death! (Leviticus 10:1-4)

> *If you hear it said about one of the towns the LORD your God is giving you to live in that troublemakers have arisen among you and have led the people of their town astray, saying, "Let us go and worship other gods" (gods you have not known), then you must inquire, probe and investigate it thoroughly. And if it is true and it has been proved that this detestable thing has been done among you, you must certainly put to the sword all who live in that town. You must destroy it completely, both its people and its livestock. You are to gather all the plunder of the town into the middle of the public square and completely burn the town and all its plunder as a whole burnt offering to the LORD your God. That town is to remain a ruin forever, never to be rebuilt, and none of the condemned things are to be found in your hands. Then the LORD will turn from his fierce anger, will show you mercy, and will have compassion on you. He will increase your numbers, as he promised on oath to your ancestors—because you obey the LORD your God by keeping all his commands that I am giving you today and doing what is right in his eyes* (Deuteronomy 13:12-18).

The irony is that the very punishment reserved for cities that worshipped idols is the same penalty that now falls upon Jerusalem. The Temple and the city had become synonymous with idolatry.

Beginning in Revelation 8:6, trumpets sound signifying action. Trumpets figured prominently in the life of Israel. In this case, the trumpets were intended to sound the alarm and warn Israel of impending judgment (cf. Jeremiah 4:5-8; Ezekiel 33:1-6; Joel 2:1-15). Sadly, the warning would ultimately go unheeded (Revelation 9:20). The first four trumpets/plagues had to do with nature, i.e. indirect judgment (8:7-12). We know that in the years leading up to the final destruction of Jerusalem, the land itself suffered terribly from drought, famine, darkness, earthquakes, and the ravages of the Roman army.[149] Despite the horrific suffering that these judgments brought, God remained merciful, limiting the destruction and suffering to only "a third" of those in the land (8:7-12). This also confirmed that the vision did not have the end of the world in view. We know that the *final* judgment will fall on the entire earth.

Chapter 8 closes with the appearance of an eagle which sounded an ominous alarm: *"Woe! Woe! Woe to the inhabitants of the earth, because of the trumpet blasts about to be sounded by the other three angels!"* (8:13). The eagle portended the death and rotting corpses that would soon litter the landscape of Jerusalem (Matthew 24:28; Luke 17:37). Echoing Ezekiel 17, the eagle stood for foreign armies that would once again invade Israel as an instrument of judgment in God's hands.

The last three plagues, introduced in chapter 9, were called "woes" because they pertained directly to people. The first two woes were clearly symbolic of invading forces, which we may assume had to do with the actual invasion and subsequent destruction of Jerusalem by the Roman General Titus. It is not insignificant that Josephus again recorded events surrounding the final assault on the Temple with

---

[149] Josephus described how the land itself was laid waste. In Book 6, Chapter 1, Paragraph 2 he wrote: *"And truly the very view itself of the country was a melancholy thing; for those places which were before adorned with trees and pleasant gardens were now become a desolate country every way, and its trees were all cut down: nor could any foreigner that had formerly seen Judea and the most beautiful suburbs of the city, and now saw it as a desert, but lament and mourn sadly at so great a change: for the war had laid all the signs of beauty quite waste: nor if any one that had known the place before, had come on a sudden to it now, would he have known it again..."*

words that mirror Revelation. He wrote *a certain prodigious and incredible phenomenon appeared: I suppose the account of it would seem to be a fable, were it not related by those that saw it, and were not the events that followed it of so considerable a nature as to deserve such signals; for, before sun-setting, chariots and troops of soldiers in their armor were seen running about among the clouds, and surrounding of cities.*[150] It would appear that the legions of Rome were an earthly mirror of the heavenly armies in the clouds.

That Satan was part of the carnage that ensued is made clear from verse 1. He is the "star that had fallen from the sky." Just as the armies of God hovered over the land as recounted by Josephus, so the armies of Hell (the Abyss of v. 2) attended the armies of Rome. The cryptic limitation in verse 5 seems out of place. In a vision so rife with symbolism, why this very specific reference to "five months?" Unlike the numerals 6, 7, and 12, five has no particular symbolic significance. Once again, the history of the first century AD may provide the answer.

The Jewish War of 66 A.D. was fought between Jewish dissidents and the Roman Empire. What precipitated this war? In 64 AD, Emperor Nero appointed a new procurator for Judea named Gessius Florus. His avarice was only outdone by his loathing of the Jewish people. Noticing Florus' proclivity for favoring Greeks over Jews, many Greeks in Judea began publically harassing Jews, going so far as to sacrifice animals outside the Jewish synagogue in Caesarea making it unclean. Despite the Jewish outcry, Florus did nothing. He then proceeded to steal a good sum of money

---

[150] Josephus, *Wars of the Jews.*, Book 6, Chapter 5, paragraph 3, pp. 889-890

from the Temple in Jerusalem, claiming it was for the Emperor and personal friend, Nero. Reacting to the inevitable Jewish outcry, Florus responded by imprisoning, flogging and crucifying a number of the Jewish leaders of the protest, many of whom were Roman citizens. These atrocities culminated in the murder of 3,600 Jews, including women, children, and infants, at the Upper Market Place in Jerusalem. *By Florus' own admission, he did these things to incite the Jews to revolt against Rome. His reign of terror lasted precisely five months, from May-September of 66 A.D. Josephus credits this five-month period with starting the Jewish War.* "And what need I say any more upon this head, since it was this Florus who necessitated us to take up arms against the Romans, while we thought it better to be destroyed at once, than by little and little."[151] The five months of suffering referenced in Revelation 9:5 may well be speaking of Florus' five-month reign of terror.

Chapter 9 goes on to describe the marauding creatures as "locust" (9:3ff). The symbolic relationship between locust and invading armies has significant Biblical pedigree. In Judges, the Midianites were described *"like swarms of locusts. It was impossible to count them or their camels; they invaded the land to ravage it"* (Judges 6:5). Jeremiah warned of an impending invasion. *"The LORD Almighty has sworn by himself: I will surely fill you with troops, as with a swarm of locusts, and they will shout in triumph over you"* (Jeremiah 51:14). The most extensive comparison of invading armies to locust is found in Joel 1-

---

[151] Josephus, *The Antiquities of the Jews*, Book 20, chapter 11, section 1, p. 649.
Support for the other details of the reign of Florus can be found in Josephus, *The Wars of the Jews*, Book 2, Chapters 14-15, pp. 737-742.

2. It is important to note that at first, God warned Israel that *"a nation has invaded my land, a mighty army without number"* (Joel 1:6). But in Joel 2:25, God concluded *I will repay you for the years the locusts have eaten— the great locust and the young locust, the other locusts and the locust swarm— **my great army** that I sent among you"* (emphasis added). Appearances to the contrary, it is always God who is pulling the strings and it is always His purposes that are being served. As the Legions of Rome (locust) descended upon Jerusalem, God Himself was moving them along to display His glory. The fact that they were lead by Satan (Revelation 9:11) belies the fact that Satan is only able to do this because "he was **given** the key to the shaft of the Abyss." Satan, then as now, never *takes* anything beyond what he is *given* by the Lord Himself. The invading armies are described as having teeth like that of a lion. The prophet Joel, using the same locust metaphor, described them in precisely the same way:

> *A nation has invaded my land, a mighty army without number; it has the teeth of a lion, the fangs of a lioness...They have the appearance of horses; they gallop along like cavalry. With a noise like that of chariots they leap over the mountaintops, like a crackling fire consuming stubble, like a mighty army drawn up for battle. At the sight of them, nations are in anguish; every face turns pale. They charge like warriors; they scale walls like soldiers. They all march in line, not swerving from their course. They do not jostle each other; each marches straight ahead. They plunge through defenses without breaking ranks. They rush upon the city; they run along the wall. They climb into the houses; like thieves they enter through the windows. Before them the earth shakes, the heavens tremble, the sun and*

> *moon are darkened, and the stars no longer shine"* (Joel 1:6; 2:4-10).

Revelation 9:6 contains language that is clearly reminiscent of Jesus' warning in Luke 23:27-30:

> *A large number of people followed him, including women who mourned and wailed for him. Jesus turned and said to them, "Daughters of Jerusalem, do not weep for me; weep for yourselves and for your children. For the time will come when you will say, 'Blessed are the childless women, the wombs that never bore and the breasts that never nursed!' Then "'they will say to the mountains, "Fall on us!" and to the hills, "Cover us!"'*

In both Luke and Revelation, the destruction of Jerusalem is in view.

Revelation 9:12 provides a brief interlude after which the altar of chapter 8 is reintroduced—only now a voice emanates from it. The connection between the prayers of the saints (symbolized by the incense altar) and the judgment that followed is reinforced. God hears the cry of His People! The voice from the altar commanded the sixth angel to *"release the four angels who are bound at the great river Euphrates"* (9:14). The number "four" symbolized the complete scope of their work, as in the "four corners" of the earth.

The fact that the "four angels" who were released with the sounding of the sixth trumpet are said to have been "bound at the great river Euphrates" (9:14) is significant. As Caird notes, *"to the Jew it (the Euphrates) was the northern frontier of Palestine, across which Assyrian, Babylonian and Persian invades had come to impose their pagan sovereignty on the people of God. All the scriptural warning about a foe from the north, therefore, find their echo in John's blood-curdling vision (Isaiah 14:31; Jeremiah 1:14ff; 6:1, 22; 10:22; 13:20; 25:9; 46:20, 24; 47:2; Ezekiel 26:7; 38:6, 15; 39:2)"*[152]

Chapter 10 introduces us to yet another angel of judgment, who pronounced the expected outcome of 9:20-21.

> *There will be no more delay! But in the days when the seventh angel is about to sound his trumpet, the mystery of God will be accomplished, just as he announced to his servants the prophets* (Revelation 9:20-21).

Again and again, God had warned His people. Again and again, prophet after prophet had appealed to Israel to repent and once again embrace their calling as a light to the nations and to live out the commandments of God. The "little scroll" that marked the final destruction of Jerusalem and the Temple was "eaten" by John. Just as his prophetic counterpart Ezekiel had experienced (Ezekiel 3:1-3), the scroll at first tastes like honey. It quickly turns his stomach sour. On the one hand, the sweet vindication of the Saints and the judgment of God upon their enemies is complete. On the other hand, that judgment would come upon John's own people. It is this very message that John was called upon to bring to the nations.

Chapter 11 describes the destruction of Jerusalem and the Temple in vivid detail. Measuring things is often used in

---

[152] Caird, *The Revelation of Saint John the Divine*, p.122.

association with judgment and death (cf. 2 Sam 8:2; Amos 7:7-8; Hab. 3:6). It is also in this chapter that we are first introduced to "the beast." With no introduction or explanation, this beast "comes up from the Abyss" (11:7) and attacks the "two witnesses (11:3ff). Who is this Beast, and who are these two witnesses?

Before we explain the two witnesses, we need to keep our beasts straight. The term "beast" (θηριον) should not be confused with the four "creatures" before God's throne (4:6ff). In Scripture, as in Revelation, "beast" is a term reserved for a being/entity that seeks autonomy from God. Daniel 4:33 portrayed Nebuchadnezzar as a "beast." Christ's tormentors are assigned "beastly" characteristics (Psalm 22:12-13, 16). Pagan nations are often referred to as "beasts" (Psalm 87:4; Isaiah 51:9; Daniel 7:3-8, 16-25). We will provide specific rationale/justification for each "Beast" as we proceed, but in every case, anything/anyone identified as a "beast" epitomizes resistance to and rebellion against God. The following is a listing of every reference to a "beast" in Revelation, with a corresponding description of who that beast represents in that passage. In the first instance, the Beast is Satan himself. The following chart will serve as a helpful reference as we continue to read through Revelation.

WINSOME WARRIORS

Usages of "The Beast" and Their Meaning

Revelation 11:7	Revelation 13:14
Revelation 13:1	Revelation 13:15
Revelation 13:2	Revelation 13:15
Revelation 13:3	Revelation 14:11
Revelation 13:4	Revelation 15:2
Revelation 13:5	Revelation 16:10
Revelation 13:8	Revelation 16:13
Revelation 13:11	Revelation 17:3
Revelation 13:12	Revelation 17:7
Revelation 17:13	Revelation 17:8
Revelation 17:16	Revelation 17:11
Revelation 17:17	Revelation 17:12

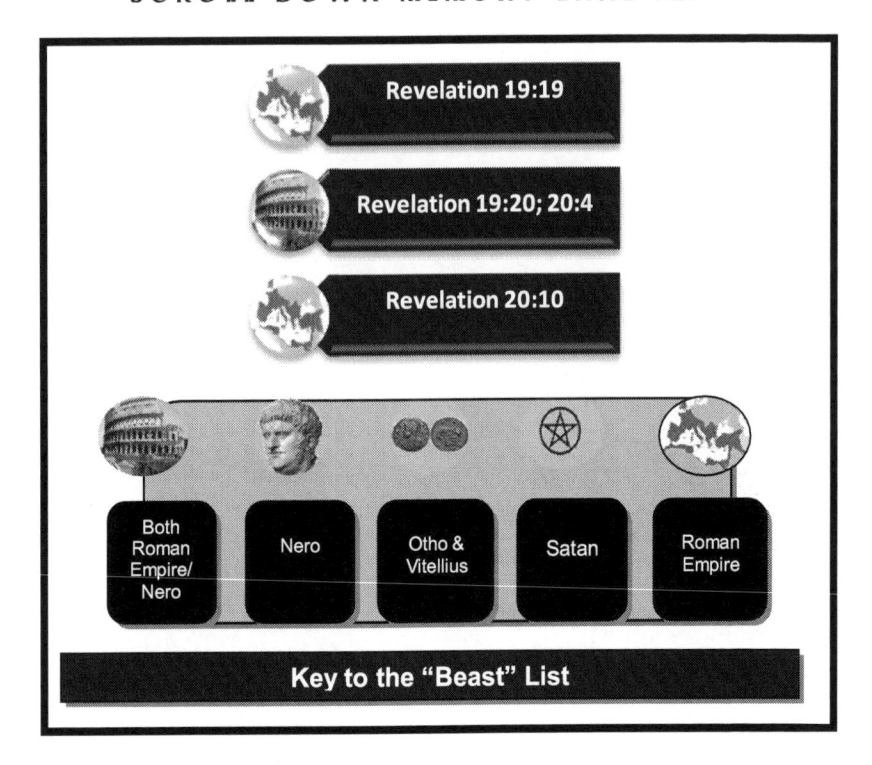

Diagram: Key to the "Beast" List

Revelation 19:19	Both Roman Empire/Nero
Revelation 19:19	Nero
Revelation 19:20; 20:4	Otho & Vitellius
Revelation 19:20; 20:4	Satan
Revelation 20:10	Roman Empire

The "two witnesses" that appear in chapter 11 have prompted a number of interpretations. Some argue that they refer to Peter and James, both of whom were martyred for the faith.[153] But the text (Revelation 11:4) **tells us** who these witnesses were! *"They were "the two olive trees" and the two lampstands, and "they stand before the Lord of the earth"* (11:4). Drawing upon the imagery of Zechariah (Zechariah 4), we are told that the lampstands and the trees represented the "kingly" function of God's people and the priestly blessing they brought in the form of the oil that continually flowed from the trees. The one witness, Zechariah was told, stood for Zerrubbabel, the anointed king, and the other for Joshua, the

---

[153] Warren, *The Book of Revelation*, pp. 148-153.

anointed priest.[154] If these witnesses were opposed, *"fire comes from their mouths and devours their enemies"* (Revelation 11:5). This fire symbolized the prophetic truth spoken by the Church as it called its first century audience to repentance. In speaking the word of God, they called down judgment upon their hearers just as the prophet Jeremiah had:

> *Therefore this is what the LORD God Almighty says: "Because the people have spoken these words, I will make my words in your mouth a fire and these people the wood it consumes"* (Jeremiah 5:14).

The Two Witnesses also represented the Word of Christ, as contained in the Law and the Prophets. We know this because the two witnesses are identified with both Moses and Elijah. In Revelation 11:6 we read that the witnesses *"have power to shut up the heavens so that it will not rain during the time they are prophesying; and they have power to turn the waters into blood and to strike the earth with every kind of plague as often as they want,"* making the connection between themselves and Elijah & Moses unmistakable (2 Kings 1:9-12; Numbers 16:35). The two witnesses represented the Church in both its priestly and prophetic role, speaking the word of Christ as they called ethnic Israel to repentance and as they preached the Gospel of the Kingdom first to Israel and then to the nations.

Under the direction of Satan (the Beast), an unholy alliance between Judaism and Rome (Luke 23:12) resulted in the persecution/death of the Two Witnesses. The derisive treatment of the first-century Church is symbolized by the

---

[154] Caird, *The Revelation of St. John*, p. 134.

fact that their "bodies" remained unburied (11:9). John's first-century readers would have understood the lack of internment as the final indignity that the martyred saints would suffer (Jeremiah 8:1-2; 16:3-4; Psalm 79:1-3). For "three-and-a-half days," or a broken-seven, their corpses were gloated over and the co-conspirators of Rome and Judaism celebrated (Revelation 11:10). Verse 10 specifically referred to them as "prophets," highlighting their role as harbingers of the coming judgment. Like Christ, who was the "firstfruits" (1 Corinthians 15:20), those who died in Christ rose again and enjoyed the reign of Christ along with Him (Revelation 11:11-12).

In summary, the two witnesses *were "representative characters, standing for all those Christian witnesses for the truth of whom Jesus himself was at the head, and his faithful disciples and apostles, walking in his steps, filling up the ranks till the fall of Jerusalem...The witnesses were men working in the spirit and power of Elijah and Moses and in somewhat analogous circumstances—like them having to do with mighty hostile forces, and withstanding them in the strength of the Lord of Hosts."*[155] By drawing upon the imagery of Zechariah 4, John is undoubtedly telling his first-century readers and us to take to heart the "point" of the vision Zechariah received: *"Not by might nor by power, but by my Spirit, says the Lord Almighty"* (Zechariah 4:6). Verses 11 and 12 of Revelation 11 confirm that the Church, symbolized in the Two Witnesses, is triumphant. Like the first Adam, the "breath of life" was breathed into them (11:11) and those who opposed them were "terrified." Just as Christ ascended with

---

[155] Henry Cowles, *The Revelation of John*, pp. 92-94.

His disciples looking on, so the Church followed suit "while their enemies looked on" (11:12). The Church wins!

On the heels of the triumph of the Church, the beginning of **the** decisive transition in the history of Christ's Kingdom commences. Up until this time, Christianity was viewed as a Jewish sect. All of that changed with the destruction of Jerusalem, the beginning of which is described in 11:13. It is at this point that the Kingdom that God had always envisioned is said to truly begin, a fact borne out by the words of 11:15ff. From that moment on, the Kingdom of God no longer had borders. From that moment on, EVERY place that the feet of the saints touched was "holy ground." The language of verse 15 is decisive. It is not the "Kingdoms" of this world, but the "Kingdom" of this world that "HAS" become the KINGDOM of our Lord. The denouement of this critical transition is reinforced as John moved from the now "marked for destruction" Temple on earth, to the True Temple in Heaven (11:19). The old, earthly Temple was gone, and the true heavenly Temple, offering access to all nations, was now opened.

Chapter Summary

The book of Revelation is not the mystery that many have made it. Using a simple, historically proven method of interpretation, the veil of obscurity that covers this book can be pulled back, providing us with great historical insight. The book can be divided into a prologue and two halves. The prologue includes all of the major themes of the book: a message of hope in the face of fierce persecution, resistance to compromise and a call to endure, the vindication of martyrs and the ultimate victory of the Saints and the Kingdom.

The seven churches of chapters 2-4 represent the wider Church and, specifically, those who were undergoing threats to property and life. As the cry of the Saints reaches heaven, Christ offers words of hope, encouragement, and victory. The great persecutors of the Church would not go unpunished, the Kingdom would prevail, and those who had given their lives for Christ would ultimately reign over the very ones who had previously threatened them.

The first half of Revelation, chapters 4-11, deals specifically with the fate of the first great persecutor of the Church, Judaism. The God of Heaven pounds the land with thunderous "sevens" as He restores Shalom. In vivid detail, these chapters chronicle the judgment of ethnic Israel, culminating in the destruction of Jerusalem and the Temple in 70 A.D.

Relying almost exclusively on Old Testament imagery, Revelation makes explicit what was implied in earlier prophecies—the longsuffering of God had reached its end. The failure of Israel to live out its covenant responsibilities, coupled with the rejection of the Messiah, culminated in unparalleled suffering for the generation that had missed the hour of their visitation. Chapters' 4-11 breathe new life into Jesus' words as recorded in the Olivet Discourse. As chapter 11 closes, the Temple lies in ruin, and the first great wave of resistance to the Kingdom of God comes to its inevitable end—destruction.

What can we learn from all this? Originally identified as a Jewish sect, Christianity was forever distinguished as unique with the destruction of Jerusalem. Although deeply rooted in the history of ethnic Israel, the ever-expanding "rock" of the Kingdom could not be contained in one country or one building. The iconoclastic lightning-strike of God's judgment zeroed in on the Temple. Never again would God's People be segregated into groups. Never again would the True Israel need the blood of lambs and goats to atone for sin. God's prerogatives stretch far beyond any one people and any one place.

As always, we see in Revelation 4-11 the fate of all those who resist the Kingdom juggernaut. Christ could not have been clearer: "Repent! The Kingdom is here." Stop building your own kingdoms—Stop creating your own personal fiefdoms with religion or politics or wealth or pleasure! Anyone or anything that is not committed to the praises of God and His Anointed will be crushed. Whether willingly or forced, every knee will bow, and every tongue will confess—"Christ is Lord!"

In addition, Revelation 4-11 reminds us that the eyes of sight are dubious organs for understanding what is really happening. Look all you want with them, but only the eyes of faith will enable you to see what is truly there; looking at history through the lens of Revelation offers up a very different reality. Surrendering is the path to victory. Those who have lost everything are truly rich. Those who have given up their lives have found the only life worth living. Dominion-smashing power is in the hands of those who kneel and those who bleed. The Comforter is never as deeply experienced as in times of discomfort. Those who appear to be pulling the strings are mere marionettes in the hands of God. The fiercest beast is a slain Lamb. The greatest dignity awaits those who received none in this life. While the list is endless, the point is obvious—don't trust the eyes of sight. Our vision needs to be filled with the very things that John saw and then recorded. Unlike the eyes of sight, the vision of Revelation only grows keener with age.

CHAPTER 13

A Scroll Down Memory Lane (3)

THE KINGDOM COMES

We come, then, to the New Testament asking what to do, seeking a program of action. And the New Testament answer is: there shall no program be given you—except to be *the Church*!
JOHN BRIGHT, *THE KINGDOM OF GOD*

For I am already being poured out like a drink offering, and the time has come for my departure. I have fought the good fight, I have finished the race, I have kept the faith. Now there is in store for me the crown of righteousness, which the Lord, the righteous Judge, will award to me on that day—and not only to me, but also to all who have longed for his appearing.
2 TIMOTHY 4:6-8

Soldiers of Christ, arise, and put your armor on; Strong in the strength which God supplies through His eternal Son. Strong in the Lord of hosts, and in His mighty power; Who in the strength of Jesus trusts is more than conqueror.
ISAAC WATTS, *AM I A SOLDIER OF THE CROSS?*

SCROLL DOWN MEMORY LANE (3)

CHAPTER 12: "LET'S REVIEW"

As noted earlier, this is a transitional chapter. We move from one enemy to the next. We move from one city to the next. We move from one culture to the next. It is a long way no matter which trip you take! John takes us back to the Jewish roots of Christianity and the early attempts of the next great enemy (Rome) to try and destroy the true King. The *"woman clothed with the sun"* (12:1) is Israel. The *"enormous red dragon with seven heads and ten horns"* (12:3) is none other than the Roman Empire. We have already explained how Rome was described in this way in chapters 13 and 17. Having failed in its earliest attempts (Herod and Pilate), the dragon now unleashed its greatest fury in the form of persecution that made even the Jewish assault pale by comparison. In anticipation of this day, the Psalmist wrote,

> *Why do the nations conspire and the peoples plot in vain? The kings of the earth take their stand and the rulers gather together against the Lord and against his Anointed One...the One enthroned in heaven laughs; the Lord scoffs at them...Therefore, you kings, be wise; be warned, you rulers of the earth. Serve the Lord with fear and rejoice with trembling. Kiss the Son, lest he be angry and you be destroyed in your way...* (Psalm 2:1-2, 4, 10-12).

Revelation 12:7 and following introduce us to another "dragon," distinct from the "red dragon" of verse 3. This dragon is named: *"That ancient serpent called the devil or Satan"* (12:9). What happened to Satan in Revelation 12 fits perfectly with what Christ described during His earthly ministry. As the seventy disciples returned from being sent out with reports of the seismic power shift they had experienced, Jesus explained, *"I saw Satan fall like lightning from heaven"* (Luke 10:18). John himself described how he heard a voice from Heaven as Jesus predicted His death. Jesus explained, *"This voice was for your benefit, not mine. Now is the time for judgment on this world; now the Prince of this world will be driven out"* (John 12:30-31). These events from the life of Christ are what are being described in Revelation 12. What were the consequences of Satan's expulsion from Heaven?

> Now have come the salvation and the power and the Kingdom of our God, and the authority of his Messiah. For the accuser of our brothers and sisters, who accuses them before our God day and night, has been hurled down. They triumphed over him by the blood of the Lamb and by the word of their testimony; they did not love their lives so much as to shrink from death. Therefore rejoice, you heavens and you who dwell in them! But woe to the earth and the sea, because the devil has gone down to you! He is filled with fury, because he knows that his time is short (Revelation 12:10-12).

The good news is that Satan has been thrown down. The bad news is that the place where He landed also happens to be the same place where we live! Satan recognized that this was more than just a change of address. This spelled ultimate defeat for Him! As a result, He was furious. He knew that His time of ruling over the nations "was short" (12:12b). Despite his feverish attempts to the contrary, the saints triumphed over Him. Note carefully **how** they defeated Him. The very thing that prompted God's judgment upon Satan's Roman ally, the persecution of the Saints, is the same thing that rendered Satan a defeated enemy! It is *"the word of their testimony; they did not love their lives so much as to shrink from death"* (Revelation 12:11).

It cannot be overstated: Satan is a pawn in the hands of God! **The fruit of the fury of Satan, the persecution of the Saints, is the very means that God used to defeat him!** Enraged that his efforts to destroy Israel and the Son of David had failed, Satan proceeded *to "wage war against the rest of her offspring—those who keep God's commands and hold fast their testimony about Jesus"* (12:17). John is very precise in his use of the word "offspring." It is literally the word for "seed." He clearly had in mind the original judgment pronounced over Satan in Genesis 3:15: *"And I will put enmity between you and the woman, and between your offspring and hers."* Thinking that He had found a capable ally in the Roman Empire, Satan now prepared to launch his last-ditch effort to destroy the nascent Church.

Chapter 13-19: The Second Great Enemy Falls

Like the first section (Revelation 4-11), chapters 13-19 give us pictures of judgment and vindication—Rome is judged, the martyrs are vindicated. Chapter 13 introduces us to the Dragon's partner in His futile effort to reclaim the throne. It is described as "a beast" that rises from the sea. The fact that its origin is the sea is significant. Earlier (9:1-3) we saw that the sea is associated with the Abyss, the habitation of demons. Biblical imagery often associates the sea with the wicked: *"But the wicked are like the tossing sea, which cannot rest, whose waves cast up mire and mud"* (Isaiah 57:20). This beast parallels the beasts described by Daniel as coming up "out of the sea" (Daniel 7:2). The sea represented the ultimate destiny of all those who opposed Christ and His Kingdom (Revelation 18:21).

Like the beast of Daniel 7, this beast/empire was frightening and blasphemous. As we learn later, the "ten horns" were ten provincial governors (17:12) and the "seven heads" were seven Roman emperors (17:9-11). Fueled by the power of the dragon, this beast proceeded to *"wage war against God's holy people and to conquer them. And it was given authority over every tribe, people, language and nation"* (13:7-8). As ruler of the entire known world, Rome used its power, under the direction of Emperor Nero, to persecute the Church and spread its unique brand of idolatry. As always, the power of the Beast was derived. Neither the Dragon nor the Beast does anything outside the permissive will of God.[156]

Although we have discussed the cult of emperor worship already,[157] it is significant that Nero's legacy fits perfectly with the description of the "image" in 13:11ff. One of Nero's greatest accomplishments was the construction of the *Colossus Neronis,* a nearly 100 foot high statue of himself that was surrounded by a worship complex known as "The Golden House." This "over-the-top" deification of Nero, coupled with the rumor that he had not actually committed suicide but had simply fled to the East, fueled the idea that Nero would "come back to life" (Revelation 13:3-4).[158]

13:11 introduces us to a "second beast" which comes "out of the earth" (Cf. The previous "Beast Chart"). We are clearly meant to understand this beast as distinct from the

---

[156] "Four times in verses 5 through 7 we read the passive, "was given," emphasizing the subordinate role of the beast." Mounce, The Book of Revelation, p. 254.

[157] "Nowhere was the Caesar-cult more popular than in Asia" Henry B. Swete, *The Apocalypse of St. John*, as quoted by Jay Adams, *The Time Is At Hand*, p. 73.

[158] George H. VanKooten, *The Year of the Four Emperors and the Revelation of John*, Journal for the Study of the New Testament, 2007; 30; 205, p. 207.

first beast which came "out of the sea." *Two of the emperors who followed Nero, Otho and Vitellius, could well be this "second beast."* With "two horns like a lamb, but (it) spoke like a dragon" suggests a paradox (not unlike the Lion of Judah who looked like a Lamb that was slain). In saying that it (they) "exercised all the authority of the first beast on its behalf" is consistent with their role as Emperor but their short-lived reigns made them less imposing. (A possible explanation for the "lamb-like appearance"?) The verses that follow suggest that this second beast and the first beast were closely connected, and that the second beast actively promoted the worship of the first. History provides some tantalizing support for their candidacy (Otho and Vitellius) as the "second beast."

Both of them modeled their reigns after Nero. Roman historian Suetonius is quick to note that "Otho, a former friend of Nero, easily held the first place among the emperor's friends because of the similarity in their characters."[159] Plutarch added that "in his desire to please the multitude, he did not refuse at first to be hailed in the theatres by the name of Nero, and when statues of Nero were produced in public, he did not prevent it."[160]

It was Otho who made one of his first orders of business the task of completing the Golden House of Nero. Tacitus, in his *Roman History*, recorded that *"Otho brought up the question of celebrating Nero's memory with the hope of winning over the Roman people; and in fact some set up*

---

[159] Ibid., p. 215.

[160] Ibid.

statues of Nero. Moreover, on certain days the people and soldiers, as if adding thereby to Otho's nobility and distinction, acclaimed him as Nero Otho."[161]

Vitellius also reigned in the tradition and memory of Nero. Suetonius observed that Vitellius made worship of Nero part of his routine. He *"clearly wished to imitate Nero and offered him a sacrifice to the dead."*[162] These practices by Otho and Vitellius are completely consistent with what John described as a two-horned beast *that...*

> *exercised all the authority of the first beast* **on its behalf***, and made the earth and its inhabitants* **worship the first beast***, whose fatal wound had been healed... it deceived the inhabitants of the earth. It ordered them to* **set up an image in honor of the beast who was wounded by the sword*** and yet lived* (Revelation 13:11-12, 14).

It is likely that the two emperors, Otho and Vitellius, were the "two-horned" second beast. Their devotion to Nero and their role as Emperor put them in an ideal position to promote the cult of emperor worship and to "breath" life into the legacy of Nero.

Revelation 13 closes with John's reference to the number of the Beast. As we have already explained, this cryptic allusion to "666," matched perfectly with Emperor Nero. That John saw the sum "666" as a number that must be arrived at via a formula is made clear by his use of the word "calculate" in verse 18. By describing the number as the "the number of man," John made it clear that this "beast" stood for

---

[161] Ibid. p. 216.

[162] Ibid.

everything that was not God, or everything that was "anti-God."[163] Despite the Beast's best efforts, the Church remained intact, albeit shaken.

Revelation 14: The Glory of the Coming of the Lord

A "trinity of hostility" embodied in the two beasts and the Devil himself had joined forces. Just as in the first section (chapters 3-11), the same question plagued the saints in this section—"can the Church survive?" Heaven answers: *Then I looked, and there before me was the Lamb, standing on Mount Zion (*14:1). For John and his original readers this could have meant only one thing—God was laughing. In fact, He was scoffing at the efforts of the beasts and the Devil. The fact that Jesus was standing on Mount Zion meant that the words of Psalm 2 had come to pass.

> *Why do the nations conspire and the peoples plot in vain? The kings of the earth take their stand and the rulers gather together against the LORD and against his Anointed One. "Let us break their chains," they say, "and throw off their fetters." The One enthroned in heaven* **laughs; the Lord scoffs at them**. *Then he rebukes them in his anger and terrifies them in his wrath, saying,* **"I have installed my King on Zion, my holy hill."** (Psalm 2:1-5).

Not only can the saints survive, they will "overcome" under the leadership of the newly "installed" King.

---

[163] Caird, *A Commentary on The Revelation of St. John the Divine*. Pp. 175-177 for a good description of all the negative implications of the number 666.

Chapter 14 also reintroduces us to the elect Jews who made up the early Church (the 144,000). These are the "People within a people" that Paul spoke of in Romans 9-11, the Remnant of which Isaiah and Jeremiah and Amos and Joel were so concerned. The contrast between those who received the mark of the Beast on their forehead in Revelation 13 is set off against those who not only rejected that mark, but who had the words "Lamb" and "Father" written on their foreheads.

The replacement of the Old System and the defeat of organized Judaism in chapters 4-11 is now met with a celebration (14:1-5). As the sounds of harps filled Heaven, God's Children were said to sing a "new song" (14:3). What other kind of song could they sing? The "old way" and the "old wineskins" would no longer do, any more than an "old song" would! These saints had not "prostituted" themselves with the whore of Rome (14:8), but had instead remained "virgins" (14:4), saving themselves for their true love, the Lamb Himself. We are told that "no lie was found in their mouths; they were blameless," a clear reference to Zephaniah's words regarding the "remnant of Israel:

> *Of Jerusalem I thought, 'Surely you will fear me and accept correction!' Then her place of refuge would not be destroyed, nor all my punishments come upon her. But they were still eager to act corruptly in all they did. Therefore wait for me," declares the LORD, "for the day I will stand up to testify...On that day you, Jerusalem, will not be put to shame for all the wrongs you have done to me, because I will remove from you your arrogant boasters. Never again will you be haughty on my holy hill. But I will leave within you the meek and humble. The remnant of Israel will trust in the name of*

> *the LORD. They will do no wrong; they will tell no lies. A deceitful tongue will not be found in their mouths. They will eat and lie down and no one will make them afraid."* (Zephaniah 3:7-8, 11-13 emphasis added)

The 144,000 are this "remnant," members of the True Israel.

They are also described as the "firstfruits," being offered to God and the Lamb (14:4), a term that is always reserved for the first of its kind or the mark of something new. Jesus is called the "first fruits of the dead" (1 Corinthians 15:20), signifying that He was the pledge of a greater harvest to come. In the same way, *these first "Jewish" believers symbolized the hope of a greater harvest to come,* a harvest taken from "every nation, tribe, language, and people" (14:6).

This was the very next thing that John saw—an angel bringing the "eternal Gospel" (14:6) to the very people for whom the 144,000 had been the first fruits. This same angel then announced that, along with the Gospel, judgment was coming (14:7). A cavalcade of angels followed the first, each with an ominous warning. The second angel identified the object of God's wrath: *"Babylon the Great, which made all the nations drink the maddening wine of her adulteries"* (14:8). A third angel returned to the themes of "the beast and its image" and the "mark" of the beast (14:9), making a clear connection between the Babylon referred to in the previous verse and the beast, understood as both the Roman Empire and the Emperor Nero.

There is still some debate over whether the "Babylon" of Revelation 14 was Rome or Jerusalem. Although the overwhelming view of the earliest Christian commentators was that Babylon was Rome,[164] recent interpretations have favored seeing Babylon as Jerusalem. A number of factors favor the more traditional view that "Babylon" is Rome.

As we have seen, there is a strong connection between the Beasts, the image of the Beast, and Babylon. The penalty for resisting the Beast is said to be both "the sword" (13:10) and the axe ("beheading" 20:4), two common forms of Roman execution, but unheard of under the Jewish persecution, the latter using stoning to execute its victims (cf. Acts 7:55-59). Second, the "Babylon is Jerusalem" proponents argue, the terms "harlot" and "adulteries" were common in describing what Israel had done in relationship to her Husband. Since the Babylon of Revelation was repeatedly referred to in this way, it must be speaking of Jerusalem. But these terms were not exclusively used to describe Israel in the Old Testament. For example, both Tyre (Isaiah 23:17) and Ninevah (Nahum 3:4) were described in this way. Most important, Israel's adultery was most often described as a result of her *being corrupted* by worshipping the gods of **other** nations. In Revelation, it was Babylon that was doing the corrupting, drawing others into illicit relations with **herself**. The Babylon of Revelation was the one initiating the "affair" while Old Testament Israel was usually the one responding to the enticements of others. To think of Israel/Jerusalem as the "Mother of Prostitutes" (17:5) and other nations committing "adultery WITH HER" (18:3) is

---

[164] The earliest surviving copy of a commentary on Revelation is that of Victorinus, Bishop of Poetovio who wrote during the mid-late 3rd century. A more complete list of other early fathers who favor the Babylon-is-Rome view are found in G. Biguzzi, Biblica: Pontifical Biblical Institute, Rome; Vol. 87 (2006). *Is the Babylon of Revelation Rome or Jerusalem.*. p. 374, footnotes 11, 12.

simply not accurate. Notice as well that "Babylon" was said to have "made all the nations drink the maddening wine of her adulteries." This accurately describes the pervasiveness of the cult of emperor worship throughout the Empire which was composed of "all the nations."

The geography of "The Woman" and "The Beast" as described in Revelation 17 was almost certainly Rome. As we have discussed, the "city of seven hills" in the ancient world was always Rome. The political realities surrounding Babylon also fit more precisely with Rome. As Biguzzi rightly observed, *"The Beast of Rev. 13, rises from the sea (v. 1), has authority over or is adored by "all the earth" (v. 3), "every tribe and people and tongue and nation" (v. 7), and "all the inhabitants of the earth" (v. 8). The Babylon of Revelation 17-18 has corrupted, or has enriched, or is mourned by "all the nations" (18:3), "the kings and merchants of the earth" (18:3b, 9, 11, 17), and "all those who had ships at sea" (18:19). "Such a sea, that bathes many regions with their many people of different languages and cultures, is recognizable as the Mediterranean sea, whereas the multi-ethnic reign and its capital city, are recognizable as the Roman empire and Rome, much more conveniently than as Jerusalem."*[165] Jerusalem could never be said to exercise that kind of influence over the entire known world of the first century. Nor was Jerusalem ever the center of trade or the economic hub of the ancient world (18:9-17).

That the Babylon of the latter half of Revelation is Rome makes the most sense of the text of Revelation. Again,

---

[165] G. Biguzzi, Ibid. p. 381.

Revelation becomes much easier to interpret when we take seriously the time frame references in the book itself, and use the dual-judgment template to divide the book. Rome is clearly in view in the second section (chapters 14-19).

In 14:14ff we are introduced to two "sickle-bearing" beings. Although the instrument for reaping is the same for both, the outcomes are very different. Seated on a "white" cloud, as distinct from the dark cloud that enshrouded Sinai, the first angel is "one like a son of man," wearing the customary head-gear of Christ (a crown). He used His sickle to reap a harvest of the righteous. John may well have had in mind the metaphor Jesus had used after talking with the Samaritan woman. The fields that were ripe for the harvest are not being reaped (John 4:34-38).

The second angel (14:17ff) gathered "grapes" to be "thrown into the great winepress of God's wrath." Christ had earlier explained this exact scene to his disciples.

> Then he left the crowd and went into the house. His disciples came to him and said, "Explain to us the parable of the weeds in the field." He answered, "The one who sowed the good seed is the Son of Man. The field is the world, and the good seed stands for the people of the Kingdom. The weeds are the people of the evil one, and the enemy who sows them is the devil. The harvest is the end of the age, and the harvesters are angels. "As the weeds are pulled up and burned in the fire, so it will be at the end of the age. The Son of Man will send out his angels, and they will weed out of his Kingdom everything that causes sin and all who do evil. They will throw them into the blazing furnace, where there will be weeping

> *and gnashing of teeth. Then the righteous will shine like the sun in the Kingdom of their Father. Whoever has ears, let them hear"* (Matthew 13:36-43).

"Ripe grapes" (14:18) symbolized the "fullness of time" for the angel's deadly harvest. The "winepress of God's wrath" was filled, and Rome (the "city" of 14:20) was awash in the blood of her people.

Revelation 15-19

In this section, we see the particulars of what God's "winepress" includes. Chapter 15 introduces us to the "beginning of the end" for Rome. Seven more angels, each with a "plague," (15:1) are commissioned to finish the pouring out of "God's wrath" (15:1). The coming judgment was witnessed by those who *"had been victorious over the beast and its image and over the number of its name"* (15:2). Another triumphant song was sung over the vanquishing of the second great enemy, and God's purposes for "all nations" were extolled (15:3-4). Unlike the seals and the trumpets, which saw an interlude between the sixth and seventh of each, there was no such pause with the seven bowls of chapter 16. The apostasy of Rome was complete, and there would be no offer of redemption.

Like bats emerging from a cave at night, the seven angels poured out of the heavenly Temple, each one representing a plague, and each one equipped with a bowl "filled with the wrath of God" (15:7). Access to the heavenly Temple was denied until the judgment of Rome was complete (15:8). Chapter 16 chronicles the just judgments of God as each angel visited the earth. Unlike the earlier judgment of Jerusalem and Israel which was limited to "one-third" of the land and its inhabitants, this judgment covered the whole earth, indicative of the far reach of the Roman Empire. Revelation 16:17 announced that the angels' work "was done." As one would expect, with the fall of the Roman Empire, *"the cities of the nations collapsed"* as well (16:19). The glue that had held the Empire together was now gone.

As we reach chapter 17, John was given the most definitive explanation thus far as to the nature of God's judgment. John was not only shown the outcome of God's sentence but also the object of His wrath. In clear, unequivocal statements, the angel explained that the reason that "Babylon" was being judged was because she *"was drunk with the blood of God's holy people, the blood of those who bore testimony to Jesus"* (17:6). The angel then proceeded to explain the features of the Beast, understood both collectively (the Roman Empire) and individually (Emperor Nero). Rome, an empire composed of many nations and peoples and tongues, fell apart from within, and was ultimately destroyed by its own citizens (17:15-17). Vandals, Goths, Angles, Saxons and Jutes invaded and ultimately destroyed Rome in 476. Despite the Beast's attempts to destroy the Lamb and His People, in the end, *"the Lamb will triumph over them because he is Lord of lords and King of kings—and with Him will be his called, chosen and faithful followers"* (17:14).

Chapter 18 is both a lament and a victory song. The chapter describes the decadent worldwide influence of the Roman Empire and the shock felt throughout the world at the fate of Rome. As the political and economic center of the earth, Rome had always symbolized the best and most beautiful that the Western world had to offer. *"Was there ever a city like this great city"* (18:18) was clearly the sentiment of everyone who knew anything of Rome. The fact of her decline and ultimate invasion was more than many could bear. It is intriguing that, like the seven angels, the seven plagues and the seven bowls, most historians identify seven as the number of times that Rome was "sacked" or experienced a major invasion.

- Battle of the Allia (387 B.C.) – Rome is sacked by the Gauls after the Battle of the Allia.
- Sack of Rome (410) – Rome is sacked by Alaric, King of the Visigoths.
- Sack of Rome (455) – Rome is sacked by Geiseric, King of the Vandals.
- Sack of Rome (546) – Rome is sacked and depopulated by Totila, King of the Ostrogoths, during the war between the Ostrogoths and the Byzantines.
- Sack of Rome (846) – The Arabs attack Rome and loot old St. Peter's Basilica, though the Roman City walls prevent further damage to the city itself.
- Sack of Rome (1084) – Rome is sacked by the Normans of Robert Guiscard.
- Sack of Rome (1527) – Rome is sacked by the mutinous troops of Emperor Charles V.

Despite the possible historical parallels, the fact remains that chapter 18 detailed the final judgment of Rome.

Chapter 19 resurrects another familiar theme—the vindication of the saints. God had come through as promised. *"He has avenged on her (Babylon/Rome) the blood of his servants"* (19:2b) Many readers have mistaken the latter part of chapter 19 as a description of Christ's second appearing. Instead, John is revisiting the action taken by Christ on behalf of His Church to destroy the Roman Empire. We know that

WINSOME WARRIORS

the second appearing of Christ will be like His departure, according to the angels of Acts 1. He did not leave on a horse, so we should not expect Him to return on one. The battle described here is spiritual in nature. Beginning in Revelation 19:9, notice that Rome was defeated by the power of the sharp sword that came out of the Rider's mouth. From a tactical and practical standpoint, this would be a very poor way to hold a sword. Clearly, it is a spiritual weapon, and we know from Scripture exactly what this sword is–*The sword of the Spirit, which is the Word of God"* (Ephesians 6:17b); *"For the word of God is alive and active. Sharper than any double-edged sword, it penetrates even to dividing soul and spirit, joints and marrow; it judges the thoughts and attitudes of the heart"* (Hebrews 4:12). So the battle was won both then and now, not by clever strategies and powerful displays of force, but by the faithful proclamation of the Word of Christ, coming out of our mouths and being put on display in our lives.

The "finality" of the destruction of the Beast (The Roman Empire) as described in chapter 19 should not throw us off. Its destruction should not be understood as "immediate" as much as "ultimate." Although the Roman Empire endured for another four centuries, the consequences of its initial and prolonged persecution of the Church were final. Even the "Christianizing" of the empire under Constantine (272-327 A.D.) could not undo the judgment heaped upon it due to its earlier alliance with Satan.

CHAPTER 20

Like chapter 12, Revelation 20 is a transitional chapter. Where does the Church go from here? What will the fate of the Kingdom of God be? How will Satan respond to his failure to destroy the infant Church? What is left to do for the now well established Church? We have already looked with some detail at parts of this chapter, but its pivotal nature demands another look.

The fact that our Bible provides a chapter division between 19 and 20 is unfortunate. Chapter 20 is the natural and immediate outcome of the victory won in chapter 19. As the Word of God, the Gospel of the Kingdom, is wielded by the Rider on the white horse and His followers, we see in chapter 20 the consequences of the worldwide triumph of the Gospel.[166] The defeat of the Beast and the False Prophet left only one enemy to deal with: Satan. Chapter 12 explained that Satan's reign of terror would be "short" (12:12). Chapter 20 details what occurred **after** that short time, and what, ultimately the fate of Satan and the Saints would be. Like everything that John has seen thus far, Revelation 20:1-6 describes events that are past. We are *currently* living during the "thousand years" that John spoke of in chapter 20. Satan is "bound" now. At some point in the future, Satan will enjoy a brief "parole," during which He will return to His old ways. Then, the End will come. The Eternal State will begin. With that summary, let's look at each verse of Revelation 20.

v. 1: And I saw an angel coming down out of heaven, having the key to the Abyss and holding in his hand a great chain.

An unnamed angel is seen descending from heaven. The angel must come "down" in order to lay hold of Satan, because his dwelling is no longer in Heaven, but on earth (12:9). The same key that was earlier "given" to Satan (9:1)

---

[166] Both Warren and Adams make the case that chapter 20 cannot be understood without reading it as an extension of chapter 19. Cf. Warren, *The Book of Revelation*, pp. 239-240 and Adams, *The Time Is At Hand*, p. 83.

is now in the hands of its rightful owner. Like a thurible in the hands of a priest, the angel held a "great chain" as he moved from Heaven to earth. The "Abyss" should not be confused with the "lake of burning sulfur" of verse 10. The latter is Satan's final destination. The "binding" to the Abyss is not ultimate, but temporary.

> *v. 2: He seized the dragon, that ancient serpent, who is the devil, or Satan, and bound him for a thousand years.*

All the monikers used to describe Satan in Revelation are used in this verse. There will be no escaping his sentence because of a technicality! Let it be known with crystal clarity who is being punished.

The word for "bind" (δεο) here is used 41 times in the New Testament. Jesus used this word to describe His relationship to Satan on three occasions, all of which are recorded in the synoptic Gospels. They are as follows:

> *Knowing their thoughts, he said to them, "Every Kingdom divided against itself is laid waste, and no city or house divided against itself will stand. And if Satan casts out Satan, he is divided against himself. How then will his Kingdom stand? And if I cast out demons by Beelzebul, by whom do your sons cast them out? Therefore they will be your judges. But if it is by the Spirit of God that I cast out demons, then the Kingdom of God has come upon you. Or how can someone enter a strong man's house and plunder his goods, unless he first **binds** the strong man? Then indeed he may plunder his house* (Matthew 12:25-29).

> *And he called them to him and said to them in parables, "How can Satan cast out Satan? If a Kingdom is divided against itself, that Kingdom cannot stand. And if a house is divided against itself, that house will not be able to stand. And if Satan has risen up against himself and is divided, he cannot stand, but is coming to an end. But no one can enter a strong man's house and plunder his goods, unless he first **binds** the strong man. Then indeed he may plunder his house* (Mark 3:23-27).
>
> *But he, knowing their thoughts, said to them, "Every Kingdom divided against itself is laid waste, and a divided household falls. And if Satan also is divided against himself, how will his Kingdom stand? For you say that I cast out demons by Beelzebul. And if I cast out demons by Beelzebul, by whom do your sons cast them out? Therefore they will be your judges. But if it is by the finger of God that I cast out demons, then the Kingdom of God has come upon you. When a strong man, fully armed, guards his own palace, his goods are safe; but when one stronger than he attacks him and **overcomes him**, he takes away his armor in which he trusted and divides his spoil* (Luke 11:17-22).

What is interesting is that in the first two cases, the word for "bind" (δεο) was used. But in Luke's account, that word was substituted for the word "overcomes" (νικαω). It is the same word that was used repeatedly to describe the calling of each of the seven churches in chapters 2 and 3. This broadens our understanding of what it means that Jesus "bound" Satan, **and** *our ongoing role as winsome warriors.* Satan is not incapacitated, he is defeated, or "overcome!" To bind someone in this sense is to render them restricted and overcome, not immobilized. As we have already seen in both Revelation 12 and Luke 10, Satan has indeed "fallen," from his position of authority specifically as it related to his ability to "deceive the nations." He is "bound" in that sense.

On the heels of Christ's ascension, as the Church experienced Pentecost, Jerusalem was marked for a Holocaust.[167] Then, the Satanically inspired efforts of Rome to crush the Church were themselves crushed. The finishing touches on the binding of which Jesus spoke of were made complete with those events. Let the plundering begin!

We are told that Satan's binding lasts "a thousand years." The mention of "a thousand years" is limited to this chapter alone. Nowhere else in Scripture do we see a time connected with the reign of Christ and His Bride. There are a number of good reasons why we should understand this number symbolically.

First, this number appears in a book that is rife with symbolism and metaphors. From the number of the Elders (24) to the sealing of the first-century believers (144,000), from the number of the Beast (666), to the number of seals, trumpets, and bowls (7), it is hard to imagine that John suddenly intended his readers to grab their desk calendars to prepare for a millennial "countdown."

Second, the wider Biblical use of the number 1,000 provides a symbolic precedent. None of us would consider searching for 1,000 bovine-inhabited hills, only to declare upon reaching hill 1001, that the cows on that hill belonged to someone other than God (Psalm 50:10). Who

---

[167] Chilton, *Days of Vengeance*, p. 90.

could imagine God using a Sharpie marker to place a large 'X' over each "heavenly" day after 365,000 days had passed on earth? (Psalm 90:4; 2 Peter 3:8). Woe to the one-thousand and first generation that follows the 1,000 to which God showed His love (Exodus 20:6). Imagine the dismay of the armies of Israel as they encountered the inhabitants of Canaan. Each warrior was promised to rout "a thousand," but what of the enemy 1,001? (Joshua 23:10). In each case, the number 1,000 is meant to be understood symbolically. We should expect nothing different here.

Third, the sometimes painfully long genealogies in Scripture are conspicuous by what they DON'T include. No human is ever recorded as living beyond 969 years (Genesis 5:27). The number '1,000' is a number that is clearly beyond the reach of man. For these reasons, it would appear that the number '1,000' is intended to convey the idea of a complete, full, long, God-centered time. We are 'in' the thousand years now. The full expression of the reign of Christ and the Saints takes time. Just as it takes time for yeast to work its way through the dough (Matthew 13:33), and just as the great Rock of Daniel's vision grows to fill the whole earth (Daniel 2:35), so the Kingdom takes time to fully develop and cover the earth. It will not be fully accomplished until the perfect amount of "God-time" has passed.

v. 3: He threw him into the Abyss, and locked and sealed it over him, to keep him from deceiving the nations anymore until the thousand years were ended. After that, he must be set free for a short time.

We have already commented on the specific nature of Satan's imprisonment. It is hard for us to imagine that Satan is "locked" and "sealed" in any real sense of the words. But the clear qualifier of those things was "to keep him from deceiving the nations anymore..." The reign of Christ over the Gentile nations is now possible. Paul's commentary on Isaiah is completely consistent with what John saw:

> *For I tell you that Christ has become a servant of the Jews on behalf of God's truth, so that the promises made to the patriarchs might be confirmed and, moreover, that the Gentiles might glorify God for his mercy. As it is written: "Therefore I will praise you among the Gentiles; I will sing the praises of your name." Again, it says, "Rejoice, you Gentiles, with his people." And again, "Praise the Lord, all you Gentiles; let all the peoples extol him."* ***And again, Isaiah says, "The Root of Jesse will spring up, one who will arise to rule over the nations; in him the Gentiles will hope"*** (Romans 15:8-12 emphasis added).

Were it not for what John described here, the work of the great Apostle Paul would not have been possible. At his commissioning on the road to Damascus, Paul was told,

> *I will rescue you from your own people and from* ***the Gentiles. I am sending you to them*** *to open their eyes and* ***turn them from darkness to light, and from the power of Satan to God****, so that they may receive forgiveness of sins and a place among those who are sanctified by faith in me* (Acts 26:17-18).

The bad news for one nation, Israel, was good news for the rest. *"Therefore I want you to know that God's salvation has been sent to the Gentiles, **and they will listen!**"* (Acts 28:28). What had been impossible before, that the Gentile nations would listen, was now possible because Satan's dominion over them had ended![168]

Unfortunately, as convicts go, Satan is the quintessential recidivist. Upon His release, he immediately returns to his old ways. As we will see, with Satan, very little changes.

> **v. 4:** *I saw thrones on which were seated those who had been given authority to judge. And I saw the souls of those who had been beheaded because of their testimony about Jesus and because of the word of God. They had not worshiped the beast or its image and had not received its mark on their foreheads or their hands. They came to life and reigned with Christ a thousand years.*

Verse 4 seems to suggest that John saw two groups: *"those seated on thrones given authority to judge,"* and the *"souls of those who had been beheaded."* The Greek here is a bit tricky. There is no "full stop" in the Greek, no "I also saw..." The idea seems to be that John saw one group, not two, seated on thrones, and those thrones were occupied by martyrs.[169] The flow of the verse goes something like

---

[168] Chilton provides a great summary of the teaching of the early Church Fathers regarding the defeat of Satan at Christ's first coming. Cf. Chilton, *Days of Vengeance*, pp. 199-200.

[169] Wilcox, *The Message of Revelation*, (Leicester, England & Downers Grove, Illinois: Intervarsity Press, 1975), pp. 191-192. Caird, *The Revelation of St. John the Divine*, pp. 251-252. Cowles, *The Revelation of John*, p. 153. Adams, *The Time Is At Hand*, pp. 88-

this: "And I saw thrones on which were seated those who had been given authority to judge—the souls of those who had been beheaded..." The fact that John saw only "souls" suggests that the resurrection he later spoke of (verse 5) should not be viewed as the final resurrection. When we die, we immediately enjoy the presence of God in Paradise (Luke 23:43). But our enjoyment will be tempered by the fact that we do not have bodies. The body/soul dualism of the Greeks in which the body is bad and the soul is good is unknown in Scripture. When God created us, he breathed the breath of life into us and we became "living beings," not souls wrapped in temporary and somehow superfluous bodies (Genesis 2:7).

We will only be able to *fully* enjoy God's presence when we receive the bodies that are as important to our eternity as our souls. As Paul explained, the resurrection of the dead (the final resurrection) involves receiving our "imperishable," "glorified," "powerful," "spiritual" bodies (1 Corinthians 15:42-44). The problem is not that we have bodies, but that we have bodies that are corrupted by sin. Our desire should not be to get rid of our bodies, but to receive our heavenly bodies! (2 Corinthians 5:1-4). The fact that John saw only "souls" (don't bother asking how one "sees" a soul) suggests that these people were in their pre-final-resurrection-state, in other words, they exist now, seated on thrones, judging.

These souls are said to represent those who were "beheaded," which was a common form of Roman

---

89. Mounce, *The Book of Revelation*, pp. 354-356. Warren, *The Book of Revelation*, pp. 247-252.

execution. It is not correct to think that only martyrs who died in this way are included.[170] The text goes on to say that this group included all those who did not worship the Beast. That martyrs in general are in view here is completely consistent with everything we have read thus far. The "key" to Revelation that we identified at the outset was the cry of the martyrs and their subsequent vindication. What John saw was the **ultimate** vindication.

They were given "authority to judge" and they "reign with Christ." In a very real sense, this is the lot of all believers, martyrs or not. Spiritually, we all "come to life" as we are resurrected in Christ (Romans 6:3-5), and we all "reign" with Him now.

> *...Because of his great love for us, God, who is rich in mercy, made us alive with Christ even when we were dead in transgressions—it is by grace you have been saved. **And God raised us up with Christ and seated us with him in the heavenly realms in Christ Jesus**... (Ephesians 2:4-6 emphasis added).*

But John cannot be describing this general sense in which all believers are "resurrected." John saw martyrs seated on thrones. Clearly, they had not worshipped the Beast. This was why they lost their lives in the first place. But it is **after** they died that we are told they "came to life and reigned with Christ a thousand years." If they had not

---

[170] "The word translated "beheaded" was no longer specific in John's day. It included those who were thrown to lions, or ignited as torches in Nero's garden, etc. James Moffatt *Expositors Greek Testament*, Vol. 5, Grand Rapids: n.d., p. 475, says, "Under the empire citizens were usually beheaded by the sword. The archaic phrase (beheaded) lingered on, like our own 'execution.' Here it is probably no more than a periphrasis for 'put to death.'" Adams, *The Time Is At Hand*, pp. 88-89, note #6.

already been resurrected as in regeneration they would not have given their lives for Christ in the first place. They had **already** been united with Christ in His death and resurrection at their baptism. They had **already** been "raised up" with Christ and "seated" with Him in the Heavenlies at the moment they were saved. John must have had something else in mind other than the resurrection and reign that is the lot of all believers. *As we will see, their "coming to life" was a special privilege reserved for those who had given their lives for the cause of Christ. Despite the fact that all Christ-followers reign with Him now, and despite the similarities to the language describing regeneration, John appears to have martyrs in view here, not all believers.*

A final observation—the only places in Revelation where thrones have been mentioned are in Heaven (4:4; 11:16). There is no mention in verse 4 of the earth. There is nothing to indicate that these thrones are located anywhere but in Heaven. The notion that there will be a future, *earthly* Kingdom with people seated on thrones and Christ Himself seated on a throne is contrary to everything we have read in Revelation.

> ***v. 5:*** *(The rest of the dead did not come to life until the thousand years were ended.) This is the first resurrection.*

John expanded on the theme of this "special" resurrection with a parenthetical observation. "The rest of the dead did not come to life until the thousand years were ended." John then returned to the topic of the martyrs' coming to life, calling it the "first resurrection." The "coming to life" (the 'first resurrection') must speak of something special given to the martyrs which other Christians do not receive until the thousand years have passed. This interpretation presupposes that the phrase "rest of the dead" *refers to all other non-martyred Christians.*[171] The verse would then read, "the rest of the dead Christ-followers did not enjoy this special "coming to life" until the thousand years were ended, only those saints who died a martyr's death did." This special martyr resurrection is called the "first resurrection."

In John's writings, his use of the word "life" (as in "come to life" in Revelation 20:5) or "live" are used in a qualitative sense. For John, "life" meant the fullness of life that could only be found in Christ. For example, John frequently wrote about "eternal life" as in John 3:16. "There it expresses not duration (or the unbeliever as easily could be said to possess "eternal life") but blessedness. Eternal life is life at its richest."[172] When John wrote that *"the rest of the dead did not come to life until the thousand years were ended..."* he meant that the non-martyred dead (in Christ) would not enjoy the kind of reign the martyr's enjoyed **now** until **after** the millennium is over. There is a special fullness to life that is reserved for those who give their lives for the cause of Christ. It is as if martyrs participate *more* fully in the nature of Christ, who suffered and sacrificed Himself for the very people who hated Him. "The glory of God shines through the beauty and splendor of self-sacrifice as nowhere else, and

---

[171] Adams, *The Time Is At Hand*, p. 91.

[172] Ibid., p. 92.

most importantly, this glory of God, the glory of His self-sacrificing love, shine out in each martyrdom."[173]

This idea that the "first resurrection" is a special or unique privilege for martyrs has been acknowledged by a number of commentators.[174] There does seem to be a sense in which the Scriptures speak of a resurrection that can be distinguished from the general resurrection at the end of time or the spiritual resurrection that occurs at conversion. The writer of Hebrews spoke of a "better" resurrection (Hebrews 11:35). The word translated "better" is κρειττονοό from the root word κρεισσών which is the comparative form of the word "good." The writer seems to distinguish between those whose dead were given back to them, "being raised to life again," and others who enjoyed a "better resurrection." Who was part of this latter group, the "better-resurrection" folk? Martyrs who were *"tortured and refused to be released...they were stoned, sawed in two; they were put to death by the sword"* (Hebrews 11:35-37). Apparently, people who die a "natural" death experience one kind of resurrection, and those who are martyred experience another kind, a "better" resurrection. What makes the latter better is that it gives that person an opportunity to reign with Christ in this present age in a special way.

---

[173] Josef Tson, *Perspectives on the World Christian Movement*, "Suffering and Martyrdom: God's strategy in the World," p. 184.

[174] Cf. Mounce, p. 359. Adams, 92-93. Caird, 254-255. Warren, p. 249. Cowles, 153-157. Wilcox, pp. 191-192.

SCROLL DOWN MEMORY LANE (3)

The Apostle Paul wrote:

> *But whatever were gains to me I now consider loss for the sake of Christ. What is more, I consider everything a loss because of the surpassing worth of knowing Christ Jesus my Lord, for whose sake I have lost all things. I consider them garbage, that I may gain Christ and be found in him, not having a righteousness of my own that comes from the law, but that which is through faith in Christ—the righteousness that comes from God on the basis of faith. I want to know Christ—yes,* **to know the power of his resurrection and participation in his sufferings, becoming like him in his death, and so, somehow, attaining to the resurrection from the dead** (Philippians 3:7-11).

Commentators have tried to explain the apparent doubt Paul expressed in *"attaining to the resurrection from the dead"* by his use of the word "somehow." Most suggest that Paul was simply expressing humility, while others say that he was expressing intense concern or involvement. Those suggestions seem strained and weak. Paul was not expressing doubt as to whether he would enjoy the "general" resurrection as much as doubt over whether he would enjoy the "first resurrection" of Revelation 20. Again, notice the context. Paul was talking about suffering for Christ and dying a martyr's death. He had no doubt that he would experience the "power of His (Christ's) resurrection" (3:10) in a general sense. But when it came to "becoming like Him in His death" (3:11), Paul could not be sure. Paul was expressing doubts as to **how** he would die, not whether he would rise. Paul knew that it was only in *"sharing in His sufferings, becoming like Him in His* *death"* that would permit him to participate in "the resurrection from the dead" in the sense that John described in Revelation. The idea that this "first resurrection" is something special is borne out in the next verse in Revelation 20.

> ***v. 6:** Blessed and holy are those who share in the first resurrection. The second death has no power over them, but they will be priests of God and of Christ and will reign with him for a thousand years.*

John is not suggesting in verse 6 that *only* martyrs are "blessed and holy." All believers are "blessed" (Rev. 1:3; 14:13; 16:15; 19:9). By singling out those who share in the first resurrection as being blessed and holy, John confirmed their unique status. The "second death" is specifically identified in verse 14 as "the lake of fire." The martyrs' identification as "priests of God and of Christ" also point to the unique way in which they filled a role that is the lot of all believers. The difference between all believers and the martyrs is made explicit in that they "will reign with Him for a thousand years." In one sense, every Christ-follower is reigning with Christ now. In another sense, only some Christ-followers are seated on thrones in Heaven during the period from 70 A.D. to the final appearing of Christ. That is what sets "first resurrection" Saints apart from "spiritual" or "general" resurrection Saints. They enjoy a unique sovereignty (for 1,000 years) because of their unique sympathy with the suffering of Christ.

> ***v. 7:** When the thousand years are over, Satan will be released from his prison...*

SCROLL DOWN MEMORY LANE (3)

Why is Satan released again? We might as well ask, "why is there evil in the world? Or "why does God postpone the judgment of His enemies—why not simply destroy them outright?" God's glory is central to the book of Revelation. God's glory is at the heart of all He does. We can only answer that all God does, including the release of Satan from the Abyss (his prison), will somehow garner God greater glory. "It is obvious that one part of God's design in permitting this last development of Satan in our world may have been to exhibit His agency before our race and before the moral universe with far more distinctness and prominence than ever before."[175] God is waiting for one final display of His glory in the final defeat of Satan against overwhelming odds.

The fact that this final assault occurs after the reign of Christ and the martyrs, after the triumph of the Gospel, and after the flourishing of the cultural influence of God's people should not surprise us. Alongside the spread of the Gospel, alongside the ever-expanding nature of the Kingdom, the Kingdom of darkness also continues to grow. During the "thousand years" Satan still exercises some influence—evil persists and sin still corrupts. Satan is still able to gather followers, still able to deceive, and still directing spiritual traffic. This is borne out in the next verse.

> *v. 8: and will go out to deceive the nations in the four corners of the earth—Gog and Magog—and to gather them for battle. In number they are like the sand on the seashore.*

---

[175] Cowles, *The Revelation of John*, p. 158.

WINSOME WARRIORS

Upon his release, Satan will pick up precisely where he left off. Once again, he will scour the earth (the four corners) looking for willing partners in his last ditch effort to reclaim his rule over the nations. His intentions are clear: "to gather them for battle." The notion that this is a physical rather than spiritual battle flies in the face of everything we have read thus far.[176]

In this verse, John alludes to Ezekiel 38-39 in describing Satan's futile efforts.

> *The word of the LORD came to me: "Son of man, set your face against Gog, of the land of Magog, the chief prince of Meshek and Tubal; prophesy against him and say: 'This is what the Sovereign LORD says: I am against you, Gog, chief prince of Meshek and Tubal"* (Ezekiel 38:1-3).

In a backhanded way, John was describing an alliance of Gentile nations that is a "type" of rebellion against God, not a literal alliance of nations. We know from the genealogies in Genesis that Gog and Magog (the chief prince of Meshek and Tubal) spawned Gentile peoples.

> *Now these are the generations of the sons of Noah, Shem, Ham, and Japheth: and unto them were sons born after the flood. The sons of Japheth; Gomer, and Magog, and Madai, and Javan, and Tubal, and Meshech, and Tiras. And the sons of Gomer; Ashkenaz, and Riphath, and Togarmah. And the sons of Javan; Elishah, and Tarshish, Kittim, and Dodanim. By these were the isles of the Gentiles*

---

[176] Charles Taylor, *Commentary of Revelation* (Online Books: Netadvantage Christian Publishers, 1996), p. 128

> *divided in their lands; every one after his tongue, after their families, in their nations* (Genesis 10:1-3).

The suggestion by some that Gog and Magog refer to a Russian-led alliance is demanding far too much of the text. Caird's observation is correct: Gog and Magog are the Biblical equivalent of the nations in Psalm 2.[177] The brevity of John's treatment of Gog and Magog is because these events are not germane to the point of the Revelation. Events surrounding the Second Appearing are not central to what John is being shown.

> ***v. 9:*** *They marched across the breadth of the earth and surrounded the camp of God's people, the city he loves. But fire came down from heaven and devoured them.*

"The camp of God's people, the city He loves" is clarified in the next two chapters. The "camp" and the "city" are parallel descriptions of the same thing. It is the People of God, the Church, the Bride of Christ that John has in mind here.[178] There is no dramatic tension in this account, no "silence in heaven," no cries of "how long?" Satan's efforts are immediately crushed. Unlike the battle of chapter 19, where the enemies of the Kingdom are "killed" (converted) by the sword of God's word, these enemies are "devoured." "Fire" is a common means that God uses to "purify" by completely destroying (Ezekiel 38:22; Genesis 19:24-25; 2 Kings 1:10-12).

---

[177] Caird, *The Revelation of St. John the Divine*, pp. 256-257.

[178] Caird, p. 257; Chilton, p.208.

> ***v. 10:*** *And the devil, who deceived them, was thrown into the lake of burning sulfur, where the beast and the false prophet had been thrown. They will be tormented day and night for ever and ever.*

The devil meets his end. His identification as the one "who **deceived** them" is fitting. In calling out the Pharisees, Christ exposed Satan's M.O.

> *You belong to your father, the devil, and you want to carry out your father's desires. He was a murderer from the beginning, not holding to the truth, for there is no truth in him. When he **lies**, he speaks his native language, for he is a liar and the father of **lies*** (John 8:44).

For Satan there will be no future release, no "little season." He will be "tormented day and night forever and ever."

> ***v. 11:*** *Then I saw a great white throne and him who was seated on it. The earth and the heavens fled from his presence, and there was no place for them.*

This is the "end" of the beginning. What began in a garden somewhere in the Near East, now culminates in the throne room of Heaven. This is the moment to which Christ referred when He said in Matthew 25:34, *"Come, you who are blessed by my Father; take your inheritance, the Kingdom prepared for you since the creation of the world."* The identification of this throne as "white" leaves little doubt as to its inhabitant: it is Christ Himself. He has traveled upon a white cloud (Chapter 14), and ridden on a white horse (chapter 19), and now sits on a white throne.

The fact *that "the earth and the heavens fled from His presence"* speaks to the "moral grandeur of God, because they were unfit for His continued presence, because they were contaminated beyond the possibility of cleansing."[179] The wider context of these words is prefigured in Psalm 114. There, the Psalmist spoke of God's covenant love for His people and the "holy terror" of God. The Psalmist wrote,

> *When Israel came out of Egypt, Jacob from a people of foreign tongue, Judah became God's sanctuary, Israel his dominion. The sea looked and fled, the Jordan turned back; the mountains leaped like rams, the hills like lambs. Why was it, sea, that you fled? Why, Jordan, did you turn back? Why, mountains, did you leap like rams, you hills, like lambs?* (Psalm 114:1-6).

The void left by the departure of earth and heaven is not a problem. A new heaven and earth are coming.

> ***v. 12:*** *And I saw the dead, great and small, standing before the throne, and books were opened. Another book was opened, which is the book of life. The dead were judged according to what they had done as recorded in the books.*

All the dead now stand before the Christ. This is the great "general resurrection" at the end of time. The mention of "books being opened" has caused evangelicals to look twice. Are we not saved by grace alone through faith alone in Christ alone? What of these "books" that are opened? Notice, there are two kinds of books that are referred to:

---

[179] Caird, pp. 258-259.

"books" and "*the* book of life." The dead are judged according to what is in the "books." A quick peek ahead to verse 15 reveals the fate of those whose names are not written in the book of life, and, by contrast, to those whose names **do** appear in that book. So then, upon what basis is judgment handed out?

Imagine two queues. In one line are those who die in Christ. Their names are written in the book of life. It is on the basis of this **one** fact that individuals escape the "lake of fire." The rest of humanity in the other line is judged "according to what they had done." Their "fruit" exposes their vain trust. It is not as if Christ is looking for enough evidence in the "books" to defer judgment. He is looking for confirmation that the "lake of fire" is the only possible sentence. "The point of the text is not, of course, 'salvation by works.' The point is *damnation by works*."[180] Those who die in Christ need not fear that somehow there might be data in the "books" that will lead to the lake of fire. All that is needed is to have one's name written in THE book, the book of life.

v. 13: *The Sea gave up the dead that were in it, and death and Hades gave up the dead that were in them, and each person was judged according to what they had done.*

As we have seen all along, "the sea" never represents anything good. The "dead" there are given up. We should not imagine that this refers to those who were buried at sea. This refers to the unbelieving dead who have been consigned to the sea, the home of the Beast and the home of Godless people. So as not to miss anyone, the only two remaining

---

[180] Chilton, p. 210.

potential resting places for the dead are also emptied, "death and Hades." Everyone has been gathered. Every person who has ever lived now stands before the great White Throne. Judgment is passed, and all verdicts are all final.

> *v. 14: Then death and Hades were thrown into the lake of fire. The lake of fire is the second death.*

The apostle Paul left no doubt as to where Christ's reign would ultimately take Him. *For he must reign until he has put all his enemies under his feet. The last enemy to be destroyed is death* (1 Corinthians 15:25-26). This is clearly the "end" to which Paul referred to earlier in 1 Corinthians 15. The last enemy is defeated. In stark contrast to the "first resurrection," the "second death" is held out as the "special" destination for everything that has ever opposed Christ and His rule.

> *v. 15: Anyone whose name was not found written in the book of life was thrown into the lake of fire.*

Like the haunting sound of a cell door slamming shut, the door closes for all eternity on those who die without Christ. Numerous attempts have been made over the years to "soften" the finality of God's punishment. In order to "let God off the hook" we have created countless arguments and expressions suggesting that if "love" truly defines God, then eternal damnation cannot be a possibility. Somewhere in the ineffable nature of God, perfect love and perfect justice coexist without contradiction. "Anyone" includes "those who have never heard," those who have lived a "good life," and those who were far more pleasant in this life than followers of Jesus Christ. In the end, all that matters is "The Book."

Chapter 21-22: Everything New

If Revelation means anything it means the triumph of Christ's cause both on earth and in heaven. John saw a "new heaven and earth," which replaced the old heaven and earth which had "fled from His presence (20:11). The fact that there is "no longer any sea" (21:1) is a fitting conclusion to the Lord's work. The appearance of the "Holy city, the new Jerusalem" is also intended as a replacement of the now destroyed "old" Jerusalem," center of the failed system of Judaism. **As we will see in the next chapter of Revelation, this city is not a 'what' but a 'who!'** The "newness" that characterizes things in these chapters is καινοσ, "new" as in "superior," not the more common νεοσ, which is the opposite of "old." Heaven, earth, and Jerusalem are not simply rebuilt; they are replaced with superior versions of their old selves.

John may well have cupped his hands over his ears as a voice thundered through Heaven:

> *Look! God's dwelling place is now among the people, and he will dwell with them. They will be his people, and God himself will be with them and be their God. 'He will wipe every tear from their eyes. There will be no more death' or mourning or crying or pain, for the old order of things has passed away* (Revelation 21:3-4).

Finally! What God could have accomplished instantly and with no effort, has finally come to pass—God "tabernacles" with His people.[181]

A textual variant[182] in verse 3 is significant. The greatest support among ancient copies of Revelation is for the

---
[181] Mounce, pp. 371-372

translation of the word λαοι, "peoples" in the phrase "God's dwelling place is now among the **peoples**."[183] This is more consistent with the overall theme of Revelation and the Scriptures in general—that ultimately God has been concerned with "peoples" rather than a "people."

Verse 5 is the key to chapter 21: *"I am making everything new."* There is more than a faint echo here of the words of Paul in 2 Corinthians 5.

> *We are not trying to commend ourselves to you again, but are giving you an opportunity to take pride in us, so that you can answer those who take pride in what is seen rather than in what is in the heart. If we are out of our mind, it is for the sake of God; if we are in our right mind, it is for you. For Christ's love compels us, because we are convinced that one died for all, and therefore all died. And he died for all, that those who live should no longer live for themselves but for him who died for them and was raised again. So from now on we regard no one from a worldly point of view. Though we once regarded Christ in this way, we do so no longer. Therefore, if anyone is in Christ, he is a new creation; the old has gone, the new has come! All this is from God, who reconciled*

---

[182] There are hundreds of *textual variants* among copies of the Scriptures. As copies of Old and New Testament Scriptures continue to pile up, textual criticism seeks to compare those copies, noticing particularly any differences between copies. Most of those differences are minor. More interesting than the differences is the unbelievable consistency among the copies. When variations do occur, editions of the Scriptures in the original languages include a "rating" system for each variation. The older variations, and the variations that have the greatest numerical support, are the ones that usually make their way into our English translations.

[183] E.g. the NASB, ASV and ESV translate the word as "men" or "man" as in "mankind." The most reliable Greek edition of the New Testament, (ed. Aland, Black, Martini, Metzger and Wikgren) prefers λαοι over λαοσ.

> *us to himself through Christ and gave us the ministry of reconciliation: that God was reconciling the world to himself in Christ, not counting men's sins against them. And he has committed to us the message of reconciliation. We are therefore Christ's ambassadors, as though God were making his appeal through us. We implore you on Christ's behalf: Be reconciled to God. God made him who had no sin to be sin for us, so that in him we might become the righteousness of God* (2 Corinthians 5:12-21).

These words came on the heels of Paul's encouragement to live by faith and not by sight. His appeal, like John's, was to be confident in what was in "the heart" rather than what "is seen."

Verse 8 rounds out the first section of chapter 21, completing thoughts first raised by Isaiah in chapter 65 and 66. God would not tolerate disobedience in the new earth anymore than He did in the old earth.

> *But as for you who forsake the LORD and forget my holy mountain, who spread a table for Fortune and fill bowls of mixed wine for Destiny, I will destine you for the sword, and all of you will fall in the slaughter; for I called but you did not answer, I spoke but you did not listen. You did evil in my sight and chose what displeases me* (Isaiah 65:11-12).

But just as Isaiah had foretold, God's faithfulness to His people would explode in an unprecedented expression of His love in the creation of a New Jerusalem.

> *See, I will create new heavens and a new earth. The former things will not be remembered, nor will they*

> *come to mind. But be glad and rejoice forever in what I will create, for I will create Jerusalem to be a delight and its people a joy. I will rejoice over Jerusalem and take delight in my people; the sound of weeping and of crying will be heard in it no more* (Isaiah 65:17-19).

Isaiah went on to describe the new heaven and earth as a place where *"he who dies at a hundred will be thought a mere youth,"* and *"my chosen ones will enjoy the works of their hands,"* and *"they will not toil in vain,"* and finally *"The wolf and the lamb will feed together, and the lion will eat straw like the ox, but dust will be the serpent's food."* Although Isaiah was describing an idyllic state, it was clearly not "paradise" or the eternal state. People still died, people still toiled, and some creatures still felt the effects of the fall.

It would seem that there is a sense in which the new heaven and earth are, like The Kingdom, both a present and a future reality. On the one hand, the Kingdom will only find its perfect expression in Eternity. On the other hand, the Kingdom continues its march now. As the yeast spreads and the mustard seed sprouts and grows, the Kingdom, through the triumph of the Gospel and humble submission of its citizens to the Kingdom way of life, continues to have an increasingly positive impact spiritually AND culturally. As God declared,

> *As the new heavens and the new earth that I make will endure before me," declares the LORD, "so will your name and descendants endure. [23] From one New Moon to another and from one Sabbath to another, all mankind will come and bow down before me," says the LORD* (Isaiah 66:22-23).

Drawing upon imagery from Ezekiel 48:31-34, Isaiah 54:11-12 and Isaiah 60, John was shown a picture of the New Jerusalem. He was invited to come and see the "Bride, the wife of the Lamb" at which point he was shown the New Jerusalem (21:9-10). The "city" was not a place but a People. It was not an earthly city, but the People of God, His Church, composed of Gentile and Jew alike. Like the old Jerusalem, this "city" had a Temple (21:22), but this "city" contained the true Temple, which is "The Lord God Almighty and the Lamb" (21:22). What John saw and what we are exposed to here is what all the prophets of old had spoken of. Ethnic Israel, with its earthly city and earthly Temple was never intended to usher in the "Kingdom of God." In fact, the prophets had made it clear that ethnic Israel was no True People of God! (Amos 9:8; Hosea 1:9). It was not that something "new" was needed. Something new had ALWAYS been God's desire. No nation, no people, no religion could ever bring in the Kingdom through political or social or religious means. But the True People of God, the New Jerusalem, the True Temple could! And they are!

Chapter 22 takes us back to the future. Our story ends precisely where it began, in the Garden of Eden. John directs us to the Tree of Life and its healing effects (22:1-2). Unlike Eden's initial pair, who were driven away from the Tree of Life (Genesis 3:24), now the people of the earth come in droves to be healed at not one, but two such trees! Unlike the curse that fell upon mankind at the fall, greatly inhibiting its ability to serve God (Genesis 3:14, 17), the curse is now lifted and God's people delight in serving Him (22:3). Unlike the "mark" that was placed on Cain to protect him from being murdered (Genesis 4:15), now the mark of God's perfect ownership is placed on all His servants (22:4b). Unlike

Eden's original inhabitants who hid their faces from God in the shadows of the trees (Genesis 3:8-9), now God's people look Him full in the face in the light of His perfect holiness (22:4-5). And what of the 1,000 year reign of the martyrs from chapter 20? Apparently 1,000 years is a drop in the bucket. In the consummated Kingdom, all God's people will "reign for ever and ever!" (22:5)!

The same angel from 21:9 now urged John to believe that the vision he had seen had the authority of the prophets (22:6). Once again, John was reminded that the things he saw were things that "must soon take place." (22:6, 10) The vision concluded with the soaring rhetoric of the One True King Himself.

> *I am the Alpha and the Omega, the First and the Last, the Beginning and the End. "Blessed are those who wash their robes, that they may have the right to the tree of life and may go through the gates into the city..."* (Revelation 22:13-14).

With one final nod to the Old Testament, Christ reminds us of the words of Isaiah 55—

> The *Spirit and the bride say, "Come!" And let the one who hears say, "Come!" Let the one who is thirsty come; and let the one who wishes take the free gift of the water of life"* (Revelation 22:17).

What is there left to say?

> *He who testifies to these things says, "Yes, I am coming soon." Amen. Come, Lord Jesus* (Revelation 22:20).

Chapter Summary

The second half of Revelation, chapters 13-20, gives us a vivid description of the judgment of the Roman Empire, the second great enemy of the Church. Describing events that have already come to pass, God once again makes clear to John's readers that they will be vindicated, that their pleas for help have been heard, and that nothing, not even the might of the Roman Empire, can stop the expansion of Christ's Kingdom.

This section also deal at length with "beasts," both the first beast, characterized as both the Roman Empire and the emperor Nero. The two-horned "second" beast is most likely two of the emperors that followed Nero, Otho and Vitellius. Inspired by Satan himself, these beasts conspire to crush the Kingdom of God and in its place, institutionalize emperor-worship as the religion of the day. Centered in the great image of Nero himself and the worship center around it (The Colossus), the cult of emperor worship found particularly strong expression in the region of the seven churches to which John wrote.

But God's plans cannot be thwarted by temporal or spiritual rulers. Chapters 15-19 provide graphic images of the vengeance of God visited upon the Roman empire and its leaders. The calamitous crescendo of this section comes in chapter 19, where we see the triumphant Christ, riding the white horse of victory, and "slaying" His enemies with the power of the gospel and God's word.

The all-important 20th chapter provides a perfect description of what is happening in our day. Christ is on the throne, the martyred saints are His *de facto* co-regents, and Satan is severely limited in His potential to do harm. Specifically, he is finally relieved of his post as "ruler of the nations," and he is shut up for a "thousand-years," a figurative time period symbolizing the time it takes for God's plans to find their perfect consummation.

We are living in the millennium now. While still active and powerful, Satan is a defeated foe. As winsome warriors, we, like our Warrior-King, carry on the work of The Kingdom by wielding the Sword of the Spirit from our mouths. Eschewing violence, we seek to champion the Lordship of Christ in every area of life. Rather than simply trying to make converts, we make disciples of every nation, just as surely as we watch the triumph of the gospel transform every culture.

The second half of chapter 20, and chapters 21 and 22 give us an inspiring picture of what we can expect in our lifetime and the lifetimes of our children and grandchildren. The faux capitals of Jerusalem and Rome are being displaced by the Holy City, the "New Jerusalem," which is in fact no city at all, but The Church, the People of God. With every day that passes, the distance between that city and the kingdoms of the earth grows less and less. Heaven is coming to earth! As the New Jerusalem descends, it settles upon and crushes every power that opposes it. Of course, the completion of its descent is both gradual and future, but it will come.

In light of those coming realities, what is there left to say and pray but, *The Spirit and the bride say, "Come!" And let the one who hears say, "Come!" Let the one who is thirsty come; and let the one who wishes take the free gift of the water of life...Amen. Come, Lord Jesus* (Revelation 22:17, 20)!

CHAPTER 14

HOW THEN SHALL WE LIVE?

OUR GLORIOUS HOPE

In the service of the victorious and already present Kingdom of God the church is given a joyful and triumphant task. The New Testament church saw itself, as we have said, as the people of that Kingdom, the "eschatological community" which was living already in the age to come. It was, then, to busy itself in those last days between the Resurrection and the expected end in proclaiming the Kingdom in the entire world and in summoning men to its rule.
JOHN BRIGHT, *THE KINGDOM OF GOD*

He who testifies to these things says, "Yes, I am coming soon." Amen. Come, Lord Jesus.
REVELATION 22:20

The next time you are taking a stroll near St. Peter's Basilica in the Vatican, look for an obelisk. It is located just outside the main entrance to the Basilica. The obelisk was removed from the Circus Maximus, scene of some of the bloodiest and most grotesque torture of Christians under the reign of Nero. Nero has long since passed away, but the obelisk remains. Chiseled on the base of the obelisk are words from a hymn that was often sung by Christians as they awaited their fate at the hands of gladiators or wild beasts. It reads, CHRISTUS VINCIT, CHRISTUS REGNAT, CHRISTUS IMPERAT, which translated is, "Christ is conquering, Christ is reigning, Christ rules over all." Is it possible that our first century forefathers and mothers knew something we do not? Despite what we see, despite how things appear, one unshakeable truth remains: Jesus is on the throne, and He is putting everything under His feet. He has invited us to join Him in this grand, sweeping movement of redemption and transformation.

The final and complete break with the old occurred in 70 A.D. By "old" we do not mean the Old Testament, or the teaching of "old" books." We mean the Old Covenant, The old Order, the grotesque caricature of humble obedience that the Temple and its practices represented. A New Covenant, written in the blood of Christ Himself (1 Corinthians 11:25) had replaced the old. The Kingdom, under the rule of the One True King is advancing. The Gospel is triumphing. How long it will take to complete that task, we cannot say. But until Christ comes again, our calling as winsome warriors could not be more important. As we have seen, much of what gets passed off as "end times truth" is nothing more than flights of fancy from well-intentioned Christ followers for whom "their days" are always the "last days." But if the last days are behind us then what should we expect to unfold in front of us?

The Final Resurrection

The most extensive Biblical treatment of the final resurrection is found in 1 Corinthians 15. One would be hard pressed to find a local assembly with more problems than the believers in Corinth. We can see that early "antichrist" teachings had already infected this assembly. The notion that the material world was "bad" and that sins committed in the body were unimportant had already begun to creep into the church. Sexual sin of a kind *"that does not occur even among pagan"* (1 Corinthians 5:1) was not only tolerated, it was celebrated.

Paul's frustration was compounded by the fact that the Corinthian believers saw themselves as spiritual heavyweights. They took great pride in the manifestations of the Spirit that were present in Corinth. For many of them, they had already "arrived." They had reached the pinnacle of spirituality. Paul's response dripped with sarcasm:

> *For who makes you different from anyone else? What do you have that you did not receive? And if you did receive it, why do you boast as though you did not? Already you have all you want! Already you have become rich! You have begun to **reign**—and that without us! How I wish that you really had begun to **reign** so that we also might **reign** with you!* (1 Corinthians 4:7-8).

In trying to warn against the dangers of using pagan Temple prostitutes, Paul affirmed that our *"bodies are members of Christ Himself"* (6:15). Given the denigration of the physical that was so popular in Corinth, and the unteachable spirit that their pride had fostered, Paul was faced with a great challenge. How could he address the issue of the final resurrection in the context of this pride-filled congregation that was heavily influence by its pagan roots? He formulated the question like this: *"But if it is preached that Christ has been raised form the dead, how can some of you say that there is no resurrection of the dead?"* (15:12).

Paul built his case for the final resurrection of our bodies by linking Christ's resurrection to our own. *"By His power God raised the Lord from the dead, and He will raise us also"* (6:14). If God thought enough of the Son's body, why would He not do the same for us? In fact, any hope that we might have for future redemption was tied to the bodily resurrection of Christ! (15:1-19). Paul employed a theologically loaded term in describing the connection between the two: *"But Christ has indeed been raised from the dead, the **firstfruits** of those who have fallen asleep."* In other words, Christ's resurrection was not "one-of-a-kind," but the "first" of its kind. Just as the wave-offering of grain symbolized all the harvest that followed (Leviticus 23:9-14), so Christ's resurrection was the first of many to follow.

Paul then responded to a potential objection: *"But someone will ask, "How are the dead raised? With what kind of body will they come?"* (15:35). Paul began his answer by stating the obvious. The necessary precondition to resurrection was death! *"What you sow does not come to life unless it dies"* (15:36). Once we die, it is up to God to decide what kind of body we will receive upon our resurrection. Although the specifics of the kind of body we will receive are unknown, some things are certain: *"The body that is sown is perishable, it is raised imperishable; it is sown in dishonor, it is raised in glory; it is sown in weakness, it is raised in power; it is sown a natural body, it is raised a spiritual body"* (15:42-44). In other words, our bodies are not bad; they just feel the effects of sin! Our bodies are not unimportant; they are just limited in the here and now! Someday, they will enjoy their original destiny! Regardless of the kind of bodies we will have at the final resurrection, one thing is certain; those bodies will be amazing! And when will this amazing transformation take place?

> *Listen, I tell you a mystery: We will not all sleep, but we will all be changed—in a flash, in the twinkling of an eye, at the last trumpet. For the trumpet will sound, the dead will be raised imperishable, and we will be changed. For the perishable must clothe itself with the imperishable, and the mortal with immortality. When the perishable has been clothed with the imperishable, and the mortal with immortality, then the saying that is written will come true: "Death has been swallowed up in victory." "Where, O death, is your victory? Where, O death, is your sting?" The sting of death is sin, and the power of sin is the law. But thanks be to God! He gives us the victory through our Lord Jesus Christ.* (15:51-57)

This is the only "rapture" to which the Bible alludes. It will not be followed by a "tribulation" or a "Beast" and it will most certainly not be a secret.

It is no accident that Paul ends his discussion of the final resurrection on a note of victory. That God would go to such lengths to redeem our bodies should inspire us to righteous, hope-filled, victorious living! The price that

Jesus paid on the cross was enough to save not only our souls, but our *bodies* as well. *"...You were bought at a price. Therefore, honor God with your bodies"* (1 Corinthians 6:20). As winsome warriors, we look forward to and long for the day when our bodies are redeemed. *Not only so, but we ourselves, who have the firstfruits of the Spirit, groan inwardly as we wait eagerly for our adoption to sonship, the redemption of our bodies* (Romans 8:23). Although we don't know the particulars, we can be sure that someday, Christ will return, at which time our bodies will be changed. That change will coincide with the defeat of the final enemy, death. We know from Paul's earlier comments in this chapter that when death is defeated, time will end and the eternal state will begin. The Kingdom will be consummated, and then *"the end will come"* (1 Corinthians 15:24).

The Final Judgment

Somewhere near my ninth birthday, I remember hearing a sermon on the final judgment. I don't remember anything from that message, except the illustration the pastor used. He suggested a large projector screen (that dates the message!) would be hauled out, and every thought, imagination and action of my life would be put on display for all to see. I was horrified. The mere thought of such a thing sent me scrambling for the nearest rock under which to crawl. Is that the reality of the final judgment? Thankfully, no! That there will *be* a final judgment is without question. Projectors? HD plasma screens? No.

Before we look at what the Bible says about the final judgment, we should first ask another question: Why a final judgment at all? Why does God need to line us up, open books, and pronounce a final verdict over our lives? Does He not already know the content of our hearts? In this study, when you are stumped for an answer, it is usually a good bet to guess "God's glory." And in this case, you would be correct. Like everything else He does, God's singular aim is to put His glory on display. So it will be at the final judgment.

The great theologian Louis Berkhof provides an excellent observation. *"It (the final judgment) will serve **the purpose rather of displaying before all rational creatures the declarative glory of God** in a formal, forensic act, which magnifies on the one hand His holiness and righteousness, and on the other hand, His grace and mercy. Moreover, it should be borne in mind that the judgment at the last day will differ from that of the death of each individual in more than one respect. It will not be secret, but public; it will not pertain to the soul only, but also to the body; it will not have reference to a single individual, but to all men."*[184]

The nail has been hit on the proverbial head. The "declarative glory of God" will be put on display as all humankind, past and present, are exposed to the white-hot justice of God. As we have already observed, Christ Himself will sit upon a great white throne. Before Him, the "nations" will stand. That we will be grouped as "nations" or "peoples" is without question.

When the Son of Man comes in his glory, and all the angels with him, he will sit on his glorious throne. All

---

[184]Louis Berkhof, *Systematic Theology* (Carlisle, PA: Banner of Truth, 1958), p. 731

> *the nations will be gathered before him, and he will separate the people one from another as a shepherd separates the sheep from the goats* (Matthew 25:31-32).

As "the books" are opened, Christ will separate us into two groups, the "sheep" on His right and the "goats" on His left. The final determining factor will not be our **actions**, but our **action**: did we put our trust in the righteousness of Christ, or in our own righteousness? For those who, in that one, eternity-altering moment were justified forever in Christ, the fully-consummated Kingdom awaits (Matthew 25:34). For the rest, their end will be *"eternal fire prepared for the devil and his angels"* (Matthew 25:41).

There can be no doubt that our behavior in this life will provide proof-positive of our destiny in the next. Although we are not saved by our works, our works provide confirmation that we are saved. Even those "works" are the fruit of God's working both in us and through us. *"For we are God's handiwork, created in Christ Jesus to do good works, which God prepared in advance for us to do"* (Ephesians 2:10).

While the debate over the reality of Hell will continue to be waged until Christ appears, God's word speaks unequivocally. Both the reality and eternal nature of Hell are spoken to again and again (Daniel 12:2, 3; Matthew 25:46; John 5:28; Revelation 20:14, 15; Hebrews 9:27; Matthew 13:50; Mark 9:48; Revelation 14:11). **We cannot imagine such a punishment precisely because we cannot imagine how great our sin is and how great an**

affront it is to the glory of God. A real Hell with real and eternal consequences only magnifies our understanding of the glory God. If the punishment fits the crime, how great indeed must the crime of "falling short" of God's glory be? Our only recourse in this life is to fall on our faces before a holy God and cry out, *"God be merciful to me, a sinner"* (Luke 18:13). We should be stunned into action as we are not only invited to stand, but actually encouraged to *"approach God's throne of grace with confidence, so that we may receive mercy and find grace to help us in our time of need"* (Hebrews 4:16).

Reigning With Christ

Carolyn Arends, in the February 2011 issue of *Christianity Today*, recounted a story from her youth that captures our current reality.

> *"As a kid, I loved Mission Sundays, when missionaries on furlough brought special reports in place of a sermon .... There is one visit I've never forgotten. The missionaries were a married couple stationed in what appeared to be a particularly steamy jungle. I'm sure they gave a full report on churches planted or commitments made or translations begun. I don't remember much of that. What has always stayed with me is the story they shared about a snake.*
>
> *One day, they told us, an enormous snake—much longer than a man—slithered its way right through their front door and into the kitchen of their simple home. Terrified, they ran outside and searched frantically for a local who might know what to do. A machete-wielding*

neighbor came to the rescue, calmly marching into their house and decapitating the snake with one clean chop.

The neighbor reemerged triumphant and assured the missionaries that the reptile had been defeated. But there was a catch, he warned: It was going to take a while for the snake to realize it was dead.

A snake's neurology and blood flow are such that it can take considerable time for it to stop moving even after decapitation. For the next several hours, the missionaries were forced to wait outside while the snake thrashed about, smashing furniture and flailing against walls and windows, wreaking havoc until its body finally understood that it no longer had a head.

Sweating in the heat, they had felt frustrated and a little sickened but also grateful that the snake's rampage wouldn't last forever. And at some point in their waiting, they told us, they had a mutual epiphany.

I leaned in with the rest of the congregation, queasy and fascinated. "Do you see it?" asked the husband. "Satan is a lot like that big old snake. He's already been defeated. He just doesn't know it yet. In the meantime, he's going to do some damage. But never forget that he's a goner."

The story [still] haunts me because I have come to believe it is an accurate picture of the universe. We are in the thrashing time, a season characterized by our pervasive capacity to do violence to each other and ourselves. The temptation is to despair. We have to remember, though, that it won't last forever. Jesus has already crushed the serpent's head."

Oh that we would live as if we believed that were true! We are living in the *final* days, the time between Christ's appearings. Like the great rock of Daniel and the yeast of which Christ spoke, the Kingdom is advancing and growing. BEFORE Christ's second appearing, EVERY enemy will be defeated, save one—death (1 Corinthians 15:25-26)! Armed with the sword of God's word and the weapons of prayer and love and worship, Christ continues to stun the world into submission, and He calls us to join Him in this great reclamation of the world that He is committed to redeeming! It should come as no surprise that the New Jerusalem is NOT in Heaven—rather, it descends TO THE EARTH (Revelation 21:1-3).

As we saw in Revelation 20, there is a unique reign enjoyed by those who have given their lives for the King and His Kingdom. But this does not mean that we do not also reign with Christ now, both while we are alive and when we die! *"...If we endure, we will also reign with Him"* (2 Timothy 2:12)! Just as the role of "apostles" was unique and limited to those who lived and worked in the first century,[185] our role today is similar as we continue to extend the rule of Christ to the nations. While there can never again be "apostles" in the same way that they existed then, our calling is just as binding and just as glorious today.

---

[185] Apostles were those who were "with Jesus" during his earthly ministry (Acts 1:21-22). They functioned in an unrepeatable way in that era of redemptive history (Hebrews 9:26-28)

THE definitive moment in history has come and gone. Christ's death, resurrection and ascension have crushed the head of the serpent. We saw in Revelation the clear connection between Christ's death, our prayers, and our role as co-regents over the earth:

> *Then I saw a Lamb, **looking as if it had been slain**, standing at the center of the throne, encircled by the four living creatures and the elders. The Lamb had seven horns and seven eyes, which are the seven spirits of God sent out into all the earth. He went and took the scroll from the right hand of him who sat on the throne. And when he had taken it, the four living creatures and the twenty-four elders fell down before the Lamb. Each one had a harp and they were holding golden bowls full of incense, **which are the prayers of God's people**. And they sang a new song, saying: "You are worthy to take the scroll and to open its seals, **because you were slain, and with your blood you purchased for God persons from every tribe and language and people and nation. You have made them to be a Kingdom and priests to serve our God, and they will reign on the earth**"* (Revelation 5:6-10).

As we wait for Christ's Second Appearing, we gladly embrace our role, not as survivalists but as subversives, winsome warriors who will not rest until every enemy is defeated. "Christians who are aware of redemptive history, therefore, anticipate the Second Coming as a time when they will see their Lord face to face (Rev. 22:4), and when the work of worldwide Christianization will receive its final catapult into definitive earthly perfection. The Second Coming is the destination of redemptive history; and the desire for it burns within knowledgeable believers, not because they wish an escape from the world, but precisely because they wish a more Christian world... *"'The Last Days' is the time of the great harvest, of Christ's incrementally trampling down His enemies by the power of the Gospel. The definitive victory on the Cross gives way to the final "mop-up operation" that will conclude at Christ's Second Coming. 'The Last Days' is a time of excitement and ecstasy, of trial and hardship, of temporary defeat and permanent victory, of the worldwide expansion of the Kingdom of God."*[186]

Our talk of being "warriors" and the war-like imagery we use should not confuse us. We are a different breed of warrior.

> *For though we live in the world, we do not wage war as the world does. The weapons we fight with are not the weapons of the world. On the contrary, they have divine power to demolish strongholds. We demolish arguments and every pretension that sets itself up against the knowledge of God, and we take captive every thought to make it obedient to Christ* (2 Corinthians 10:3-5).

Although it is beyond the scope of this work, we have already alluded to the weapons that Paul refers to. The nagging problem that God's People face is that we continue to fight the wrong war against the wrong enemy with the wrong weapons. The battle is spiritual, the enemy is Satan

---

[186] Andrew Sandlin, *"Those Long-Lived Last Days,"* December, 2001, http://www.preteristarchive.com/PartialPreterism/2001_sandlin_last-days.html, pp. 3-4

and Sin and the World system that follows the Evil One, and the weapons are prayer and truth and worship and love and yes, even death, to name only a few. Systematically, cunningly, we are called to infiltrate every area of life and to transform it. Steadily, shrewdly, we are called to bring the Gospel to the nations, using business start-ups, or "English-as-a-second-language" classes, or whatever means are at our disposal. Our calling is not to run, but to reign! Our hope is not to survive but to subvert! Our mission is not to fold, but to fight! Like our spiritual mothers and fathers, it may cost us our lives, but if that is the worst that the World can do, then they play right into the hands of our Warrior-King, because to *"live is Christ, but to die is gain"* (Philippians 1:21).

What About Israel?

To those who hold a similar view to my own regarding the end times, a criticism is often levied: we are anti-Semitic. NOTHING COULD BE FURTHER FROM THE TRUTH! God's word leaves no doubt as to my and all Christ-followers indebtedness to historic Israel. Romans 9:3-4,

> *"For I could wish that I myself were accursed, separated from Christ for the sake of my brethren, my kinsmen according to the flesh, who are Israelites, to whom belongs the adoption as sons, and the glory and the covenants and the giving of the Law and the Temple service and the promises."* Or Romans 9:5, *"whose are the fathers, and from whom is the Christ according to the flesh, who is over all, God blessed forever. Amen."* Or John 4:22, *"Salvation is of the Jews."*

Unfortunately, bad theology has moved from these clear teachings to an unbiblical commitment to the modern-day state of Israel. A critical distinction needs to be made. There is no country in the Middle-East where democracy flourishes as it does in Israel. Politically, the United States must continue to support the modern state of Israel as the best hope for the spread of democracy in that region. But the notion that ethnic Israel and the country that currently bears that name is destined to rule the world from an earthly headquarters in Jerusalem is false and dangerous. The Kingdom cannot be contained by any ethnicity or any nation, people, denomination, agenda or worldview. The Scriptures have made that abundantly clear. Tragically, the history of the Church is replete with times when anti-Semitism was justified on the grounds that "they" crucified Christ. That, too, is bad theology. *This man (Jesus) was handed over to you (the Jews)* **by God's set purpose and foreknowledge**... (Acts 2:23). In the truest sense, it was God who killed Jesus. *Yet it was* **the Lord's will** *to crush Him and cause Him to suffer*... (Isaiah 53:10). Christ "bore the sin of many" (Isaiah 53:12), not the sin of one race or one people. The Gospel of the Kingdom is for ALL people and for all races. To the shame of many Gentiles, we have encouraged anti-Semitism and must repent of that. Where does this leave the Church in our relationship to the modern state of Israel?

In 2003, Knox Theological Seminary published a statement that clearly reflects the Bible's teaching on the state of Israel, salvation, and the Kingdom. This statement has been signed and endorsed by a number of evangelical luminaries who have forgotten more than I will ever know regarding God's word. They include men like R.C. Sproul, O. Palmer Robertson, Michael Horton, Richard B. Gaffin, and Rev. Robert Dillard, to name only a few. A complete copy of this statement is included in the appendix. The statement affirms that there is no special favor upon any people or ethnic group, and that apart from Christ, salvation is not possible. All the spiritual benefits available to mankind come only through a personal relationship with Christ. The "True Israel" is the Church, composed of Jews and Gentiles alike.

The "true Temple" is Christ Himself, and the new, heavenly Jerusalem has once for all replaced the old Jerusalem. The destruction of Jerusalem and the Temple in 70 A.D. represented God's definitive declaration that these things are so. The "regathering" of Israel that the Old Testament prophets spoke of pertained to their return to the land after their captivity in 586 B.C. To expect a still future regathering or to suggest that we must support the current state of Israel on Biblical grounds is misguided and dangerous. The current reign of Jesus Christ is over the nations, and that rule will continue to grow and expand to include the whole earth. There is nothing in Scripture to suggest that the political or territorial fortunes of the state of Israel will ever be restored. True peace, both in the Middle East and throughout the world, will come only as peoples and cultures are transformed by the power of the Gospel of the Kingdom.

Final Implications

We serve a Divine Warrior. Our calling is to serve as winsome warriors. The Old Covenant, headquartered in Jerusalem and cemented in the cultic practices surrounding Herod's Temple, was insufficient to hold the New Order under the leadership of the True King. The definitive break with that Order occurred in 70 A.D. with the destruction of that Temple. Christ's complete work once and for all wrested the rule of the Kingdoms of the earth from Satan's hands to His own. Now, Christ is winning back the nations, systematically bringing everything under His rule and authority. The Kingdom, always God's priority, has now become accessible in ways never imagined possible to Israel.

God's desire to "tabernacle" with His people has also remained constant. Through the work of Christ, the Father is moving us ever closer to the "Kingdom come, on earth, as it is in heaven." In Christ, we have been delivered from this present evil age (Galatians 1:14). In Christ, we have tasted of the powers of the coming age (Hebrews 6:5). Our citizenship is already in Heaven (Philippians 3:20). We have been rescued from the dominion of darkness (Colossians 1:13). We have been reconciled to Christ (2 Corinthians 5:19). We have been adopted as sons and daughters (Galatians 4:5-7). We have the mind of Christ (1 Corinthians 2:16). We reign with Christ (Ephesians 2:6). In Christ, we live with the confidence that the Gospel will prevail, that the nations will come to Him, and that a final day will come when God's Anointed will receive His due. There is much to be done.

Just as the Old Covenant people of God misunderstood the Kingdom and their place in it, we run that same risk today. No nation corresponds to it. No country can contain it. Our calling is to look again to the model of our great Warrior-King who showed us how the Kingdom comes—through selfless acts of service, through embracing and living out the ethic He left us in the Sermon on the Mount, through retiring to a quiet place to abide with Him, and in suffering, even dying for the very people who would kill us. Our calling is to do that with joy and gladness, to be engaging and winsome, to put "swords" in our mouths and pads on our knees. Our calling is to unequivocally declare "Repent! The Kingdom is here" just as surely as we wet our cheeks with the tears of those who have yet to enter the New Jerusalem. In the meantime, we look for and long for the Day when even the stones will cry out:

> *Gather together and come; assemble, you fugitives from the nations. Ignorant are those who carry about idols of wood, who pray to gods that cannot save. Declare what is to be, present it— let them take counsel together. Who foretold this long ago, who declared it from the distant past? Was it not I, the LORD? And there is no God apart from me, a righteous God and a Savior; there is none but me. "Turn to me and be saved, all you ends of the earth; for I am God, and there is no other. By myself I have sworn, my mouth has uttered in all integrity a word that will not be revoked: Before me every knee will bow; by me every tongue will swear. They will say of me, 'In the LORD alone are deliverance and strength.'" All who have raged against him will come to him and be put to shame. But all the descendants of Israel will find deliverance in the LORD and will make their boast in him* (Isaiah 45:20-25).

MARANATHA!

Appendix 1 : The Early Church

The following is a brief list of those Church Fathers and writers who taught: That the Church is the True Israel, that many of the prophetic writings of the New Testament (most especially the Olivet Discourse) were fulfilled in the destruction of Jerusalem in 70 A.D. and that the Final Resurrection and Judgment represent the end of time and the beginning of the Eternal State.

Not every person listed here would be in complete agreement with everything contained in *Winsome Warriors*. What this list *does* illustrate is that the historical position of the early Church was *very little* like what the popular teaching is today. Many readers are at this point muttering to themselves, "Why have I never heard this stuff before? *Winsome Warriors* represents a radical new perspective." The fact is that the only thing that is radical and new is the teachings of dispensationalism. The history of the Church is replete with thinkers and theologians who embraced much of what you have learned here. Readers are encouraged to look in more detail at the writings of the authors listed below. Prior to each name is the presumed date of authorship. The words following the names refer to the specific document (if known) where their teaching can be found.

Approximately 70-150 A.D.

- 40-60 : Didache: Teaching of the Twelve
- 60-: Acts of the Apostles : Western Text

- 70: 1 Clement
- -c. 70?: The Epistle of Mathetes
- 75: Barnabas
- 75-: Apocalypse Of Baruch
- -c. 85: Shepherd of Hermas
- 70-80: Esdras 2 (4 Ezra)
- 70-160: Gospel of Peter
- 100: The Odes of Solomon

Approximately 150-500 A.D.

- 150: Justin Martyr - Dialogue with Trypho, a Jew
- 150: Pseudo Clement: Recognitions
- 150: Melito - Homily of the Pascha
- 175: Irenaeus - Against Heresies
- 185: Clement of Alexandria - The Stromata
- 198: Tertullian - An Answer to the Jews
- 200: Tertullian - Against Marcion
- 230: Origen - The Principles
- 235: Hippolytus
- 248: Cyprian - Testimonies Against the Jews
- 250: Origen - Against Celsus | John | Matthew
- 260: Victorinus - Apocalypse Commentary
- 273: Alexander of Alexandia - Epistle on Arianism
- 306: Peter of Alexandria - Letter to the Church at Alexandria
- 310: Eusebius - Theophania
- 310: Peter of Alexandria - Fragments
- 312: Eusebius - Demonstratio Evangelica
- 319: Eusebius - Proof of the Gospel
- 319: Athanasius - On the Incarnation | Refutation of the Jews

APPENDICES

- 320: Eusebius - History of the Martyrs
- 325: Eusebius - Ecclesiastical History
- 330: Lactantius
- 345: Aphrahat the Persian Sage - Excerpts from Select Demonstrations
- 359: Gregory of Nyssa - On Virginity
- 360: Ephrem the Syrian - Selected Works Translated out of the Original Syriac
- 367: Athanasius - Festal Letters
- 370: Pseudo Hegesippus - On The Ruin of the City of Jerusalem
- 386: Chrysostom - Homilies Against the Jews
- 387: Chrysostom - Homilies on Matthew 24
- 388: Chrysostom - Homilies on Second Timothy
- 390s: Epiphanes
- 390s: Pseudo Chrysostom
- 390: Ambrose of Milan
- 401: Sulpicius Severus - Sacred History
- 408: Jerome - Commentary on Daniel
- 410: Jerome - The Nativity of Christ
- 412: Isidore of Pelusium
- 417: Augustine - On Pelagius
- 420: Augustine - On Doctrine | The Bondage of the
- Jews
- 420: Cassian - Conferences
- 426: Augustine - City of God
- 428: Augustine - Harmony of the Gospels

From 500-1000 A.D.

- 500: Andreas
- 507: Joshua the Stylite - Syriac Chronicle
- 540: Arethas
- 550: St. Remigius - Commentary (On Rev. 7:1)
- 600: Veronica" - The Avenging of the Saviour
- 731: Venerable Bede
- 851: Maurus Rabanus
- 999: St. Symeon

Appendix 2 : Israel and The Church

The People of God, the Land of Israel, and the Impartiality of the Gospel
(Numbered footnotes appear after the statement)

I. The Gospel offers eternal life in heaven to Jews and Gentiles alike as a free gift in Jesus Christ. Eternal life in heaven is not earned or deserved, nor is it based upon ethnic descent or natural birth.[4]

II. All human beings, Jews and Gentiles alike, are sinners,[5] and, as such, they are under God's judgment of death.[6] Because God's standard is perfect obedience and all are sinners, it is impossible for anyone to gain temporal peace or eternal life by his own efforts. Moreover, apart from Christ, there is no special divine favor upon any member of any ethnic group; nor, apart from Christ, is there any divine promise of an earthly land or a heavenly inheritance to anyone, whether Jew or Gentile.[7] To teach or imply otherwise is nothing less than to compromise the Gospel itself.

III. God, the Creator of all mankind, is merciful and takes no pleasure in punishing sinners.[8] Yet God is also holy and just and must punish sin.[9] Therefore, to satisfy both his justice and his mercy, God has appointed one way of salvation for all, whether Jew or Gentile, in Jesus Christ alone.[10]

IV. Jesus Christ, who is fully God and fully man,[11] came into the world to save sinners.[12] In his death upon the cross, Jesus was the Lamb of God taking away the sin of the world, of Jew and of Gentile alike. The death of Jesus forever fulfilled and eternally ended the sacrifices of the Jewish Temple.[13] All who would worship God, whether Jew or Gentile, must now come to him in spirit and truth through Jesus Christ alone. The worship of God is no longer identified with any specific earthly sanctuary. He receives worship only through Jesus Christ, the eternal and heavenly Temple.[14]

V. To as many as receive and rest upon Christ alone through faith alone, to Jews and Gentiles alike, God gives eternal life in his heavenly inheritance.[15]

VI. The inheritance promises that God gave to Abraham were made effective through Christ, Abraham's True Seed.[16] These promises were not and cannot be made effective through sinful man's keeping of God's law.[17] Rather, the promise of an inheritance is made to those only who have faith in Jesus, the True Heir of Abraham. All spiritual benefits are derived from Jesus, and apart from him there is no participation in the promises.[18] Since Jesus Christ is the Mediator of the Abrahamic Covenant, all who bless him and his people will be blessed of God, and all who curse him and his people will be cursed of God.[19] These promises do not apply to any particular ethnic group,[20] but to the church of Jesus Christ, the true Israel.[21] The people of God, whether the church of Israel in the wilderness in the Old Testament[22] or the Israel of God among the Gentile Galatians in the New Testament,[23] are one body who through Jesus will receive the promise of the heavenly city, the everlasting Zion.[24] This heavenly inheritance has been the expectation of the people of God in all ages.[25]

VII. Jesus taught that his resurrection was the raising of the True Temple of Israel.[26] He has replaced the priesthood, sacrifices, and sanctuary of Israel by fulfilling them in his own glorious priestly ministry and by offering, once and for all, his sacrifice for the world, that is, for both Jew and Gentile.[27] Believers from all nations are now being built up through him into this Third Temple,[28] the church that Jesus promised to build.[29]

VIII. Simon Peter spoke of the Second Coming of the Lord Jesus in conjunction with the final judgment and the punishment of sinners.[30] Instructively, this same Simon Peter, the Apostle to the Circumcision,[31] says nothing about the restoration of the Kingdom to Israel in the land of Palestine.[32] Instead, as his readers contemplate the promise of Jesus' Second Coming, he fixes their hope upon the new heavens and the new earth, in which righteousness dwells.[33]

IX. The entitlement of any one ethnic or religious group to territory in the Middle East called the "Holy Land" cannot be supported by Scripture. In fact, the land promises specific to Israel in the Old Testament were fulfilled under Joshua.[34] The New Testament speaks clearly and prophetically about the destruction of the second Temple in A.D. 70.[35] No New Testament writer foresees a regathering of ethnic Israel in the land, as did the prophets of the Old Testament after the destruction of the first Temple in 586 B.C.[36] Moreover, the land promises of the Old Covenant are consistently and deliberately expanded in the New Testament to show the universal dominion of Jesus,[37] who reigns from heaven upon the throne of David, inviting all the nations through the Gospel of Grace to partake of his universal and everlasting dominion.[38]

X. Bad Christian theology regarding the "Holy Land" contributed to the tragic cruelty of the Crusades in the Middle Ages. Lamentably, bad Christian theology is today attributing to secular Israel a divine mandate to conquer and hold Palestine, with the consequence that the Palestinian people are marginalized and regarded as virtual "Canaanites."[39] This doctrine is both contrary to the teaching of the New Testament and a violation of the Gospel mandate.[40] In addition, this theology puts those Christians who are urging the violent seizure and occupation of Palestinian land in moral jeopardy of their own bloodguiltiness. Are we as Christians not called to pray for and work for peace, warning both parties to this conflict that those who live by the sword will die by the sword?[41] Only the Gospel of Jesus Christ can bring both temporal reconciliation and the hope of an eternal and heavenly inheritance to the Israeli and the Palestinian. Only through Jesus Christ can anyone know peace on earth.

[4] Luke 3:8, "And do not begin to say to yourselves, 'We have Abraham as our father.' For I tell you that out of these stones God can raise up children for Abraham." Ephesians 2:8-9, "For it is by grace you have been saved, through faith—and this not from yourselves, it is the gift of God—not by works, so that no one can boast."

[5] Romans 3:22-23, "There is no difference; for all have sinned and fall short of the glory of God."

[6] Romans 6:23, "The wages of sin is death."

[7] Romans 3:9-10, "Are we better than they? Not at all; for we have already charged that both Jews and Greeks are all under sin; as it is written, 'There is none righteous, not even one.'"

[8] Ezekiel 18:23, 32, "Do I take any pleasure in the death of the wicked? ... I take no pleasure in the death of anyone, declares the Sovereign Lord."

[9] Exodus 34:7, "He does not leave the guilty unpunished."

[10] Acts 4:12, "Salvation is found in no one else, for there is no other name under heaven given to men by which we must be saved." John 14:6, "Jesus answered, 'I am the way and the truth and the life. No one comes to the Father except through me.'"

[11] John 1:1, 14, "In the beginning was the Word, and the Word was with God, and the Word was God. ... And the Word became flesh and dwelt among us, and we beheld his glory, the glory as of the only begotten of the Father, full of grace and truth."

[12] 1 Timothy 1:15, "Christ Jesus came into the world to save sinners."

[13] Hebrews 9:11-12, "But Christ came as High Priest of the good things to come, with the greater and more perfect tabernacle not made with hands, that is, not of this creation. Not with the blood of goats and calves, but with his own blood he entered the Most Holy Place once for all, having obtained eternal redemption." Hebrews 10:11-12, "And every priest stands ministering daily and offering repeatedly the same sacrifices, which can never take away sins. But this man, after he had offered one sacrifice for sins forever, sat down at the right hand of God."

APPENDICES

[14] John 4:21, 23, "Jesus said to her, 'Woman, believe me, the hour is coming when you will neither on this mountain, nor in Jerusalem, worship the Father. ... But the hour is coming, and now is, when the true worshipers will worship the Father in spirit and truth; for the Father is seeking such to worship him. God is Spirit, and those who worship him must worship in spirit and truth.'" John 2:19-21, "Jesus answered and said to them, 'Destroy this Temple, and in three days I will raise it up.' Then the Jews said, 'It has taken forty-six years to build this Temple, and will you raise it up in three days?'" But he was speaking of the Temple of his body."

[15] Romans 1:16, "For I am not ashamed of the Gospel of Christ, for it is the power of God to salvation for everyone who believes, for the Jew first and also for the Greek [Gentile]." John 1:12-13, "But as many as received him, to them he gave the right to become children of God, to those who believe in his name: who were born, not of blood, nor of the will of the flesh, nor of the will of man, but of God."

[16] Galatians 3:16, "Now to Abraham and his Seed were the promises made. He does not say, "And to seeds," as of many, but as of one, "And to your Seed," who is Christ."

[17] Romans 4:13, "The promise to Abraham that he would be the heir of the world was not to his seed through the law, but through the righteousness of faith."

[18] Galatians 3:7, 26-29, "Therefore, be sure that it is those who are of faith who are sons of Abraham. ... For you are all sons of God through faith in Christ Jesus. There is neither Jew nor Greek, there is neither slave nor free, there is neither male nor female, for you are all one in Christ Jesus. And if you are Christ's, then you are Abraham's seed, and heirs according to promise."

[19] Genesis 12:3, "I will bless those who bless you, And I will curse him who curses you." Galatians 3:7-8, "Therefore, be sure that it is those who are of faith who are sons of Abraham. The Scripture, foreseeing that God would justify the Gentiles by faith, preached the Gospe

beforehand to Abraham, saying, 'All the nations will be blessed in you.'"

[20] Galatians 3:22, "But the Scripture has shut up everyone under sin, so that the promise by faith in Jesus Christ might be given to those who believe." Matthew 21:43, "Therefore I say to you, the Kingdom of God will be taken away from you and given to a people producing the fruit of it."

[21] Romans 2:28-29, "For he is not a Jew who is one outwardly, nor is circumcision that which is outward in the flesh; but he is a Jew who is one inwardly; and circumcision is that of the heart, in the Spirit, not in the letter; whose praise is not from men but from God." Philippians 3:3, "For we are the true circumcision, who worship in the Spirit of God and glory in Christ Jesus and put no confidence in the flesh."

[22] Acts 7:38, "This [Moses] is the one who was in the church in the wilderness together with the angel who was speaking to him on Mount Sinai."

[23] Galatians 6:16, "And as many as walk according to this rule, peace be upon them, and mercy, even upon the Israel of God."

[24] Hebrews 13:14, "For here we have no continuing city, but we seek the one to come." Philippians 3:20, "For our citizenship is in heaven, from which we also eagerly wait for the Savior, the Lord Jesus Christ." 2 Peter 3:13, "We, according to his promise, look for new heavens and a new earth, in which righteousness dwells." Revelation 21:9-14, "Then one of the seven angels who had the seven bowls filled with the seven last plagues came to me and talked with me, saying, 'Come, I will show you the bride, the Lamb's wife.' And he carried me away in the Spirit to a great and high mountain, and showed me the great city, the holy Jerusalem, descending out of heaven from God, having the glory of God. ... Also she had a great and high wall with twelve gates, and twelve angels at the gates, and names written on them, which are the names of the twelve tribes of the children of Israel... Now the wall of the city had twelve foundations, and on them were the names

of the twelve apostles of the Lamb." Hebrews 11:39-40, " And all these, having obtained a good testimony through faith, did not receive the promise, God having provided something better for us, that they should not be made perfect apart from us."

25 Hebrews 11:13-16, "These all died in faith, not having received the promises, but having seen them afar off were assured of them, embraced them and confessed that they were strangers and pilgrims on the earth. For those who say such things declare plainly that they seek a homeland. And truly if they had called to mind that country from which they had come out, they would have had opportunity to return. But now they desire a better, that is, a heavenly country. Therefore God is not ashamed to be called their God, for he has prepared a city for them." Hebrews 12:22-24, "But you have come to Mount Zion and to the city of the living God, the heavenly Jerusalem, to an innumerable company of angels, to the general assembly and church of the firstborn who are registered in heaven, to God the Judge of all, to the spirits of just men made perfect, to Jesus the Mediator of the new covenant, and to the blood of sprinkling that speaks better things than that of Abel."

26 John 2:19-21, "Jesus answered and said to them, 'Destroy this Temple, and in three days I will raise it up.' Then the Jews said, 'It has taken forty-six years to build this Temple, and will you raise it up in three days?'" But he was speaking of the Temple of his body."

27 Hebrews 8:1-6, "Now this is the main point of the things we are saying: We have such a High Priest, who is seated at the right hand of the throne of the Majesty in the heavens, a Minister of the sanctuary and of the true tabernacle which the Lord erected, and not man... For if he were on earth, he would not be a priest, since there are priests who offer the gifts according to the law; who serve the copy and shadow of the heavenly things... But now he has obtained a more excellent ministry, inasmuch as he is also Mediator of a better covenant, which was established on better promises." See further Hebrews 4:14-5:10; 6:13-10:18.

[28] Ephesians 2:19-22, "Now, therefore, you are no longer strangers and foreigners, but fellow citizens with the saints and members of the household of God, having been built on the foundation of the apostles and prophets, Jesus Christ Himself being the chief cornerstone, in whom the whole building, being fitted together, grows into a holy Temple in the Lord, in whom you also are being built together for a dwelling place of God in the Spirit." 1 Peter 2:4-6, "And coming to him as to a living stone which has been rejected by men, but is choice and precious in the sight of God, you also, as living stones, are being built up as a spiritual house for a holy priesthood, to offer up spiritual sacrifices acceptable to God through Jesus Christ. For this is contained in Scripture: 'Behold I lay in Zion a choice stone, a precious corner stone, and he who believes in him shall not be disappointed.'"

[29] Matthew 16:18, "And I tell you that you are Peter, and on this rock I will build my church, and the gates of Hades will not overcome it." Hebrews 3:5-6, "For [Jesus] has been counted worthy of more glory than Moses, by just so much as the builder of the house has more honor than the house. For every house is built by someone, but the builder of all things is God. Now Moses was faithful as a servant in all God's house, for a testimony of those things which were to be spoken later. But Christ is faithful as a son over God's house. And we are his house."

[30] 2 Peter 3:10-13, "But the day of the Lord will come as a thief in the night, in which the heavens will pass away with a great noise, and the elements will melt with fervent heat; both the earth and the works that are in it will be burned up. Therefore, since all these things will be dissolved, what manner of persons ought you to be in holy conduct and godliness, looking for and hastening the coming of the day of God, because of which the heavens will be dissolved, being on fire, and the elements will melt with fervent heat? Nevertheless we, according to his promise, look for new heavens and a new earth in which righteousness dwells."

[31] Galatians 2:7, "The Gospel for the uncircumcised had been committed to [Paul], as the Gospel for the circumcised was to Peter

(for he who worked effectively in Peter for the apostleship to the circumcised also worked effectively in [Paul] toward the Gentiles)."

[32] Cf. Acts 1:6-7, "Therefore, when they had come together, they asked [Jesus], saying, 'Lord, will you at this time restore the Kingdom to Israel?' And he said to them, "It is not for you to know times or seasons which the Father has put in his own authority.'"

[33] 2 Peter 3:13, "We, according to his promise, look for new heavens and a new earth in which righteousness dwells."

[34] Joshua 21:43-45, "So the Lord gave to Israel all the land of which he had sworn to give to their fathers, and they took possession of it and dwelt in it. The Lord gave them rest all around, according to all that he had sworn to their fathers. And not a man of all their enemies stood against them; the Lord delivered all their enemies into their hand. Not a word failed of any good thing that the Lord had spoken to the house of Israel. All came to pass."

[35] Matthew 24:1-2, "Then Jesus went out and departed from the Temple, and His disciples came up to show Him the buildings of the Temple. And Jesus said to them, 'Do you not see all these things? Assuredly, I say to you, not one stone shall be left here upon another, that shall not be thrown down.'" See also Mark 13:1-2; Luke 21:20-24.

[36] Luke 21:24, "Jerusalem will be trampled by Gentiles until the times of the Gentiles are fulfilled."

[37] Exodus 20:12, "Honor your father and your mother, that your days may be long upon the land which the Lord your God is giving you." // Ephesians 6:2-3, "'Honor your father and mother,' which is the first commandment with promise: 'that it may be well with you and you may live long on the earth.'" Genesis 12:1, "Now the Lord had said to Abram: "Get out of your country, from your family and from your father's house, to a land that I will show you"; cf. Romans 4:13, "The promise to Abraham that he would be the heir of the world was not to his seed through the law, but through the righteousness of faith.'

Psalm 37:11, "But the meek shall inherit the land, and shall delight themselves in the abundance of peace." // Matthew 5:5, "Blessed are the meek, for they shall inherit the earth." Psalm 2:7-8, "The Lord has said to me, 'You are my Son, Today I have begotten you. Ask of me, and I will give you the nations for your inheritance, and the ends of the earth for your possession.'"

[38] Acts 2:29-32, "Men and brethren, let me speak freely to you of the patriarch David, that he is both dead and buried, and his tomb is with us to this day. Therefore, being a prophet, and knowing that God had sworn with an oath to him that of the fruit of his body, according to the flesh, he would raise up the Christ to sit on his throne, he, foreseeing this, spoke concerning the resurrection of the Christ, that his soul was not left in Hades, nor did his flesh see corruption. This Jesus God has raised up, of which we are all witnesses."

[39] Deuteronomy 20:16-18, "Only in the cities of these peoples that the Lord your God is giving you as an inheritance, you shall not leave alive anything that breathes. But you shall utterly destroy them, the Hittite and the Amorite, the Canaanite and the Perizzite, the Hivite and the Jebusite, as the Lord your God has commanded you, so that they may not teach you to do according to all their detestable things which they have done for their gods, so that you would sin against the Lord your God." See also Leviticus 27:28-29.

[40] Matthew 28:19, "Go therefore and make disciples of all the nations."

[41] Matthew 26:52, "But Jesus said to him, 'Put your sword in its place, for all who take the sword will perish by the sword.'"

Appendix 3 : The Church Is The True Israel

God's People have always been the "True Israel," often referred to by the prophets as the "remnant." The notion that the Church has somehow *replaced* Israel as God's people is misguided. There has *only ever been* one People of God. The "People within a people" in the Old Testament, the True Israel, expanded and reached a point where it included individuals from every tribe, nation and tongue. That People is called the Church in the New Testament.

The continuity between the True Israel of the Old Testament and the Church of the New Testament is given unequivocal confirmation in the Bible. The way that the names, titles, privileges and responsibilities of both groups are described in God's Word is identical. Charles D. Provan has contributed an essential study in this regard. In his book, *The Church Is Israel Now,* Provan has gathered these terms and appellations and charted them. What follows is a summary of the content of that book. I urge every reader to consider purchasing a copy of that book (I have NO vested interest in such a purchase and receive no compensation connected with a purchase.) Ordering information is provided at the end of this appendix.

OLD TESTAMENT TITLES AND ATTRIBUTES OF ISRAEL WHICH ARE, IN THE NEW TESTAMENT, REFERRED TO THE CHRISTIAN CHURCH

THE BELOVED OF GOD
A) Israel Is Beloved Of God:
- Ex. 15:13, Deut. 33:3, Ezra 3:11
B) Disobedient Israel Is Not Beloved Of God:
- Lev. 3:16, Jer. 12:8, Jer. 16:5, Hos. 9:15
C) Christians Are Beloved Of God:
- Rom. 9:25, Eph. 5:1, Col. 3:12, 1 John 3:1

THE CHILDREN OF GOD
A) Israel Are The Children Of God:
- Ex. 4:22, Deut. 14:1, Isa. 1:2,4, Isa. 1:2,4, Isa. 63:8, Hos. 11:1
B) Disobedient Israel Are Not The Children Of God:
- Deut. 32:5, John 8:39, 42, 44
C) Christians Are The Children Of God:
- John 1:12, John 11:52, Rom. 8:14,16, 2 Cor. 6:18, Gal. 3:26, Gal. 4:5,6,7, Phil. 2:15, 1 John 3:1

THE FIELD OF GOD
A) Israel Is The Field Of God:
- Jer. 12:10
B) Christians Are The Field Of God:
- 1 Cor. 3:9

THE FLOCK OF GOD AND OF THE MESSIAH
A) Israel Is The Flock Of God And Of The Messiah:
- Psa. 78:52, Psa. 80:1, Isa. 40:11, Jer. 23:1,2,3, Jer. 31:10, Eze. 34:12, 15, 16, Mic. 5:4, Zec. 10:3
B) Christians Are The Flock Of God And Of The Messiah:
- John 10:14,16, Heb. 13:20, 1 Pet. 2:25, 1 Pet. 5:2,3

THE HOUSE OF GOD
A) Israel Is The House Of God:
- Num. 12:7
B) Christians Are The House Of God:
- 1 Tim. 3:15, Heb. 3:2,5,6, Heb. 10:21, 1 Pet. 4:17

THE KINGDOM OF GOD
A) Israel Is The Kingdom Of God:
- Ex. 19:6, 1 Chr. 17:14, 1 Chr. 28:5
B) Disobedient Israel Is Not The Kingdom Of God:
- Matt. 8:11,12, Matt. 21:43
C) Christians Are The Kingdom Of God:
- Rom. 14:17, 1 Cor. 4:20, Col. 1:13, Col. 4:11, Rev. 1:6

THE PEOPLE OF GOD
A) The Israelites Are The People Of God:
- Ex. 6:7, Deut. 27:9, 2 Sam. 7:23, Jer. 11:4
B) Disobedient Israelites Are Not The People Of God:
- Hos. 1:9, Jer. 5:10
C) The Christians Are The People Of God:
- Rom. 9:25, 2 Cor. 6:16, Eph. 4:12, Eph. 5:3, 2 Th. 1:10, Tit. 2:14

THE PRIESTS OF GOD
A) The Israelites Are The Priests Of God:
- Ex. 19:6
B) Disobedient Israelites Are Not The Priests Of God:
- 1 Sam. 2:28,30, Lam. 4:13,16, Eze. 44:10,13, Hos. 4:6, Mal. 2:2,4,8,9
C) The Christians Are The Priests Of God:
- 1 Pet. 2:5,9, Rev. 1:6, Rev. 5:10

THE VINEYARD OF GOD
A) Israel Is The Vineyard Of God:

- Isa. 5:3,4,5,7, Jer. 12:10
B) Christians Are The Vineyard Of God:
- Luke 20:16

THE WIFE (OR BRIDE) OF GOD
A) Israel Is The Wife (Or Bride) Of God:
- Isa. 54:5,6, Jer. 2:2, Eze. 16:32, Hos. 1:2
B) Disobedient Israelites Is Not The Wife (Or Bride) Of God:
- Jer. 3:8, Hos. 2:2
C) The Christians Are The Wife (Or Bride) Of God:
- 2 Cor. 11:2, Eph. 5:31,32

THE CHILDREN OF ABRAHAM
A) The Israelites Are The Children Of Abraham:
- 2 Chr. 20:7, Psa. 105:6, Isa. 41:8
B) Disobedient Israelites Are Not The Children Of Abraham:
- John 8:39, Rom. 9:6,7, Gal. 4:25,30
C) The Christians Are The Children Of Abraham:
- Rom. 4:11,16, Gal. 3:7,29, Gal. 4:23,28,31

THE CHOSEN PEOPLE
A) The Israelites Are The Chosen People:
- Deut. 7:7, Deut. 10:15, Deut. 14:2, Isa. 43:20,21
B) Disobedient Israelites Are Not The Chosen People:
- Deut. 31:17, 2 Ki. 17:20, 2 Chr. 25:7, Psa. 78:59, Jer. 6:30, Jer. 7:29, Jer. 14:10
C) The Christians Are The Chosen People:
- Col. 3:12, 1 Pet. 2:9

THE CIRCUMCISED
A) The Israelites Are The Circumcised:
- Gen. 17:10, Jud. 15:18
B) Disobedient Israelites Are Not The Circumcised:
- Jer. 9:25,26, Rom. 2:25,28, Phil. 3:2

C) The Christians Are The Circumcised:
- Rom. 2:29, Phil. 3:3, Col. 2:11

ISRAEL
A) Israel is Israel
B) Disobedient Israelites Are Not Israelites:
- Num. 15:30,31, Deut. 18:19, Acts 3:23, Rom. 9:6
C) The Christians Are Israel:
- John 11:50,51,52, 1 Cor. 10:1, Gal. 6:15,16, Eph. 2:12,19

JERUSALEM
A) Jerusalem Is the City And Mother Of Israel:
- Psa. 149:2, Isa. 12:6, Isa. 49:18,20,22, Isa. 51:18, Lam. 4:2
B) Jerusalem Is The City And Mother Of Christians:
- Gal. 4:26, Heb. 12:22

THE JEWS
A) Israelites Are Jews
- Ezr. 5:1, Jer. 34:8,9, Zech. 8:22,23
B) Disobedient Israelites Are Not Jews:
- Rom. 2:28, Rev. 2:9, Rev. 3:9
C) The Christians Are Jews:
- Rom. 2:29

THE NEW COVENANT
A) The New Covenant Is With Israel:
- Jer. 31:31,33
B) The New Covenant Is With The Christians:
- Luke 22:20, 1 Cor. 11:25, 2 Cor. 3:6, Heb. 8:6,8,10

AN OLIVE TREE
A) Israel Is An Olive Tree:
- Jer. 11:16, Hos. 14:6

B) The Christians Are An Olive Tree:
- Rom. 11:24

OLD TESTAMENT VERSES REFERRING TO ISRAEL WHICH ARE QUOTED IN THE NEW TESTAMENT AS REFERRING TO THE CHRISTIANS

QUOTE #1
- Lev. 26:11, 12, Eze. 37:27, 2 Cor. 6:16

QUOTE #2
- Deut. 30:12-14, Rom. 10:6-8

QUOTE #3
- Deut. 31:6, Heb. 13:5

QUOTE #4
- Deut. 32:36, Psa. 135:14, Heb. 10:30

QUOTE #5
- Psa. 22:22, Heb. 2:12

QUOTE #6
- Psa. 44:22, Rom. 8:36

QUOTE #7
- Psa. 95:7-11, Heb. 3:7-11

QUOTE #8
- Psa. 130:8, Tit. 2:14

QUOTE #9
- Isa. 28:16, Rom. 10:11, Eph. 2:20, 1 Pet. 2:6

APPENDICES

QUOTE #10
- Isa. 49:8, 2 Cor. 6:2

QUOTE #11
- Isa. 52:7, Rom. 10:15

QUOTE #12
- Isa. 54:1, Gal. 4:27

QUOTE #13
- Jer. 31:31-34, Heb. 8:8-12

QUOTE #14
- Hos. 1:10; 2:23, Rom. 9:25-26, 1 Pet. 2:10

QUOTE #15
- Hos. 13:14, 1 Cor. 15:55

QUOTE #16
- Joel. 2:32, Rom. 10:13

You can order *The Church Is Israel Now* by Charles D. Provan from Ross House Books for $8 per copy. P & H are not included in the price. Please contact Mr. Provan or Ross House Books for postage rates. http://www.llg.simplenet.com California residents add 7.25% tax. Payment must accompany all orders. Ross House does not bill.

Make checks payable in U.S. funds drawn on a U.S. bank to:
Ross House Books
PO Box 67
Vallecito, CA 95251

Appendix 4 : Scripture Index

Verse(s)	Page (s)	Verse (s)	Page (s)
Genesis		14:4	131
2:7	441	15:17	391
3:8-9	460	19:3-6	156
3:14, 17	459	19:6	197
3:15	43, 420	19:9, 16-19	377n
3:24	459	20:6	438
4:15	459	25:8	93
5:27	438	30:2-3	121
6:5	134	33:19	167
8:20-21	388n	30:1-10	332
10:1-3	450	48:31-34	459
12:1-3	74, 153		
12:3	67, 134	**Leviticus**	
15:17	377n	10:1-4	400n
17:1-9, 14	153	23"9-14	467
17:18	163	25:2-7	327
18:10, 14	163	25:9	329
18:17-19	181	25:8-13	329
19:24-25	450	26:11-12	93, 197
21:12	163	26:27-29	388
25:23	164	26:27-28, 33-35, 43	330
41:27	391	26:35, 43	309
49:9-10	386		
49:17	392n	**Numbers**	
50:20	355	12:7	197
		14:34	330
Exodus		16:35	411
4:21	168	27:15-17	70
6:7	197		
7:3	168	**Deuteronomy**	
9:13-16	20	4:2	371
9:16	168	7:7	197
13:21-22	377n	12:11	93

503

Verse(s)	Page(s)	Verse(s)	Page(s)
Deut (Cont.)		*2 Kings*	
12:32	371	1:9-12	411
13:12-18	401	1:10-12	450
14:1	197		
15:1-2, 9	328	*1 Chronicles*	
28:1-2	157	16:23-25	136
28:15	157	16:29	131
30:17-18	157	24:6-19	384
31:10-13	328	29:22	337
32:36	197		
33:3	197	*2 Chronicles*	
33:26	120	20:7	197
		36:20-21	330
Joshua			
23:10	438	*Ezra*	
		3:11	197
Judges		6:14	339
6:5	404	7:11-26	338
1 Samuel		*Job*	
9:16	337	1:8-12	132
10:1	337	2:3-6	132
2 Samuel		*Psalms*	
7:23	20, 197	1:6	181
8:2	408	2:1-2, 4, 10-12	418
22:8-10	120	2:1-5	424
		18:8-14	377n
1 Kings		22:12-13, 16	408
6:11-13	94	35:17	389
19:18	182	45:3-5	387
		49:20	316

Verse(s)	Page(s)	Verse(s)	Page(s)
Ps (Cont)		**Isa (Cont)**	
50:10	437	13:9-10	115
68:4	121	14:31	407
73:22	316	19:1	377n
78:52	197	23:17	427
78:54-61	158	26:15	131
79:1-3	412	28:11	50
79:9	131	28:16	198
80:4	389	34:3-4	116
87:4	408	34:4	74, 390
89:46	389	42:8	132
90:4	438	43:20-21	197
92:12-14	391	44:22-23	149
104:2-3	121	45:20-25	481
104:3-4	391	48:10-11	149
110	12	49:6	105
114:1-6	452	49:5-6	393
119:18	30	51:9	408
		53:10	478
Isaiah		53:12	478
1:2, 4	197	53:10-12	342
1:9	173, 364	54:5-6	197
2:1	227	54:11-12	459
2:10, 19	391	57:20	420
2:10, 17-21	226	60	459
3:8	227	61	64
5:3-7	197	61:1-2	65
6:2-3	385	62:5	145
6:13	392	63:3	371
7:8	392n	65	372
9:6	141, 142	65:2	180
10:22-23	173	65:11-12	457
13-14	371	65:17-19	458

Verse(s)	Page(s)	Verse(s)	Page(s)
Isa (Cont)		*Ezekiel*	
66:18-20	270	1:5-14	384
66:22-23	458	1:26-28	388n
		2-3	372
Jeremiah		2:1,3-4, 7, 9-10	386
1:14	407	3:1-3	407
2:2	197	9	372
4:5-8	401	10-11	159
4:13-14	121n	14:21	388
5:14	411	16	372
6:1, 22	407	16:46-49	364
7:11	78	26:7	407
8:1-2	412	29:4-6	69
9:3-6	392	32:7-8	116, 377n
10:32	407	33:1-6	401
12:7-8	96	34	70
12:10	197	36:20-23	20, 149
13:20	407	36:31-32	149
15:2	256	38:6, 15	407
16:3-4	412	38-39	372
16:16-18	68	38:1-4	69, 449
17:5-8	391	38:22	450
23:1-8	72	39	372
25:1-15	325	39:2	407
25:9	407	47	372
29:1-23	325		
29:17	74	*Daniel*	
34:8-17	330	2:1	310
46:20, 24	407	2:10	311
47:2	407	2:11	311
51:14	404	2:14	311

Verse(s)	Page(s)	Verse(s)	Page(s)
Dan (Cont)		*Dan (Cont)*	
2:16	311	7:26-27	318, 323, 324
2:21-22	311, 377	7:28	323
2:27	312	8:17	40
2:27-28	40	8:26	32, 41
2:28	312, 372	8-10	40
2:34	313	8:18	377
2:35	313, 438	9:2, 12, 16-18	326
2:37-38	313	9:4	326
2:40	313	9:13-14	309
2:42	314	9:14-16	326
2:43	314	9:16-19	326, 331
2:44	127, 144, 314	9:20	327, 333
2:45	314	9:20-27	333
2:47	314	9:22	333
4-5	40	9:24	332, 334, 335
7:2	420	9:25-26	338, 339, 343
7:3-8, 16-25	408	9:27	106, 342
7:7	316, 317	10:2-3	334
7:8	317	10:14	41
7:8, 24	318	12:2-3	471
7:9	323	12:4	358, 372
7:10	323	12:6	41
7:9-11	323, 382	12:8-9	32, 344
7:13-14	119, 120, 323, 372, 377		
7:15	316, 323	*Hosea*	
7:17	316	1:8-9	189, 459
7:20	318	1:10	173
7:21	322, 369	2:12	74
7:23	317	2:23	173
7:24	317	8:7-8	184
7:25	318, 321	9:10	74

Verse(s)	Page (s)	Verse (s)	Page (s)
Hos (Cont)		*Hab (Cont)*	
10:6-8	391	*3:2*	20
11:1	197	*3:6*	408
13:4-5	181	*3:9-11*	387
13:15-16	391		
		Zephaniah	
Joel		*3:7-8, 11-13*	426
1:6	405, 406	*1:15-17*	121n
1:7	74		
2:1-2, 10	116	*Zechariah*	
2:1-15	401	*4*	372, 410
2:4-10	406	*4:6*	412
2:25	405	*10:3*	197
		11:10,14	73
Amos		*11:12-13*	73
3:1-2	181		
4:1-3	69	*Malachi*	
7:7-8	408	*1:2-3*	165
8:14	392n		
9:8	459	*Matthew*	
		1:21	336
Micah		*3:1-3*	36
5:4	197	*3:7-12*	84, 336
7:1	74	*3:11-13*	61
		3:15-17	337
Nahum		*4:8-9*	135
1:2-8	377n	*4:17*	32, 36
1:3	121n	*5-7*	140
3:4	427	*5:25*	45
		7:23	181
Habakkuk		*8:11-12*	189
1:2	389	*9:17a*	64

Verse(s)	Page(s)	Verse(s)	Page(s)
Matt (Cont)		*Matt (Cont)*	
9:36	70	23:37-39	95
10:6	88	24:1	95
10:7	36	24:1-35	51
10:23	56	24:2	96
10:37-39	27	24:3	97
11:10	121	24:4-5	98, 228
11:16	55	24:6-7	99, 389
11:25	350	24:7-8	100
12:25-29	435	24:8	389
12:41, 42, 45	55	24:9	389
13:10-15	184	24:9-11	228
13:11	275	24:9-13	101
13:11-17	183	24:12	229
13:14-15	336	24:13	229
13:33	438	24:14	101
13:36-43	430	24:15	106, 229
13:47-51	70, 276	24:16-20	108
13:50	471	24:20-21	90, 91
14:42-43	276	24:21	394
16:4	55	24:21-22	111
16:28	56	24:23-28	113, 228, 229
17:5	336	24:28	402
17:7	55	24:29	115, 390
19:28	118	24:30	117, 229, 323, 377n
21:12-22	74	24:30-31	119, 120, 228
21:33-45	336	24:36-42	284
21:42-44	144	24:40-42	286
21:43	189, 378		
23:32,35,36,38	336	24:32-34	36, 90
23:35-36	95	24:32-35	123
23:36	54, 55		

APPENDICES

Verse(s)	Page(s)	Verse(s)	Page(s)
Matt (Cont)		**Luke**	
24:34	32, 52, 55, 98	1:13-17	5
25:31-32	471	1:32	142
25:34	451, 471	1:69	142
25:41	471	2:32	351
25:46	471	4:6	131, 135
26:39	135	4:12-20	65
26:45-46	36	4:18	337
26:52	256	4:24-30	66
26:64	57, 118, 378	7:27	121
28:7	45	8:10-12	131
28:14	141	9:27	57
28:18-20	105	9:51	364
		9:52	121
Mark		10:17-18	133
1:2	121	10:18	419
1:14-15	9	11:17-22	436
2:1	104	11:47-51	336
3:23-27	436	12:39-40	286
6:34	70	12:49-56	85
9:48	471	14:26-27	26
10;32-34	364	17:20-37	113
11:12-19	74, 78	17:37	402
11:12-26	76, 78	18:1-8	399
11:17	75, 78	18:13	472
11:20-23	79	19:11	35
13:1-37	51, 390	19:27	82
13:9-11	103	19:41-44	397
13:30	53	19:45-47	74
14:62	377n	21:5-36	51, 365
		21:9	390
		21:20-24	107
		21:30-31	35

Verse(s)	Page (s)	Verse(s)	Page (s)
Luke (Cont)		*John (Cont)*	
21:32	53	*12:13*	394
21:34	286	*12:30-31*	419
22:1	37	*12:31-32*	133
23:12	411	*12:39-41*	336
23:27-30	390, 406	*14:6*	142
23:27-30	391	*17:13-19*	275
23:43	441	*19:15*	361
24:25-27	373		
24:50-53	5	*Acts*	
		1:9-11	306
John		*1:11*	119
1:1	336	*1:21-22*	474n
1:3	141	*2:5*	103
1:12	197	*2:14-21*	49
1:32	337	*2:19*	377n
1:29	142, 386	*2:32,33,38,39*	337
2:13-16	74	*2:34*	384n
3:16	444	*3:15*	141
4:34-38	429	*4:12/26, 27*	192/337
5:24-27	61	*6:5*	221
5:28	471	*7:37*	336
6:35	141	*7:52*	142
6:48	141	*7:54-60*	101
7:55-59	427	*7:55-56*	119
8:12	142	*8:9-24*	219
8:42-47	183	*10:36/37,44,45*	142/337
8:44	451	*10:43*	336
10:14	197	*11:27-28*	100
10:14-16	71	*13:44-48*	105
10:28-29	273	*14:6*	195
11:50-52	197	*17:4-15*	224
12:1	394	*17:7*	362

Verse(s)	Page(s)	Verse(s)	Page(s)
Acts (Cont)		*Rom (Cont)*	
18:6	224	9:11	161
18:12	101	9:11-13	164
21:27-26:32	255	9:12	165
23:9-10	274	9:14	171
24 & 25	101	9:17	168
25:4	46	9:19	169, 172
26:17-18	439	9:22	170, 188
28:25-27	336	9:24	172
28:28	440	9:25	197
		9:27-28	392
Romans		9:30	174, 336
1:1-2	336	9:31-32	175, 336
1:8	102	10:1	177
1:20-25	151	10:3	175
2:28-29	155, 200	10:4	176
3:10	174	10:5	175
3:20	174	10:6-7	176
3:21-24	174, 336	10:8	176
3:23	151	10:9-10	176
4:11, 16	197	10:11	198
4:13	336	10:12-13	176
4:16-17	154	10:14-15	177
5:8-11	336	10:18	102, 180
5:17-18	336	10:19	180
8:23	469	11:1	180
8:37	355	11:1-2	181
9:2	177	11:4	181
9:4-5	187, 477	11:5-6	182, 191
9:6	160, 171	11:11	186
9:7	160	11:11, 14	187
9:8	161	11:15	186

Verse(s)	Page (s)	Verse (s)	Page (s)
Rom (Cont)		*1 Cor (Cont)*	
11:16	186	8:3	181
11:18	188	10:1	197
11:20	188	14:20-22	50
11:21	189	15:1-19	467
11:22	189	15:3-5	1
11:23	189	15:12	467
11:25	190, 193,	15:19	306
11:26	141, 190, 193	15:22-26	281
11:28	193	15:24	469
11:30-31	195	15:24-26	11, 454, 474
11:32	194, 195	15:24-28	130
12:9-21	87	15:35-36	467
13:11-12	47	15:42-44	441, 468
14:17	336	15:50-57	281, 468
15:8-12	439	15:58	10
15:20	105, 412		
16:17-20	43	*2 Corinthians*	
16:25-26	336	3:12-16	48
		5:1-4	441
1 Corinthians		5:7	353
1:24	142	5:17-21	336
1:30	336	5:19	480
2:8	142	6:16	197
2:10-12	30	9:9	336
2:16	480	10:3-5	355, 476
3:9	197	12:2-4	272, 280
4:7-8	466	15:12-21	457
5:1	466		
5:7	386	*Galatians*	
6:15	466	1:6-8	218
6:20	469	1:11-12	280, 351
7:29-31	47	1:14	480

Verse(s)	Page(s)	Verse(s)	Page(s)
Gal (Cont)		*Phil (Cont)*	
1:22-23	143	*2:10*	139
1:23	14	*2:15*	197
2:1-2	127	*3:7-11*	446
2:4-6	442		
2:6	384n	*Colossians*	
2:11-17	336	*1:6, 23*	102
2:12, 19	197	*1:10*	190
2:20	141	*1:12-21*	336
3:10-11	143	*1:26*	336
4:5-7	480	*2:18*	215
4:12	197	*3:1*	384n
5:23	142	*3:12*	197
5:31-32	197		
		1 Thessalonians	
Ephesians		*1:13*	190
1:20	384n	*2:14-16*	225, 336
1:18-21	4	*4:13-18*	272, 282
2:6	480	*4:15-18*	266, 306
2:10	471	*4:16*	306
3:26-29	199	*4:17*	306
3:29	155, 393	*5:2*	306
4:8-9	181	*5:2-4*	286
4:23, 28, 31	197		
5:7-12	217	*2 Thessalonians*	
6:15-16	197, 393	*1:4*	225
6:17b	433	*1:5-12*	225, 226
		1:10	197
Philippians		*2*	289
4:4-5	37	*2:1-2*	227, 228, 230, 231
1:13	480	*2:1-12*	231
1:21	477		

Verse(s)	Page(s)	Verse(s)	Page(s)
2 Thess (Cont)		**Hebrews**	
2:3	228, 229, 230, 231, 235, 351	1:1-2	208, 336
2:4	229, 231	1:2	141
2:5	227	1:3, 13	384n
2:6	230, 231	2:14	236
2:7	229, 230, 231, 235, 255	2:17	336
2:8	236	3:7-10	56
2:9	231	4:12	433
2:15	229	4:14	141
2:16	336	4:16	472
3:6-15	227	6:5	480
		7:27	383
1 Timothy		8:1	384n
1:17	142	8:13	37, 62
2:12	474	9:6	383
3:15	197	9:11-15	63
3:16	102	9:12-14, 26	336
4:1-6	206	9:15	142
4:1-11	223	9:22-28	81, 337
4:6-8	417	9:26-28	474n
6:15	141, 142	9:27	471
		10:1-7	82
2 Timothy		10:5-18	342
2:15	2, 299	10:9-14	336
2:16-19	181	10:12	384n
2:24-3:5	207	10:21	197
3:15	16	10:25	63
		10:30	198
Titus		10:34-35	38
1:4	142	11:35	445
3:6	142	11:35-37	445

Verse(s)	Page(s)	Verse(s)	Page(s)
Heb (Cont)		*1 John Cont)*	
12:2	384n	2:18-19	202
		2:18-22	204
James		2:18-27	205, 211
5:1-3	208	2:19	212
5:7-8	38	2:22	212, 213
		2:24-25	213
1 Peter		3:1	197
1:3-5	209	3:8	11
1:9-11	336	3:23	213
1:19	386	4:2-3	204, 213
2:5, 9	197	4:3	212
2:6	198	4:13-15	213
2:9	197	5:1-5, 10-13	213
3:8	438	5:4	353
4:7	37		
5:2-3	197	*2 John*	
		7	204, 213
2 Peter		7-11	212
1:19-21	336		
2:1	278	*Jude*	
2:20	142	17-21	210
3	279	22-23	273
3:3-13	278		
3:10	306	*Revelation*	
		1:1	43, 349, 357, 377
1 John		1:1, 19	372
1:1-3	213	1:1-8	374
1:7	213	1:3	39, 239, 357
2:1	141, 142	1:4, 19-20	240
2:2	141, 213	1:4	351

Verse(s)	Page (s)	Verse (s)	Page (s)
Rev (Cont)		*Rev (Cont)*	
1:6	197	4:2	382
1:7	57	4:2-3	383, 388
1:8	141	4:4	443
1:9	240, 352	4:4, 6-8	384
1:9-3:22	374	4:6	408
1:12-16	372	4:8	385
1:13	377	4:11	385
1:17	377	5	372
1:19	357	5:1	385
1:20	378	5:3-4	386
2-3	379	5:5	142, 381
2:3	240	5:6-10	475
2:6	222	5:6	386
2:6, 15	221	5:9-10	387
2:7, 11, 17, 26	240, 354, 381	6:2	381, 387
2:9	352	6:9-11	352, 389
2:10	380	6:10	398
2:13	352, 380	6:11	384, 389, 394
2:16	42, 357	6:16	391
2:17	355	7	372
2:20, 24-25	380	7:1-3	391
2:26-28	382	7:4	392
2:26-27	4, 355	7:5-8	392
3:5, 12, 21	240, 355, 380	7:9	384, 393, 394
3:8	380	7:12	398
3:10	357, 381	7:13-17	352
3:11	42, 357	7:14	394
3:14	141	7:15-17	398
3:21	355, 381	8:4	399
4:1-11:19	374	8:5	400
4-11	413-415	8:6	401
		8:7-12	401, 402

Verse(s)	Page(s)	Verse(s)	Page(s)
Rev (Cont)		*Rev (Cont)*	
8:13	402	12:6	434
9:1	434	12:7	418
9:1-3	420	12:9	418
9:3	404	12:10-12	419
9:5	404	12:11	352, 374, 420
9:11	405	12:12b	419, 434
9:12	406	12:17	262, 420
9:14	406	13:1-19:21	376
9:20	401	13:1	409, 428
9:20-21	407	13:2	245, 409
10:5-7	42	13:3	257, 258, 260, 409, 428
11	372	13:3-4	421
11:1-2	363	13:4	409
11:3	408	13:4, 8, 14-15	239
11:4	125, 410	13:5	409
11:5	411	13:5-7	239, 249
11:6	411	13:7	352, 428
11:7	408, 409	13:7-8	239, 421
11:8	372	13:8	409, 428
11:9	412	13:8-10	256
11:10	412	13:9-10	239
11:11-12	412, 413	13:10	427
11:13	413	13:11, 12, 14	423
11:14	42	13:11	409, 421
11:15	279, 413	13:12	409
11:16	443	13:14	384, 409
11:19	413	13:15	409
12	375	13:18	239, 240, 423
12:1	418	14:1	424
12:3	418	14:1-5	425
12:5	272	14:3	425

Verse(s)	Page(s)	Verse(s)	Page(s)
Rev (Cont)		*Rev (Cont)*	
14:4	425, 426	17:9-11	421
14:6	426	17:11	257, 260, 409
14:7	426	17:12	409, 421
14:8	425, 426	17:12-14	239
14:9	426	17:13	409
14:11	409, 471	17:14	431
14:12, 13	352	17:15-17	431
14:14	387, 429	17:16-17	409
14:17	429	18	371
14:18	430	18:3, 9, 11, 17	428
14:20	430	18:3	427
15:1	430	18:9-17	428
15:2	409, 430	18:18	431
15:3	142	18:20, 24	352
15:3-4	430	18:21	420
15:7	430	19	372
15:8	430	19:2	432
16:5-6	352	19:2-3	352
16:10	409	19:6	125
16:13	409	19:9	433
16:15	286	19:11	141
16:17	431	19:11-16	368, 381
16:19	431	19:13	142, 372
17:3	409	19:16	142
17:3, 9	238	19:19	410
17:4-6	352	19:20	239, 410
17:5	427	20	376
17:6	431	20:1	434
17:8	409	20:1-3	137
17:9, 10	238, 239, 241, 243, 258, 261, 361	20:1-6	434

Verse(s)	Page(s)	Verse(s)	Page(s)
Rev (Cont)		*Rev (Cont)*	
20:1-10	129	22:4	459, 475
20:2	435	22:5	460
20:3	438	22:6	44, 357, 460
20:4	352, 410, 427, 440	22:6, 10	460
20:5	443, 444	22:7	357
20:6	447	22:10	32, 39, 41, 357, 358, 372
20:7	447	22:12	357
20:7-8	137	22:13	141, 460
20:7-9	372	22:13-14	460
20:8	448	22:16	142
20:9	450	22:17	460
20:10	410, 451	22:17, 20	463
20:11	451, 455	22:18-19	372
20:11-15	306	22:20	357, 460, 464
20:12	452		
20:13	453	*Apocrypha*	
20:14	454, 471	1Ma 13:49-52	395
20:15	454	2Ma 10:1-8	396
21:1	80, 455		
21:1-3	474		
21:1-22:21	376		
21:3-4	455		
21:5	456		
21:7-8	392n		
21:8	457		
21:9	145		
21:9-10	459		
21:22	80, 459		
22:1-2	459		
22:3	459		

Made in the USA
Lexington, KY
21 November 2018